CONTRIBUTIONS
TO
ECONOMIC ANALYSIS

146

Honorary Editor
J. TINBERGEN

Editors
D. W. JORGENSON
J. WAELBROECK

NORTH-HOLLAND PUBLISHING COMPANY
AMSTERDAM · NEW YORK · OXFORD

ON THE INTERACTION BETWEEN STATE AND PRIVATE SECTOR

ON THE INTERACTION BETWEEN STATE AND PRIVATE SECTOR

a study in political economics

F. A. A. M. VAN WINDEN
Utrecht University, The Netherlands

1983

NORTH-HOLLAND PUBLISHING COMPANY
AMSTERDAM · NEW YORK · OXFORD

ISBN: 0 444 86667 1

Publishers:
NORTH-HOLLAND PUBLISHING COMPANY
AMSTERDAM · NEW YORK · OXFORD

Sole distributors for the U.S.A. and Canada:
ELSEVIER SCIENCE PUBLISHING COMPANY, INC.
52 VANDERBILT AVENUE
NEW YORK, N.Y. 10017

PRINTED IN THE NETHERLANDS

Introduction to the series

This series consists of a number of hitherto unpublished studies, which are introduced by the editors in the belief that they represent fresh contributions to economic science.

The term 'economic analysis' as used in the title of the series has been adopted because it covers both the activities of the theoretical economist and the research worker.

Although the analytical methods used by the various contributors are not the same, they are nevertheless conditioned by the common origin of their studies, namely theoretical problems encountered in practical reserch. Since for this reason, business cycle research and national accounting, research work on behalf of economic policy, and problems of planning are the main sources of the subjects dealt with, they necessarily determine the manner of approach adopted by the authors. Their methods tend to be 'practical' in the sense of not being too far remote from application to actual economic conditions. In addition they are quantitative rather than qualitative.

It is the hope of the editors that the publication of these studies will help to stimulate the exchange of scientific information and to reinforce international cooperation in the field of economics.

The Editors

Aan mijn moeder

Aan Jos en Lara

PREFACE

This book deals with the interface of economics and politics. It is a study in political economics. It's main concern is the modelling, and explicit incorporation in an economic model, of the behaviour of the state and of political activities by private sector agents in capitalist economies of the Western type.
The improvement of our knowledge of the interaction between the state and the private sector is of obvious importance for the understanding of present-day economies. The book gives a comprehensive and systematic treatment of the problems involved in studying this interaction. A number of general politico-economic models, of increasing complexity, with a fully articulated private sector are worked out, and studied by means of analytical as well as computer simulation techniques. Along with these models a series of partial models dealing with state behaviour, voting (allowing for multi-party systems), government coalition formation, and pressure group activity, are developed, which - it is hoped - are also of interest in themselves.
In the course of the argument a new approach to the study of politico-economic phenomena is suggested, which is related to but differs from the existing Marxian and public choice approaches in the field. It starts from the recognition that distributional conflicts are inherent to politics. A distinction is made between the interests of members of different social classes, which allows the behaviour of (individual, collective) agents in the economic as well as political sphere to be modelled in a unified way.
This book should, in our view, be of interest to anyone concerned with the study of the state, the study of political activities by private sector agents, or the development of (general) politico-economic models. Only some basic mathematical training is required for the understanding of the models and their analysis.

The content of this book served as my Ph.D.-thesis, which was delivered at Leyden University in May 1981. Only some minor, mainly textual, modifications have been made.
Of all those deserving my gratitude for their contribution, in one way or another, to whatever makes this book worth reading, I especially would like to mention here the following persons.
I am, first of all, indebted to my supervisor Bernard van Praag who not only contributed to this book as co-author of one of the articles on which it is based, but also monitored the quality and progress of the thesis.
Wim Driehuis and Pieter Ruys, the official referees of the thesis, read through the whole manuscript and suggested significant improvements for which I am very grateful.
The same holds for Ben van Velthoven, to whom I am also indebted for in-

teresting discussions and comments during the preparation of the thesis.
I further want to acknowledge the useful comments on Chapter 5 by R.J.M. Mokken, who willingly refereed the thesis from a political scientific point of view.
The computational burden was skilfully lightened by Joost Cohen Tervaert and, in particular, by Huib van de Stadt and Eitel Homan.
I am grateful to José Kooyman and the "Centrale Tekstverwerking" of the Faculty of Law of Leyden University for typing parts of the manuscript, and, especially, to Lucia van der Tol who produced the typescript used in the preparation of this book.
The larger part of the research reported in this book was carried out while I was affiliated with the Economic Institute and the Centre for Research in Public Economics at Leyden University. The research project was started in 1974, and is presently continued at the Economic Institute of Utrecht University. It is a pleasure to acknowledge the support that I received from my (former) colleagues at these universities. Apart from Ben van Velthoven, I particularly would like to thank Arie Kapteyn for his critique and encouragement during the formative stage of the project.

Utrecht, December 1982 Frans van Winden

CONTENTS

3. STATE AND PRIVATE SECTOR RECONSIDERED, THE INTRODUCTION OF TIME

4. AN ALTERNATIVE APPROACH: INTERESTS AND INTEREST FUNCTIONS

5. ON POLITICAL ACTIVITIES

LIST OF FIGURES

LIST OF TABLES

LIST OF SYMBOLS

Only symbols the occurrence of which is not restricted to one section of a chapter are listed. The page of introduction is shown in parentheses.

$\sim$: denotes expectations (p. 53);
$\hat{}$: indicates that hypothetical outcomes - party promises - are involved (p. 143);

Superscripts

c : consumption (p. 59);
d : demanded (p. 23);
i : investment (p. 56);
p : pivot state (p. 34);
s : supplied (p. 23);
t : transacted (p. 53);

-, + : minimum, maximum, respectively (pp. 23, 41);

Subscripts

b : business (p. 22);
c : collectivity (p. 95);
g : denotes argument in elementary interest function (p. 93);
k : denotes economic position of agent; k = 1 for state sector worker, k = 2 for private sector worker, k = 3 for capital owner (capitalist), k = 4 for unemployed (dependant) (p. 92);
o_i : option or political party index (pp. 139, 141);
s : state (p. 21);

Variables, parameters: Greek symbols

α : labour productivity (p. 55);
β : output-capital ratio (p. 62);
Γ_{ko_h} : abstention rate of k-agents who voted for o_h at previous election (p. 152);
$\bar{\bar{\gamma}}$: positive-alienation threshold (p. 152);
δ : depreciation rate of private capital (p. 62);

ε, ε_{kg}	: interest function parameters (pp. 22/53, 93, respectively);
ζ	: depreciation rate of state capital (p. 56);
η	: labour productivity function parameter (p. 56);
θ	: state employment growth rate target of bureaucrats (p. 52);
κ	: job preference parameter (p. 58);
λ_s, λ_{kc}	: interest function parameters (pp. 53, 95, respectively);
μ_{ko_h}	: average of party valuations $V_{ko_h o_i}$ (p. 152);
ν	: labour productivity function parameter (p. 56);
ρ	: time preference parameter of firms (p. 61);
σ	: fraction of excess funds reserved for investment by firms (p. 57);
$\sigma^2_{ko_h}$	: variance of party valuations $V_{ko_h o_i}$ (p. 152);
τ	: income tax rate (p. 55);
τ_1, τ_2, τ_3, $\underline{\tau}$	: value added tax rate, profit tax rate, private wage sum tax rate, tax rate structure [$\underline{\tau} = (\tau_1,\tau_2,\tau_3)$], respectively (pp. 22, 23);
ϕ	: state wage rate parameter (p. 57);
ψ	: dole rate parameter (p. 22);

Variables, parameters: Latin symbols

$a_{ko_h o_i}$, $b_{ko_h o_i}$	: floating rate function parameters (p. 143);
$\bar{c}_{ko_i}$, c_{ko_i}	: weights attached to incumbencies and periods within incumbencies, respectively (p. 143);
D	: accumulated debts (p. 56);
E_k, E	: number of k-agents, total population (labour force), respectively (pp. 21/22/56/96, 95), $E = \Sigma_k E_k$;
E_{ko_i}, E'_{ko_i}	: number of k-agents that voted for o_i as measured just after and just before an election, respectively (p. 144);
E_{o_i}	: constituency of o_i (p. 144);
$\bar{E}_1$	: minimum state employment level, minimum state size (p. 23);
E^*	: total employment target (p. 22);
e_k	: relative number of k-agents (p. 91), $e_k = E_k/E$;
F	: excess funds of firms (p. 22);
$f_{ko_h o_i}$	: floating rate of k-agents from o_h to o_i (p. 140);
G	: production function (p. 24);

K : capital stock (p. 56); in Chapter 2 K_b stands for capital rented by firms (p. 24), and $\bar{K}_b$ for the existing capital stock (p. 26);

L : total dependent labour force (p. 22), $L = E - E_3$;

M, MM : within period generated money supply, total money supply, respectively (p. 60);

m : incumbency index (p. 142);

N : (value of) surplus constraint function (p. 29);

n_m : number of periods covered by incumbency m (p. 142);

o_i : option or political party index (pp. 139, 141);

P, P_k, P_k^* : (value of) interest function, elementary interest function of k-agent, argument in P_k, respectively (pp. 21/23/53/61/95, 93, 93);

p : (private) product price (p. 56);

q : minimum profit margin (p. 26);

r : rate of return on capital (p. 69), rental of capital in Chapter 2 (p. 23);

S : private product stocks (p. 55);

t, T : indices denoting time periods and election dates, respectively (pp. 52, 141);

t_m : last period of incumbency m (p. 143);

$V_{ko_ho_i}$: valuation of o_i by k-agent whose previous choice was o_h (p. 140);

w_k, $\bar{w}_k$, $\bar{\bar{w}}_k$: income of k-agent, real-, real disposable-, respectively (pp. 56/104, 95, 92): $\bar{\bar{w}}_k = (1 - \tau)\bar{w}_k = (1 - \tau)w_k/p$; w stands for real wage rate in Chapter 2 (p. 21);

X : output (p. 21);

x_b^{c-} : minimum consumption level (p. 57);

x_{sk} : bundle of state goods available to k-agent (p. 93);

Z_{ko_i} : interest realization rating of o_i by a k-agent (p. 140).

CHAPTER 1

INTRODUCTION

1.1. Interaction between State and Private Sector

In this book a *non-normative*, explanatory, *theoretical* analysis is given of the interaction between state and private sector in a *capitalist economy*, that is, a private enterprise economy of the Western type. The interaction between the *state sector* - which comprises the state - and the *private sector* - which comprises all agents or institutions (households) other than the state - follows from the interdependence of these two sectors. The *state* - defined as an institution that has the monopoly of legitimate violence and taxation within a certain territory [1)] - is typically dependent on the private sector for its financial means (taxes) and political support (e.g., votes); the private sector on the other hand, is dependent on the state for such things as infrastructure, internal and external security (police, defense) and legal order (e.g., private property rights).

It should be clear that this interdependence has always been of great significance to the functioning and understanding of capitalist economies. A fact that has so well been documented for the Mercantilist period, for example [see Dobb (1972), Heimann (1968), MacIver (1966), Roll (1973)]. A glance at the literature, moreover, reveals that the intensity and, say, visibility of this interdependence has fluctuated over time (think of war periods) and across countries [see Shonfield (1970)]. Since the second world war, however, a general, steady and significant increase in this intensity has occurred. Symptoms are: state expenditures (including transfers) growing faster than GNP and in some countries approaching or even exceeding a 50 per cent share [OECD (1978); see also Fig. 1.1.]; industrial sectors (energy, aerospace, for example) being widely dependent on the state for product demand, basic research or highly qualified labour; an increasing number of tax-incentives and regulatory activities by the state. All these well-known phenomena testify to the enlarged role of the state.
The recently revived interest in subjects like the limits to taxation, tax capacity, and the restrictions on the size of the non-market sector is one of the outgrowths of this state of affairs [2)].
There have also been developments within the private sector, however, that should be mentioned. These developments can, for our purposes, be summarized under the headings: concentration and globalization - or internatio-

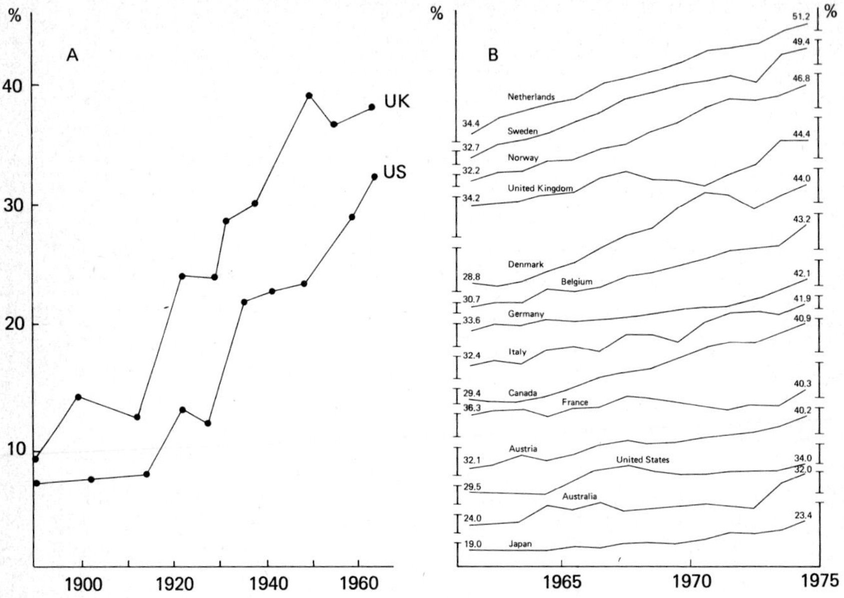

Fig. 1.1. State expenditure as percentage of GNP
[A: Musgrave (1969, pp.96-97); B: OECD (1978, p.16)].

nalization - of economic activities, giantism, technological development, and organization (interest groups) [see, e.g., Cameron (1978), Jacquemin and De Jong (1976); see also Fig. 1.2.].
The consequences have been that the state becomes not only more and more involved in the private sector by its own initiative - in order to stimulate and to sustain technological developments or to canalize international influences - but it is also forced or manipulated into such greater involvement by powerful organizations.

The relationships between state and private sector participants have become less and less anonymous. Bargaining has grown in importance. The seriousness of, especially, this trend towards bigness in both sectors may be indicated by the following two citations:

> "The trouble with this country is that you can't win an election without the oil bloc, and you can't govern with it" [Franklin D. Roosevelt, quoted in Sampson (1976, p. 104)]
>
> "we might wind up in an economic system where good contacts with government officials and politicians become more important for successful operations by firms than the ability of the management to pursue efficient production, innovations and marketing" [Lindbeck (1975, p. 38); see also Johansen (1979), Nieburg (1966)].

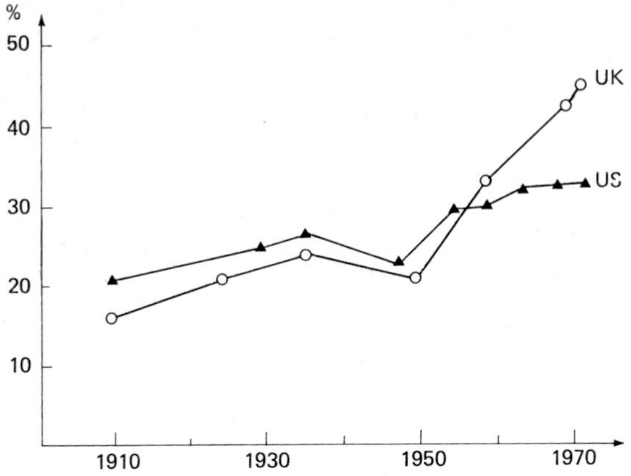

Fig. 1.2. Share of the 100 largest enterprises in manufacturing net output in the UK and the US [Prais and Reid (1976, p.80)].

Of course, any other 'bloc' may be the reason of similar worries as worded in the first citation.

In the light of all this, one would expect that the interaction between state and private sector is a major subject of study in economics. However, this turns out to be true in a very limited sense only.

1.2. Review and Critique of Current Approaches

1.2.1. Mainstream Economics

As a matter of fact, mainstream economics has been concerned with the relationships between state and private sector from such different angles as: welfare economics [Arrow and Scitovsky (1969), Samuelson (1954, 1955) Scitovsky (1971)], the theory of economic policy [Fox, Sengupta and Thorbecke (1973), Mosley (1976), Tinbergen (1956)], public finance/economics [Johansen (1968), Musgrave and Musgrave (1973), Musgrave and Peacock (1967)], the theory of economic systems [Halm (1970), Pryor (1968)], industrial organization [Bain (1959), Scherer (1970)], econometric models [Evans (1969), Lucas (1976)] [3]. However, these studies are, on the whole, *normative* in character and/or ignore *political processes*, i.e. the way that the behaviour of the state is determined [4].

A typical approach has been to look for the conditions of an optimal allocation of public and private goods (welfare economics), or to view the state as a benevolent dictator who maximizes a somehow concocted 'social welfare' function (theory of economic policy). Quite often also - as in macro-economic and econometric models - the behaviour of the state is treated as exogenous, notwithstanding the fact that up to 50 per cent of national income is allocated by the state [5)].

Non-normative studies, on the other hand, are typically concerned with the history or the effects/incidence of taxes, tax structure and state expenditures (public finance), or with such topics as competition policy or state-procurement policy (industrial organization). Political processes are neglected. The following remark by Morgenstern is instructive in this respect:

> "Economic theory assumes that allocation of resources is *only* through markets (...). This view completely overlooks the existence of governments, national and local, where allocations are made not through the medium of markets but by means of *voting* (...). Congress, parliaments, governments vote *how much* is to be invested in capital goods, *when* and *where* the investment should take place. They vote the income of millions of persons (government employees, the military personnel, welfare recipients, etc.). Clearly the movement of these funds - a respectable percentage of national income - sets forth flows of money, determines demand, influences prices and thus affects the 'free economic sector' of the whole economy with its prices, incomes, allocations" [Morgenstern (1972, p. 1174)].

The state of the art is even less satisfactory if one realizes that voting is just one of a number of instruments that may be available to agents. Lobbying, corruption, leaving the jurisdiction and self-provision may be equally or even more important activities for the allocation of resources [see Breton (1974, Ch. 5)]. These activities should particularly gain in importance in a time-period in which big organizations manifest themselves and try to have their interests promoted by the state.

The alleged shift in power from the legislature to the executive also points at the potential weight of allocation mechanisms (such as bargaining) other than voting procedures and markets [6)].

1.2.2. Marxist Approach/Public Choice Approach

Although the theoretical status of the *non-normative* study of the interaction between state and private sector, with which we will be concerned, leaves much to be desired, there are some old strands of economic thought and some new theoretical developments over the past two decades that deserve our attention. Two main approaches can be distinguished, the Marxist Approach and the Public Choice Approach.

Marxist Approach

Writers and topics. Marx himself did not formulate a full-fledged theory of the relationship between state and private sector in capitalist societies. His insights into this matter are spread over his texts. Nevertheless, according to Schumpeter (1972, p. 433):

> "Marx's theories of history, of social classes, and of the state (government) constitute (...) the first serious attempts to bring the state down from the clouds (...)".

In a most condensed form Marx's view was that, in general:

> "Die moderne Staatsgewalt ist nur ein Ausschusz, der die gemeinschaftlichen Geschäfte der ganzen Bourgeoisklasse verwaltet" [Marx and Engels (1848, p. 14)] [7].

The class character of the state was further elaborated upon by Engels (1892) [for an anthology of Marx's and Engels' contributions, see Hennig *et al.* (1974)], Lenin (1918, 1919) and Gramsci (1971), and has remained the starting point of all Marxist theories of the state ever since. These classical works do not exhibit a systematic and sustained analysis of the state. It is most of the time treated as an instrument of the 'ruling class', but at times it is also presented as an epiphenomenon of the system of property relations (a rigid interpretation of the 'base-superstructure' theory) or, more actively, as a factor of cohesion in the class struggle, or as an institution for political domination, in which case attention is shifted to political representation and state intervention [Jessop (1977, pp. 354-357)].

The last mentioned approach clearly allows for a relative autonomy of the state [8]. The relative autonomy of the state has taken an important place in more recent Marxist studies.
Starting at the end of the sixties a great number of studies on the state in capitalist societies has appeared, attacking such diverse problems as: the genesis of the state, the development and structure of state expenditures/taxes, ideology, economic crises, state intervention in the economy, the impact of big business (monopoly capital), the consequences and determinants of the internationalization of economic activities (imperialism), inflation [9]. Apart from O'Connor (1973), the Marxist Approach has particularly profited by the works of Miliband (1973a) and Poulantzas (1978a, 1978b) and the discussion between these two writers [see Miliband (1970, 1973b) and Poulantzas (1969, 1976)].
It is impossible here to give a detailed exposé of all these studies and to do justice to all the theoretical shades involved. Instead we will try to epitomize those pieces of theory that would especially seem to be im-

portant for a study of the interaction between state and private sector 10).

Theory. The relevant theory can be summarized as follows.

1. In a capitalist economy, as in any other mode of production, the production process (production playing the determinant role in the economic sphere) is constituted by interdependent productive forces (means of labour: e.g., machines, technology) and social relations of production; the latter consisting, on the one hand, of the relationships between the agents of production and the means of labour, and, on the other hand, through these relationships, of the relations between the agents themselves.
2. The relations between the agents are class relations; classes being social groupings that are principally defined by their position in the production process, more specifically by their economic control of the means of production (their economic power or real economic ownership, to be distinguished from legal ownership). Classes may consist of different fractions. In a capitalist economy the main classes are: the bourgeoisie (the exploiting, dominant, owning class) and the working class (the exploited, dominated class); we furthermore have the so-called middle classes.
3. Classes involve class antagonisms and class struggles that not only take place on the economic level but also on the political and ideological level.
4. Classes may have standpoints in concrete cases that differ from their class interests; the latter follow from their position in the economic process.
5. Class struggle is the motor of history.
6. A mode of production is an abstract object. In reality we have social formations formed by several (forms of) modes of production. Normally, there will be a dominant mode of production (unless we are in a transition phase) and remnants of previous (dominant) modes of production.
7. Although the economic plays the determinant role in any mode of production or social formation (the 'dominance in the last instance' assumption), the political and ideological (the superstructure) also have a constitutive, relatively autonomous, role.
8. The complex of old and new dominant classes is called the 'power bloc'. The dominant fraction within the power bloc is coined the 'hegemonic' fraction. In the last instance the hegemonic fraction is not only economically but also ideologically and politically dominant in a social formation. At the present stage of capitalism the power bloc, formed by the bourgeoisie as a whole, is under the hegemony of monopoly capital.
9. Through the internationalization of the accumulation process there is an internationalization of class relations and class struggle which influences the political and ideological class struggle that largely develops

within nation states.

10. The state is neither a thing or instrument that can be freely disposed of by anyone who (formally) seizes state power, nor a subject with a unified will and complete autonomy. The state is the institutional materialization and condensation of the class struggle on the political level. State 'functions' cannot be neutral, therefore. On the other hand, it is precisely its position within the class struggle that establishes its relative autonomy. It is not fully controlled by any fraction.

11. Class contradictions also show themselves in the actions and policies of the different apparatuses that make up the state organization (administrative departments, judiciary, government, and others). The result is a complex of policies, the degree of coordination of which depends on the character of the class struggle (especially interesting is of course its crystallization on the governmental level).

12. The dominant class(es) need not be the governing class(es). One of the means by which the dominance of the power bloc and its hegemonic fraction is secured are the structural restrictions on the actions of the state which originate in the private sector. Other means are: personal ties with state apparatuses and the activities of representative interest groups. In the last analysis the long term interests of monopoly capital are at present served by the state, implying a strategy of compromise towards non-monopoly capital.

13. The basic function of the state is to (help) (re-)produce the conditions for the accumulation of capital; this further involves political, ideological (legitimation) and economic functions.

Fig. 1.3 presents some of the more important relationships between state and private sector according to the Marxist Approach [11)]. The arrows indicate influences emanating from, and affecting class struggles on, the economic, ideological (here: political parties, some state apparatuses), and political level; m.o.p. stands for modes of production.

Critique. In our opinion, *important* and *valuable* aspects of the Marxist Approach are:

1. the search for the most central class (and, thus, power) relationships in society - which is interesting from a social-research strategic point of view - and related to this, the interest in the structure of the economy;
2. the emphasis on the intricacy of the dominance of a dominant class or power bloc, which demands a continuous reproduction of its economic, ideological and political conditions;
3. the emphasis on the relative autonomy of the political and ideological spheres in society, and, in particular, on the importance of the role played by the state and of determinants of its behaviour (class relation-

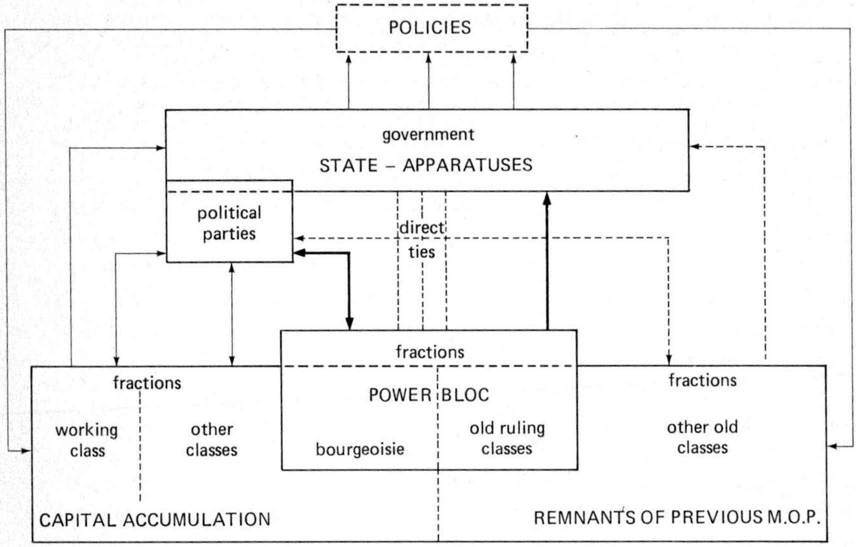

Fig. 1.3. Marxist Approach.

ships, interest group activity, economic structure).

As yet the *most serious weakness* in the Marxist Approach seems to be its lack of specificity, notwithstanding its stress on the relevance of historical and situation-specific details. This, especially, shows up in:
1. the treatment of classes, in particular those other than bourgeoisie and working class;
2. the delimitation of the relative autonomy of the political and ideological levels, given the last instance or determination assumption with respect to the economic level;
3. the role played by individual agents *vis-à-vis* impersonal structures.

Due to this lack of explicitness it occurs, on the one hand, that theories get in fact void of social content by over-emphasizing the impact of structures, and, on the other hand, that theories get a structural functionalist overtone, thereby either falling back into a simple instrumentalism or reductionism, or even going so far as to assume the predominance of the superstructure in certain aspects. As Foley (1978, pp. 233-234) puts it:

> "to achieve convincing explanation Marxist theory faces two major hurdles. First, at point after point, clear models of the mechanisms through which relations of production influence other aspects of economic life (clear models of the operation of money, labor markets, price formation, political influence, for example) are lacking. This leaves important gaps in the general arguments, since very often the thrust of an explanation depends critically on the details of some mechanism (...). If we are to have convincing accounts of the links between production and State policy, we need a better understanding of the modern dynamics of accumulation" [12].

Public Choice Approach

Writers and topics. In Mueller (1976, p.395) Public Choice is defined as "the economic study of nonmarket decision-making, or, simply the application of economics to political science".
Alternative labels of this field of research are: social (collective) choice, (new) political economy, economic theory of political decision making. Related approaches from the side of political science go under the names of mathematical political theory and positive political theory.
Seminal contributions to this approach are the works of Arrow (1963), Black (1958), Buchanan and Tullock (1962), Downs (1957), Olson (1965). The by now already vast amount of literature in this field is surveyed by Frey (1978), Mueller (1976), Taylor (1971). See also the textbooks by Bernholz (1972, 1975, 1979), Frey (1977a), Mueller (1979), Riker and Ordeshook (1973), Van den Doel (1978).

The literature may roughly be said to address four topics. The *first* concerns the ultimate reasons for state activities [13]. The *second* concerns the different aspects of voting, such as the properties of voting rules [14], party competition and the significance of the median voter [15], and the behaviour of the voter [16]. The *third* topic regards the behaviour of politicians in a representative government [17], the behaviour of bureaucrats [18], the interrelationships between government and bureaucracy [19]. The *fourth* topic, finally, concerns the relationships between the economy and the state and the mediating role played by voters; there are three approaches: non-formal studies [20], formal analytical or simulation models focusing primarily on the behaviour of the government (politicians) and its impact and dependence on politico-economic outcomes [21], and econometric studies which have particularly been concerned with the relationship between vote-shares of political parties, or government popularity, and general economic conditions (*scil.*, inflation, unemployment, per capita income)[22].

Theory. Although there are differences in accentuation, the Public Choice Approach with respect to the aforementioned topics, in so far as it is relevant to a non-normative study of the interaction between state and private sector, can be characterized as follows.

1. The approach is individualistic. The behaviour of organizations like the state, or private interest groups, is related to the behaviour of their individual members.

2. The basic behavioural postulate is that every individual acts rationally, is self-interested, and maximizes utility.

3. Democratic capitalist economies are examined.

4. The main actors in the political sector are the government (politicians), bureaucracy (bureaucrats), parties, and voters.

5. Government and parties aim at winning elections (through the maximization of votes, vote shares, the probability of re-election, etc.); in fact they want to govern at all cost, the realization of the goals (e.g., power, ideology) of politicians and party members is considered to be completely conditional on the attainment of state power. Apart from this political constraint on the behaviour of politicians, there are administrative constraints, mainly due to the presence of a (self-interested) bureaucracy, and economic constraints, originating from the general economic structure (with its consequences for the state budget, for example) and the activities of interest groups (e.g., contributions to political campaign expenditures). The popularity index determined from popularity polls is taken to be the best current indicator that the government has for assessing its vote getting capacity at the next election. Given the aforementioned constraints, politicians try to reassure their election by using all instruments available, including (discriminatory) economic policies (concerning transfers, taxes, exhaustive expenditures), and psychological distortion with respect to their achievements by claiming responsibility for beneficial politico-economic outcomes and denying it for disadvantageous ones [23].

Political parties will use and adapt their party programmes and propaganda to the same purpose.

6. Bureaucrats try to maximize output, budgets, or the size of their bureaus; these activities are taken to be conducive to the maximization of their utility, which is considered to be dependent on such items as prestige and power. Financial means - budgets - are obtained in a bargaining process with politicians. The position of the bureaucrats in this process is strengthened by the fact that they are the sole suppliers of their goods and services (at least within the state organization); the bargaining process resembles the situation of a bilateral monopoly.

7. Voters are rational and will only vote if the expected utility of voting exceeds that of abstaining. This utility differential is dependent on the difference in expected utility to be derived from the incumbency of the different candidate parties, the voter's subjective appraisal of the probability that her/his vote will affect the outcome of the election, the

utility that the voter derives from participating in the electoral process, and the costs involved.

8. Important for the relationship between government and voters are: constitutional arrangements, decision rules (such as the majority rule), the length of the period between elections, the comprehensiveness of the policy-bundle (degree of full-line supply) that the voter automatically votes for when voting for a representative at elections.

9. Voting is not the only instrument of political participation, however. Other instruments are: participation in interest groups, corruption, moving to another jurisdiction, etc.

10. The specific structure of the economy is important for the government's selection of (economic) policies, as the consequences of these policies for the government's re-election chances may differ depending on their incidence. Labour intensive industries, for example, with - *ceteris paribus* - more potential voters may be more interesting for beneficial treatment than relatively capital intensive industries.

Fig. 1.4 pictures the relationships between state and private sector that are, as yet, focused upon in so-called general politico-economic models within the Public Choice Approach. These models - still a very small number - concentrate on the macro-relationship between the economic sector and the political sector [24].

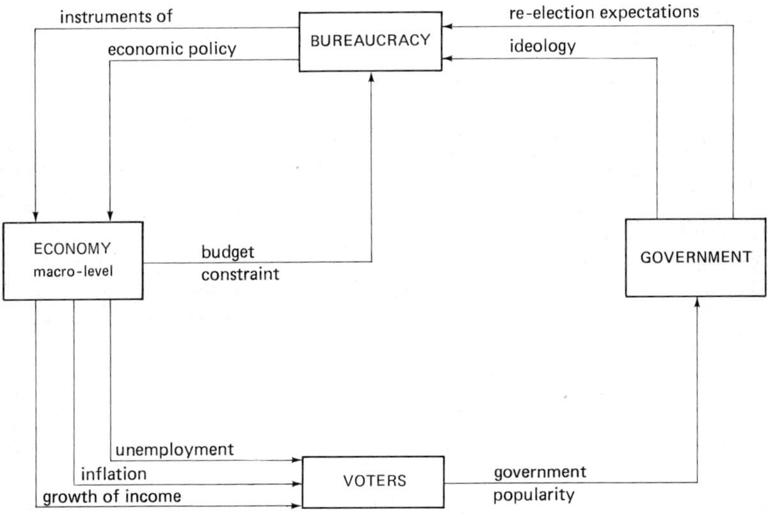

Fig. 1.4. General politico-economic model (Public Choice Approach).

Critique. In our view, *valuable* and *important* aspects of the Public Choice Appoach are:

1. the emphasis on the role played by bureaucrats, politicians/parties and voters in economic processes [25];
2. the attempt to root explanations of politico-economic phenomena in individual motivations;
3. the clear preference for formalization.

Unsatisfactory in this approach - at least in its present form - is, though:

1. the neglect of broader class or power relationships in society; generally, no distinction is made between socio-economic groups or classes, which may be important in view of the distributional aspects of economic events (take inflation, for instance) [26];
2. the predominant attention for macro-economic relationships in politico-economic models; most of the time, only agents in the political sphere but no identifiable agents in the economic sphere play a part [27];
3. the almost exclusive interest in voting as a means of political participation [28];
4. the assumption that politicians and parties want to govern at all costs, while from a political strategic point of view a deliberate choice for going into the opposition cannot *a priori* be ruled out; moreover, ideology, party line, electoral promises, information problems, and bureaucratic influences are discounted.

1.3. Political Economics

Overlooking the contributions of the Marxist Approach and the Public Choice Approach it appears that a lot of ground in the research area of the relationship between state and private sector is still left to be uncovered. With this book we intend to make a contribution to this uncovering. Our *point of departure* thereby is that the indicated valuable elements as well as the shortcomings of both approaches should be taken care of. This means that in studying the interaction between state and private sector, attention should be paid to:

- social *classes*, and the impact of class/power relationships on political and economic processes;
- the way that social *power structures* (involving the real control over state activities) are maintained or altered;
- the *relative autonomy* of political processes (involving the state) and its consequences for, as well as its dependence on economic processes;
- individual *motivations*;
- the possibility of mathematical *formalization*.

Political economics seems to be an appropriate name for this type of study; it deals with the intersection of politics and economics [29].

1.4. Approach and Scope of the Book

Largely by means of a series of formal models it will be attempted to give a rather rigorous *non-normative analysis of the relationships between state and private sector in capitalist economies, thereby taking into account the analytical requirements enumerated in the previous section* [30]. The following *two sets of problems* are addressed:

1. the impact of the political and socio-economic structure, the activities of political parties and other 'pressure groups', and the interests represented by state-personnel, on the behaviour of the state;
2. the impact of the state - and changes in the type of state - on the behaviour of firms and households (as consumers, suppliers of labour, political agents).

The analysis has the following *features.*

- The state, which we defined in Section 1.1 as an institution, in fact comprises "a number of particular institutions which, together, constitute its reality, and which interact as parts of what may be called the state system" [Miliband (1973a, p. 46)]. In the sequel, we will speak of the *state organization.*
  The different institutions or apparatuses (among which: the military, the judiciary, the cabinet, the parliament) [31] that the state organization consists of will be subsumed under two headings: government and bureaucracy. The term *bureaucracy* is used to denote all the state-apparatuses except for the (central, sub-central) 'representative' bodies (forming the formal decision-making centre), which are all subsumed under the heading *government*; thus, also a parliament is part of the government [32]. The bureaucracy is made up by bureaucrats, the government by politicians.

- No comprehensive theory of the state can, of course, be given. Although the behaviour of the state is endogenous in the models to be considered, this is only partly so. The general traits of the political system and the instruments that the state has at its disposal, for example, are assumed to be given. Moreover, the range of instruments available to the state is restricted to *taxation* (the setting of tax tariffs, that is) and *state employment* (which is, presumably, generally the main component determining state consumption) [33]. Activities such as regulation (laws), selling and buying (procurement, state-enterprises), and the shaping of ideology will not be dealt with. Apart from the state wage

sum, state expenditure also includes *transfers* of unemployment benefits, though.
Another simplification is that the bureaucracy is, generally, treated as a homogeneous state-apparatus. Nevertheless, it is one of the special features of this study compared with other studies that employ formal models that the *behaviour of bureaucrats* is *endogenous* [34)].
Another special feature is the introduction of a relationship between state-activities and *technology*, involving an *endogenous* level of labour productivity in the private sector. This relationship is clearly of great importance (think of education, research).

- Attention is restricted to capitalist economies [35)]. These economies are supposed to be *closed*, which is an important assumption as the openness of economies may clearly have substantial consequences for the behaviour of state and private sector participants as well as for their relationship [36)].
  The size of the *labour force* is assumed to be *fixed*. Although an endogenous development of technology is allowed for, its character is such that the possibility of long-term non-zero growth is excluded by this assumption.
  Four types of goods will be dealt with: private (marketed) goods, collective (non-marketed) goods, labour services, and money.
  There are mainly four types of decision makers (agents); the state, political parties, firms, and households in the role of consumers, suppliers of labour, and of political agents.
  Financial intermediation only occurs in a very rudimentary form.
  Private production takes place in *one production sector* [37)]. In the politico-economic models to be developed, *atomistic competition* is assumed to hold for the private sector; moreover, apart from political parties, agents trying to influence the state - *pressure groups* - are supposed to be absent. The consequences of the presence of pressure groups in the private sector will be studied in a separate chapter. This will confront us again with the limited reach of contemporary economic theory, because of its almost exclusive concern with market behaviour. For our interest here is, particularly, in the impact of such groups on the interaction between state and private sector outside any market (see Section 1.6).

- The models are of increasing complexity. Except for state and firms, our concern is not so much with a detailed construction of the constitutive parts rather than with the integratedness and the working of a model as a whole. The heuristic value of these models is what we are basically interested in.
  The study is *theoretical* and *explorative* in character. There is no empirical testing or estimation. Possibilities for empirical work are in-

dicated along the way, though.

Apart from the first model in Chapter 2, all models are *dynamic* - in which case time is treated as a discrete variable [38] - and *non-stochastic*. Expectations are formed in a simple adaptive way, may not be fulfilled, and need not be 'rational' in the sense of Muth (1961) [39]. Markets may be in disequilibrium, i.e. need not clear, even in case of stationariness. The analysis is *micro-orientated* and explicitly refers to *motivating interests* of individual agents.

The basic research methods used are that of *comparative statics* and *computer simulation*. Both methods have their obvious limitations. However, they enable us to formulate the models according to our wishes, which is at least at this stage of the analysis an important advantage. Whenever this is possible, though, additional information on the dynamical properties of the models will be given.

1.5. Outline of the Book

After some general remarks on social relationships and activities in the following section, we start, in Chapter 2, with a simple *static model* by means of which some general aspects of the interdependence of state and private sector are studied. Attention is focused upon the interaction of state and firms. In Chapter 3 *time* is introduced and the structure of the private sector is further worked out. In addition, the behaviour of the state is reconsidered in the light of some existing hypotheses on the *behaviour of bureaucrats and politicians*. The interdependence of state and private sector is particularly shaped by the assumption of a minimum consumption level in terms of private product, the assumption of a relationship between accumulated state production and labour productivity, and the job preferences of labour. Chapter 4 presents an alternative approach that hinges upon the notion of an *interest function*; the latter is a representation of the interests of agents, associated with the *position* that they have with respect to production in the economy. This approach - which is coined the *Interest Function Approach* - is maintained in the following chapters. Chapter 5 is concerned with the modelling of *political activities*, such as voting and government coalition formation by parties. In Chapter 6 we present and analyze a model for a *representative democracy* with political parties and elections; it is based on the model developed in Chapter 4. Chapter 7 deals with some issues that were already pointed at in Chapter 2; it is particulary concerned with the various consequences of the presence of influential organizations - *pressure groups* - in the private sector for the relationship between the state and these organizations.

Chapter 8 concludes.

1.6. Market and Non-Market Activities and Social Relationships

1.6.1. Introduction

In order to gain a clear understanding of the interaction between state and private sector it is necessary to look beyond the *market*. A distinction should be made between *market* and *non-market activities* of agents, and *market* and *non-market social relationships* between agents.
As these concepts are fundamental to a politico-economic study of a capitalist economy, it is appropriate to discuss and define them first.
The present section is devoted to that purpose [40)].

1.6.2. Activities and Social Relationships

Agents - individual or collective decision-making units, such as consumers or firms, in the state or private sector - are supposed to *represent interests*, that is to have preferences with respect to the outcomes of political and economic processes. The promotion, or realization, of these interests is restricted. An agent is confronted with constraints on the set of ways (to be specified) in which he/she can further his/her interests. The ways that remain determine the *activity set* from which the agent can choose.
An *activity* is defined as the realization of choice. In the sequel, the words *activity*, *action* and *behaviour*, will be used interchangeably.
A distinction is made between constraints that are due to *structural coercion*, and constraints that are due to *pressure*. Structural coercion stands for the behavioural constraints (inclusive of instrumental constraints) that stem from the nature (structure) of the environment in which the agent acts, *in so far* as these do not result from influence attempts - directed at that agent - by other agents in the environment; in the latter case we speak of pressure.
For example, the existing body of technical know-how is part of the structural coercion that shapes the activity set of a firm, while the restrictions on that set resulting from a threat by a labour union to strike are subsumed under pressure.
The incorporation of pressure into the analysis of the behaviour of an agent demands that the analytically complicating phenomena of strategic behaviour and bargaining will have to be dealt with.
As determinants of the behaviour (activities, actions) of an agent we, thus, consider: the *representation of interests* (or *representation*, for short), *structural coercion*, and *pressure*.

Activities will be distinguished into market activities and non-market activities. In order to arrive at a neat distinction between these two kinds of activities we need a clear concept of a market. Although being a central concept in economic theory, a casual examination of textbooks shows that no generally accepted definition exists [41].

Here, a *market* will be defined as:

a. the social process of agents negotiating the exchange

b. of well-defined products (goods)

c. that is voluntary in nature (agents have the opportunity to opt out)

d. and - more or less frequently - recurrent (although not necessarily between the same agents [42].

Exchange may be *direct or indirect*. The difference is that in the latter case money (and prices) are involved: goods are exchanged for money, and money is exchanged for goods; the rate of exchange expressed in money being the price of a good [43].

Market activities (MA) then are defined as activities involved in the exchange-negotiation process in markets. Any other type of activity is called a *non-market activity* (NMA) [44].

Examples of MA are: supplying and demanding of marketed goods, pricing [45].

Examples of NMA are: (threat of) violence, lobbying, taxation, enactment of laws, public relations activities [46]. We admit that the definition of MA is still rather loose, but it will suffice for our purposes.

Consider two agents, i and j. Let the activity sets of the two agents be denoted by A_i and A_j with as typical elements a_i and a_j, respectively. The Cartesian product of these sets, denoted by $A_i \times A_j$, is the set of all ordered pairs (a_i,a_j), i.e. $A_i \times A_j \equiv \{(a_i,a_j) | a_i \in A_i, a_j \in A_j\}$.

Assume, furthermore, the existence of, say, *utility functions* P_i: $A_i \times A_j \to R$ and P_j: $A_i \times A_j \to R$ (where R denotes the one-dimensional Euclidean space), which associate a level of utility (satisfaction) with each pair of activities, for agents i and j, respectively.

A *social relationship* [or relation(ship), for short] between i and j, *then*, is said to exist if and only if the activities of one of them influence the utility level of the other; formally it is defined by the existence of activities $a_i, a_i' \in A_i$ and $a_j, a_j' \in A_j$ such that $P_i(a_i,a_j) \neq P_i(a_i,a_j')$ and/or $P_j(a_i,a_j) \neq P_j(a_i',a_j)$. It is called *one-sided* if only one of the inequalities holds, *two-sided* if both inequalities hold.

What matters for the behaviour of agents is, of course, their *perception* of a social relationship, and not the assessments of an outside observer.

In this context, we note that *interaction* between two agents will be said to occur if the activities of one of them have consequences for the activities of the other. Formally, agent i is said to interact with agent j if and only if there exists a function r_i: $A_j \to A_i$ such that $r_i(a_j) \neq r_i(a_j')$ for some $a_j, a_j' \in A_j$; r_i may be called a *reaction function*.

The definition allows for complete asymmetry in interaction. Interaction is called *one-sided* or *two-sided* dependent on whether only for one or both agents a reaction function, as defined, exists. Its occurrence is taken to imply that the agent who reacts on the activities of the other perceives a social relationship with the other agent; on the other hand, the perception of a social relationship is not taken to imply that interaction takes place (it may be too costly to take the behaviour of a specific agent into account) [47].

A *market social relationship* (MSR) between the agents i and j exists if and only if there is exchange-negotiation between these agents in a market and a social relationship between them is constituted by the MA, pertaining to that market, in their activity sets (given the utility functions P_i and P_j).
Any other type of social relationship that may exist between those agents is labelled a *non-market social relationship* (NMSR).
A MSR is exclusively constituted by MA, and not by NMA; NMA can only constitute a NMSR. However, MA may also establish a NMSR; this is not restricted to NMA. Consider the following example. There exists a NMSR between a large firm and the state if layoffs by that firm would be perceived by the state to affect the attainment of a given employment target. In that case, the social relationship is established through MA (by the firm in the labour market), but it should, nevertheless, be labelled a NMSR as it does not arise from exchange-negotiation between that firm and the state in a market.

Note that MSR and NMSR may at the same time exist between agents, that agents may have an option between the use of MA and NMA, and that an activity does not necessarily consist of a single act, it may comprise a number of MA and/or NMA. Note, furthermore, in this context that *political activities* - defined as activities by agents that affect or are intended to affect the behaviour of the state [cf. Milbrath and Goel (1977, p. 2)] - may involve MA as well as NMA, in MSR as well as NMSR with the state.

Fig. 1.5 sums up the social relationships and activities that may play a role in the interaction between state and private sector participants.

In this book attention will particularly be focused upon NMSR between state and private sector as these are most fundamental to the interdependence of these two sectors. After all, the activities of the state are basically financed by means of taxation (NMA), are basically associated with the provision of non-market goods, and predominantly determined through NMSR with the private sector (voting, pressure group activities, structural coercion originating from the structure of the economy).
This is not to deny the importance of MSR as a subject of study in this

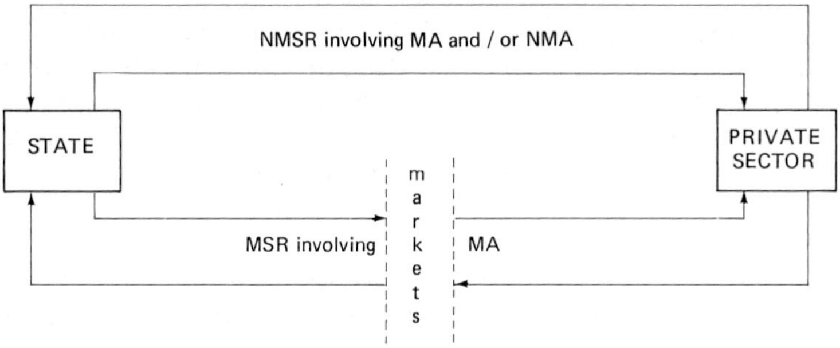

Fig. 1.5. Interaction between state and private sector: activities and social relationships.

context. One need only think of nationalized industries.
However, each study has its limitations. As indicated in Section 1.4, the only market that the state, in this book, will be actively involved in, is the labour market (only a rudimentary capital market will be considered). And even there our main interest will not be in the way that the state behaves as a buyer of labour services, but in side-effects such as the crowding out of firms in that market (which refers to a NMSR between state and firms).

CHAPTER 2

A FIRST APPROACH

2.1. Introduction

In this chapter some *general aspects* of the relationship between state and private sector are studied by means of a simple static model [1].
Attention is focused upon the interaction between state and firms that follows from a non-market relationship between them. The impact, on this relationship, of *structural coercion*, *representation* and *pressure* (see the previous chapter) is particularly studied. Apart from pressure directed at the state on the side of the firms, we will not explicitly deal with influential political actions emanating from outside the state sector.
We start with the presentation of the model which is cast in a game theoretical framework (Section 2.2). Characteristics of the game are then given (Section 2.3), after which a numerical example is worked out (Section 2.4). This is followed by an analysis of the consequences of alternative behavioural strategies of the firms (Section 2.5). The chapter ends with a summary (Section 2.6).

2.2. A Simple Static Model: The Dominant Player Game.

2.2.1. General Aspects of the Model

We consider a closed capitalist economy with a state sector and a private sector. The state sector comprises two sorts of households, the *state* itself and the households that are represented by people employed by the state (state sector workers). The private sector is made up by *capitalists* (people owning the stock of capital goods or controlling the firms) *private sector workers* (workers employed by business), and *unemployed*. The state produces solely non-marketed goods (services), using labour as the only input. The firms produce a homogeneous marketed good (private product), using labour and capital goods as inputs. Assumed is a large and constant number of relatively small identical firms. Capital goods - of which there is a given stock - are rented by the firms and do not wear out. Capital stock and total labour supply are fixed; rent and wage-rate are fixed as well. Private product is used as *numéraire*.
The state levies taxes for the payment of unemployment benefits and wages for state sector workers; the dole rate is taken to be proportional to the wage rate. There are no other state expenses. The state budget is balanc-

ed.
Disposable income is wholly consumed. Private product demand and supply are balanced. Input demand and supply (capital goods, labour) need not match, however.
Fig. 2.1 pictures the *flows of money* in the model.

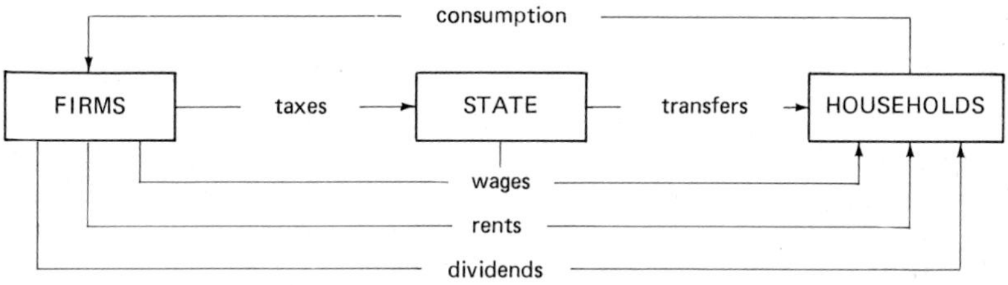

Fig. 2.1. Structure of the model: money flows.

2.2.2. The State

The state comprises a government and a bureaucratic apparatus. In order to be able to explain the activities of the state we need to know four things:

1. the interests of the politicians and the bureaucrats that make up the government and the bureaucratic apparatus, respectively;
2. the distribution of power within the state;
3. the instruments that are available to politicians and bureaucrats;
4. the constraints on the activities of the state.

Interests. With respect to the first point, we simply start from the fact that, due to the existence of the state, private product is split up into one part that goes to the state sector [to be consumed by state sector workers (politicians and bureaucrats)] and another that remains in the private sector. It is assumed that the interests that are represented within the state can be expressed as a function of these two parts of *private* product, whatever the ultimate goals of bureaucrats and politicians may be. Now in order to allow, in a yet simple way, for a possible inequality in the relative strength with which the interests are represented it is further assumed that the state acts in accordance with the maximization of a function P_s, specified as

(2.1) $$P_s = \varepsilon[wE_1] + (1 - \varepsilon)[X_b - wE_1] \quad , \; 0 \leqq \varepsilon \leqq 1,$$

where w (> 0) stands for the fixed real wage rate (assumed to be equal for private sector workers and state sector workers), E_1 for the number of state sector workers, and X_b for total private product. Recall that private product is used as numéraire. The part of private product that goes to the state sector is equal to the state wage sum wE_1, and may be seen as an indicator for the size of the state as well as for the amount of state goods produced.

State goods are taken to be purely collective in character [2].

The parameter ε indicates the relative strength with which the interests indicated by wE_1 and $X_b - wE_1$ are furthered; it is used to characterize, what we will call, the *type of state*. Since ε is defined on the [0,1]-interval an infinite number of types of states can be distinguished. For example, if $\varepsilon = 0$ then eq. (2.1) shows that the state exclusively serves the interests of those who want to promote the 'welfare' of the private sector, indicated by $X_b - wE_1$. As will be shown below, this type of state will - under the conditions of model - strive after a maximum amount of private product; we call it, therefore, a *pure private product biased state*. On the other hand, if $\varepsilon = 1$ then the interests of those favouring the state sector are exclusively met; this type of state will, consequently, be called a *pure state goods biased state*. If one endorses the hypothesis proposed by students of bureaucracy that bureaucrats are strongly, or even predominantly, interested in their budgets or the size of their bureaus [3], then the latter type of state may also be labelled a pure bureaucratic state in case it is fully controlled by the bureaucrats, or if the interests of the politicians are identical with the interests of the bureaucrats.

Instruments. It is assumed that the state has four instruments (disregarding any constraints on the use of them for the moment): its demand for labour E_1, a value added tax τ_1, a profit tax τ_2 (not effective in case of losses), and a private wage sum tax τ_3. All taxes are paid by business.

Constraints. The activities of the state (no matter what type it is) are supposed to be restricted by the following constraints:

firstly, a balanced budget demanding that total state outlays (state wage sum plus transfers) are equal to total tax revenues:

$$(2.2) \qquad wE_1 + \psi w(L - E_1 - E_2) = \tau_1 X_b + \tau_2 F + \tau_3 wE_2 \quad (\equiv R),$$

where ψw $(1 > \psi \geqq 0)$ denotes the dole rate, L total labour supply, E_2 the number of private sector workers, F the total excess funds of business (see the next subsection), and R the total tax sum;

secondly, a fixed total employment target E^* $(0 < E^* \leqq L)$,

$$(2.3) \qquad E_1 + E_2 = E^* \quad ;$$ [4]

thirdly, a minimum state size, indicated by E_1^- (> 0) or wE_1^-, thus

$$(2.4) \qquad E_1 \geqq E_1^-;$$

fourthly, the constraints resulting from the behaviour of business which will be given below [see (2.9)].

2.2.3. Business

Assumptions. As no goods are marketed between state and firms, there are no market relationships between them to be considered. There certainly exists a non-market relationship, however, since the state influences the firms' after-tax profits (in which they are interested, see below) by the tax structure $\underline{\tau} = (\tau_1, \tau_2, \tau_3)$, while the firms determine the size of the tax base as they decide on employment and production. This situation may give rise to market activities by firms, such as changes in employment and capital use, as well as non-market activities, such as lobbying, in order to force the state to promote their interests. However, as we assumed a large number of relatively small identical firms, an individual firm will not be able to particularize the tax structure in accordance with its interests [5]. For the same reason, moreover, it seems acceptable to ignore the possibility of collusive or overtly co-operative behaviour for the moment [6]. It is first assumed, therefore, that the firms act like *tax-price takers*. Moreover, under the given conditions (see also Subsection 2.2.1) we may as well study the aggregate behaviour of the firms instead of the behaviour of the individual firm. In the sequel *aggregate variables* will, therefore, be used.

It is supposed that the firms expect that their demand for labour and capital will be met and that they can sell whatever they supply. As private product supply X_b^s and demand X_b^d will be balanced [see eq. (2.10)], supply is assumed to equal production, i.e. $X_b^s = X_b$.

Interests. Given the tax structure $\underline{\tau}$, let the firms maximize expected after-tax profits, denoted by P_b, which will equal actual after-tax profits as the firms' expectations are realized:

$$(2.5) \qquad P_b = (1 - \tau_2)F,$$

where F - the firms' excess funds that are subject to profit taxation - is given by

$$(2.6) \qquad F = (1 - \tau_1)X_b - (1 + \tau_3)wE_2 - rK_b,$$

where r (> 0) stands for rent, and K_b denotes the quantity of capital goods rented. After-tax profits are paid out as dividends to those who control the firms.

Instruments. The instruments of business are its demand for labour E_2 and capital K_b.

Constraints. Production is constrained by an at least twice continuously differentiable production function G with positive first-order partial derivatives and a negative definite matrix of second-order partial derivatives, while positive amounts of both inputs are needed for production:

$$X_b = G(E_2, K_b). \tag{2.7}$$

Demand for capital and labour. The first-order conditions for a maximum of (2.5) when $\tau_1 < 1$, $\tau_2 < 1$, and $\tau_3 > -1$ (as will be the case, see the following section) are:

$$(1 - \tau_1)\partial G/\partial K_b = r \quad \text{and} \quad (1 - \tau_1)\partial G/\partial E_2 = (1 + \tau_3)w, \tag{2.8}$$

that is, marginal revenue (adjusted for value added tax) should equal marginal costs [7]. The properties of the production function G ensure that the necessary and sufficient conditions for a unique maximum are fulfilled (that is if $\tau_1 < 1$, $\tau_2 < 1$, $\tau_3 > -1$). Using (2.8) and the properties of G it follows that input demand and intended production can be written as functions of τ_1 and τ_3 (for notational convenience, the functions are denoted by the same symbols as the function values) [8]:

$$E_2 = E_2(\tau_1, \tau_3), \quad K_b = K_b(\tau_1, \tau_3), \quad X_b = X_b(\tau_1, \tau_3). \tag{2.9}$$

The specification of the behaviour of the state will be such that input demand and intended production are realized [see eqs. (2.3) and (2.13)]. Let capital income and wage-related income be fully consumed, and let profit-related consumption demand be equal to P_b [9].
Using eq. (2.2) and $X_b^s = X_b$, equilibrium on the product market then follows from:

$$X_b^b = P_b + rK_b + w[\psi L + (1 - \psi)(E_1 + E_2)] = X_b = X_b^s. \tag{2.10}$$

The second equality indicates the equality of total income and total private product.

2.2.4. The Dominant Player Game

The interaction between state and firms, that follows from their non-market relationship, may be described as a game. To sketch this game by means of an illustration, suppose there are m different courses of action (strategies) open to the state regarding the tax structure $\underline{\tau}$ and demand for labour E_1 [among which the one determined by the maximization problem comprising eqs. (2.1)-(2.4), (2.9)] and n different courses of action with respect to input demand to the firms [including the one given by eq. (2.9), the tax-price taker strategy].
Let the first set of strategies be denoted by $\{\alpha_1,..,\alpha_m\}$ and the second set by $\{\beta_1,...,\beta_n\}$.
Then, the game between state and firms can be pictured by the following payoff matrix:

firms

$$
\begin{array}{c}
\quad\quad \beta_1 \dots\dots\dots\dots\dots\dots\dots \beta_k \dots\dots\dots\dots\dots\dots\dots \beta_n \\
\begin{array}{c} \alpha_1 \\ \vdots \\ \text{state } \alpha_h \\ \vdots \\ \alpha_m \end{array}
\left[\dots\dots\dots\dots [P_s(\alpha_h,\beta_k) \quad, \quad P_b(\alpha_h,\beta_k)] \dots\dots\dots\dots \right]
\end{array}
$$

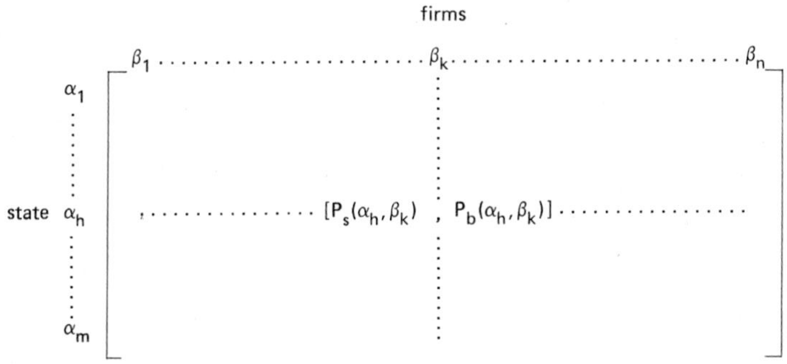

where $[P_s(.), P_b(.)]$ indicates the payoff [10].
An *equilibrium* is defined as the situation in which it is not possible for any player to improve its payoff by using a different strategy, given the strategies of the other players (Nash equilibrium). Formally, if A and B^1, B^2,...denote the strategy sets of the state and the firms, respectively, then an equilibrium is defined by a pair of strategies, labelled α_e ($\in$ A) and $\underline{\beta}_e = (\beta_e^1, \beta_e^2, ...)$ with $\beta_e^f \in B^f$ (f = 1,2,...), for which the following holds: $P_s(\alpha_e, \underline{\beta}_e) \geq P_s(\alpha_i, \underline{\beta}_e)$ for all $\alpha_i \in A$, and $P_f(\alpha_e, \bar{\underline{\beta}}_e^f, \beta_e^f) \geq P_f(\alpha_e, \bar{\underline{\beta}}_e^f, \beta_j^f)$ for all $\beta_j^f \in B^f$, where P_f denotes the after-tax profits of firm f and $\bar{\underline{\beta}}_e^f$ indicates the vector of equilibrium strategies of firms other than f.

In the game between state and firms that we will study here, the state takes the *reactions* of business on its activities as given, while the firms take the *actions* of the state as given. Because of the peculiar 'hierarchical' decision structure of this game, we call it a *dominant player game*, with the state as the dominant player [11)]. Since the state takes account of the equilibrium strategy of the firms, see eq. (2.9), any solution to the programming problem for the state, as exposed in Subsection 2.2.2 and summarized below, establishes an equilibrium for this game.

Before summarizing the programming problem for the state, however, a few more *constraints* on its behaviour will be introduced. First observe that the following should hold:

(2.11) $\tau_1 < 1, \tau_3 > -1.$

If $\tau_1 \geqq 1$ then the maximization of P_b [eq. (2.5)] by business demands that no production takes place (irrespective of τ_2 - which is not effective in case of losses - and τ_3, given $\tau_3 > -1$), which implies that the state cannot balance its budget as tax receipts are zero and outlays equal $wE_1 + \psi w(L - E_1) > 0$. If $\tau_3 \leqq -1$ then we have an insatiable demand for labour by business which runs counter to the total employment constraint and the minimum state size constraint for the state [see (2.3) and (2.4)]. As regards τ_2, notice that the marginal product equations (2.8) do not follow in case that $\tau_2 = 1$. Now instead of assuming that (2.8) also holds in that special case it is assumed that after-tax profits should exceed some fixed proportion q of private product, ensuring that $\tau_2 < 1$:

(2.12) $P_b = (1 - \tau_2)F \geqq qX_b \quad , 0 < q < 1.$

This condition may be justified by observing that, as the firms are interested in after-tax profits, production may become endangered or the non-co-operative behaviour of the firms may vanish and, consequently, coalitions against the state may be formed when after-tax profits are pressed too low. It is assumed that the state tries to avoid such a confrontation and that it (correctly) demands, to that purpose, that (2.12) is satisfied. Notice that negative tax rates (subsidies) are permitted. Finally, the state is constrained in its activities by the fact that the firms cannot employ more capital goods than the available capital stock $\bar{K}_b$:

(2.13) $K_b \leqq \bar{K}_b.$

As $E_2 < L$ by (2.3) and (2.4) and $K_b \leqq \bar{K}_b$ by (2.13), input demand will be satisfied, while intended and actual production will be equal [see (2.9)].

Using (2.1)-(2.4) and (2.11)-(2.13), and recalling that E_2, K_b, and F

$[= (1 - \tau_1)X_b - (1 + \tau_3)wE_2 - rK_b]$ are functions of τ_1 and τ_3 according to (2.6) and (2.9), the programming problem for the state can be written as:

$$
\begin{aligned}
(2.14)\quad & \max_{\underline{\tau}, E_1} P_s(\underline{\tau}, E_1) = \varepsilon[wE_1] + (1 - \varepsilon)[X_b(\tau_1,\tau_3) - wE_1] = \\
& \qquad = (2\varepsilon - 1)wE_1 + (1 - \varepsilon)X_b(\tau_1,\tau_3) \\
& \text{subject to:} \\
& E_1 - E_1^- \geqq 0 && \text{, state size constraint (2.4),} \\
& \bar{K}_b - K_b(\tau_1,\tau_3) \geqq 0 && \text{, capital constraint (2.13),} \\
& (1 - \tau_2)F(\tau_1,\tau_3) - qX_b(\tau_1,\tau_3) \geqq 0 && \text{, profit constraint (2.12),} \\
& 1 - \tau_1 > 0 \\
& && \text{, tax constraints (2.11),} \\
& \tau_3 + 1 > 0 \\
& wE_1 + \psi w[L - E_1 - E_2(\tau_1,\tau_3)] - \tau_1 X_b(\tau_1,\tau_3) + \\
& - \tau_2 F(\tau_1,\tau_3) - \tau_3 wE_2(\tau_1,\tau_3) = 0 && \text{, budget constraint (2.2),} \\
& E_1 + E_2(\tau_1,\tau_3) - E^* = 0 && \text{, employment constraint (2.3),} \\
& X_b(\tau_1,\tau_3) - G[E_2(\tau_1,\tau_3), K_b(\tau_1,\tau_3)] = 0 \\
& && \text{, production constraint (2.7).}
\end{aligned}
$$

A few *remarks* are in order.

1. As indicated above, solving (2.14) is equivalent to finding an equilibrium for the dominant player game.
2. The feasible set of tax structures $\underline{\tau}$ determined by the constraints may be more or less restrictive, depending on the specification of the production function, the employment target E^*, the minimum state size E_1^- and the minimum profit margin q, for example. However, it is easily seen from the employment constraint and the budget constraint that in any case no more than two tax instruments can be freely varied.
3. The employment constraint is particularly important since labour is the only input that is used in both the private sector and the state sector. The labour market is the only market where a crowding out effect may occur, as the state adjusts itself to the demand for labour by business due to the employment target E^*. The outlays on unemployment benefits being fixed by E^*, it is the employment of labour by the state, furthermore, that eventually determines the tax burden for business [see (2.2)]. The importance of the assumption made with respect to the strategy that the firms will use *vis-à-vis* the state - whether they

will determine E_2 according to a tax-price taker strategy in reaction to the tax manipulations by the state or use a different strategy, as will be assumed in Section 2.5 - becomes already apparent now.

4. Note that the part of private product that goes to the private sector equals: $P_b + rK_b + w[\psi(L - E_1) + (1 - \psi)E_2]$ [see (2.10)]. Using (2.3) it follows that eq. (2.1) can be rewritten as: $P_s = \varepsilon[wE_1] + (1 - \varepsilon)\{(P_b + rK_b - wE_1) + w[\psi L + (1 - \psi)E^*]\}$, that is, for each ε P_s is a function of wE_1 and $(P_b + rK_b - wE_1)$. Thus, if $\varepsilon = 0$ (the pure private product biased state) then $P_b + rK_b - wE_1$, i.e. the difference between disposable profit and capital income, on the one hand, and the state wage sum, on the other hand, is maximized. In that case, as will be shown below, private output, and the total of profit and capital income are maximized, while the state size is minimized ($E_1 = E_1^-$). If $\varepsilon = 1$ (the pure state goods biased state) then the state wage sum wE_1 is maximized. This clearly suggests the importance to capitalists of the strength with which the different interests are represented within the state organization (and, consequently, the importance also of personal ties and ideology).

2.3. *Equilibrium Characteristics of the Game; Restrictiveness of an Economy*

The properties of the production function (2.7) warrant that any combination of E_2 and K_b that may be of interest - i.e., for which $0 < E_2 \leqq L$, and $0 < K_b \leqq \bar{K}_b$ can be effectuated by the state through an appropriate choice of $\tau_1 < 1$ and $\tau_3 > -1$ [12]. Notice, furthermore, that τ_2, E_1 and X_b can be eliminated in (2.14) by using the equality constraints (2.2), (2.3), and (2.7); for F, see eq. (2.6). In solving this programming problem we may as well concentrate on E_2 and K_b, and the first three inequality constraints, therefore. The problem can be rewritten as:

(2.14a) $$\max_{E_2,K_b} P_s(E_2,K_b) = (2\varepsilon - 1)w(E^* - E_2) + (1 - \varepsilon)G(E_2,K_b),$$

subject to:

$$E^* - E_1^- - E_2 \geqq 0,$$

$$\bar{K}_b - K_b \geqq 0 \ ,$$

$$(1 - q)G(E_2,K_b) - rK_b - w[E^* + \psi(L - E^*)] \equiv N \geqq 0,$$

$$E_2,K_b \geqq 0,$$

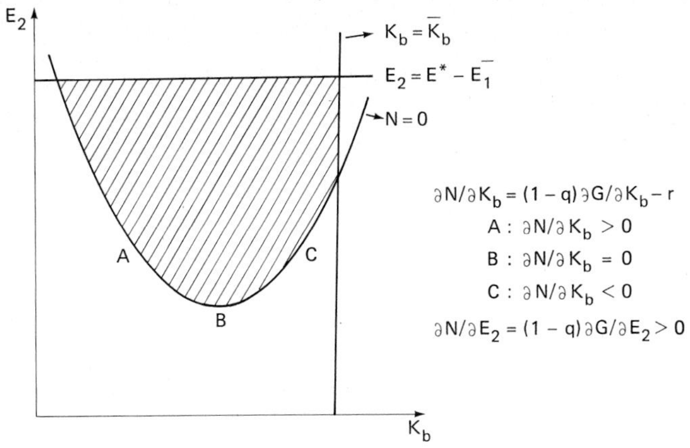

Fig. 2.2. The opportunity set.

where the last but one constraint concerns the surplus of private product in the economy - in the sequel indicated by N - when all income claims have been taken into account [13)]; we will call this constraint the *surplus constraint*. The surplus is a function - for notational convenience also indicated by N - of E_2 and K_b, $N = N(E_2,K_b)$; this function will be called the *surplus constraint function*.

The problem can be illustrated geometrically by measuring the instrumental variables E_2 and K_b along the axes of a Cartesian diagram, showing the opportunity set - i.e., the intersection of the sets of (E_2,K_b) pairs defined by the inequality constraints - and indicating the nature of the function P_s via contours (iso-value curves) and the preference direction (i.e., the direction in which the value of P_s is increasing fastest) [14)]. The opportunity set is illustrated by the shaded area of Fig. 2.2. The figure also shows the strict convexity of the contours of the surplus constraint function $N(E_2,K_b)$ [15)].

As regards the contours of P_s it is useful to distinguish between three classes of states on the [0,1]-interval for ε which may be coined the *political scale*; see Fig. 2.3.

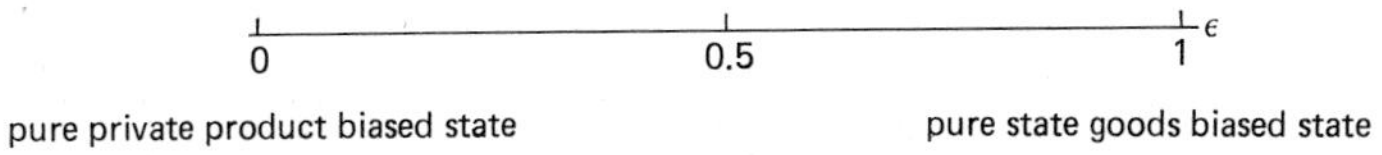

Fig. 2.3. The political scale.

$$\partial P_s/\partial E_2 = w + \partial G/\partial E_2 - \epsilon(2w + \partial G/\partial E_2), \quad \partial P_s/\partial K_b = (1 - \epsilon)\partial G/\partial K_b$$

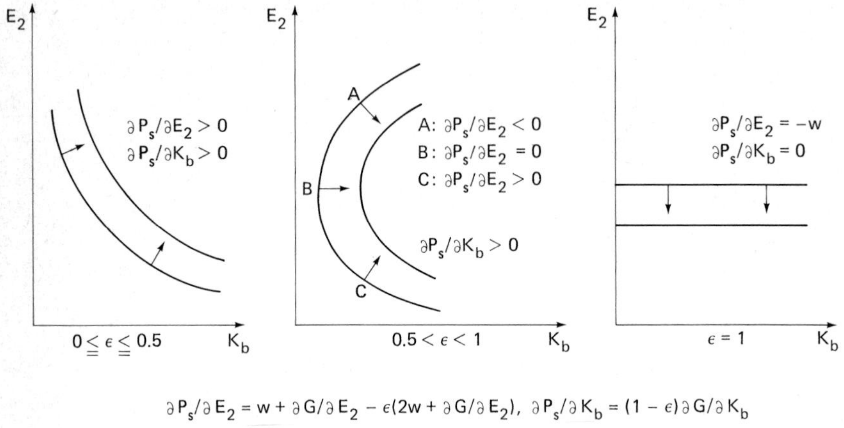

Fig. 2.4. Contours of P_s and preference direction for different ϵ.

It can be shown that the contours of P_s for types of states for which $0 \leqq \epsilon \leqq 0.5$, $0.5 < \epsilon < 1$, or $\epsilon = 1$, are shaped as illustrated in Fig. 2.4; arrows indicate the preference direction [16].

Although Fig. 2.2 shows a non-empty opportunity set, this need not be so, of course. In fact we have three possibilities: the set is empty, the set contains one point only, the set contains more than one point.

Empty opportunity set

Let us start with the case that there are no (E_2, K_b)-combinations satisfying all of the inequality constraints. In that case there is *no solution* to (2.14a). Given the available capital stock and the size of the total labour force the economy cannot meet the income claims of the different agents involved.

One-point opportunity set: a perfectly restrictive economy

In that case there exists only one feasible (E_2, K_b)-combination. The surplus constraint curve in Fig. 2.2 must either be tangent to the state size constraint curve or go, with the downward sloping part, through the intersection of state size and capital constraint curves as shown in Fig. 2.5.

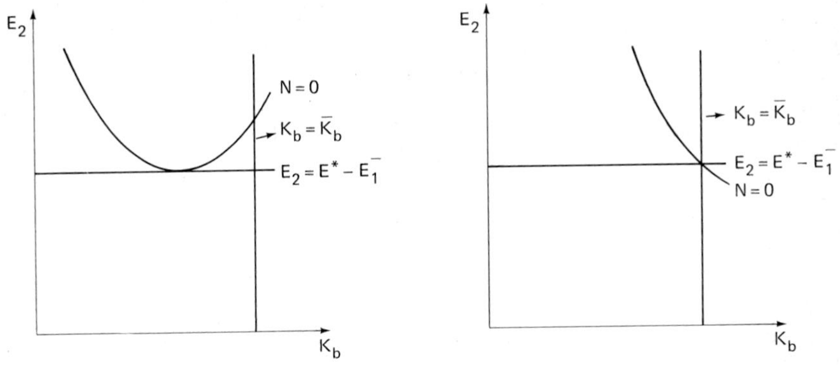

Fig. 2.5. One-point opportunity sets.

As the solution is unique for all $\varepsilon \in [0,1]$ we will speak of a perfectly restrictive economy.

Definition. A *perfectly restrictive economy* is an economy in which the state - whatever type it is - is forced by the constraints that it faces to act in one particular way [that is, here, to choose one particular $(\underline{\tau},E_1)$-combination].

In such an economy the solution $(E_2,K_b) \to (\underline{\tau},E_1)$ to (2.14a) has the following *characteristics*:

either

a. for $0 \leqq \varepsilon \leqq 1$: $E_1 = \bar{E}_1$, $K_b < \bar{K}_b$, $N = 0$, $\partial N/\partial K_b = 0$ ($\tau_1 = q$);

or

b. for $0 \leqq \varepsilon \leqq 1$: $E_1 = \bar{E}_1$, $K_b = \bar{K}_b$, $N = 0$, $\partial N/\partial K_b \geqq 0$ ($\tau_1 \geqq q$);

see Fig. 2.6, where a and b refer to the aforementioned sets of characteristics (for τ_1, see below).

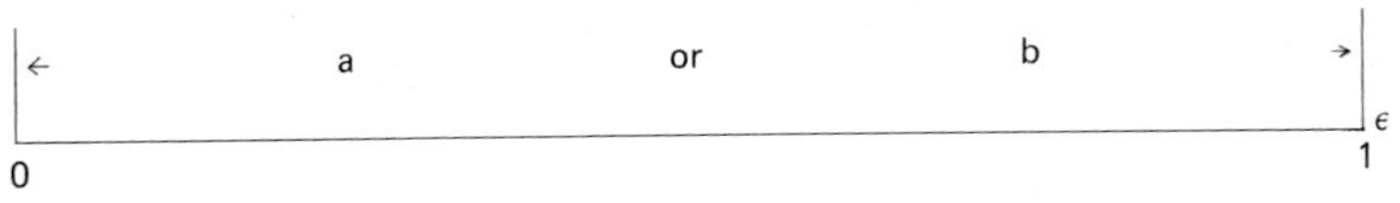

Fig. 2.6. The political scale and equilibrium characteristics for a perfectly restrictive economy.

The state is compelled to keep state employment and, thus, the state size at its minimum, and to choose the particular tax structure that follows from the aforementioned characteristics. With respect to the equilibrium characteristics the following should be noticed.

First, $N = 0$ should hold, for, otherwise, there would be either no feasible point at all ($N < 0$, for all E_2, K_b) or more than one point ($N > 0$), as is easily seen from Fig. 2.5.

A zero surplus in the economy, $N = 0$, implies that after-tax profits are minimal, i.e. $P_b = qX_b$ [see (2.14a)]. Since $P_b + rK_b + w[E^* + \psi(L - E^*)] = X_b$, the share of capital income in total income, rK_b/X_b, as well as the share of profits and capital income together in total income is positively related to the level of private output X_b.

Second, regarding to $E_1 = \bar{E_1}$ and $K_b \leqq \bar{K}_b$, recall that $\partial N/\partial E_2 > 0$ for all E_2, K_b, while $\partial N/\partial K_b \gtreqless 0$. Although a change in private employment does not change the total outlays for business (due to the total employment target, the uniform wage rate, the balanced state budget, and the fact that all taxes are paid by business), the surplus N is changed by the positive marginal productivity of labour adjusted for the minimum profit margin (q) on this marginal product. Thus, changes in N and E_2 are in the same direction. This clearly does not hold for N and K_b, as the firms' outlays are affected by changes in capital use (there is no capital employment target for the state); the rental rate of capital (r) should then be taken into account. As a consequence, the available capital stock in the economy need not be fully employed.

Third, the three (or even four) equations that are (possibly) part of the set of equilibrium characteristics are all in terms of τ_1 and τ_3, implying the existence of functional dependence among them.

Fourth, the equality $\partial N/\partial K_b = 0$ and the (in)equality $\partial N/\partial K_b \geqq 0$ can be substituted by $\tau_1 = q$ and $\tau_1 \geqq q$, respectively, since $\partial N/\partial K_b = (1 - q) \partial G/\partial K_b - r$, and $(1 - \tau_1)\partial G/\partial K_b - r = 0$ because of eq. (2.8).

The opportunity set contains more than one point: restrictive and permissive economies

In this case the state has a choice between different combinations of E_2 and K_b, which it is able to effectuate by manipulating the tax structure $\underline{\tau} = (\tau_1, \tau_2, \tau_3)$. Fig. 2.7 illustrates the different structures that the opportunity set may have in (E_2, K_b)-space (the thick parts of the curves will be referred to below). Figure a differs from b in that $K_b < \bar{K}_b$ for all E_2, K_b in a. The figures a and b differ from c in that it is possible to have $E_1 = \bar{E_1}$, $K_b = \bar{K}_b$ and $N > 0$ in c. Figures a, b and c, finally, differ from d in that only the downward sloping part of the surplus constraint curve lies in the opportunity set in d. The terms 'permissive' and 'restrictive economies' in the figure will be explained below.

In order to establish the equilibrium characteristics for different types of states, we first write problem (2.14a) in Lagrangean function form:

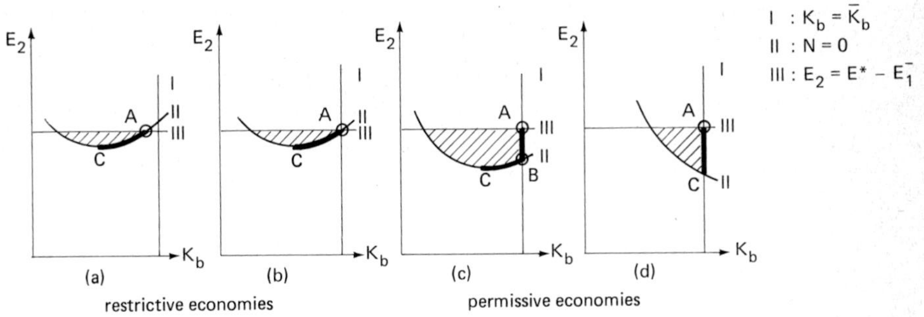

Fig. 2.7. Opportunity sets containing more than one point.

$$(2.15)\quad L(E_2,K_b) = (2\varepsilon - 1)w(E^* - E_2) + (1 - \varepsilon)G(E_2,K_b) + \\ + \ell_1(E^* - E_1^- - E_2) + \ell_2(\bar{K}_b - K_b) + \\ + \ell_3\{(1 - q)G(E_2,K_b) - rK_b - w[E^* + \psi(L - E^*)\},$$

where ℓ_i $(i = 1,2,3)$ denotes the Lagrange multiplier. The necessary and sufficient (Kuhn-Tucker) conditions for a unique global maximum are [17]:

$$(2.16)\quad \frac{\partial L}{\partial E_2} = 0,\ \frac{\partial L}{\partial K_b} = 0,\ \frac{\partial L}{\partial \ell_i} \geqq 0,\ \ell_i \cdot \frac{\partial L}{\partial \ell_i} = 0,\ \ell_i \geqq 0,\quad i = 1,2,3.$$

Using these conditions the equilibrium results that are presented below can be proved. For reasons of exposition, however, we will refer to Figs. 2.4 and 2.7 in establishing these results.

First notice from the shape of the contours of P_s and the preference direction as shown in Fig. 2.4 that only the thick part of the boundary of the opportunity sets shown in Fig. 2.7 is of interest for an equilibrium. If $0 \leqq \varepsilon \leqq 0.5$ the equilibrium is situated in the north-east corner of the sets (point A). If $0.5 < \varepsilon < 1$ the equilibrium may be anywhere between the north-east corner (including the corner itself) and the lowest point of the surplus constraint curve (point C). If $\varepsilon = 1$ the equilibrium is located at the lowest point of the surplus constraint curve in the opportunity set.

It appears that we cannot have an interior solution. For all ε at least the capital constraint and/or the surplus constraint should be active, irrespective of the nature of the opportunity set.
This is not surprising. If none of the constraints is active or if the state-size constraint is active only, it is feasible and advantageous to

the state, depending on the value of ε, to stimulate the demand for capital (thereby increasing X_b, and, thus $X_b - wE_1$) and/or to increase E_1 (thereby increasing wE_1, and lowering X_b due to E^*). It is also clear from Fig. 2.7 that the capital constraint is the only constraint that may never be active, irrespective of the value of ε. A full utilization of the available capital stock may be blocked by the surplus constraint.

Comparing the figures a and b with c and d it shows that in the economies represented by a and b the surplus constraint will always be active, while in the economies represented by c and d it will only be so for types of states for which ε is sufficiently high. For the latter, c and d, at least $\varepsilon > 0.5$ should hold, for, otherwise, the equilibrium is located at A; at any rate, the surplus constraint will be active if $\varepsilon = 1$ (see above). The former types of economies will be called restrictive, the latter types permissive.

Definition. A *restrictive economy* is an economy in which the surplus constraint is active for all types of states (ε).
Definition. A *permissive economy* is an economy in which the surplus constraint is inactive for at least one type of state.
For the sake of completeness we also give the following definition.
Definition. A *perfectly permissive economy* is an economy in which the surplus constraint is inactive for all types of states.
The last definition will not be relevant for our model as the surplus constraint will, at any rate, be active when $\varepsilon = 1$.

I. *Restrictive economy*. Denoting the marginal products of labour and capital when measured at the intersection of $N = 0$ and $E_2 = E^* - E_1^-$ by $(\partial G/\partial E_2)_1$ and $(\partial G/\partial K_b)_1$, respectively, and putting $\{r(\partial G/\partial E_2)_1 + w[r - (1 - q)(\partial G/\partial K_b)_1]\}/\{r(\partial G/\partial E_2)_1 + 2w[r - (1 - q)(\partial G/\partial K_b)_1]\} = \varepsilon^p$, the following equilibrium *characteristics* hold for this type of economy:

a. for $0 \leqq \varepsilon \leqq \varepsilon^p$: $E_1 = E_1^-$, $K_b \leqq \bar{K}_b$, $N = 0$, $\partial N/\partial K_b < 0$ $(\tau_1 < q)$;

b. for $\varepsilon^p < \varepsilon < 1$: $E_1 > E_1^-$, $K_b < \bar{K}_b$, $N = 0$, $\partial N/\partial K_b < 0$ $(\tau_1 < q)$;

c. for $\varepsilon = 1$: $E_1 > E_1^-$, $K_b < \bar{K}_b$, $N = 0$, $\partial N/\partial K_b = 0$ $(\tau_1 = q)$;

see Fig. 2.8, where a, b and c, refer to the aforementioned sets of equilibrium characteristics (the term pivot state in that figure will be explained below).

Types of states for which $0 \leqq \varepsilon \leqq \varepsilon^p$ try to maximize private output and keep the state sector as small as possible. Full utilization of

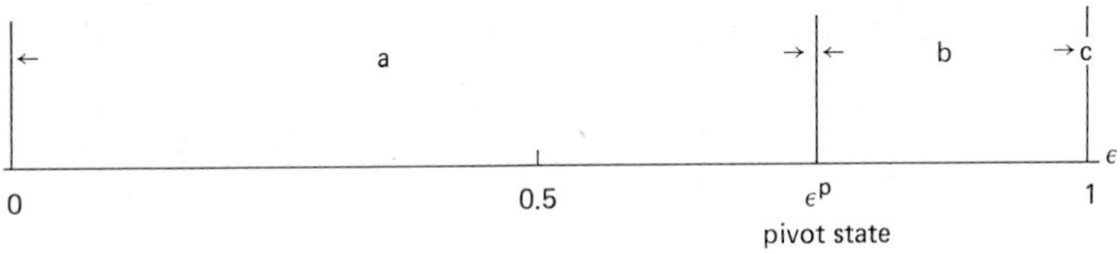

Fig. 2.8. Political scale and equilibrium characteristics for a restrictive economy.

the capital stock may, however, be blocked by the surplus constraint, causing $K_b < \bar{K}_b$ to hold in that case. As long as $0 \leqq \varepsilon \leqq \varepsilon^p$ the equilibrium is located at the intersection of state size and surplus constraint curve (point A in the figures a and b of Fig. 2.7). Note that $\varepsilon^p > 0.5$ as $r - (1 - q)(\partial G/\partial K_b)_1 > 0$ [18].

The reason why E_1 is minimized even if $0.5 < \varepsilon \leqq \varepsilon^p$ is that the reallocation of a worker from the private sector to the state sector implies not just a reallocation of a constant X_b between wE_1 and $X_b - wE_1$ but has at the same time a negative effect on private output X_b through the positive productivity of the worker ($\partial G/\partial E_2 > 0$), while there is *no* effect - in this model - of state production on private production. The weight attached to wE_1 [see (2.1)] needs to be sufficiently higher than 0.5 to make such a reallocation attractive.

When $\varepsilon = \varepsilon^p$ the equilibrium is located at the tangency point of a P_s-contour and the surplus constraint curve, which point then coincides with A. From $\varepsilon = \varepsilon^p$ on, this tangency point, determining the equilibrium location, follows the thick part of the surplus constraint curve in the direction of C, which point is attained when $\varepsilon = 1$ (in that case the P_s-contour is a horizontal line; see Fig. 2.4). The resulting increase in E_1 beyond $\bar{E}_1$ is achieved by discouraging the use of capital. As $(1 - q)\partial G/\partial K_b - r < 0$ along that part of the surplus constraint curve, the marginal product of capital is less than what is claimed in the form of rent and profits. A decrease in K_b raises the surplus N, therefore, to be used for the increase in state employment.

The type of state characterized by $\varepsilon = \varepsilon^p$ marks off, on the political scale, the class of states that all try to maximize private output X_b from the class of states that, along with a rise in ε, step up state employment and increase the amount of private product that goes to the state sector, thereby raising wE_1/X_b as X_b decreases. This state will be called a pivot state (hence the superfix p). It is defined in the following way.

Definition. Let the set of ordered pairs (ε, E_1), indicating the optimal state employment level associated with a particular type of state ε, be represented by the function $E_1(\varepsilon)$. A *pivot state* is defined as a type of state ε^p, $\varepsilon^p \in (0,1)$, at which $E_1(\varepsilon)$ is not differentiable. Fig. 2.9. gives an illustration.

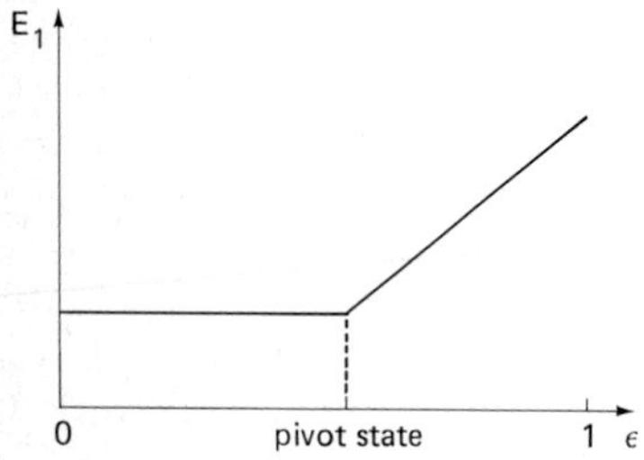

Fig. 2.9. Illustration of a pivot state.

It may be clear that the pivot state phenomenon has to do with the angularity (non-smoothness) of the relevant part of the opportunity set (see also below) [19].

In contrast with a perfectly restrictive economy the type of state that governs in a restrictive economy is of importance for the distribution of labour over state and private sector, the distribution of private product over these sectors and the shares of wage-related income, and profit and capital income, in total income. As $N = 0$ (implying that $P_b = qX_b$) it is the share of capital income that will fall if private product is no longer maximized, since wage-related income - equal to $w[E^* + \psi(L - E^*)]$ - is constant.

II. *Permissive economy.* The marginal products of labour and capital when measured at the intersection of $E_2 = E^* - \bar{E}_1$ and $K_b = \bar{K}_b$ will be denoted by $(\partial G/\partial E_2)_2$ and $(\partial G/\partial K_b)_2$, and when measured at the intersection of $K_b = \bar{K}_b$ and $N = 0$ by $(\partial G/\partial E_2)_3$ and $(\partial G/\partial K_b)_3$, respectively. Putting $[(\partial G/\partial E_2)_2 + w]/[(\partial G/\partial E_2)_2 + 2w] = \varepsilon^{p1}$, $[(\partial G/\partial E_2)_3 + w]/[(\partial G/\partial E_2)_3 + 2w] = \varepsilon^{p2}$, and $\{r(\partial G/\partial E_2)_3 + w[r - (1 - q)(\partial G/\partial K_b)_3]\}/\{r(\partial G/\partial E_2)_3 + 2w[r - (1 - q)(\partial G/\partial K_b)_3]\} = \varepsilon^{p3}$, one of the following two sets of equilibrium *characteristics* will hold for a permissive economy:

either

a. for $0 \leqq \varepsilon \leqq \varepsilon^{p1}$: $E_1 = \bar{E}_1,\ K_b = \bar{K}_b,\ N > 0,\ \partial N/\partial K_b \gtreqless 0\ (\tau_1 \gtreqless q)$;

b. for $\varepsilon^{p1} < \varepsilon < \varepsilon^{p2}$: $E_1 > \bar{E}_1,\ K_b = \bar{K}_b,\ N > 0,\ \partial N/\partial K_b \gtreqless 0\ (\tau_1 \gtreqless q)$; 20)

c. for $\varepsilon^{p2} \leqq \varepsilon \leqq \varepsilon^{p3}$: $E_1 > \bar{E}_1,\ K_b = \bar{K}_b,\ N = 0,\ \partial N/\partial K_b < 0\ (\tau_1 < q)$;

d. for $\varepsilon^{p3} < \varepsilon < 1$: $E_1 > \bar{E}_1,\ K_b < \bar{K}_b,\ N = 0,\ \partial N/\partial K_b < 0\ (\tau_1 < q)$;

e. for $\varepsilon = 1$: $E_1 > \bar{E}_1,\ K_b < \bar{K}_b,\ N = 0,\ \partial N/\partial K_b = 0\ (\tau_1 = q)$;

or

a. for $0 \leqq \varepsilon \leqq \varepsilon^{p1}$: $E_1 = \bar{E}_1,\ K_b = \bar{K}_b,\ N > 0,\ \partial N/\partial K_b > 0\ (\tau_1 > q)$; 21)

b. for $\varepsilon^{p1} < \varepsilon < \varepsilon^{p2}$: $E_1 > \bar{E}_1,\ K_b = \bar{K}_b,\ N > 0,\ \partial N/\partial K_b > 0\ (\tau_1 > q)$;

c. for $\varepsilon^{p2} \leqq \varepsilon \leqq 1$: $E_1 > \bar{E}_1,\ K_b = \bar{K}_b,\ N = 0,\ \partial N/\partial K_b \geqq 0\ (\tau_1 \geqq q)$;

see Fig. 2.10, where the letters between arrows again refer to the aforementioned characteristics.

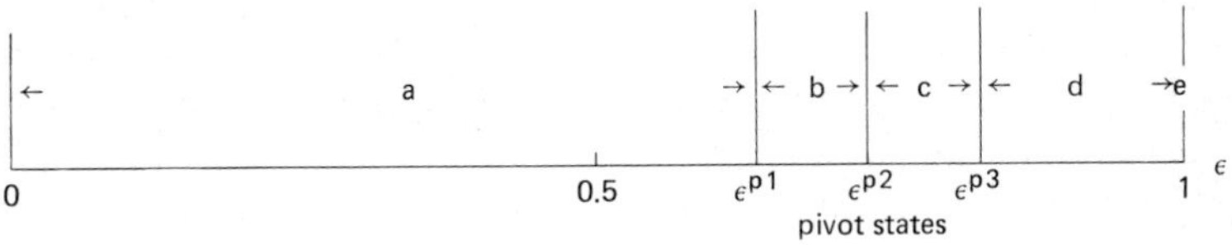

or :

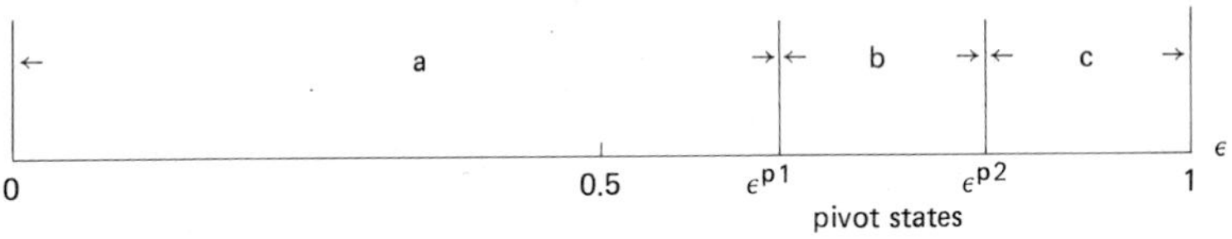

Fig. 2.10. Political scale and equilibrium characteristics for a permissive economy.

For the types of states characterized by $0 \leqq \varepsilon \leqq \varepsilon^{p1}$ the equilibrium is located at the intersection of the state size and capital constraint curves (point A in Figs. 2.7c and d). These states all maximize private output as well as the part of it that stays in the private sector. Capital stock is fully employed. The state size is kept at its minimum. The aggregate of profit and capital income as well as its share in total income is maximized.

When $\varepsilon^{p1} \leqq \varepsilon \leqq \varepsilon^{p2}$ the equilibrium is determined by the tangency point of the highest feasible P_s-contour (see Fig. 2.4: $0.5 < \varepsilon < 1$) and the capital constraint curve. For $\varepsilon = \varepsilon^{p1}$ this point coincides with the intersection of the state size and capital constraint curves (see above), for $\varepsilon = \varepsilon^{p2}$ with the intersection of the capital and surplus constraint curves (point B in figure c and point C in figure d of Fig. 2.7). State employment increases along with ε when $\varepsilon > \varepsilon^{p1}$, until $\varepsilon = \varepsilon^{p2}$ (notice the pivot character of the state for which $\varepsilon = \varepsilon^{p1}$). The use of capital need not be discouraged this time to make this increase financially possible, as appeared to be necessary in a restrictive economy. The shares of capital income and wage-related income in total income will be larger than under the regime of a state characterized by $0 \leqq \varepsilon \leqq \varepsilon^{p1}$, since private output is no longer maximized while $K_b = \bar{K}_b$ still holds; the share of profit income will, consequently, be smaller. The more E_1 is increased and, thus, X_b is lowered, the tighter the surplus constraint becomes.

The state characterized by $\varepsilon = \varepsilon^{p2}$ is again a pivot state. In case of an opportunity set as illustrated by Fig. 2.7d, all types of states for which $1 \geqq \varepsilon > \varepsilon^{p2}$ will behave in exactly the same way as this pivot state. The capital constraint as well as the surplus constraint will be active. If the opportunity set is shaped like the one shown in Fig. 2.7c, however, then this identity of behaviour will only hold for the class of states for which $\varepsilon^{p2} \leqq \varepsilon \leqq \varepsilon^{p3}$. When $\varepsilon^{p3} \leqq \varepsilon < 1$ the equilibrium is - in that case - determined by the tangency point of a P_s-contour (see again Fig. 2.4: $0.5 < \varepsilon < 1$) and the surplus constraint curve.

State employment increases again along with ε when $\varepsilon > \varepsilon^{p3}$, until $\varepsilon = 1$ (note the pivot character of the state for which $\varepsilon = \varepsilon^{p3}$). This time the use of capital has to be decreased in order to make a higher level of E_1 financially possible (observe that $\partial N/\partial K_b < 0$).

As $N = 0$ and, thus, $P_b = qX_b$, it is now the share of capital income that necessarily falls when private output further decreases through the decline in private employment and capital use.

In case of the pure state goods biased state, $\varepsilon = 1$, state employment is maximized, as $P_s = w(E^* - E_2) = wE_1$ in that case. The equilibrium is then located at the lowest point of the feasible part of the surplus constraint curve (point C in Figs. 2.7c and d).

Remarks

We conclude this section with some remarks.

1. The analysis suggests that an economy in which the type of state (ε) changes - which may be called a politically unstable economy (see section 5.8) - *might* (and, thus, need not) experience marked changes in state policies, such as with respect to tax rates. In case of a perfectly restrictive economy there would be no change at all (*in so far as* equilibria are concerned). In restrictive and permissive economies the passing of pivot states would, particularly, stand out. A good theory of the state - dealing with its composition, interests, constraints - is especially useful and in fact necessary for the study of such types of economies.

2. A distinction should be made between the *tax-capacity* of an economy, defined by the maximum amount of tax revenues that can be extracted from the economy, and its *carrying capacity* as regards state and private sector, defined by the maximum size of, respectively, the state and the private sector that can be borne by the economy.
   In our model the tax capacity is obtained by maximizing $(1 - q)G(E_2,K_b) - wE_2 - rK_b$ subject to the inequality constraints in (2.14a). For an interior solution: $(1 - q)\partial G/\partial E_2 - w = 0$ and $(1 - q)\partial G/\partial K_b - r = 0$ should hold.
   In order to obtain the carrying capacity for an economy as regards the *size of the state sector* (measured by E_1, or wE_1) one should maximize E_1 subject to the constraints in (2.14a). In that case the relevant point in the opportunity set is the lowest point of the surplus constraint curve (point C in Fig. 2.7). This carrying capacity may be measured (given w) by the largest distance between the state size and surplus constraint curves in the opportunity set (such as AC in Fig. 2.7d). The carrying capacity of an economy as regards the *size of the private sector* - measured by the level of private output, say - is obtained by maximizing X_b subject to the constraints in (2.14a). Since it is assumed in the present model that state activities have no impact on production technology (which is a very important assumption in this context), E_2 and K_b should be as large as possible; the relevant point of the opportunity set is then the north-east corner (point A in

Fig. 2.7). The state sector would have its minimum size.
Note the difference between the tax capacity of an economy and its carrying capacity as regards the size of the state sector. State activities, which are not referred to in measuring the tax capacity, may and probably will have an impact on the economy. In our model, for example, the state will crowd out the firms in the labour market, which affects the level of private output that can be produced. Assuming that state activities are financed out of taxes, the carrying capacity will then be smaller than the tax capacity.

3. In general, it can be said that the following factors are determinant for the restrictiveness, as well as the tax and carrying capacity, of an economy:
   a. *technical factors*, such as the technology of production, or a physically determined subsistence wage level;
   b. *socio-economic* and *political factors*, such as the economic system (in our case, the production and employment decisions of the firms cannot directly be determined by the state), the 'minimum' wage level, the 'minimum' profit margin, the dole rate and the total employment target.

   We will return to this later on.

4. Observe from (2.14) that, for $\varepsilon > 0$, P_s can be written as: $P_s = \varepsilon[\alpha (wE_1) + (1 - \alpha)X_b]$, where $\alpha = (2\varepsilon - 1)/\varepsilon$. The expression between hooked brackets shows a confrontation of the sizes of state and private sector, with α and $(1 - \alpha)$ denoting the weights attached to the sizes of these sectors. For those who would prefer this expression as a representation of the interests of politicians and bureaucrats, the following is noted.
   Let $P'_s = \alpha(wE_1) + (1 - \alpha)X_b$, then the equilibrium results for $0 \leqq \alpha \leqq 1$ using P'_s in (2.14) will be identical to the results obtained from $0.5 \leqq \varepsilon \leqq 1$, using P_s, with $\varepsilon = 1/(2 - \alpha)$, as, for each α, the maximization of P'_s implies the maximization of P_s $(= \varepsilon P'_s)$ for the corresponding ε. The pivot states will, consequently, move towards the left on the political scale determined by the $[0,1]$-interval for α.

5. Of course, more specific equilibrium characteristics for different types of states can be obtained if the production function is further specified. The characteristics presented above can then be further worked out [22].

2.4. A Numerical Example

The solution to (2.14) for different types of states and two different types of economies will be presented under the assumption of a Cobb-Douglas type of production function: $X_b = AK_b^{\mu}E_2^{\nu}$, $\mu + \nu < 1$. The first economy (E-I) is a permissive economy, the second (E-II) a perfectly restrictive economy. The following parameter values are chosen [23]:

E-I	:	$\mu = 0.1$,	$A = 24.55$	
E-II	:	$\mu = 0.2$,	$A = 9.74$	
E-I and E-II	:	$\psi = 0.8$,	$L = 100$,	$E^* = 95$, $q = 0.55$, $w = 10$,
		$\nu = 0.7$,	$\bar{K}_b = 3200$,	$E_1^- = 1$, $r = 0.04$.

The economies are chosen to differ only with respect to the shift parameter A and the partial production elasticity of capital μ. Instead of technical parameters we could also have selected socio-political parameters such as the minimum profit margin q and the employment target E^* [24]. As the profit margin equals: $P_b/X_b = (1 - \tau_1)(1 - \tau_2)(1 - \mu - \nu)$, where use has been made of the production function specification and (2.8), it follows that E-II has the smallest profit margin for given levels of τ_1 and τ_2 (note that the profit margin is independent of τ_3). For each economy the upperbound on the profit tax, denoted by τ_2^+, is given by: $\tau_2^+ = 1 - q[(1 - \tau_1)(1 - \mu - \nu)]^{-1}$. In E-II, $\tau_2 = \tau_2^+$ holds for any type of state, as N = 0 for all ε.

The relation between types of states and equilibrium tax rates for E-I and E-II is illustrated by Fig. 2.11 [25]. Table 2.1 shows some other equilibrium results for the economies. In this table X_b^+ denotes the level of private output that is obtained if $E_2 = E^* - E_1^-$ and $K_b = \bar{K}_b$.
The permissive character of E-I and the restrictiveness of E-II clearly show up. As there is not much to say about E-II (for the impact of the different parameters on the equilibrium tax rates, see note 24), attention is restricted to E-I.
The equilibrium characteristics that were presented in the previous section are shown by the results for this type of economy. First, for all ε we have the activeness of the capital constraint and/or the surplus constraint (see Table 2.1). Second, the relationship between types of states and the activeness of constraints as pictured in the upper part of Fig. 2.10 is confirmed (though not shown in the table, it appears that for $0.66 < \varepsilon < 0.67$ - where the figures are rounded - the capital constraint is active only).
Third, Fig. 2.11 clearly shows the position of the pivot states. Under the present parameter choice: $\varepsilon^{p1} = 0.66$, $\varepsilon^{p2} = 0.67$, $\varepsilon^{p3} = 0.9$. Finally, the results show that $\tau_1 \{ {< q \atop = q}$ when $\varepsilon \{ {< 1 \atop = 1}$ and the surplus constraint is active.

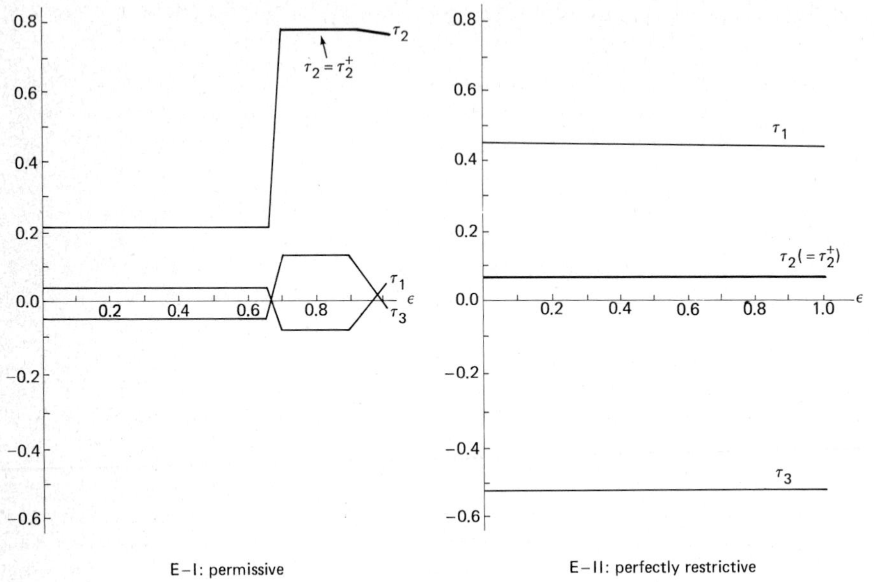

Fig. 2.11. The relationship between types of states and tax structures for two different economies.

Table 2.1. Some equilibrium results for E-I and E-II.

	ϵ	E_1/L	$K_b/\bar{K}_b$	P_b/X_b	wE_1/X_b	wE_2/X_b	X_b/X_b^+	rK_b/X_b
	0.0 - 0.6	0.01	1.00	0.16	0.01	0.71	1.00	0.10
E-I	0.7 - 0.9	0.15	1.00	0.05	0.13	0.68	0.89	0.11
	1.0	0.16	0.86	0.05	0.14	0.69	0.87	0.10
E-II	0.0 - 1.0	0.01	1.00	0.05	0.01	0.80	1.00	0.11

Because of the tax structure, the private product shares of real capital income rK_b/X_b and real wage income wE^*/X_b [= $w(E_1 + E_2)/X_b$] are not given by the partial production elasticities μ [= $(\partial G/\partial K_b)(K_b/X_b)$] and ν [= $(\partial G/\partial E_2)(E_2/X_b)$] - see the marginal productivity equations (2.8) - but by $(1 - \tau_1)\mu$ and $(1 - \tau_1)\nu/(1 + \tau_3)$, respectively.

When $\varepsilon \to 1$, the share of real wage income in private product rises since wE^* is constant and X_b decreases as labour goes from the private sector to the state sector (and eventually also K_b diminishes). The increase in the share of wage income is, in particular, realized through a decrease of the after-tax profit share P_b/X_b (this is no wonder, because as much capital as possible is employed; recall that $\partial P_s/\partial K_b > 0$ if $\varepsilon < 1$); the lower q the more this will be the case in our example, as τ_1 is related to q for high values of ε (see the previous section) and the share of capital rent income is given by $(1 - \tau_1)\mu$.

2.5. *Other Strategies for the Firms*

In this section we drop the assumption that the firms behave as tax-price takers. There may be circumstances under which a different strategy becomes attractive. Co-operative behaviour, for example, cannot be totally excluded (recall the discussion with respect to after-tax profits in Subsection 2.2.4) [26]. The impact of two alternative types of strategies on the outcome of the game between state and business will be investigated. As before, it is assumed that these strategies are equilibrium strategies for the firms and that the *state* - although *no longer a dominant player* - takes the strategy choice of business into account when determining its own strategy.

First we discuss what happens when the *firms do not react to taxes* (apart from demanding the minimum after-tax profit margin q). This strategy is called the *null-strategy*. The stickiness of E_2 and K_b with respect to the behaviour of the state may be due to binding agreements between labour and capitalists, for example, or any other (non-governmental) restriction on the adjustment of the employment of labour and capital. *Secondly*, a *group-rational strategy* is analyzed, defined as a strategy for the firm that *maximizes total after-tax profits* for business. As the firms are identical it also maximizes the after-tax profits of each single firm. As will become clear below, the (non-co-operative) tax-price taker strategy is not necessarily a group-rational strategy, although it may be perfectly rational from the point of view of an individual firm (see note 6). By co-ordinating their activities (implicitly or explicitly) after-tax profits may be increased.

It is interesting to see to what extent the behaviour of the state and the firms is curbed by these new strategies in comparison with the tax-price taker strategy. Information on this subject may point at tensions or conflicts within the politico-economic system that might be interesting for further study.

2.5.1. The Null-Strategy

If business does not react to taxes then the tax rates τ_1 and τ_3 will not appear in the input demand functions (2.9).
Using $\partial G/\partial K_b = r$ and $\partial G/\partial E_2 = w$ instead of (2.8), E_2 and K_b will only be functions of the parameters of the production function and the input prices r and w. The actions of the state are again taken to be conditional on the actions of business (which are no longer reactions on the policies of the state, however). It is assumed that the opportunity set determined by the constraints in (2.14a) is non-empty under the null-strategy. The result is an identical state size for all ε, to wit: $wE_1 = w(E^* - E_2)$. State outlays are also identical for all ε; they are equal to $w(E^* - E_2) + \psi w(L - E^*)$. Given the balanced budget condition, tax revenues R, and, consequently, after-tax profits P_b are the same under the regime of any type of state, and are determined by E_2, E^*, L, w, and ψ. There is no uniquely determined tax structure $\underline{\tau}$, however. A set of optimal tax structures is determined by the balanced budget constraint: $\tau_1 X_b + \tau_2 F + \tau_3 w E_2 = w(E^* - E_2) + \psi w(L - E^*)$.
In *real terms*, the economy may be called *perfectly restrictive* [27)].

In order to compare the impact of the null-strategy on the outcome of the game with the impact of the tax-price taker strategy, a distinction is made between the types of states that try to maximize the employment of labour and capital goods in the private sector and those that do not (see Section 2.3). As will be demonstrated in Subsection 2.5.2, the maximization of E_2 has a favourable effect on P_b. The maximization of K_b, however, has an unfavourable effect if this would imply that $\partial G/\partial K_b \neq r$, unless $K_b = \bar{K}_b$ and $\partial G/\partial K_b > r$.
It follows that it is uncertain whether business will profit from leaving the null-strategy for the tax-price taker strategy. The state, on the other hand, cannot loose. By choosing the right tax structure in response to a tax-price taker strategy the state can always effectuate the (E_2,K_b)-combination that is arrived at when business uses its null-strategy.
For the types of states that do not maximize private output there holds, again, that the state cannot loose from a switch to the tax-price taker strategy; the higher ε the less chance there is for business, however, to profit from such a shift (it is even zero when $\varepsilon = 1$, for in that case

$P_b = qX_b$). If K_b is changed and/or E_2 is decreased compared with the levels that business would choose under the null-strategy, business will loose.

To summarize:

a. for $0 \leqq \varepsilon < 1$, it is uncertain (that is, dependent on the parameter values) whether the firms will profit or not from a switch from the null-strategy to the tax-price taker strategy; if $\varepsilon = 1$, the firms will not benefit from it;

b. the state cannot loose and will most probably win when the firms switch to the tax-price taker strategy;

with this knowledge the state will, in general, disfavour any stickiness of E_2 and K_b.

2.5.2. A Group-Rational Strategy

A group-rational strategy for the firms was defined as a strategy that maximizes total after-tax profits P_b for business. In order to derive that strategy, first observe that the marginal sensitivity of tax revenues ($R = \tau_1 X_b + \tau_2 F + \tau_3 wE_2$) with respect to the employment of labour ($\partial R/\partial E_2$) and capital ($\partial R/\partial K_b$) that the optimal strategy of the tax-prixe taker takes account of can be written as

$$\partial R/\partial E_2 = w[(1 + \tau_3)/(1 - \tau_1) - 1], \qquad (2.17)$$

$$\partial R/\partial K_b = r[1/(1 - \tau_1) - 1];$$

see eqs. (2.6) and (2.8). Because of the balanced budget constraint and the total employment constraint on the behaviour of the state, which demand that $R = w(E^* - E_2) + \psi w(L - E^*)$, the real marginal tax sensitivity, denoted by $(\partial R/\partial E_2)^*$ and $(\partial R/\partial K_b)^*$, respectively, equals,

$$(2.18) \qquad (\partial R/\partial E_2)^* = -w \quad \text{and} \quad (\partial R/\partial K_b)^* = 0.$$

As $\partial R/\partial E_2 > (\partial R/\partial E_2)^*$ the firms overestimate - as tax-price takers - the marginal cost of an increase of E_2, and would profit by employing more labour. Along the same lines, a change in capital employment would be profitable as long as $\tau_1 \neq 0$ [in that case $\partial G/\partial K_b \neq r$, see (2.8)]. Using (2.18), a maximum of P_b would demand:

$$(2.19) \qquad \partial G/\partial E_2 = 0 \quad \text{and} \quad \partial G/\partial K_b - r = 0.$$

Since $\partial G/\partial E_2 > 0$ it follows that a group-rational strategy for the firms demands that $E_2 = E^* - E_1^-$ and that $\partial G/\partial K_b = r$ (or $\partial G/\partial K_b \geqq r$ if $K_b = \bar{K}_b$).

It should be clear from the aforegoing that the tax-price taker strategy only leads to these outcomes under special conditions (among which political).

If there is no opportunity for the state to bargain with the firms (see below) then it will be forced by this strategy (irrespective of the type of state) to keep the state size at its minimum level.
As was obtained for the null-strategy, only a set of optimal tax structures can be determined in that case (from the balanced budget equation; it is assumed that the opportunity set is non-empty). Again, the economy may be called *perfectly restrictive in real terms*.

We conclude this subsection with some *remarks*.

1. Although the maximization of total after-tax profits is in accordance with the interest of those who control the firms, it need not further the interests of those who own the stock of capital goods. Rentiers are interested in the rent total (i.e., rK_b), and thus, in maximal employment of capital goods (as the rental rate is fixed). This need not be the case under the group-rational strategy for the firms, as the latter demands that $\partial G/\partial K_b = r$ holds. It follows that there may be a conflict among rentiers and those who control the firms with respect to the best strategy *vis-à-vis* the state.
2. Notice, that it is important for the behaviour of the state in what way the group-rational strategy comes about. If it occurs through implicitly co-operative behaviour or collusion, the state may have no other choice than to take the reactions of business as given when determining its strategy, as it sees itself confronted with a large number of relatively small firms. If it results from a coalition that can be called upon by the state, then the state may have the opportunity to bargain with business (forcing the firms to become engaged in non-market activities). In that case, the possibility of *threats* should be taken into account [28]. The action space of the state may thereby be enlarged. It is beyond the scope of this chapter, however, to pursue this line of thought in greater detail (see Chapter 7).
3. Finally, it may be useful to note that, although the interaction between state and business has been studied within a very simple framework, the analysis demonstrates that the *carrying capacity of the economy* as regards the size of the state sector (or non-market sector, for that matter) is not only determined by technical factors (such as the production capacity of an economy) but also by the power that state and private sector may have to enlarge or restrict each other's action spaces.

2.6. Summary

From our first approach to the analysis of the interaction between state and private sector, where we focused upon the relationship between state and firms, the following more general conclusions emerge.

- Differences in behaviour between types of states depend on the *restrictiveness* of the economy. The restrictiveness of an economy is, given its *interest structure*, determined by *structural coercion* and *pressure*. Structural coercion stems from the restrictions set by technology as well as the relationships between agents participating in the economy (think of the consequences of decentralized decision making, for example; in this context see Appendix 2A on the Marxist notions of 'dominance' and 'dominance in the last instance'). Due to structural coercion economies may be perfectly restrictive, forcing all types of states to behave in exactly the same way. The less restrictive (or more permissive) an economy is, the more room there is for discretionary behaviour by the state. Economies may also become perfectly restrictive by pressure, however, as was shown by the group-rational strategy for business.

- In analyzing the *carrying capacity* of an economy as regards the size of the state sector one should, in the same perspective, not only take into account the restrictions set by technology (say the productive capacity of the private sector) but also the structural coercion that the state is confronted with [such as the way that price and wage decisions are made; see, in this context, Watson (1978)], as well as the pressure that is, or can be, exerted on the state.

- The type of state may have a great impact on the outcome of the game between state and firms in case of economies that are not perfectly restrictive. In that case the phenomenon of the so-called *pivot state* may be encountered; that is, a type of state that marks off different classes of states, classified according to the sort of behaviour they show. Significant changes in representation may - and when involving the passing of a pivot state they will - lead to so-called 'shift points', 'step effects' or 'displacement effects' in state activities, as has been observed for state expenditures [see Davis, Dempster, and Wildavsky (1966), Johansen (1968), Peacock and Wiseman (1961)] [29]. It is especially for these economies that knowledge with respect to the staffing of the state apparatuses (giving information on the leading positions, the leading interests, and so on) is needed, and where empirical studies on representation as put forward by Domhoff, Galbraith, Mills and Miliband, for example, become important [30]. On the other hand, realistic politico-economic models are needed to determine whether a change in government - more generally, a change in the staffing of the state apparatuses - would make any difference. One of the greatest difficulties to be surmounted here will be the incorporation of pressure (see Chapters 5, 6 and 7).

APPENDIX 2A

DOMINANCE, AND DOMINANCE IN THE LAST INSTANCE

In the context of the restrictiveness of economies reference can be made to the Marxist notion of 'dominance in the last instance'. According to the Marxist Approach political phenomena are 'in the last instance' dependent on the structure of the production process (see Subsection 1.2.3). In a famous passage in the preface of '*Zur Kritik der Politischen Ökonomie*' [Marx (1859)] Marx assigned a predominant role to the productive forces of the economy. As one cannot live by politics alone and as the complex of productive forces can be considered as a stock variable that can in fact only marginally be changed at will at any moment of time by the state, it may indeed be expected that these forces somehow basically shape and delimit the political action space. To some extent this is illustrated in our model by the impact of the production function on the activities of the state. By changing the parameter values of the production function alone it is possible to alter the variety in behaviour of different types of states.

However, not all Marxists subscribe to the predominance of the productive forces any longer. Poulantzas, for example, designated the predominant role to the relations of production in the economic sphere [Poulantzas (1978b, Introduction)] [31)]. Moreover, he distinguished between dominance in the last instance ('determination') and dominance as such. In any mode of production the economic is dominant in the last instance; however, the political or the ideological may play the dominant role in a concrete situation, assigned to it by the economic [Poulantzas (1978a, pp. 14-15)]. Now this is all rather cryptic, ill-defined and subject to dispute [32)], and we certainly do not want to go into this matter very deeply at this place. Only a few remarks will be made.

Let us first consider the role played by the relations of production. These relations comprise class/power relations. In a capitalist economy the main relations are between capitalists and workers; they are moulded by the character of the accumulation process (the concentration and centralization of capital, the socialization of the production process, etc.). In terms of our model these relations might be said to express themselves in the parameters q, r and w that the state is confronted with; and it is shown in Section 2.3 that they may cause the economy to be perfectly restrictive - in some well-defined sense - apart from the pure technological aspects of production.
The other reason for perfect restrictiveness that is mentioned (the null-

strategy or the group-rational strategy of the firms) may in fact also be considered to be rooted in the relations of production.
Thus, within the confines of our model we might say that the relations of production - together with the productive forces - basically define the boundaries of the state's action space, and in particular cases completely determine the state's actions. Is this dominance in the last instance? The question remains to be answered then whether - in a more realistic setting than our simple model - it would be possible to significantly change the relations of production by political activities. We will not try to answer this question here, nor even in this book, as the operationalization of the different notions alone (if possible) would lead us too far. Nevertheless, the question seems important enough to return to it when we have taken a closer view of political activities (see Section 5.8).

Suppose for the moment that one could say in some clearly defined way that the economic is determinant, would it then make sense to assert that not the economic but the political may play the dominant role? Our model suggests that it could. Even when the economy is perfectly restrictive the state may be a dominant player, in the sense that the state takes into account the reactions of the agents in the economic sphere, while the latter react to the actions of the state as if they were fixed. The reason why the state can play a dominant role in our model is the atomistic nature of the production process [33)]. The structural coercion emanating from the economic sphere may be such, though, that the state cannot display any form of discretionary behaviour. Parenthetically, recall that even in a permissive economy a dominant role for the state does not imply that it acts against the interests of the capitalists; representation - in addition to structural coercion and pressure - becomes an important factor, then.

CHAPTER 3

STATE AND PRIVATE SECTOR RECONSIDERED, THE INTRODUCTION OF TIME

3.1. *Introduction*

In this chapter we start developing a *dynamic* and more realistic model of the interaction between state and private sector [1]. The model serves as a basis for the models to be developed in subsequent chapters. Within the state, the positions of bureaucrats and politicians are more clearly delimitated. Use is made of some existing hypotheses regarding the interests of these agents. For simplicity, taxation is restricted to a general income tax. The behaviour of labour and firms, and the functioning of labour and product markets will be carefully specified.
The capital stock is no longer fixed, and will be owned by those who control the firms (the capitalists). From now on also a *linear production technology* with no substitutability between capital and labour will be assumed to hold for the firms. This assumption is analytically convenient, and does not seriously seem to detract from the realism of the model. Technology is made *endogenous* by the assumption of a relationship between (accumulated) *state production* and *private labour productivity*; labour productivity in the state sector is taken to be constant [2]. Although the empirical determination of technological change is fraught with many difficulties [3], it is generally recognized that the state has a significant part in it through its activities in such areas as health, education, infrastructure, research and development [4]. Nevertheless, relatively little attention has been paid to this relationship in formal economic models [5]. As the impact of technological change on the capital-output ratio is less clear, this ratio is supposed to be constant [6].

Only a relatively few formal politico-economic models - all within the Public Choice Approach - have been developed as yet (see Subsection 1.2.2 for references).
In these models it is the behaviour of politicians acting under a re-election constraint within a democratic political setting and a macro-economic context that is focused upon. They have, particularly, been used to show the possibility of a *'political business cycle'*, i.e. an economic cycle deliberately generated by politicians attempting to secure their re-election [7]. The model to be presented below differs from the aforementioned models in the following respects. First, the activities of the state are determined by the direct confrontation of the interests of *politicians* (in our definition including the members of parliament) with those of *bu-*

reaucrats. Second, a micro-economic framework is used in which the behaviour of the constitutive parts is made explicit. Third, there are *no elections* [8]. As in the previous chapter, political actions emanating from outside the state are neglected. The analysis of the impact of political actions - such as voting - on the behaviour of the state is postponed to Chapter 5. It is preferable to study the simpler case first.
The chapter is arranged as follows. The model is presented in Section 3.2. Some parts of it are discussed in Section 3.3. Section 3.4 is concerned with the characteristics of equilibria. A few simulation results are presented in Section 3.5. Section 3.6 summarizes.

3.2. A Dynamic Model

3.2.1. General Structure of the Model

The model comprises:

- a *private production sector*, which produces a (marketed) good that can be used for investment as well as consumption;
- a *state*, which levies an income tax on and pays unemployment benefits to households; the bureaucratic apparatus consists of one department whose (non-marketed) product may influence the technology of the private production sector;
- *households*, which supply one homogeneous labour service to the private production sector and the state, and are the sole buyers of goods from the private sector;
- a rudimentary *bank*, which supplies the money in the economy; it employs neither capital goods nor labour.

Time is treated as a discrete variable; it is divided into periods indicated by the symbol t. Fig. 3.1 illustrates the structure of the economy. The assumed sequence of events per period is shown in Table 3.1. This sequence will be followed in the exposition of the model.

3.2.2. The Behaviour of the State: Bureaucrats and Politicians

Interests. In line with hypotheses and some findings put forward by students of bureaucracy (see Subsection 1.2.2 for references) it is assumed that the interests of bureaucrats - whatever their ultimate goals may be - in fact boil down to a continuous and gradual expansion of the state apparatus. This expansion will be represented by the growth rate of the number of state employees. Let θ denote the growth rate target that the bureau-

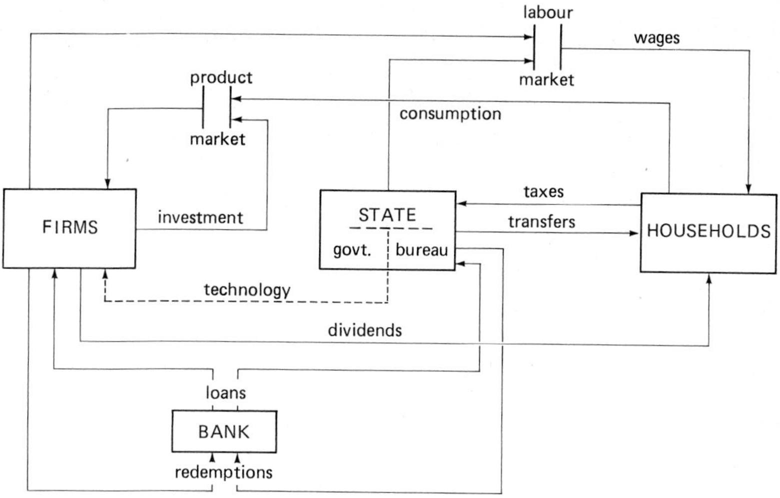

Fig. 3.1. Economic structure: money flows ⟶, and supply of technology - - - ►

crats aim at. The interests of politicians are - in the spirit of the previous chapter - taken to be divided between private output and state output, but now with a changing rate of substitution, which seems to be more plausible.

As in the previous model, it is supposed that the state acts as if it maximizes the value of a variable P_s, now (as an expectation) specified as:

$$(3.1) \qquad \tilde{P}_s(t) = \lambda_s\{-[ln\tilde{E}_1(t) - lnE_1(t-1) - \theta]^2\} + $$
$$+ (1 - \lambda_s)\{\varepsilon ln\tilde{X}_b^t(t) + (1 - \varepsilon)ln\tilde{X}_s(t)\}$$
$$, \theta > 0, 0 \leqq \lambda_s \leqq 1, 0 \leqq \varepsilon \leqq 1,$$

where E_1 stands for the number of state sector workers, X for output, the superfix t for transacted, and the suffices b and s for business and state, respectively. The tilde (~) indicates that we have to do with expected values of variables. The relative weight of the different interests of politicians within the government is denoted by ε [note that - in contrast with eq. (2.1) - ε is here attached to private output]; ε characterizes the *type of government*. The relative weight of the interests of the bureaucrats *versus* the interests of the politicians within the state is indicated by λ_s. A *type of state* is characterized by the ordered pair (λ_s,ε). A future time horizon of one period is assumed.

Table 3.1
Sequence of events for period t.

start									end
State	Labour market		Bank	State/firms	Product market		Firms		State/firms	Bank
Tax rate announced	Wage bargaining	Trans-actions	Loans for wages and doles	State outlays on labour	Consumption demand	Trans-actions	Price deci-sion	Investment deci-sion + Reservation of funds	Distribution of excess funds by firms	Debt account adjustment for firms and state
Demand for labour	Labour demand			Firms' out-lays on labour	Investment demand				Dividend taxes	
	Labour supply			Taxes over wage related income						

Instruments. The state has two instruments at its disposal: its demand for labour $E_1^d(t)$ and a uniform income tax rate $\tau(t)$.

Constraints. The relations determining the relationship between $P_s(t)$ and both instrumental variables of the state - together making up the economic model that is implicitly or explicitly employed by the state - will now be given, in addition to some constraints on the use of the instruments. We start with some - in the context of our model economy - objective, true relations, which will be presented without tildes.
The state's demand for labour, E_1^d, is restricted by the size of the total labour force L and a minimum level E_1^- (the minimum state size), which are assumed to be fixed:

$$(3.2) \qquad E_1^- \leqq E_1^d(t) \leqq L \qquad , L > E_1^- > 0.$$

Labour is the sole input in the production of state goods; its productivity α_s is supposed to be constant. State production equals:

$$(3.3) \qquad X_s(t) = \alpha_s E_1(t) \qquad , \alpha_s > 0.$$

For $\tilde{E}_1(t)$, see eq. (3.16).
A linear production function is also assumed for private production.
As will become clear in Subsection 3.2.5, there will be no idle labour in the firms. Private labour productivity, α_b, is taken to be variable (see below). More specifically:

$$(3.4) \qquad X_b(t) = \alpha_b(t)E_2(t),$$

where E_2 stands for private employment; for $\tilde{\alpha}_b(t)$ and $\tilde{E}_2(t)$, see (3.17) and (3.18). Private product supply is supposed to equal production plus private output stocks S (see below):

$$(3.5) \qquad X_b^s(t) = X_b(t) + S(t).$$

Assuming voluntary exchange and exhaustion of all mutually advantageous trades [Barro and Grossman (1976, p.40)], private product transactions equal

$$(3.6) \qquad X_b^t(t) = \min \{X_b^d(t), X_b^s(t)\},$$

where the superscripts d and s stand for demanded and supplied, respectively; for $\tilde{X}_b^d(t)$, see (3.18).

Stocks result from a discrepancy between supply and transactions:

(3.7) $S(t) = X_b^s(t-1) - X_b^t(t-1).$

Private labour productivity is related to accumulated state production, denoted as state capital K_s, in the following way:

(3.8) $\alpha_b(t) = vK_s(t)^\eta \qquad ,v > 0,\ \eta \geqq 0,$

(3.9) $K_s(t) = (1 - \zeta)K_s(t-1) + X_s(t-1) \qquad ,0 < \zeta < 1,$

where ζ denotes the rate of depreciation of state capital. The parameter η indicates the elasticity of labour productivity with regard to state capital. If $\eta = 0$, we have a fixed coefficients technology with $\alpha_b(t) = v$, for all t. State capital K_s and state output X_s can be considered as 'public intermediate goods' as the whole amount supplied enters the production function of each firm [9]. As $\eta \geqq 0$ we may speak of public 'goods' rather than public 'bads'. It will be assumed here that the state has no exact knowledge of (3.8) and (3.9); see (3.18).

The state is supposed to strive after a balanced budget (see below). State expenditures consist of wage payments and payments of unemployment benefits, for which *loans* - free of interest - can be contracted with the bank. Loans have to be paid off as soon as possible [10].

State revenues are derived from the income tax on wages, unemployment benefits and dividends. Dividends are equal to the firms' excess funds F adjusted for reservations made for investment. The excess funds of the firms comprise the difference between sales revenues on the one hand, and wage costs and accumulated debts, D_b, on the other, augmented by the money reserved for unfulfilled investment orders, if that should be the case [for the expected value of this remainder, see under (3.18)]:

(3.10) $F(t) = p(t)X_b^t(t) - w_2(t)E_2(t) - D_b(t) + p(t)[X_b^{id}(t) - X_b^{it}(t)],$

where p stands for product price, w_2 for private wage rate, and the superfix i for investment; for $\tilde{p}(t)$ and $\tilde{w}(t)$, see (3.18),

The debt burden of business, D_b, equals:

(3.11) $D_b(t) = \max\{0, -F(t-1)\}.$

The debt burden of the state, D_s, equals:

(3.12) $$D_s(t) = w_1(t-1)E_1(t-1) + w_4(t-1)E_4(t-1) + D_s(t-1) - \tau(t-1).$$
$$.[w_1(t-1)E_1(t-1) + w_2(t-1)E_2(t-1) + w_4(t-1)E_4(t-1) +$$
$$+ \max\{0, [1 - \sigma(t-1)]F(t-1)\}],$$

where E_4 denotes the number of unemployed, w_1 the state wage rate, w_4 the dole rate, and σ the fraction of F that is reserved for investment; for $\tilde{\sigma}(t)$, see (3.18) [11].

The state wage rate and the dole rate are taken to be proportionally related to the private wage rate:

$$(3.13)\qquad w_1(t) = \phi w_2(t) \text{ and } w_4(t) = \psi w_2(t) \qquad , \ \phi > \psi > 0,\ \psi < 1.$$ [12]

The income tax rate is bounded from above by a statutory minimum (subsistence) consumption basket x_b^{c-}. [13] The maximum tax rate τ^+ - which may be violated as the state does not have all the relevant information when $\tau(t)$ is determined - equals:

$$(3.14)\qquad \tau^+(t) = 1 - p(t)x_b^{c-}/w_4(t) \qquad , \ x_b^{c-} > 0.$$

The following relations are more particularly assumed to hold for the state; they do not necessarily hold when the tildes are deleted.

The state aims at balancing its expected tax revenues with its expected expenditures and debts (balanced budget):

$$(3.15)\qquad \tau(t)[\tilde{w}_1(t)\tilde{E}_1(t) + \tilde{w}_2(t)\tilde{E}_2(t) + \tilde{w}_4(t)\tilde{E}_4(t) + \max\{0,$$

$$[1 - \tilde{\sigma}(t)]\tilde{F}(t)\}] = \tilde{w}_1(t)\tilde{E}_1(t) + \tilde{w}_4(t)\tilde{E}_4(t) + D_s(t).$$

As regards *expectations* it is assumed, for the state, with respect to employment that

$$(3.16)\qquad \tilde{E}_1(t) = E_1^d(t),$$

$$(3.17)\qquad \tilde{E}_2(t) = \min\{\tilde{E}_2^d(t),\ L - E_1^d(t)\},$$

$$\tilde{E}_2^d(t) = \max\{0,\ [\tilde{X}_b^d(t) - S(t)]/\tilde{\alpha}_b(t)\},$$

Note that $\tilde{E}_4(t) = L - \tilde{E}_1(t) - \tilde{E}_2(t)$. Furthermore, it is assumed that

$$(3.18)\qquad \tilde{p}(t) = p(t-1),\ \tilde{w}_2(t) = w_2(t-1),\ \tilde{\alpha}_b(t) = \alpha_b(t-1),\ \tilde{\sigma}(t) = \sigma(t-1),$$

$$\tilde{X}_b^d(t) = X_b^t(t-1),\ \tilde{p}(t)[\tilde{X}_b^{id}(t) - \tilde{X}_b^{it}(t)] \text{ in (3.10) is neglected.}$$

Clearly, more sophisticated expectation patterns - involving different lag structures or least squares adjustments, for example - could be employed.

Observe from (3.15) through (3.18) that the tax rate can be written as a function of the state's demand for labour, to be denoted by $\tau(t) = \tau[E_1^d(t)]$.

Tax rate and demand for labour. Whenever it is impossible for the state to meet its budget constraint (3.15) - through normal taxation - it is assumed that the tax rate is put at its highest level and state employment is curtailed as much as possible [14]; in that case $E_1^d(t) = E_1^-$ and $\tau(t) = \tau^+(t)$. Apart from such a situation of state 'bankruptcy', $E_1^d(t)$ and $\tau(t)$ are determined by maximizing $\tilde{P}_s(t)$ using (3.1) through (3.18), which renders the following program:

$$\text{(3.19)} \quad \underset{E_1^d(t),\tau(t)}{\text{maximize}} : \quad \tilde{P}_s[E_1^d(t),\tau(t)] \quad \text{subject to}$$

$$E_1^- \leqq E_1^d(t) \leqq L,$$

$$\tau(t) = \tau[E_1^d(t)],$$

$$\tau(t) \leqq \tau^+(t).$$

As it is impossible, in general, to find an explicit analytical solution to this program, the optimal values for $E_1^d(t)$ and $\tau(t)$ are in the numerical experiments determined by a search-procedure.

3.2.3. Labour and Labour Market

Assumptions. The following assumptions are made.

1. There is a large number of suppliers of labour.
2. Coalitions inside or outside the market (i.e., directed at the state) are excluded.
3. Except for job preferences workers are identical; for whatever reasons, one part of the labour force (κ, $0 < \kappa < 1$) prefers to be employed by the state, the other part by business [15].
4. Employment is preferred to being idle; thus, workers that prefer to work in the state sector, for example, do accept jobs in the private sector when state jobs supply is inadequate.

Employment. Under the assumption of voluntary exchange and the exhaustion of mutually advantageous trades, labour market transactions result in:

$$\text{(3.20)} \quad E_1(t) = \min\{E_1^d(t),\ E_1^s(t)\} \qquad \text{and}$$

$$E_2(t) = \min\{E_2^d(t), E_2^s(t)\}, \qquad \text{where}$$

$$E_1^s(t) = \max\{\kappa L, L - E_2^d(t)\} \qquad \text{and}$$

$$E_2^s(t) = \max\{(1-\kappa)L, L - E_1^d(t)\}.$$

Wage rate. Within the context of the present model (homogeneous labour force, one production sector with identical firms) it is reasonable to assume that the wage rate is bounded from above by the value of labour productivity. This upperbound will be denoted by w_2^+. Moreover, in line with the statutory minimum consumption assumption - see the previous subsection, in particular eq. (3.14) - it is demanded that $[1 - \tau(t)]w_4(t) \geqq \tilde{p}(t)x_b^{c-}$ should hold. In view of the numerical experiments in Section 3.5, let $\tilde{p}(t) = p(t-1)$. The corresponding wage rate is denoted by w_2^-. For the special case that $w_2^-(t) > w_2^+(t)$ it is supposed that the market overrides the law, so that $w_2(t) = w_2^+(t)$. Within these bounds the wage rate should reflect the relative bargaining strength of worker and firm. A plausible assumption is that the relative change in the wage rate is a continuous monotonically increasing function (g) of the relative excess-demand for labour (Phillips curve). Let the corresponding wage rate be denoted by w_2^0. Thus, it is obtained that

(3.21) $$w_2(t) = \min\{\max[w_2^-(t), w_2^0(t)], w_2^+(t)\},$$

where $$w_2^-(t) = p(t-1)x_b^{c-}/\{[1-\tau(t)]\psi\},$$

$$w_2^0(t) = w_2(t-1)\left[1 + g\left(\frac{E_1^d(t-1) + E_2^d(t-1) - L}{L}\right)\right], \quad g(.) > -1, \quad g(0) = 0,$$ [16]

$$w_2^+(t) = p(t)\alpha_b(t).$$ [17]

3.2.4. Product Market

Demand and supply. The amount of money at the disposal of households when consumption demand is determined consists of disposable wage related income, disposable dividend income (from the previous period), and forced savings, if any, due to supply shortages in previous periods. There are no voluntary savings. As households aim at balancing their budgets, real consumption demand, x_b^{cd}, equals:

(3.22) $$x_b^{cd}(t) = \frac{1}{p(t)}\Big\{[1-\tau(t)][w_1(t)E_1(t) + w_2(t)E_2(t) + w_4(t)E_4(t)] +$$

$$+ \max\{0, [1 - \tau(t-1)][1 - \sigma(t-1)]F(t-1)\} +$$
$$+ p(t-1)[X_b^{cd}(t-1) - X_b^{ct}(t-1)]\Big\}.$$

Nominal investment demand equals the amount of money that is reserved for investment orders by the firms, $\sigma(t-1)F(t-1)$ [see (3.27)]. Thus, neglecting forced savings, all the money that is available to households and firms is spent on private product. It appears that this total amount of money - to be denoted by MM - can be subdivided into a part M, representing the money that is transferred from the previous period, and a part representing the money that is generated within the current period (to wit, wage-related income). It will be assumed that, apart from wage related income for which loans can be contracted with the bank, some money is available on a long term base in the economy [18]. For total product demand it is, consequently, obtained that

$$(3.23) \quad X_b^d(t) = MM(t)/p(t),$$
$$MM(t) = M(t) + [1 - \tau(t)][w_1(t)E_1(t) + w_2(t)E_2(t) + w_4(t)E_4(t)],$$
$$M(t) = \max\{0, [1 - \tau(t-1)][1 - \sigma(t-1)]F(t-1)\} + \sigma(t-1)F(t-1) +$$
$$+ p(t-1)[X_b^{cd}(t-1) - X_b^{ct}(t-1)].$$

Total supply $X_b^s(t)$ is given by eq. (3.5).

Transactions. With respect to transactions - see also (3.6) - it is assumed that investment demand is first handled as it is based on orders [19]:

$$(3.24) \quad X_b^{it}(t) = \min\{X_b^{id}(t), X_b^s(t)\},$$

$$(3.25) \quad X_b^{ct}(t) = \min\{X_b^{cd}(t), X_b^s(t) - X_b^{it}(t)\}.$$

3.2.5. The Behaviour of the Firms

Assumptions. The following is assumed.

1. A homogeneous good, that can be used for consumption as well as investment, is produced by a large and constant number of identical small firms.
2. Firms do not expect to have any influence on the state; coalitions inside of outside the market are excluded.
3. Within the boundaries of their relatively small production capacity, firms expect to sell whatever they supply at the expected market clearing price.
4. Investment orders and demand for labour are expected to be met.
5. Investment is totally self-financed.

6. Investment orders are to be executed in the next period, otherwise they are reconsidered [see the last term of (3.10)].
7. Loans, free of interest, can be contracted with the bank for the advance payment of wages, but have to be paid off as soon as possible.
8. Buyers are evenly distributed over the firms.

Under the given conditions, our object of study may as well be the industry, or business, rather than the individual firm. In the sequel, aggregate variables will, therefore, be used.

Interests. It is postulated that the firms act as if they maximize a time preference discounted expected flow of dividends, indicated by $\tilde{P}_b$; moreover, a three-period planning horizon is assumed (see below):

$$(3.26) \qquad \tilde{P}_b(t) = \sum_{n=0}^{2} \rho_n \ln\{[1 - \sigma(t,t+n)]\tilde{F}(t+n)\},$$

$$\rho_n \geqq 0, \ \Sigma_n \rho_n = 1, \ 0 \leqq \sigma(t,t+n) \leqq 1,$$

where F is defined by (3.10) [20]. Double time indices - that will only be used for instrument variables such as σ - are employed to distinguish between the period that a decision on the value of an instrument variable is made (denoted by the first index) and the period for which it is made (denoted by the second index). If the value of the second index exceeds that of the first, this is to indicate, moreover, that the instrument value under consideration may be revised in subsequent periods, until the final decision is made.

Dividends are paid out to those who control the firms (the capitalists); we will not further specify here who exactly these people are.

Instruments. Three instruments are available to the firms: demand for labour, product price, and the investment ratio $\sigma(t,t+n)$.

Constraints. In addition to the aforementioned assumptions, and the relations (3.4) through (3.7), (3.10) and (3.11), the following relations are used. We start with two - within the context of our model economy - objective, true relationships where tildes should be thought added for future periods. Investment orders are tied up with the reservation of funds that are made after the determination of the new product price (see Table 3.1 and below) at the end of the previous period:

$$(3.27) \qquad X_b^{id}(t) = \sigma(t-1)F(t-1)/p(t).$$

Newly acquired capital goods cannot sooner be used for production than in the period following transactions. Capital stock equals

$$(3.28) \qquad K_b(t) = (1 - \delta)K_b(t-1) + X_b^{it}(t-1) \qquad ,0 < \delta < 1,$$

where δ stands for the depreciation rate of private capital; for $X_b^{it}(t)$, see (3.24).

The following relations, (3.29) and (3.30), do not necessarily hold when the tildes are deleted.

As regards *expectations* it is obtained from assumptions 3 and 4 concerning the firms that

$$(3.29) \qquad \tilde{E}_2(t+n) = E_2^d(t,t+n),\ \tilde{X}_b^{it}(t+n) = \tilde{X}_b^{id}(t+n),\ \tilde{X}_b^{t}(t+n) = \tilde{X}_b^{s}(t+n) \qquad , n = 1,2.$$

It is , furthermore, assumed that

$$(3.30) \qquad \tilde{w}_2(t+n) = w_2(t)\ ,\ \tilde{\alpha}_b(t+n) = \alpha_b(t) \qquad , n = 1,2.$$

Product price, demand for labour, investment ratio. A plausible assumption for a firm operating under conditions of atomistic competition seems to be that it sets its *product price* in accordance with what it believes to be the market clearing price, using the excess demand for its product over the last period as an indication for the situation on the market [21]. The rate of price change is taken to be a continuous monotonically increasing function h of the excess demand. Thus,

$$(3.31) \qquad p(t+1) = p(t)\left[1 + h\left(\frac{X_b^d(t) - X_b^s(t)}{X_b^s(t)}\right)\right] \quad , h(.) > -1,\ h(0) = 0.$$

As $\tilde{X}_b^d(t+1) = \tilde{X}_b^s(t+1)$, given $p(t+1)$, it follows that $p(t,t+2) = p(t+1)$.

Given the 'fixed' coefficients technology [see (3.4)] and the condition that loans have to be paid off as soon as possible, it is readily seen that whenever the expected value of labour productivity exceeds the expected wage costs, i.e. $p(t,t+n)\tilde{\alpha}_b(t+n) > \tilde{w}_2(t+n)$, *labour demand* will be determined by the size of the capital stock. It is supposed that this will also be the case if an equality holds. Thus,

$$(3.32) \qquad E_2^d(t,t+n) = [\beta/\tilde{\alpha}_b(t+n)]\tilde{K}_b(t+n) \quad \text{if} \quad p(t,t+n)\tilde{\alpha}_b(t+n) \geq \tilde{w}_2(t+n) \qquad , n = 0,1,2,$$

where β stands for the fixed output-capital ratio. As $p(t)\alpha_b(t) \geq w_2(t)$, see (3.21), eq. (3.32) at least holds for period t (n = 0, tildes deleted)

[23]. Workers that have been contracted by a firm will always be fully employed. However, as labour supply may fall short of labour demand [see (3.20)], the available capital stock need not be fully utilized. Using (3.4), it follows that $X_b(t) = \alpha_b(t)E_2(t) = \beta K_b^u(t)$, where K_b^u stands for utilized private capital.

Because of the time lag for the completion of investment projects [see (3.27) and (3.28)], a firm's *investment* decision in period t is relevant only for the production capacity from period t+2 on, and not for that of period t+1. It follows that the expected excess funds contribution of period t+1, $\tilde{F}(t+1)$, is independent of the investment decision in period t. For $\tilde{F}(t+2)$ it is obtained, using eqs. (3.27)-(3.32), that

$$\tilde{F}(t+2) = [p(t+1)\alpha_b(t) - w_2(t)].[\beta/\alpha_b(t)].[(1-\delta)K_b(t+1) + \sigma(t)F(t)/p(t+1)], \quad (3.33)$$

where the first two factors indicate the expected rate of return on capital, and the third the expected size of the capital stock. Because of the investment lag and the three-period time horizon (on which more in the following section), only $\sigma(t)$ [$= \sigma(t,t)$] need be considered.
Assuming that $\rho_0 + \rho_2 > 0$, let

$$\rho = \rho_0/(\rho_0 + \rho_2). \quad (3.34)$$

Then s(t), defined by

$$s(t) = 1 - \rho[1 + (1-\delta)K_b(t+1)p(t+1)/F(t)], \quad (3.35)$$

gives the value of $\sigma(t)$ that is obtained from the first-order condition for a maximum of (3.26) if, for rather obvious reasons, $F(t) > 0$, $p(t+1)\alpha_b(t) > w_2(t)$ [see (3.33)], and $\rho > 0$ (due to the strict concavity of $\tilde{P}_b$ a global maximum is obtained in that case) [24]. Now, clearly $\sigma(t) = 0$ when either $F(t) \leqq 0$ or $p(t+1)\alpha_b(t) \leqq w_2(t)$ holds, and $\sigma(t) = 1$ when $\rho = 0$. It follows that

$$\sigma(t) \begin{cases} = 0 & \text{if } F(t) \leqq 0 \text{ and/or } p(t+1)\alpha_b(t) \leqq w_2(t), \\ = \max\{0, s(t)\} & \text{,otherwise.} \end{cases} \quad (3.36)$$

3.3. *Some Remarks on the Behaviour of State and Firm*

The behaviour of the state

1. With respect to the *state's time horizon* - which extends only one period into the future, see eq. (3.1) - it should be noticed that it excludes a direct feed-back on the behaviour of the state of the impact of state activities on labour productivity [see eqs. (3.8) and (3.9)]. As it is generally believed that the time horizon of governments is rather short, this may do for our present purposes [the consequences of a longer time horizon are studied in Van Winden (1979b)].

2. Disregarding the time dimension, the *specification* of P_s in (3.1) differs from that in the previous chapter, (2.1), in the following respects:
   a. it is more specific with respect to the interests of bureaucrats, taking into account some general hypotheses that have been put forward in the literature on bureaucracy;
   b. as regards the interests of politicians it incorporates a changing, instead of a constant, rate of substitution between private output and state output, which seems to be more plausible [25].

3. The *interests* chosen for the politicians, viz. state production (and, thus, because of the balanced budget condition, expenditures) and private production, are in line with what is typically assumed if 'ideology' apart from some form of vote getting is considered at all for politicians.
   In the few cases that ideology has been given separate attention in formal models, the familiar distinction is made between governments from the 'left' of the political spectrum that like to step up state expenditures, and governments from the 'right' that are pro-private-sector and try to curb state expenditures [see Frey (1977b), Frey and Schneider (1978a,b)] [26].

4. *Types of states* are defined as points on the unit square spanned by λ_s and ε; see Fig. 3.2.
   Let us consider two broad cases: first, the case where bureaucrats fully control the state apparatus, and, second, the case where the state is controlled by the politicians (the government). The remaining cases fall in between. The first case covers the class of states defined by the set $\{(\lambda_s,\varepsilon) \mid \lambda_s = 1\}$. It is easily seen from (3.1) and (3.19) that in that case: $E_1^d(t) = E_1(t-1)e^{\theta}$, unless the total labour force constraint or the maximum tax rate constraint is violated, as will sooner or later happen, of course. If the government is in full control of the

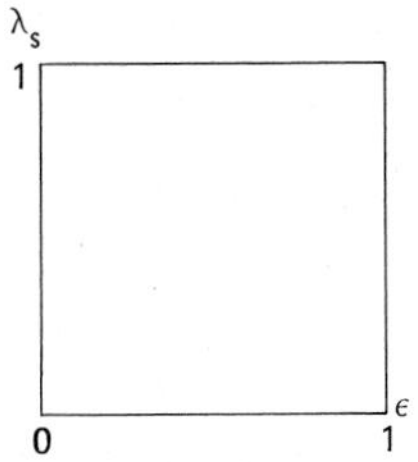

Fig. 3.2. The political space.

state - the class of states defined by $\{(\lambda_s,\varepsilon) \mid \lambda_s = 0\}$ - it is obtained, for $\varepsilon < 1$, that: $E_1^d(t) = \min\{\max[L - \tilde{E}_2^d(t), (1 - \varepsilon)(L + S(t)/\tilde{\alpha}_b(t)], L\}$ and for $\varepsilon = 1$, that $E_1^d(t) = E_1^-$ if $L - \tilde{E}_2^d(t) \leqq E_1^-$, or $E_1^- \leqq E_1^d(t) \leqq L - \tilde{E}_2^d(t)$, if $L - \tilde{E}_2^d(t) > E_1^-$ (provided that the tax constraint is inactive). If follows that for all $\varepsilon < 1$ in this case the demand for labour by the state at least equals the difference between the size of the total labour force and the expected demand for labour by the firms. The reason is that even a pro-private-sector type of government (say, $\varepsilon > 0.5$) [27)] prefers to employ labour that would otherwise be expected to be unemployed, as state production as such is positively valued if $\varepsilon < 1$ (recall that the maximum tax constraint is assumed to be inactive). The state is willing to crowd out the firms in the labour market - which is the only market in the model where crowding out may occur - for values of ε for which $(1 - \varepsilon)[L + S(t)/\tilde{\alpha}_b(t)] > L - \tilde{E}_2^d(t)$. Whether crowding out occurs or not depends, of course, on the total demand for and supply of labour as well as on the working of the market (think of the job preference parameter κ). Types of states for which ε is very low are - just as much as purely bureaucratic states ($\lambda_s = 1$) - bound to run into financial troubles due to the maximum tax rate, although the positive impact of state production on private labour productivity may give some temporary relief [28)]. In case of a small difference between the state wage rate and the dole rate there is not much manoeuvring room for the state to balance its budget whenever a decrease in its demand for labour implies an increase in the expected rate of unemployment. An influential bureaucracy may then have a mitigating impact on the state's demand for labour for some time. For example, for $\varepsilon = 0$ and $\lambda_s > 0$ it is obtained that: $E_1^d(t) = E_1(t-1) \exp[\theta + (1 - \lambda)/(2\lambda)]$. [29)] The more influential the bureaucrats are, the more the growth target θ is approached.

5. Restricting attention to the class of states defined by $\{(\lambda_s,\varepsilon) \mid \lambda_s = 0\}$ - implying a powerless, subservient bureaucracy - one can say that

(taking S(t) = 0 on average) the state characterized by ($\lambda_s = 0$, $\varepsilon = 1 - E_1^-/L$) performs a *pivotal* role in the sense that it marks off a class of states that are only prepared to crowd out the firms in the labour market if $L - \tilde{E}_2^d(t) < E_1^-$ in order to safeguard the minimal size of the state (for these states $\varepsilon > 1 - E_1^-/L$), and a class of states that may even do so if $L - \tilde{E}_2^d(t) > E_1^-$ [in which case $\varepsilon < 1 - E_1^-/L$; see 4]. In the following section it will be shown that there also exists a class of states with a pivotal position in the political space (see Fig. 3.2) in the sense that it divides that space into a set of states for which $\tau(t) = \tau^+(t)$ is a necessary condition for an equilibrium in the economy (which, as we shall see, makes them likely to produce economic cycles), and another set for which this is not a necessary condition (see Section 3.4, point 13).

The behaviour of the firms

1. The log-linear specification of P_b in eq. (3.26) implies a changing rate of substitution between the expected dividend contribution of the periods involved. In case of a linear form one would have obtained a step function for the investment ratio, with $\sigma(t)$ alternating between one and zero, depending on the time discount parameter ρ and the expected rate of return on capital [30]. As can be seen from eqs. (3.35) and (3.36) a positive expected rate of return on capital is demanded for investment in the log-linear version as well, but its level does not further play a part in the determination of $\sigma(t)$ [see also (3.33) where the first two factors on the right-hand side indicate the expected rate of return]. Apart from ρ, the expected size of the capital stock, the price of capital goods and the funds available for investment are determinant in this respect.

2. The time discount parameter ρ determines the importance that is attached to the expected dividend contribution of period t+2, which may be seen as an indicator of the contribution of periods further extending into the future. If needed, the weights ρ_n can be transformed into 'normal' discount rates, and the time horizon can be extended to include more than 3 periods [31].

3. It is readily seen from eq. (3.26) that the same behaviour of the firm results when real or disposable (after-tax) dividends are considered [32].

3.4. Equilibrium Analysis

Definition. An *equilibrium* is defined by the constancy of all variables over time [33].

The *necessary* and *sufficient* conditions for an equilibrium are enumerated in Appendix 3A. From these conditions, a number of equilibrium characteristics can be derived that will be presented below. Proofs are straightforward and will be given in Appendix 3B, if necessary. To indicate equilibrium values of variables the time index will be omitted, whenever this is non-confusing.

1. *An equilibrium need not exist; more than one equilibrium may exist*. For the first part, see (3B1); it is ultimately due to the minimum consumption level x_b^{c-}, which may be too high. Important in this respect are the time discount parameter of capitalists (see 8 below) and the type of state (see 13 below). As the numerical experiments will illustrate, however, equilibria may exist. The latter part of the characteristic is due to the wage rate inequality condition (3A4), and the fact that corner solutions may be obtained for programming problem (3.19), which means that multiple equilibria may be sustained by the same type of state (see below).

2. Figs. 3.3 and 3.4, respectively, show the impact of the type of state on the demand for labour, and the relationship between money supply and product demand in equilibrium.

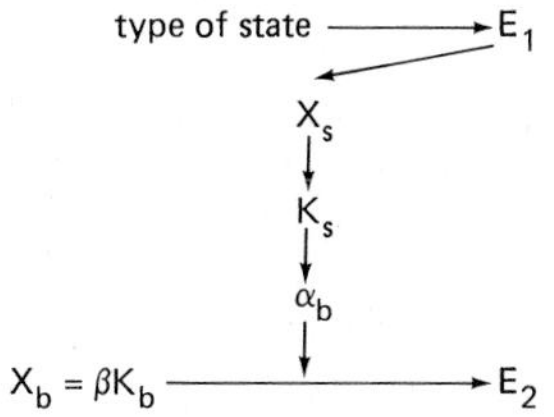

Fig. 3.3. Type of state and labour demand.

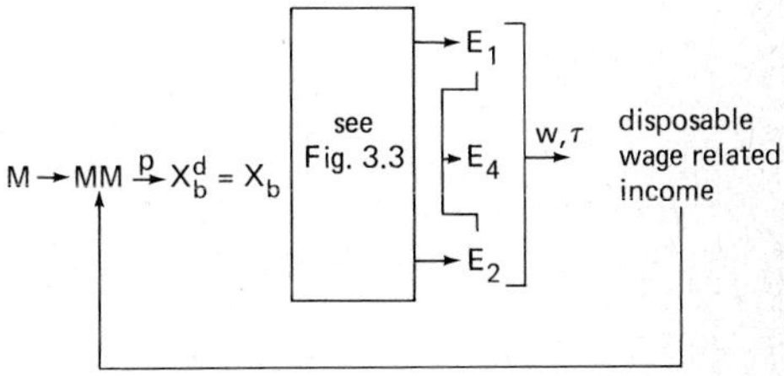

Fig. 3.4. Money supply and product demand.

Fig. 3.3 illustrates the relationship between type of state and labour productivity, through the state's demand for labour, when $\eta > 0$ [i.e., when the elasticity of private labour productivity with respect to state capital is positive; see (3.8)] [34]. Labour productivity determines the firms' demand for labour, given the stock of capital of the firms. There are no labour or financial bottlenecks in equilibrium [35]. Fig. 3.4 shows the relationship between money supply and product demand [see (3.23)]. Wage related income is generated within a period; M equals the amount of money that is available in the economy at the start of a period [36]. Using (3A2), (3A3), (3A6) and (3A7), it is obtained that:

$$(3.37) \qquad pX_b = \left[\frac{\beta(1-\rho)}{(1-\tau)\rho + \delta(1-\rho)}\right].M,$$

a rather familiar expression if we call the ratio between brackets [.] the 'velocity of circulation'. As $0 < \tau < 1$, and $0 \leqq \rho < (\beta - \delta)/(1 + \beta - \delta)$ [see (3.41)], it follows that: $1 < [.] \leqq \beta/\delta$, i.e. the velocity of circulation is greater than 1 and smaller than or equal to the ratio of the output-capital ratio and the depreciation rate of private capital. This is easily seen, as total income pX_b exceeds, of course, profit-related income, which is equal to M, and for any given level of pX_b the stock of money M is smallest if $\sigma = 1$ $(\rho = 0)$, in which case there is no dividend income and $M = F = p\delta K_b = p(\delta/\beta)X_b$ only [see (3A2), (3A3) and (3A6)]. Apart from the parameters ϕ, ψ, ρ, δ, and L, $1 - \tau$ depends on E_1 and E_2 [see (3A5), (3.39), (3.40), (3.42)], which means that [.] depends on the *type of state* (provided that $\rho > 0$); for example, the higher E_1, the higher τ - and, consequently, the velocity of circulation - becomes, unless it can be accompanied by an off-setting increase in E_2. This dependence on the type of state also follows from the fact that the velocity of circulation [.] can be shown to equal the reciprocal of the after-tax profit share (see 10). Notice that the equilibrium size of the *real money stock* M/p is bounded from above by the lower bound on [.], and the fixed size of the total labour force, which determines a ceiling for X_b [$X_b = \alpha_b E_2$; for α_b, see (3A2)]; it is also bounded from below, since X_b is bounded from below by the tax rate constraint [see (3A8)]. In other words, given the size of the money stock M, p must lie within a certain interval.

3. *All expectations are realized.* It is easily checked that in case of an equilibrium all expectations - see (3.16), (3.17), (3.18), (3.29) and (3.30) - are fulfilled. Product supply equals product demand, and labour demand is realized, but it may be less than labour supply [see (3A4)].

4. *Capital stock is fully utilized, but labour may be underemployed.* The utilization of capital at full capacity follows from the realization of private labour demand [see (3A2)]; as regards the possibility of unemployment, see the previous characteristic.

5. *Labour productivity in the private sector.* Equilibrium condition (3A2) shows that

$$(3.38) \qquad \alpha_b = v[(\alpha_s/\zeta)E_1]^{\eta}.$$

6. *Investment ratio.* Because of (3A3) and (3A7)

$$(3.39) \qquad \sigma = (1 - \rho)/[1 + \rho(1 - \delta)/\delta].$$

If $\rho = 0$, so that capitalists only care about future dividends, then $\sigma = 1$. If $\delta \to 1$, in which case capital becomes fully circulating, then $\sigma \to 1 - \rho$.

7. *Rate of return on capital.* The rate of return on capital r is defined as: $r \equiv F/(pK_b)$. Using (3A3) and (3.39), it is obtained that

$$(3.40) \qquad r = \delta/\sigma = \delta + \rho/(1 - \rho).$$

The first equality is not surprising; the second equality shows, however, that the equilibrium rate of return only depends on the depreciation rate δ and the time discount parameter of the firm ρ, which are exogenously determined (and independent of the type of state in the model), which implies that r is invariant in case of multiple equilibria.

8. *Time preference condition for the firm.* As $r < \beta$ should hold, it is demanded, using (3.40), that

$$(3.41) \qquad \rho < (\beta - \delta)/(1 + \beta - \delta).$$

9. *Wage rate and rate of return on capital.* Using (3A2) and (3A3), and letting $\bar{w}_2 \equiv w_2/p$, one obtains that

$$(3.42) \qquad \bar{w}_2 = (1 - r/\beta)\alpha_b.$$

This expression resembles the 'wage-profit curve', 'wage-interest frontier', or 'factor-price frontier', which plays an important role in the theory of capital [see, e.g., Harcourt (1974)]. Note, however, that as r is exogenously determined in our model (see 7) there is no trade-off relationship between the real wage rate and the rate of return in equilibrium. In this respect, the real wage rate appears as a residual [see Robinson (1970), Dobb (1973, pp. 267 *seq.*)][37)]. The real wage rate also depends, however, on labour productivity, which is positively related to state employment if $\eta > 0$ [see (3.38)].

Now, although different equilibrium levels of state employment do not necessarily require different types of states, it will be shown below [see (3.43)] that if one does not want to rely - for a particular equilibrium level of state employment - on the particular path that the economic process may take towards an equilibrium (assuming that an equilibrium directed path is followed) then the type of state does matter, which is of course important from a political point of view. Fig. 3.5 illustrates the relationship between $\bar{w}_2$ and r for different α_b ($\alpha_b^- < \alpha_b^* < \alpha_b^+$) when $r = r^*$; if $\eta > 0$, a_b^- and α_b^+, respectively, denote the approximate level of labour productivity when $E_1 \to 0$, and when $E_1 \to L$; of course, $\delta \leqq r < \beta$ should hold.

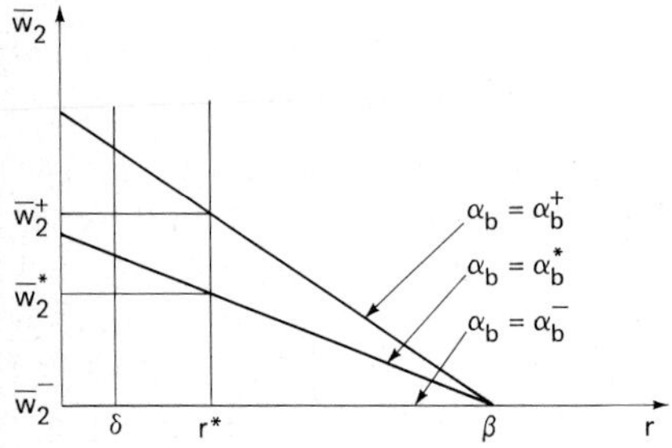

Fig. 3.5. Wage rate, rate of return, labour productivity.

10. *Income distribution*. Dividing both sides of (3.42) by α_b one obtains the share of the *before-tax* real private wage sum in private output; this share is equal to $(1 - r/\beta)$ and, thus, fixed (its complement is the before-tax profit share). The share of *total* real *disposable* wage related income (including unemployment benefits and wages for state sector workers) in private output, however, is only fixed - and equal to the aforementioned private wage sum share - if $\sigma = 1$, in which case the tax burden is fully borne by workers and unemployed [38]. If $\sigma < 1$; this share is positively related to the level of state employment, in that case part of the extra taxes are paid by the capitalists, due to the uniform tax rate. As regards the distribution of income between labour and capitalists it clearly matters then what type of state governs.

With respect to the 'size of the cake', it follows that private output should be maximized in order to maximize the before-tax private wage sum as well as total disposable wage related income when $\sigma = 1$. There will be a trade-off between the latter and the amount of private output when $\sigma < 1$; see 21.

11. *An unemployment equilibrium requires that* $\tau = \tau^{+}$; see (3A4). This follows from the way that the wage rate is determined (for another reason see 12). In case of unemployment the wage rate falls until the minimum income level is reached. An equilibrium of this type is not very likely, though, whenever the difference between w_1 (state wage rate) and w_4 (unemployment benefit) is small. In that case, the state has not much room, financially, to manoeuvre. Slight perturbations may force it to trim the state apparatus in order to meet its financial constraints (see Subsection (3.2.2).

12. *Equilibria with* $\tau < \tau^{+}$ *demand that*

$$(3.43) \qquad E_1 \geqq \left[\frac{2\theta\lambda_s + (1-\varepsilon)(1-\lambda_s)}{2\theta\lambda_s + (1-\lambda_s)}\right].L;$$

see (3B2). Equilibria with $\tau < \tau^{+}$ are full employment equilibria. This is not only due to the way the wage rate is determined, as referred to under 11. It can be shown that any type of state, apart from ($\lambda_s = 0$, $\varepsilon = 1$) for which $E_1 = E_1^{-}$ should hold, is interested in stepping up state employment whenever unemployment would be expected otherwise and no financial bottlenecks are present (recall that expectations are realized). Note that (3.43) only establishes a *lower* bound for E_1. This suggests that as far as the political part of the politico-economic system (the type of state) is concerned no unique equilibrium need exist (see below). Notice, moreover, that this lower bound is positively related to λ_s (indicating the strength with which the interests of bureaucrats are represented) for $\varepsilon > 0$, and inversely related to ε (which indicates the weight attached to private production by politicians) for $\lambda_s < 1$.

13. *There exists a (non-empty) class of states for which in equilibrium* $\tau = \tau^{+}$ *necessarily holds*; see (3B3). Where it all comes to is that, on the one hand, a certain private production level is required for the minimum consumption basket $x_b^{c-} > 0$ for which the necessary income level is guaranteed by the state, while, on the other hand, types of states exist that would try to further encroach upon the private sector when not financially constrained [see (3.43)]. The crucial equilibrium condition here is that $\tau \leqq \tau^{+}$ should hold; see (3A4), (3A5), (3A8). Note, that types of states for which - in case that $\eta > 0$ - the lower bound of E_1 given by the right-hand side of (3.43) is too small according to (3A8) are, nevertheless, compatible with an equilibrium, as any type of state sustains an equilibrium with E_1 larger than that lower bound [excepting ($\lambda_s = 0$, $\varepsilon = 1$), for which E_1^{-} should be large

enough; see 12]. The condition $\tau \leqq \tau^+$ demands that $E_1 - (A_1E_1^\eta + A_2)E_2 + A_3 \leqq 0$, where A_1, A_2 and A_3 are exogenously determined, and $A_1, A_3 > 0$, $A_2 < 0$. The relationship between $\tau - \tau^+$ and E_1, for $E_1 + E_2 = L$, is sketched in Fig. 3.6. It has at most two real roots. The downwards sloping part of the curve should be neglected for $\eta = 0$.

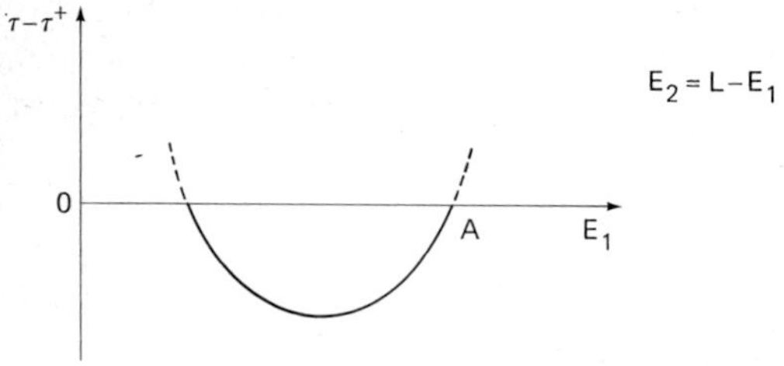

Fig. 3.6. The relationship between $\tau - \tau^+$ and E_1.

The elasticity of labour productivity with respect to state capital (accumulated state production) is clearly important in this respect. Changes in η cause changes in the size of the class of states of which the activities are curbed by the tax rate constraint; the larger η, the smaller its size will be, *ceteris paribus* [see (3A8)].

In this context it may be noted that the *carrying capacity* of the economy regarding the size of the state sector (see the concluding remarks of Section 2.3.) - defined by the maximum feasible state size as measured by E_1 or $\bar{w}_1E_1$ - is determined by the largest possible value of E_1 that still satisfies (3A8) [it is readily checked that - given the existence of an equilibrium at all for some type of state - the remaining equilibrium conditions, apart from (3A1), can be satisfied if (3A8) is satisfied]. It is clear from (3A8) that $E_2 = L - E_1$ should hold in that case. The value is indicated by A in Fig. 3.6. The carrying capacity is fully utilized in case of an equilibrium involving a type of state for which $\tau = \tau^+$ *necessarily* holds. It is, furthermore, noted that the class of states for which the right-hand side of (3.43) equals this largest possible value of E_1 performs a *pivotal* role in the political space in the sense that it divides that space into a set of states for which $\tau(t) = \tau^+(t)$ necessarily holds in equilibrium, and another set of states for which this equality does not necessarily hold (assuming that there exists an equilibrium with $\tau < \tau^+$)[39].

14. *If for an arbitrary* (λ_s, ε) *an equilibrium exists for which* $\tau = \tau^+$

holds, then it is an equilibrium for all (λ_s,ε), *except possibly for* $(\lambda_s = 0,\ \varepsilon = 1)$; see (3B4).

15. *If for an arbitrary* (λ_s,ε) *a full employment equilibrium exists with* $\tau < \tau^+$, *then there exists for all* $(\lambda_s,\varepsilon) \in \{(\lambda_s,\varepsilon) | \lambda_s > 0$ or $\varepsilon < 1\}$ *a full employment equilibrium with* $\tau = \tau^+$, *and an unemployment equilibrium. For* $(\lambda_s = 0,\ \varepsilon = 1)$ *only the latter may hold;* see (3B5).

16. *If an equilibrium exists for an arbitrary* (λ_s,ε), *then there exists an equilibrium for all* (λ_s,ε), *except possibly for* $(\lambda_s = 0,\ \varepsilon = 1)$; see 11, 14, 15.

17. *If for an arbitrary* (λ_s,ε) *an unemployment equilibrium exists, then there exists a full employment equilibrium as well;* see (3B6).

18. *More than one* (λ_s,ε) *can be associated with an equilibrium;* see (3B7). It means that, from a comparative static point of view, changes in the polity do not necessarily demand changes in the economy.

19. *More than one equilibrium may exist for a type of state;* see 15 and 17. It means that, from a comparative static point of view, changes in the economy do not necessarily require changes in the polity.

Definition. A *unique equilibrium* is defined by (a) the existence of at most one equilibrium per type of state, and (b) the identity of equilibria over types of states.

20. *If there exists only one equilibrium for an arbitrary* $(\lambda_s,\varepsilon) \in \{(\lambda_s,\varepsilon) | \lambda_s > 0$ *or* $\varepsilon < 1\}$ *then: (1) it is a full employment equilibrium with* $\tau = \tau^+$; *(2) it is a unique equilibrium for all* $(\lambda_s,\varepsilon) \in \{(\lambda_s,\varepsilon) | \lambda_s > 0$ or $\varepsilon < 1\}$; *(3) it is a unique equilibrium for all* (λ_s,ε) *if* $E_1 = E_1^-$ *happens to hold;* see 15 and 17 for (1), 14 and 15 for (2), (3B2) for (3). In case of a unique equilibrium, there is a maximum of structural coercion on the activities of the state; all equilibrium compatible types of states behave in exactly the same way (a perfectly restrictive economy).

21. *The necessary and sufficient conditions for an equilibrium with maximum private output are given by:* (3A1)-(3A7), $E_1 + E_2 = L$ *and* $E_1 = \max\{E_1^-,\ [\eta/(1+\eta)].L\}$. If $\eta > 0$, private output does not only depend on the employment of capital and labour but also on the employment of labour by the state. Obviously, $E_1 + E_2 = L$ should hold for a maximum of X_b. Using (3.4), (3.38), and $E_1 \geqq E_1^-$ it then follows from the first order condition for a maximum of X_b that $E_1 = \max\{E_1^-,\ [\eta/(1+\eta)].L\}$; a

minimum state size $E_1 = E_1^-$, is only required when: $\eta/(1+\eta) \leqq E_1^-/L$.

It may be interesting to note that a unique equilibrium does not imply maximum private output. The differential between the state wage rate and the private wage rate, and the investment ratio are important in this respect [40)].

Suppose that $\phi = \sigma = 1$, in which case there is no wage differential between state and private sector, and tax revenues from dividend income are absent, it then follows that maximum private output is implied by a unique equilibrium, as in that case the before-tax real private wage sum should obtain its maximal value, for, otherwise, it would be possible to shift labour from one of the sectors to the other, thereby increasing the wage sum beyond what is necessary for minimum consumption (recall from 10 that the equilibrium share of the before-tax real private wage sum in private output is constant)[41)].

As regards the types of states that are compatible with a maximum private output equilibrium, note from characteristic 14 that such an equilibrium, for an arbitrary type of state, would be sustained by any $(\lambda_s,\varepsilon) \in \{(\lambda_s,\varepsilon) | \lambda_s > 0 \text{ or } \varepsilon < 1\}$ if $\tau = \tau^+$; if $\tau < \tau^+$ then, because of (3.43), it is only sustained by the class of states for which

(3.44) $$\varepsilon - [2\theta\lambda_s/(1 - \lambda_s) + 1]/(1 + \eta) \geqq 0$$

or

$$\varepsilon - [2\theta\lambda_s/(1 - \lambda_s) + 1](L - E_1^-)/L \geqq 0.$$

3.5. Numerical Experiments

In this section we present the result of a number of numerical experiments with the model. The experiments are concerned with the consequences of representation of interests by the state, and the impact of structural coercion on these consequences. For notational convenience, the time index will again be deleted whenever this is non-confusing. Parameter values and initial conditions will first be given. With respect to the wage equation (3.21) and the price equation (3.31) it is, respectively, assumed that: $g(.) = [E_1^d(t-1) + E_2^d(t-1) - L]/L$, and $h(.) = [X_b^d(t) - X_b^s(t)]/X_b^s(t)$, which means that relative changes in product price and wage rate are supposed to equal the relative excess demand for product and labour, respectively.

Parameter values

$\alpha_s = 1$	$\delta = 0.1$	$\theta = 0.05$	$\phi = 0.9$	$E_1^- = 1$
$\beta = 0.5$	$\zeta = 0.1$	$v = 0.29$	$\psi = 0.8$	$L = 100$
$\kappa = 0.1$	$\eta = 1$	$\rho = 0.1$	$x_b^{c-} = 5$	

The only parameter values that remain to be specified are λ_s, which indicates the relative strength with which the interests of bureaucrats and politicians are represented by the state, and ε, which represents the weight attached by politicians to private *versus* state production. The state employment growth target of the bureaucrats (θ) is assumed to be 5%. The fraction of labour that prefers to be employed by the state if not threatened by unemployment (κ) is put at 10%. The elasticity of private labour productivity with respect to state capital (η) is assumed to be 1.

Initial conditions

$D_s(1) = 0$	$\tau(0) = 0.09$	$E_2(0) = 85$	$K_b(1) = 4500$	$p(0) = 1$	$w_2(0) = 20$
$E_1(0) = 10$	$D_b(0) = 0$	$K_b(0) = 5000$	$S(0) = 0$	$p(1) = 1$	

These initial conditions are sufficient to determine the initial values of all the remaining variables.

Four *patterns of motion* were generated by the types of states that were considered: (1) equilibria, (2) regular cycles, (3) cycles marked by a periodic 'bankruptcy' of the state forcing it to put $\tau = \tau^+$ and $E_1 = E_1^-$, and (4) shrinking private production accompanied by an accelerating inflation due to a chronic financial breakdown of the state.

Figs. 3.7, 3.8 and 3.9 show the time-paths of some of the variables for three types of states, generating the first three patterns of motion.

Fig. 3.7.: Private product biased state: ($\lambda_s = 0$, $\varepsilon = 0.99$).

This type of state consists of a government that is only marginally interested in state production whenever this is expected to interfere with private production, and an obedient, powerless, bureaucracy. It is not interested in higher levels of employment than what makes up the difference between total labour force and the expected private demand for labour (see Section 3.3). In short, the state adjusts itself to the behaviour of business in the labour market. Expecting an excess supply of labour at $t = 0$ the state steps up its demand for labour; E_1 increases accompanied by an increase of the tax-rate τ. The increase in E_1 causes labour productivity in the private sector (α_b) and, consequently, the capital-labour ratio ($K_b/E_2 = \alpha_b/\beta$) to rise. The latter effect produces a fall in private labour demand and induces a further increase in E_1. At the same time, enhanced labour productivity and a lower real wage rate (w_2/p), effectuated during the initial economic contraction, raise the profit margin ($pX_b - w_2E_b)/pX_b$ [$= 1 - (w_2/p)/\alpha_b$] [42]. The investment ratio σ increases, followed, with a lag, by an increase of $\dot{K}_b$. The latter effect gradually dominates the rise of α_b and causes private demand for labour to grow. An excess demand for labour results. State employment is forced back ($\kappa = 0.1$) and α_b declines. In the meantime w_2/p rises due to the excess demand for labour and a decrease in p induced by an excess supply on the product market (stocks reflect the budget surplus of the state and the time lag in the spending of disposable business funds). Profit margin and investment ratio, consequently, fall. The contraction, however, does not terminate into a depression. After some time an equilibrium sets in.

Fig. 3.8: Bureaucratic state : ($\lambda_s = 1$, $0 \leqq \varepsilon \leqq 1$).
This type of state is characterized by a powerless government. The figure shows a regular cycle. The growth target of the bureaucrats stands in the way of a rapid expansion of E_1 like the private output biased state effectuated (see Section 3.3). Labour productivity and, consequently, the capital-labour ratio scarcely increase. The expansion of E_1 is again checked by an increase in private demand for labour. State employment dwindles until a floor ($\kappa L = 10$) is reached.
From that time on private demand for labour is frustrated causing an underutilization of capital ($K_b^u < K_b$). Investment falls and E_1 increases again. It seems that productivity is a bottleneck to an equilibrium.
The pictures also clearly show the relationship between, on the one hand, budget surpluses and deficits, and, on the other hand, the tax rate and excess supply and demand on the product market. The share of state production in total production Y, as estimated in the national accounts [i.e., $w_1E_1/(w_1E_1 + pX_b)$], more or less follows the development of E_1. Note, finally, that contrary to what might be expected this state does not even realize the level of state employment that the private product biased state established.

Fig. 3.9: State goods biased state : ($\lambda_s = 0.5$, $\varepsilon = 0.01$).
In this case we have a government that is only marginally interested in private production, and an influential bureaucracy, say because of the dependence of politicians on the bureaucratic apparatus that goes with a strong emphasis on state production. The pictures show some interesting profiles. The very fast expansion of E_1 is brought about by a sharp decline of private demand for labour. This decline results from an increased capital-labour ratio - due to the expansion of E_1 and, consequently, α_b - and a diminishing investment level following a strong increase of the real

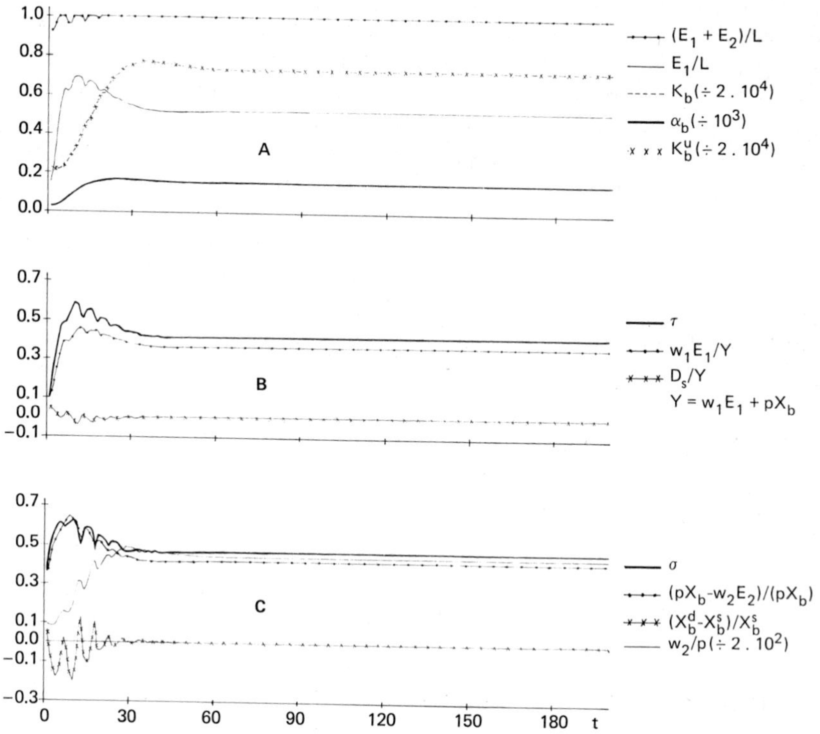

Fig. 3.7. Private product biased state: ($\lambda_s = 0$, $\varepsilon = 0.99$).

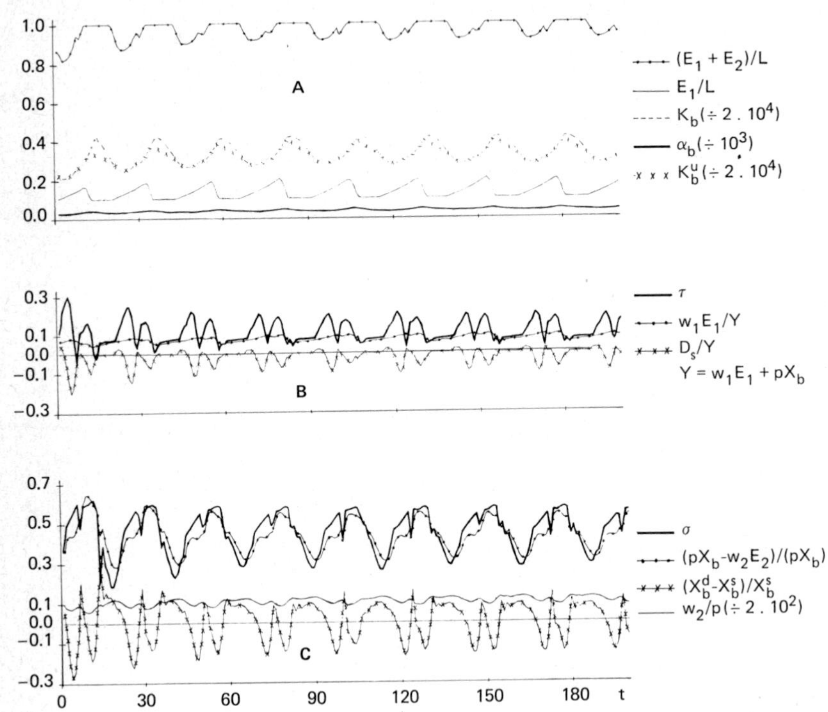

Fig. 3.8. Bureaucratic state: ($\lambda_s = 1$, $0 \leqq \varepsilon \leqq 1$).

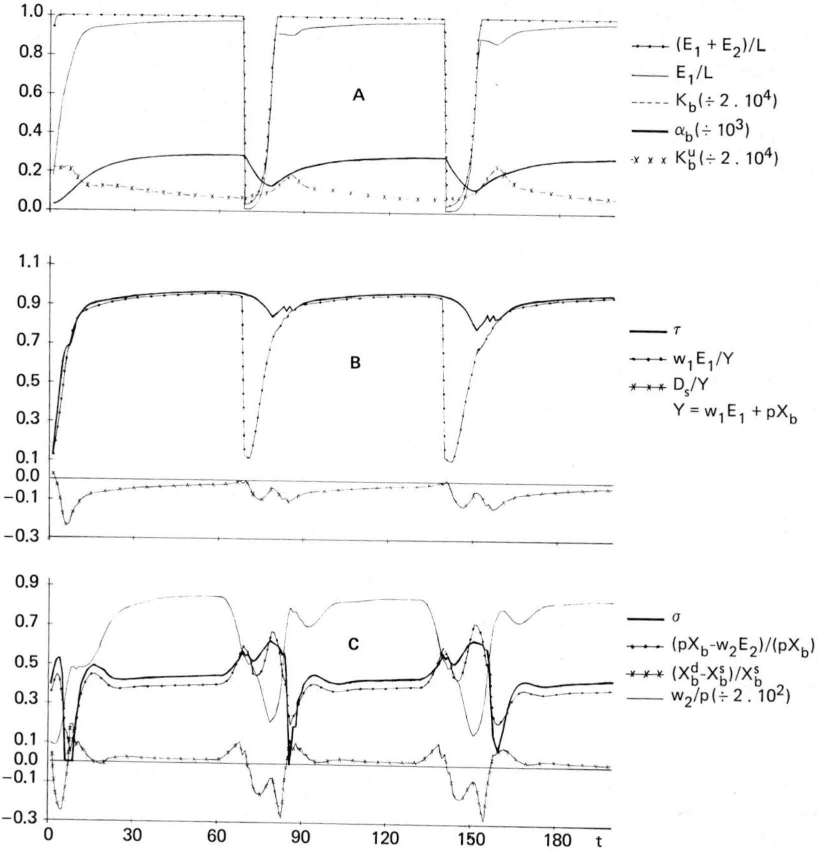

Fig. 3.9. State goods biased state: (λ_s = 0.5, ε = 0.01).

wage rate. A persistent rise of the product price, however, accompanying a shrinking private production level ultimately brings the real wage rate down (t = 60). The upper bound on the tax rate falls and, given a rate of 96%, it does not take long before it becomes active. When t = 69 the state is forced to trim its organization and to keep the tax rate at its maximum, because it cannot meet its financial constraints. After a while, the state recuperates, added by a recovery of the private sector, and the process starts again.

Sensitivity

- All in all 25 *types of states* were considered, based on the following values for ε and λ_s: $\varepsilon = 0, 0.01, 0.5, 0.99, 1$; $\lambda_s = 0, 0.25, 0.5, 0.75, 1$. Table 3.2 gives an overview of the results that were obtained; the cell numbers correspond with the aforementioned patterns of motion (see page 75) [43].

  It appears that equilibria occur when state production is mildly favoured. If it is pushed too hard then cycles marked by financial problems for the state show up, if it is too much restricted then regular cycles such as shown by the bureaucratic state occur. We have tried to describe the underlying processes in the text accompanying the Figs. 3.7, 3.8 and 3.9. The fourth motion pattern, marked by a chronic financial breakdown of the state and an accelerating inflation, shows up in case of such rather extreme types of states as ($\lambda_s = 0$, $\varepsilon = 0.01$) and ($\lambda_s = 0$, $\varepsilon = 1$); in the first case the state is almost exclusively interested in state production, which leads to an enormous expansion of the state at first, but the state is in short time financially forced to put $\tau = \tau^+$ and $E_1 = E_1^-$; in the second case the state is exclusively interested in private production which also leads to a minimal state size [44]. In all these cases, the chronic financial difficulties of the state are due to a persistent negative maximum tax rate, compelling the state to subsidize. This may be caused by a low wage (due to unemployment) and/or a high price level (due to a large money supply and a low private production level). State debts accumulate, state employment is kept at a

Table 3.2
Types of states and patterns of motion.

	λ_s				
ε	0	0.25	0.5	0.75	1
0	3	3	3	4	2
0.01	4	3	3	3	2
0.5	1	1	1	1	2
0.99	1	2	2	2	2
1	4	2	2	2	2

minimum, private output decreases as labour productivity declines, the price level increases, and still larger subsidies are called for.

- Using the parameter values and equilibrium condition (3A8), it is easily computed that the *feasible range* for E_1 in equilibrium is at any rate restricted to: $3.8 \leqq E_1 \leqq 97.5$ (rounded values).
  It follows, using (3.43), that cycles and/or severe financial problems for the state are bound to appear - irrespective of the initial conditions - if the right-hand side of (3.43) exceeds 97.5, as equilibria with $\tau = \tau^+$ are unlikely to occur (see equilibrium characteristic 11 in the previous section). In this case, the feasible range for E_1 is quite large, but it may be much smaller or even vanish for different parameter values. One of the important parameters in this respect is, of course, the minimum consumption level x_b^{c-} [see (3A8)].
  Another important parameter is the firms' time preference parameter ρ; if $\rho \geqq 0.29$ then any equilibrium is ruled out [see (3.41)], no matter what the initial conditions are [45].

- It is clear that the specific assumption that is made with respect to the *time horizon for the state* may have a significant influence on the outcome of the economic process. If it would extend over more then one period then the effects of its activities on labour productivity, for example, might have been taken into account [46]. Note, however, that a longer time horizon does not imply that either financial difficulties or cycles will disappear. Cycles may even be generated on purpose, as the literature on political business cycles has suggested [see, e.g., Frey (1978)]. Moreover, a longer time horizon need not be accompanied by a deeper understanding of the economic process [47].

- The value of the *job preference parameter* κ and the *initial conditions* are particularly important for the occurrence of regular cycles. The value of κ determines the level of state demand for labour that is protected against competition from private demand for labour in case of an excess demand in the labour market. An even development of E_1 is assured up to $E_1^d(t) = \kappa L$, which is important given the lower bound on the equilibrium value of E_1 [see (3.43)]. This even development of E_1 will be reflected in the development of private labour productivity, which is important for the firms' behaviour; moreover, a higher level of labour productivity reduces, by decreasing the labour intensity of production, the pressure under the wage rate in case of an expansion of private production [48]. Note, furthermore, that the state's expectation that private demand for labour will - on average - equal the previous period level of E_2 [see (3.17)], may easily lead to an unintentional crowding-out phenomenon on the labour market when κ is high. As long as $E_1^d(t) \leqq$

κL the firms cannot encroach upon E_1. The time path of E_2 is clearly important in this respect.

3.6. *Summary*

In this chapter we have developed a *dynamic* model of the interaction between state and private sector. The state comprises a government and a homogeneous bureaucracy. The (endogenous) behaviour of the state is related to the interests of *politicians* and *bureaucrats*. The behaviour of *firms*, *workers* and *consumers* has been carefully spelled out. A (rudimentary) financial sector has been introduced for the supply of money. The economic model will serve as a basis for the models to be developed in the following chapters. Special attention has been given to the impact of representation and structural coercion on the activities of the state, and its consequences for the economic process.

The *character of the economic process* is, particularly, influenced by an assumed relationship between state production and labour productivity in the private sector, the job preferences of labour, a minimum consumption level in terms of private product, and the fact that state and firms draw upon the same homogeneous labour force for production.

As regards the *behaviour of the state* it was, *inter alia*, obtained that:
- apart from the purely private product biased state ($\lambda_s = 0$, $\varepsilon = 1$), and the purely bureaucratic state ($\lambda_s = 1$, $0 \leqq \varepsilon \leqq 1$), all types of states practise a Keynesian type of policy; state production and employment are increased in case of an expected excess supply of labour; the reason is not, however, that politicians are interested in state employment as such, but the fact that they are interested (to whatever extent) in state production and, therefore, in employing resources that would otherwise be idle; even outspoken pro-private-sector types of states may sustain a large state sector;
- bureaucrats may have a restraining influence on governments that are primarily interested in state production when they are interested in a fixed growth rate of state employment; in the long run, however, such bureaucratic types of states are bound to be confronted with problems, given the fixed size of the labour force and the minimum consumption level in terms of private product.

Equilibrium analysis, among other things, showed that:
- the velocity of circulation of money is related to the type of state;
- the capital stock is fully utilized in equilibrium, but labour may be underemployed;

- the equilibrium rate of return on capital only depends on the depreciation rate of capital and the time preference parameter of firms; the real wage rate depends on the type of state, although there is no one-to-one relationship; the share of the before-tax real private wage sum in private output is fixed for any type of state; the share of total real disposable wage related income is positively related to the level of state employment, however, if not all profits are used for investment, so that taxes can be obtained from dividend income;
- there exists a non-empty class of states for which in equilibrium the tax rate necessarily attains its maximal value; such an equilibrium is not very likely to occur; in this context a class of states can be indicated which performs a pivotal role in the political space in the sense that it divides that space into a set of states for which the tax rate constraint is necessarily active in equilibrium, and another set of states for which this does not always necessarily hold;
- more than one type of state can be associated with an equilibrium, and more than one equilibrium may exist for a type of state; a unique equilibrium is possible, though, in which case the economy is perfectly restrictive, compelling all equilibrium compatible types of states to show exactly the same (equilibrium) behaviour.

Numerical experiments showed that equilibria occur when state production is mildly favoured. If it is pushed too hard then cycles marked by financial problems for the state appear, if it is too much restricted then regular cycles occur. In rather extreme cases even a chronic financial breakdown of the state is possible, accompanied by an accelerating inflation. As the type of state clearly matters for the occurrence of cycles, we may speak of politico-economic cycles.

The *sensitivity* of the simulation results for, for example, the minimum consumption level, the firms' time preference, the time horizon of the state, and the value of the job preference parameter, has been discussed.

APPENDIX 3A

NECESSARY AND SUFFICIENT CONDITIONS FOR AN EQUILIBRIUM

The necessary and sufficient conditions for an equilibrium are given by (3A1)-(3A7):

(3A1) $E_1 = E_1^d$ = solution of programme (3.19), implying that:
$E_1^- \leqq E_1 \leqq L$, and $\tau \leqq \tau^+$;

(3A2) $E_2 = E_2^d = (\beta/\alpha_b)K_b > 0$, where $\alpha_b = \nu[(\alpha_s/\zeta)E_1]^\eta$;

(3A3) $K_b = \dfrac{\sigma F}{\delta p} > 0$, where $F = (p\alpha_b - w_2)E_2 > 0$;

(3A4) $w_2 \geqq \dfrac{px_b^{c-}}{(1 - \tau)\psi} > 0$, $w_2 = \dfrac{px_b^{c-}}{(1 - \tau)\psi} = w_2^-$ at any rate if $E_1^d + E_2^d < L$;

(3A5) $$\tau = \left\{ 1 + \left[\frac{w_2E_2 + (1 - \sigma)F}{w_2[(\phi - \psi)E_1 + \psi(L - E_2)]} \right] \right\}^{-1},$$

$$\tau = \tau^+ = 1 - \frac{px_b^{c-}}{\psi w_2} \text{ iff } w_2 = w_2^-;$$

(3A6) $pX_b (= p\alpha_b E_2) = M + (1 - \tau)w_2[(\phi - \psi)E_1 + (1 - \psi)E_2 + \psi L]$,

$(1 - \tau)(1 - \sigma)F + \sigma F = M$,

where M is the stock of money that is permanently present in the economy;

(3A7) $\sigma = 1 - \rho[1 + (1 - \delta)pK_b/F] > 0$.

Condition (3A1) follows from (3.19)-(3.21), and $F > 0$ [see (3A3)]; the first part of (3A2) is obtained from (3.20), (3.21), (3.32), and $F > 0$, the second part from (3.3), (3.8), and (3.9); the first part of (3A3) follows from (3.24), (3.27), (3.28) and (3.31), the second part from (3.5)-(3.7), (3.10), (3.11), (3.24), (3,31), and $F > 0$; (3A4) follows from (3.21), and $F > 0$; the first part of (3A5) is obtained from (3.15), the second part from (3.14) and (3A4); (3A6) is derived from (3.5)-(3.7), (3.23), (3.27), and (3,31); (3A7) follows from (3.35), (3,36), and (3A3).

The following relations are useful in checking whether the conditions (3A2)-(3A7) are satisfied: (3.39)-(3.42), and, because of (3A4) and (3A5)

(3A8) $E_1 - (A_1E_1^{\eta} + A_2)E_2 + A_3 \leqq 0,$

where: $A_1 = \psi(1 - r/\beta)\nu(\alpha_s/\zeta)^{\eta}\{1 + (1 - \sigma)[(1 - r/\beta)^{-1} - 1]\}/$
$/[(\phi - \psi)x_b^{c-}] > 0,$

$A_2 = \{\psi - 1 - (1 - \sigma)[(1 - r/\beta)^{-1} - 1]\}/(\phi - \psi) < 0,$

$A_3 = \psi L/(\phi - \psi) > 0$; for σ and r, see (3.39) and (3.40).

Clearly, condition (3A8) is not satisfied if $E_1 \to 0$ (given E_2; if $\eta > 0$), or $E_2 \to 0$ (given E_1).

APPENDIX 3B

PROOFS OF SOME OF THE EQUILIBRIUM CHARACTERISTICS

(3B1) *Characteristic 1: An equilibrium need not exist.*

Proof: It is clear from (3.4) and (3.38) that X_b is bounded from above by X_b^+, say. Suppose $x_b^{c-} > X_b^+/L$. Then using $\dot{X}_b^{ct} = X_b^{cd}$, and (3A4): $pX_b^{ct} > (1 - \tau)\psi w_2 L \geq px_b^{c-}L > pX_b^+$, which obviously cannot hold.

(3B2) *Characteristic 12: Equilibria with $\tau < \tau^+$ demand that* $E_1 \geq L.[2\theta\lambda_s + (1 - \varepsilon)(1 - \lambda_s)]/[2\theta\lambda_s + (1 - \lambda_s)]$.

Proof: It can be checked from (3.1), (3.3)-(3.6), and (3.16)-(3.18), that any type of state, apart from ($\lambda_s = 0$, $\varepsilon = 1$) is interested in stepping up state employment as long as $E_1(t-1) < L - \tilde{E}_2^d(t)$. Thus, $E_1(t-1) = L - \tilde{E}_2^d(t)$, and, therefore, $E_1 = L - E_2$ should hold when $\tau < \tau^+$. The lower bound of E_1 then follows from the first order condition for programme (3.19) taking $\tilde{E}_2(t) = L - E_1^d(t)$. If $\lambda_s = 0$ and $\varepsilon = 1$, then $E_1 = L - E_2 = E_1^-$ should hold as there would be an indeterminateness when $L - \tilde{E}_2^d(t) > E_1^-$. The inequality sign is then due to the fact that $E_1^- > 0$.

(3B3) *Characteristic 13: There exists a (non-empty) class of states for which in equilibrium $\tau = \tau^+$ necessarily holds.*

Proof: For $\tau < \tau^+$, (3A8) should hold as a strict inequality. It is easily seen from (3.43) and (3A8), however, that there exist types of states for which the right-hand side of (3.43) exceeds, or equals, the largest possible value of E_1 that still satisfies (3A8). An equilibrium for these types of states demands, therefore, that $\tau = \tau^+$.

(3B4) *Characteristic 14: If for an arbitrary (λ_s,ε) an equilibrium exists for which $\tau = \tau^+$ holds, then it is an equilibrium for all (λ_s,ε) except possibly for ($\lambda_s = 0$, $\varepsilon = 1$).*

Proof: This follows immediately from the behaviour of the state as described under 12, and the fact that τ is positively related to E_1. It is an equilibrium for ($\lambda_s = 0$, $\varepsilon = 1$) as well, if $E_1 = E_1^-$ happens to hold; see (3B2).

(3B5) *Characteristic 15: If for an arbitrary (λ_s,ε) a full employment equilibrium exists with $\tau < \tau^+$, then there exists for all* $(\lambda_s,\varepsilon) \in \{(\lambda_s,\varepsilon) | \lambda_s > 0 \text{ or } \varepsilon < 1\}$ *a full employment equilibrium* *with* $\tau = \tau^+$ *and an unemployment equilibrium. For* $(\lambda_s = 0, \varepsilon = 1)$ *only the latter may hold.*

Proof: The first part is easily checked from the equilibrium conditions (see Appendix A), given characteristic 14, by changing E_1 and E_2.
For the second part, suppose that $E_1 = E_1^-$ for the equilibrium with $\tau < \tau^+$.

(3B6) *Characteristic 17: If for an arbitrary* (λ_s, ε) *an unemployment equilibrium exists, then there exists a full employment equilibrium as well.*

Proof: Neglecting (3A1) for the moment, it can be checked from (3A2)-(3A7) that is possible to obtain a new equilibrium for which $E_2 = L - E_1$ holds by choosing a sufficiently higher level of E_2 [in which case $\tau < \tau^+$, see (3A8)]. As regards (3A1), observe that there are always types of states for which (3.43) is satisfied, as $E_1 \geqq E_1^- > 0$ [in addition note that E_1 is bounded away from zero if $\eta > 0$; see (3A8)].

(3B7) *Characteristic 18: More than one* (λ_s, ε) *can be associated with an equilibrium.*

Proof: This follows from (3B4) for an equilibrium with $\tau = \tau^+$, and from the latter part of (3B6) for equilibria with $\tau < \tau^+$.

CHAPTER 4

AN ALTERNATIVE APPROACH: INTERESTS AND INTEREST FUNCTIONS

4.1. Introduction

In the previous chapter we made a start with the development of a dynamic model of the interaction between state and private sector. Disregarding the proposed relationship between state production and labour productivity in the private sector, the more novel aspects of the model - as a politico-economic model - are its micro-economic character, and the way the state and its activities are incorporated. The function P_s by means of which the actions of a type of state are determined [see (3.1.)] not only takes into account the usual hypothesis that bureaucrats are interested in a continuous expansion of the state, but it simultaneously allows for the equally popular dichotomy between governments that are inclined towards state expenditures (a 'socialist', 'left-wing' government), and governments that are pro-private-sector and try to restrict state expenditures (a 'conservative', 'right-wing' government).

In our view, however, these assumptions and hypotheses with respect to the behaviour of bureaucrats and politicians (governments) are not very satisfactory, for the following reasons:

1. bureaucrats may as well be supposed to be interested in their income, especially their real after-tax (disposable) income, which interest may run counter to a continuous expansion of the state [1]; in other words, they may be expected to be interested in the bundle of goods that they can obtain in the private sector [2];
2. it is not at all clear why left-wing governments would always favour state expenditures and right-wing governments would not;
3. the existence of multiple positions (for example, a bureaucrat that is also a stock-holder), which appears to be substantial [see, e.g., Domhoff (1967), Helmers *et al.* (1975), Miliband (1973a), Mills (1956)], is neglected;
4. these assumptions do not take advantage of the fact that *a priori* some less abstract interests can be distinguished for (groups of) agents in a capitalist economy (see below).

In this chapter we will, therefore, present an alternative approach [3]. *Central* to this approach is that actions of individuals and collectivities, whether in the traditional economic sphere or in the political sphere, are related to interests that make sense from the point of view of the individual agents involved. From a research strategic point of view it seems best for the problem at hand to start with the position of agents with respect to production in society, as people are typically dependent on state as well as private production for the satisfaction of even their most important needs (such as safety, food). *Four basic positions* can be distinguished in a capitalist economy; worker in the state sector, worker in the private sector, capital owner, unemployed ('dependant'). The interests attached to these positions, which will have to do with the (potential) control over state goods and private goods (more general, marketed and non-marketed goods), will be incorporated in so-called *elementary interest functions*. The actions of individual agents (such as workers, capital owners, voters) and collectivities (such as the state, firms, political parties) are then related to these elementary interest functions. In this way it appears to be possible to get a unified approach to the economic *and* political problems involved in the study of the interaction between state and private sector. As a corollary the behaviour of collectivities is determined in a way that explicitly allows for the existence of internal 'interest blocs'.

Our focusing upon interests is in line with the two earlier referred to approaches to the problem area, the Marxist Approach and the Public Choice Approach.
However, in contrast with the former the individual agent gets a more prominent place in our approach, while the specific way that interests are determined and conflicts within collectivities are dealt with makes it differ from the latter and more alike the former. We will call our approach the *Interest Function Approach*.

The organization of this chapter is as follows. We start with a discussion of interests of individual agents and collectivities (Section 4.2), which is followed by the introduction of so-called interest functions (Section 4.3). Using these interest functions, an alternative model of the interaction between state and private sector is developed (Section 4.4). Some dynamical properties of this model are then discussed (Section 4.5). We next study the characteristics of equilibria (Section 4.6), after which the chapter is summarized (Section 4.7). In an appendix to the chapter we make some comments on the Marxist theory of classes. To economize on space only those symbols that are for the first time introduced will be explained.
The reader is further referred to the List of Symbols.

4.2. Interests

In Chapter 1 it was assumed that *activities* of agents (individuals, collectivities) are related to three determinants:
1. representation,
2. structural coercion, and
3. pressure.
The first determinant has to do with, say, the internal environment of the agent, to wit the nature of the interests represented by that agent; the other two have to do with the character of the agent's external environment (see Section 1.6). This section primarily deals with *representation*. The following questions will have to be answered. *What* interests play a role and should be taken care of in our field of study? *How* do different interests if represented by one individual or by different individuals (or groups of individuals) within a collectivity work themselves out? *In what way* are activities related to interests?

Individual as well as collective actions (activities by collectivities) are, ultimately, supposed to be related to individual *interests*. Because of the apparently extreme complexity and pluriformity of the interests of individuals involved in politico-economic processes, however, we will not occupy ourselves directly with individual interests. Instead, attention will be focused upon the interests of individuals as occupants of certain economic *positions*. Our point of departure thereby is the fact that people are dependent on the production by others for the satisfaction of even their most fundamental needs, such as security and food. In our model production is divided into non-marketed goods produced by the state sector and marketed goods by the private sector. People can be assumed to be interested, in some basic sense, in their control over marketed and non-marketed goods, and, thus, in the present context, in the bundles of state goods and private goods that they (can) acquire. The opportunities, action space or power of people in this respect, and the particular forms in which their basic interests will manifest themselves are shaped by the position that they have with respect to *production* in the economy.

Four *basic positions* can be distinguished in a capitalist economy:
1. worker in the state sector,
2. worker in the private sector,
3. capital owner (capitalist), and
4. unemployed ('dependant', in a wide sense).

First we have a distinction between capitalists and workers. They differ from each other with respect to the control over means of production, while their basic interest in private output takes the particular form of

an interest in profits and wages, respectively.
Second, there is a distinction between state sector workers and workers in the private sector. Apart from the fact that taxes (forced payments) instead of proceeds of sales are the characteristic source of the wages of state sector workers, there are some important differences in the position of these groupings in the economy that should not be neglected:

a. the most important means of violence are in the hands of state sector workers (think of the police and the military);
b. state sector workers have potential control over goods that are typically more or less collective in nature, and in as much as these goods are purely collective they even affect every individual in the economy;
c. state sector workers are part of one already existing organization, which makes it relatively easy for them to promote their interests in a unified way;
d. to the extent that state departments are monopolistic suppliers, state sector workers not only obtain a strong position *vis-à-vis* politicians within the state because of expert knowledge, but they will also easily remain unaffected by political upheavals that will typically direct themselves against the government and may 'at worst' only involve a change of government (the 'survival' problem is much more urgent for a firm than for a bureaucracy);
e. state sector workers are currently, generally, not employed by a government that solely consists of capitalists - as the board of directors of a firm in the private sector typically is - but by one in which more than one basic position in the economy is represented.

For these reasons, we think it is important to distinguish - at least in the first instance - between these two types of workers.
The fourth, and last, basic position that we mentioned regards the unemployed. The unemployed ('dependants', including also pensioners, for example) occupy a marginal position with respect to production. They are not directly involved in it, and are for that reason dependent on transfers from those who are, which gives them - in this respect - the weakest position in the economy.

The set of agents in each basic position will be referred to as a *basic social class* [4)]. Due to, for example, ideological influences further divisions into social groupings may be necessary for the analysis of concrete social phenomena, of course (see also below).
Now let e_k (k = 1,2,3,4) denote the fraction of the total number of economic positions which belongs to the basic social class k. A vector $\underline{e}$ = (e_1,e_2,e_3,e_4) can then be said to indicate a *basic social class structure*; clearly $\underline{e} \geqq 0$ and $\Sigma_k\, e_k = 1$. The set of all $\underline{e}$ is a 3-dimensional unit simplex [5)]; this set will be called the *basic social class space*. Each point in this space represents a particular basic social class structure; see

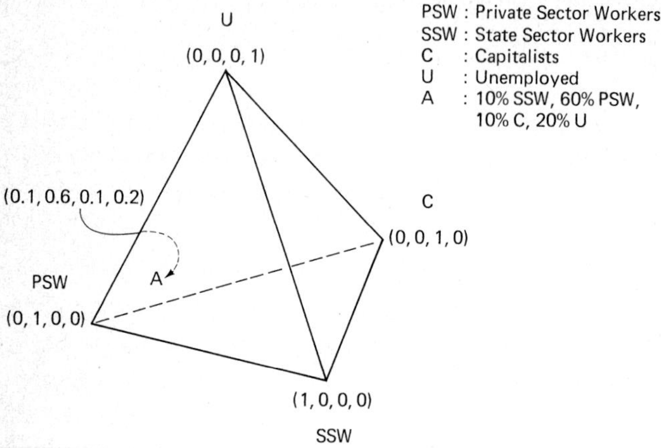

Fig. 4.1. The basis social class structure as a point in a three-dimensional unit-simplex.

Fig. 4.1.

Apart from the position of agents in the economic process there is another factor that is generally recognized as being of great importance for their action space or power in society, namely their *numerical strength*. The extent to which agents are able to realize their (class) interests, and the security of their position, may be related to their numerical share in the population [6]. It will, therefore, be assumed that people are not only, basically, interested in their direct control over marketed and non-marketed goods, but also in the relative number of people that are in the same economic position (the relative size of their class), as this, generally, facilitates an indirect control over these goods. Note that numerical strength can be regarded as a non-marketed good itself.

4.3. *Interest Functions*

4.3.1. Elementary Interest Functions

The four basic positions in a capitalist economy: worker in the state sector, worker in the private sector, capital owner, and unemployed, will be be indicated by a suffix k = 1,2,3,4, respectively. The three *basic class interests* attached to each position k are specified as: average real disposable income $\bar{\bar{w}}_k$ (indicating the bundle of goods that can be obtained in

the market), the average bundle of, non-marketed, state goods available to agents in position k, x_{sk}, and the fraction of the population in position k, e_k [7]. These interests should be further specified dependent on the problem considered.
For example, in case of class-representative collectivities, such as political parties or the state, the appropriate form of these variables would indeed be: the average real disposable income level, the average consumption level of state goods, and the numerical shares of the classes in the population.
In case of class-fraction representative collectivities (such as trade unions) or non-class representative collectivities (such as a firm) the aforementioned variables may have to be further particularized [8]. To the capitalists and workers in a particular firm it is their real disposable income rather than the class average that counts. In the sequel we will indicate this particularization by way of a suffix; for example $\bar{\bar{w}}_{2,f}$ would stand for the real disposable wage income obtained by the workers in firm f.

The interests are incorporated as arguments in so-called *elementary interest functions* P_k that will be used for the determination of the behaviour of agents in different economic positions. The following (partial) specification of P_k is suggested:

(4.1) $$P_k(t) = P_k[P_k^*(t), P_k^*(t+1), \ldots.., P_k^*(t+n)],$$

with

$$P_k^*(t) = \bar{\bar{w}}_k(t)^{\varepsilon_{k1}} . e_k(t)^{\varepsilon_{k2}} . x_{sk}(t)^{\varepsilon_{k3}} ,$$

$$\text{for all } k,\ \varepsilon_{kg} \geqq 0,\ g = 1,2,3,\ \Sigma_g\ \varepsilon_{kg} \leqq 1,$$

where $P_k(t)$ - a scalar - indicates the extent to which the class interests of an agent in position k are realized. For simplicity, the exponents ε_{kg} are taken to be constant over time. Whenever these elementary interest functions are used in the sequel to determine the behaviour of agents, it will be assumed that agents act in accordance with the maximization of the interest function that is supposed to hold for them [9].

More than one elementary interest function may be relevant for the determination of the behaviour of an individual or collective agent, due to:
a. ideology,
b. mobility,
c. multiple positions, and
d. heterogeneous membership in case of collectivities.

It is not our intention here to probe into the nature and causes of *ideology.* Complications raised by the possibility that agents may have a 'false class consciousness' or an 'altruistic' attitude will be neglected in the models developed in this book. *Mobility* refers to the fact that agents may move from one position to another. Before that, they will orientate themselves with respect to the opportunities present in different positions to satisfy their interests, and that is where the elementary interest functions for different economic positions come in. We will return to this later on.

With *multiple positions* the empirically important phenomenon is indicated that agents may occupy more than one position in the economic process; for example, managers (in the private sector) or bureaucrats holding shares in joint-stock companies, 'captains of industry' having important positions in the state as minister or advisor, executives or managers within a firm that are shareholders in the same firm, and so on. These 'hybrid' agents cannot straightforwardly be allocated to one of the basic classes, and are, therefore, a problem to those Marxist theorists who want to have every agent in society allocated to one class only [see, however, Wright (1976) who speaks of 'contradictory locations within the basic contradictory class relations' (*op. cit.*, p. 26)]. To indicate their class position Fig. 4.1 may again be used, but now for a single agent. Point A would then represent an agent who is for 20% unemployed, 60% worker in the private sector, 10% worker in the state sector, and 10% capitalist. The obvious difficulty here is to find an adequate measure by which to determine such percentages (percentages of what?). A candidate would be the fraction of income acquired in the different positions [10]. Although agents in multiple positions seem to perform an important, 'mediating', role in the social class fabric, we will not explicitly be concerned with them in this book.

Let us, therefore, proceed to the fourth case in which more than one elementary interest function may become important: heterogeneous membership in case of collectivities.

4.3.2. Complex Interest Functions

A social grouping - i.e., a set of agents with some common characteristics - possessing, formally, one decision-making centre will be called a *collectivity* [11].

The collectivities that we will, particularly, be concerned with in this book are the state, the firm and the political party. The agents that make up a collectivity may have similar interests [think of Marschak's concept of a team; see Marschak and Radner (1971), Radner (1972a,b)] or dissimilar, conflicting, interests (in which situation the concept of a game becomes more appropriate). The latter situation is, of course, the most common for the collectivities to be considered here. As regards the firm, this has effectively been brought to the fore by the managerial and behavioural theories of the firm [a survey is given in Koutsoyiannis (1979, Sections E and F)]. Now in case of conflicting interests between agents "one can easily imagine that quite complicated assumptions about anticipations and about the possibilities of coalition formation might be appropriate for a given organizational context" and that this would lead "towards a proliferation of special theories with a large element of descriptive detail" [Radner (1972a, pp. 182-183)]. This is not a very attractive prospect. As a provisional way out we propose to follow the idea that a collectivity can be considered as a coalition of interests in which class relationships express themselves. This idea can also be found in Kornai (1971, pp. 93-95), and Poulantzas (1978b, p. 25) [12]. This brings us back to our elementary interest functions. For collectivities the latter are transformed into so-called *complex interest functions* P_c, where c stands for collectivity [13]. The following specification is suggested for the collectivities to be considered in this book:

$$(4.2) \qquad P_c(t) = \Pi_k\, P_k(t)^{\lambda_{kc}(t)} \qquad , \lambda_{kc}(t) \geqq 0,\ \Sigma_k\, \lambda_{kc}(t) = 1,$$

where λ_{kc} denotes the importance of the elementary interest function P_k, and, thus, the weight assigned within the collectivity to the interests of agents in economic position k. It will be assumed in this chapter that these power-weights are constant over time - so that the time index can be dropped - and that collectivities act in accordance with the maximization of the complex interest function that is supposed to hold for them.

To elucidate the assumptions made with respect to collectivities, we give the following *example*. Suppose we have a type of state for which $\lambda_{2s} = \lambda_{4s} = 0$, where s stands for state. In that case, the interests of private sector workers and unemployed do not count, either because they are not represented within the state, or because they are dominated by the interests of capitalists and state sector workers [14]. As $\Sigma_k\, \lambda_{ks} = 1$, it follows that $\lambda_{3s} = 1 - \lambda_{1s}$, and, thus,

$$P_s(t) = P_1(t)^{\lambda_{1s}} . P_3(t)^{1 - \lambda_{1s}} .$$

It is assumed that $P_1(t) = P_1^*(t)$, $P_3(t) = P_3^*(t)$, $\varepsilon_{11} = \varepsilon_{12} = 0.5$, $\varepsilon_{31} = 1$; see (4.1). Thus, $P_1(t) = \{[1 - \tau(t)].\bar{w}_1(t)\}^{0.5}.\{E_1(t)/E\}^{0.5}$ and $P_3(t) = [1 - \tau(t)].\bar{w}_3(t)$, where $\bar{w}_k$ indicates the average real income level of people in position k, and E denotes the fixed total labour force (which is

assumed to make up the total relevant population); the remaining variables have their earlier defined meaning. For ease of notation, the time index will be suppressed from now on; since only period t is involved there cannot be any confusion. The real wage and profit income levels $\bar{w}_1$, $\bar{w}_2$, $\bar{w}_3$, the number of private sector workers E_2 and the number of capitalists E_3, are assumed to be positive and given. The state is confronted with a budget constraint: $\tau(\bar{w}_1E_1 + \bar{w}_2E_2 + \bar{w}_3E_3) \geqq \bar{w}_1E_1$, and the labour force constraint: $E_1 + E_2 + E_3 \leqq E$ (unemployment benefits are disregarded). The endogenous variables are τ and E_1.
The feasible set of P_1,P_3-combinations for this type of state is shown by the shaded area in Fig. 4.2. The line AB is alternatively called the 'joint maximal set' or the 'Pareto optimal set' [see Luce and Raiffa (1957, p.118)] as it is the locus of P_1,P_3-combinations that cannot be improved upon, in the sense that a higher P_1 (P_3) value can only be obtained by negatively affecting P_3 (P_1). For these combinations of P_1 and P_3 the budget constraint is active. The line OA is the locus of P_1,P_3-combinations for which the labour force constraint is active.

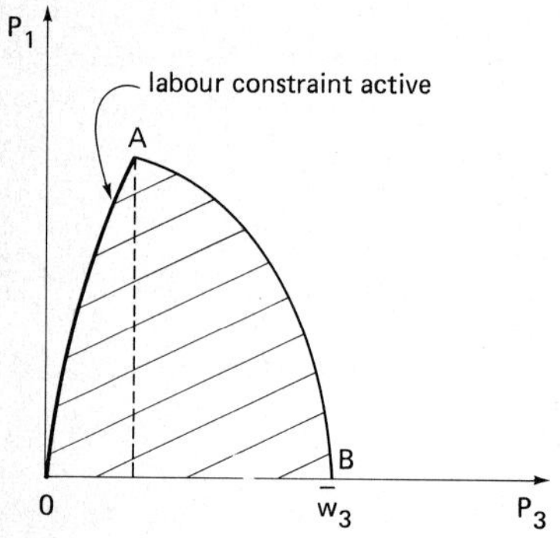

Fig. 4.2. The feasible set.

Fig. 4.3 shows the same feasible set plus three contours or iso-value curves (C_1,C_2,C_3) of P_s for a given value of λ_{1s}, $0 < \lambda_{1s} < 1$.
Higher positions of the contours correspond with higher values of P_s: The contours become vertical lines if $\lambda_{1s} = 0$, and horizontal lines if $\lambda_{1s} = 1$. The assumption that collectivities act in accordance with the maximization of the complex interest function that is supposed to hold for them in fact boils down to assuming that there are forces active within a collectivity that pushes it towards the joint maximal subset of its feasible set; put differently, there is an assumed tendency that the collectivity tries to make the best of the situation ('group rationality'). For the members of

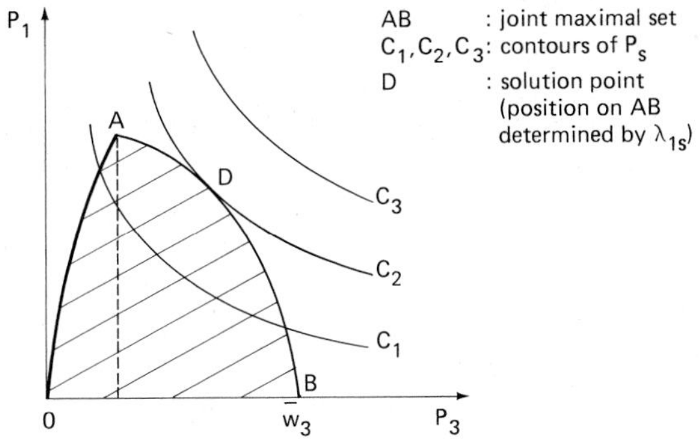

Fig. 4.3. Joint maximal set, contours of P_s, solution point.

the collectivity the joint maximal set is the real controversial part of the feasible set, as improvements in the position of an interest bloc will always negatively affect the position of at least one other bloc (distribution problem). The maximization assumption seems to be quite plausible (at least as a tendency). Neglecting the corners A and B, the maximum value of P_s is obtained where a contour of P_s is tangent to the joint maximal set (point D in Fig. 4.3) [15]. Using this information, it is easily obtained that the optimal values of the state's instrument variables equal

$$E_1 = \min\left\{\left[\frac{\lambda_{1s}}{2(1-\lambda_{1s})}\right]\cdot\left[\frac{\bar{w}_2E_2 + \bar{w}_3E_3}{\bar{w}_1}\right], \; E - E_2 - E_3\right\},$$

with $E_1 = E - E_2 - E_3$ if $\lambda_{1s} = 1$, and

$$\tau = \min\left\{\frac{\lambda_{1s}}{\lambda_{1s} + 2(1-\lambda_{1s})}, \; 1\Big/\left(1 + \left[\frac{\bar{w}_2E_2 + \bar{w}_3E_3}{\bar{w}_1(E - E_2 - E_3)}\right]\right)\right\}.$$

Thus if $\lambda_{1s} = 0$ (capitalists' interests 'rule the state'), $\tau = 0$ and $E_1 = 0$; if $\lambda_{1s} = 1$ (state sector workers' interests are exclusively furthered by the state), $\tau = 1/\{1 + (\bar{w}_2E_2 + \bar{w}_3E_3)/[\bar{w}_1(E - E_2 - E_3)]\}$ and $E_1 = E - E_2 - E_3$, in which case the state's propensity to expand - which is boundless for $\varepsilon_{11} = \varepsilon_{12} = 0.5$ - is checked by the labour force constraint.

With the foregoing example we hope to have elucidated the reasoning behind our procedure to determine the behaviour of collectivities [16].

A nested complex interest function

Before we proceed there is another aspect of collectivities that we would like to pay some attention to, namely the fact that they typically consist of factions, departments, or interest units on different decision-making levels. The occurrence of these interest blocs, as they will be called below, gives rise to a complex of decisions and non-decisions within the collectivity, and of conflicts and compromises between the interest blocs [cf. Kornai (1971, pp. 94-95), Poulantzas (1978b, p. 164)]. In order to deal with this phenomenon we introduce the notions of a *nested complex interest function* and an *interest tree* [17]. A nested complex interest function is a function of complex interest functions referring to interest blocs of a collectivity. For example, in case of the state the interest structure of each bureaucratic department can be represented by a complex interest function for that department; if these departmental complex interest functions, together with a complex interest function for the government, can somehow be aggregated into a complex interest function for the state, then the latter would be called a nested complex interest function.

Distinguishing between different decision-making or interest structure levels within a collectivity, there are two types of interest blocs;
a. *level specific blocs*, and
b. *representative blocs*.
The latter somehow aggregate the interests of lower level blocs, while the former are specific for the decision-making level under scrutiny. The interests of each bloc will be represented by a complex interest function P_{hi} where hi denotes the interest bloc i of decision-making level h; $i \in I_h = \{1,2,..,\bar{I}_h\}$, where I_h denotes the set of interest blocs - numbering $\bar{I}_h$ in total - of level h, and $h \in H = \{1,2,..,\bar{h}\}$, where H denotes the set of decision-making levels - numbering $\bar{h}$ in total - with h = 1 as top level.
Let $I_h^{h'i'}$ indicate the subset of I_h containing the interest blocs of level h that are directly represented by h'i', $h > h' \in H$, $i' \in I_{h'}$. In line with (4.2) it is assumed for representative blocs that

$$(4.3) \qquad P_{h'i'}(t) = \prod_{h > h'} \prod_{i \in I_h^{h'i'}} P_{hi}(t)^{\lambda_{hi}^{h'i'}} ,$$

where $\lambda_{hi}^{h'i'}$ denotes the relative strength with which the interests of hi are represented by h'i';

$$0 \leq \lambda_{hi}^{h'i'} \leq 1, \qquad \sum_{h > h'} \sum_{i \in I_h^{h'i'}} \lambda_{hi}^{h'i'} = 1.$$

For the level specific interest blocs, that do not represent another bloc in the collectivity, it is assumed that

$$(4.4) \qquad P_{hi}(t) = \Pi_k \, P_{k,hi}^{\lambda_{k,hi}} \quad , \quad \Sigma_k \, \lambda_{k,hi} = 1,$$

where $P_{k,hi}$ denotes the elementary interest function for economic position k, as particularized for interest bloc hi, and $\lambda_{k,hi}$ denotes the weight attached to $P_{k,hi}$ within that bloc.

The decision-making structure of a collectivity can be illustrated by an upside-down interest tree, as shown in Fig. 4.4, where, for notational convenience, the time index has been deleted [18].

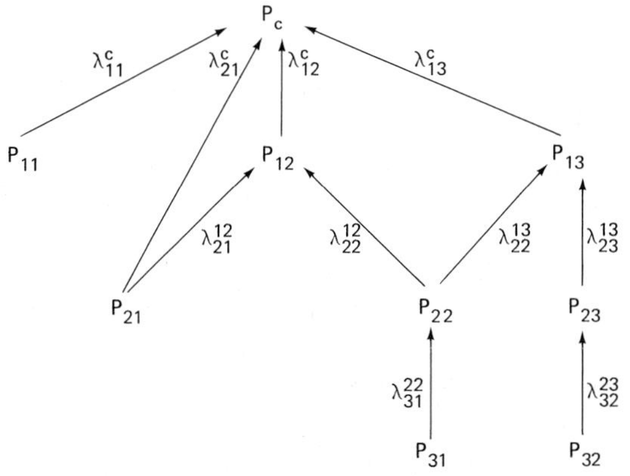

Fig. 4.4. An interest tree.

In this figure the level specific interest blocs are 11, 21, 31, and 32. The figure also illustrates that an interest bloc may be represented by more than one bloc on the same, higher, decision-making level (see P_{22}) or on more than one such level (see P_{21}).

Note that there is a complication pertaining to the representative agents that make up the representative interest blocs. As, of course, these agents have their own (say, internal) interests, the extent to which they represent other agents' interests (external interests) depends upon the structural coercion and pressure that is exerted on them by these agents (recall that the possible impact of ideology is neglected). Because of the, generally, intimate, structural relationship between representatives and represented it is implicitly assumed here that this sort of structural coercion and pressure can be dealt with in the same multiplicative way as the interests of the agents themselves (see Chapter 7 for a more general discussion). One might say that the lower level interests have been internalized on the decision-making level under consideration. Along the same lines it is assumed that those external interests with which politicians (who are, like bureaucrats, state sector workers) are intimately and structurally related - as is typically the case for the interests of the political parties that they come from - are internalized on the governmental level, and incorporated in the government's complex interest function (see the foregoing example). The internal interests of the representative agents should be considered as level specific interests [19].

To give an *example*, suppose we have a firm that is (legally) owned by a group of shareholders employing a number of workers. Suppose, furthermore, that its decision-making structure can be represented by two levels: the board of directors (the top level) and the shop floor. The firm's interest tree is pictured in Fig. 4.5, where $P_{11}(t)$ denotes the interest function of the level specific interest bloc of the shareholders, $P_{21}(t)$ that of the level specific interest bloc of the workers, and, $P_{12}(t)$ that of the representative bloc of the workers. Let,

$$P_{11}(t) = P_{3,11}(t) = \bar{\bar{w}}_{3,11}(t) ,$$

$$P_{12}(t) = P_{2,21}(t) = \bar{\bar{w}}_{2,21}(t)^{\varepsilon_{21}} . e_{2,21}(t)^{\varepsilon_{22}} ,$$

where $P_{2,21}(t)$ and $P_{3,11}(t)$, respectively, denote the elementary interest function for the workers and the shareholders (particularized for their position in the firm), $\bar{\bar{w}}_{2,21}(t)$ and $\bar{\bar{w}}_{3,11}(t)$ the real disposable income levels for these agents, and $e_{2,21}(t)$ the numerical strength of the workers;

$\bar{\bar{w}}_{k,hi}(t) = [1-\tau(t)]w_{k,hi}(t)/\hat{p}(t)$, where $\hat{p}(t)$ is the price index for consumption goods, and $e_{2,21}(t) = E_{2,21}(t)$, where $E_{2,21}(t)$ denotes the employment level of the firm [20].

Suppose that the firm expects to sell whatever it supplies to the product market, given its limited production capacity (there are no stocks), and that it operates under a fixed coefficients technology. Supposing, fur-

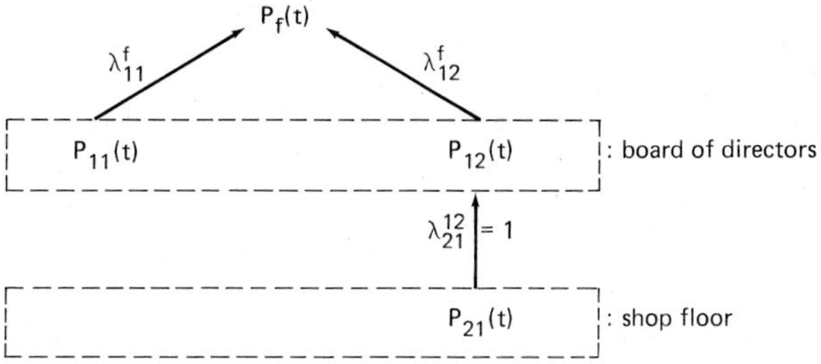

Fig. 4.5. Interest tree for a firm.

thermore, that for period t only the employment level and the distribution of expected sales revenues among shareholders and workers can be varied (there are only wage costs) then the interest function for the firm, $P_f(t)$, can be written as:

$$P_f(t) = P_{11}(t)^{\lambda_{11}^f} . P_{12}(t)^{(1 - \lambda_{11}^f)} =$$

$$= C.\{[p(t)\alpha_b(t) - w_{2,21}(t)]E_{2,21}(t)\}^{\lambda_{11}^f} .$$

$$.\{w_{2,21}(t)^{\varepsilon_{21}}.E_{2,21}(t)^{\varepsilon_{22}}\}^{(1 - \lambda_{11}^f)} ,$$

where C stands for the combined influence of the variables not shown in the expression; the other variables have their earlier defined meaning. If the shareholders have full control of the firm, $\lambda_{11}^f = 1$, then we have effectively only one decision-making level although there may be representatives of the workers on the board. If the workers' interests somehow play a role, e.g. due to co-determination laws [21)], then it is really appropriate to speak of a two-tier decision-making structure. According to our model the firm will show the following behaviour in period t. The number of workers $E_{2,21}(t)$ will be equal to the capital stock times the ratio between the output-capital ratio and the labour productivity level, irrespective of λ_{11}^f, ε_{21}, and ε_{22} (assuming that $\lambda_{11}^f > 0$ or $\varepsilon_{22} > 0$). The before-tax income level of the workers will be equal to: $w_{2,21}(t) = \varepsilon_{21}(1 - \lambda_{11}^f)p(t)\alpha_b(t)/[\lambda_{11}^f + \varepsilon_{21}(1 - \lambda_{11}^f)]$. If $\lambda_{11}^f = 1$ then, obviously, $w_{2,21}(t) = 0$; if $\lambda_{11}^f = 0$ then $w_{2,21}(t) = p(t)\alpha_b(t)$ is obtained for any value of ε_{21} greater than zero, which means that all the revenues go to the workers.

4.4. *The New Politico-Economic Model*

The general structure of the politico-economic model to be developed in this chapter is the same as that of the model presented in the previous chapter; the reader is referred to Subsection 3.2.1. The main difference with the previous model is that interest functions will be used in order to determine the activities of the agents involved in the economy. Again, political actions emanating from outside the state are neglected. Political activities such as voting will be dealt with in the following chapter. As most of the equations of the model have already been introduced in Chapter 3, the presentation of the new model will be kept as compact as possible. A full representation of the model is desirable, though, since it will also be used in Chapter 6 and can then be easily referred to.

Interest functions

The interest functions to be used in the model are based on eqs. (4.1) and (4.2). The fact that (4.2) is chosen instead of (4.3) implies that no (explicit) distinction will be made between decision-making levels within collectivities [22]. As regards the elementary interest functions, we will not entirely base ourselves on (4.1). This has to do with the fact that we do not want to become deeply involved - at this stage - into the problem of mobility. Consistency would seem to demand that elementary interest functions play a part in the transition of agents from one economic position to another, as, for example, in the transition of workers from the state sector to the private sector, or from being unemployed to being employed in either sector. However, we prefer to postpone such an approach. Instead, the following simplifying assumptions are made:

1. the number of capitalists is constant; moreover, once a capitalist means always a capitalist;
2. as was assumed in the previous model, a fixed fraction κ of the (dependent) labour force prefers to be employed by the state, the other part by business; however, employment is preferred to being unemployed; thus, workers do accept a less preferred job in case of excess labour supply;
3. in the elementary interest function for the unemployed in (4.1) $P_4^*(t)$ is respecified as

$$P_4^*(t) = \bar{\bar{w}}_4(t)^{\varepsilon_{41}}.[1 - e_4(t)]^{\varepsilon_{42}}.x_{s4}(t)^{\varepsilon_{43}}, \tag{4.5}$$

   to take the assumption into account that unemployed workers prefer to be employed [23].

The specification of the model will be such that we do not need to further particularize the interest functions. As regards the complex interest functions it is assumed that the power weights $\lambda_{kc}(t)$ are constant over time so that the time index can be deleted.

The state

Interests. Instead of (3.1) it is assumed, using (4.2), that the state acts in accordance with the maximization of the following complex interest function:

$$(4.6) \qquad \tilde{P}_s(t) = \Pi_{k=1}^{4} P_k^*(t)^{\lambda_{ks}} \qquad , \lambda_{ks} \geqq 0, \Sigma_k \lambda_{ks} = 1,$$

where $P_k^*(t)$ is defined by (4.1) and (4.5). Again, a one-period future time horizon is supposed to hold for the state. Tildes are used to indicate that the state has to rely on expectations with respect to period t, because it has to make its decisions at the start of that period (see Table 3.1). Whenever economic results of periods before t are involved these are supposed to be known by the state.

Instruments. The state's policy instruments are: its demand for labour $E_1^d(t)$, and a uniform income tax rate $\tau(t)$.

Constraints. The maximization of (4.6) is subject to the model of the economy that is, implicitly or explicitly, employed by the state [24]. We start, again, with some - in the context of our model economy - objective relations. The state has to rely here on expectations with respect to the values that the variables involved will have in period t. These relations will be presented without tildes.

The total labour force, denoted by E, is fixed and consists of the (fixed) dependent labour force L $[L = E_1(t) + E_2(t) + E_4(t)]$, plus the independent labour force E_3 (the fixed number of capitalists); thus,

$$(4.7) \qquad \begin{aligned} L &= E_1(t) + E_2(t) + E_4(t) \\ E &= L + E_3 \qquad , \text{total labour force.} \end{aligned}$$

The numerical strength of agents in economic position k is given by

$$(4.8) \qquad e_k(t) = E_k(t)/E \qquad , \text{for all } k.$$

Real disposable income equals:

$$(4.9) \quad \bar{\bar{w}}_k(t) = [1 - \tau(t)]w_k(t)/p(t) \qquad , \text{ for all } k.$$

The wage structure is given by

$$(4.10) \quad w_1(t) = \phi w_2(t) \text{ and } w_4(t) = \psi w_2(t) \qquad , \ \phi > \psi > 0, \ \psi < 1.$$

Before-tax income of capitalists, consisting of some minimum payment $w_3^-(t)$ plus dividend income, if any, equals:

$$(4.11) \quad w_3(t) = [w_3^-(t)E_3 + (1 - \sigma(t))\max\{0, F(t)\}]/E_3,$$

where

$$(4.12) \quad F(t) = p(t)X_b^t(t) - w_2(t)E_2(t) - w_3^-(t)E_3 - D_b(t) + {} + p(t)[X_b^{id}(t) - X_b^{it}(t)] \qquad , \text{ excess funds of firms,}$$

where

$$(4.13) \quad D_b(t) = \max\{0, -F(t-1)\} \qquad , \text{ firms' debt burden,}$$

$$(4.14) \quad X_b^t(t) = \min\{X_b^d(t), X_b^s(t)\} \qquad , \text{ marketed output,}$$

$$(4.15) \quad X_b^s(t) = X_b(t) + S(t) \qquad , \text{ private product supply,}$$

$$(4.16) \quad X_b(t) = \alpha_b(t)E_2(t) \qquad , \text{ private output,}$$

$$(4.17) \quad S(t) = X_b^s(t-1) - X_b^t(t-1) \qquad , \text{ stocks.}$$

Labour productivity in the private sector equals:

$$(4.18) \quad \alpha_b(t) = \nu K_s(t)^\eta \qquad , \ \nu > 0, \ \eta \geqq 0,$$

where

$$(4.19) \quad K_s(t) = (1 - \zeta)K_s(t-1) + X_s(t-1) \qquad , \ 0 < \zeta < 1, \text{ state capital stock,}$$

$$(4.20) \quad X_s(t) = \alpha_s E_1(t) \qquad , \ \alpha_s > 0, \text{ state output.}$$

It will again be assumed for this model that the state has no exact knowledge of (4.18) and (4.19); see (4.27). The non-marketed good produced by the state is taken to be purely collective in nature; thus,

(4.21) $x_{sk}(t) = X_s(t)$, for all k
, consumption of state goods.

The maximum tax rate equals:

(4.22) $\tau^+(t) = 1 - p(t)x_b^{c-}/w_4(t)$, $x_b^{c-} > 0$.

The state debt burden, for notational convenience defined for t+1, equals:

(4.23) $D_s(t+1) = w_1(t)E_1(t) + w_4(t)E_4(t) - \tau(t)\Sigma_k w_k(t)E_k(t) + D_s(t)$.

Labour demand is constrained as follows:

(4.24) $E_1^- \leqq E_1^d(t) \leqq L$, $L > E_1^- > 0$.

The following relations are more particularly assumed to hold for the state; they do not necessarily hold when the tildes are deleted.

The balanced budget constraint demands that

(4.25) $\tau(t)\Sigma_k \tilde{w}_k(t)\tilde{E}_k(t) = \tilde{w}_1(t)\tilde{E}_1(t) + \tilde{w}_4(t)\tilde{E}_4(t) + D_s(t)$.

As regards expectations it is assumed with respect to employment that

$\tilde{E}_1(t) = E_1^d(t)$,

(4.26) $\tilde{E}_2(t) = \min\{\tilde{E}_2^d(t),\ L - E_1^d(t)\}$,

$\tilde{E}_2^d(t) = \max\{0,\ [\tilde{X}_b^d(t) - S(t)]/\tilde{\alpha}_b(t)\}$;[25)]

and, furthermore, that

(4.27) $\tilde{p}(t) = p(t-1)$, $\tilde{w}_3^-(t) = \tilde{w}_2(t) = w_2(t-1)$, $\tilde{\alpha}_b(t) = \alpha_b(t-1)$, $\tilde{\sigma}(t) =$
$\sigma(t-1)$, $\tilde{X}_b^d(t) = X_b^t(t-1)$, while $\tilde{p}(t)[\tilde{X}_b^{id}(t) - \tilde{X}_b^{it}(t)]$ in (4.12)
is neglected.

Note that $\tilde{E}_4(t) = L - \tilde{E}_1 - \tilde{E}_2(t)$.

Tax rate and demand for labour. Whenever it is impossible for the state to meet its budget constraint (4.25), $\tau(t) = \tau^+(t)$ and $E_1^d(t) = E_1^-$. Otherwise, rewriting the budget constraint into $\tau(t) = \tau[E_1^d(t)]$, $E_1^d(t)$ and $\tau(t)$ are determined by maximizing $\tilde{P}_s(t)$, using (4.6) through (4.27), which renders the following program that is similar to (3.19) in the previous chapter:

$$\text{(4.28)} \quad \underset{E_1^d(t),\tau(t)}{\text{maximize}} \; : \tilde{P}_s[E_1^d(t),\tau(t)] \quad \text{subject to}$$

$$E_1^- \leqq E_1^d(t) \leqq L,$$

$$\tau(t) = \tau[E_1^d(t)],$$

$$\tau(t) \leqq \tau^+(t).$$

Labour and labour market

Exactly the same assumptions will be used here as in the previous chapter (the reader is referred to Subsection 3.2.3). To economize on space we only reproduce the eqs. (3.20) and (3.21).

$$\text{(4.29)} \quad \begin{aligned} E_1(t) &= \min\{E_1^d(t)\ ,\ E_1^s(t)\}, \\ E_2(t) &= \min\{E_2^d(t)\ ,\ E_2^s(t)\}, \\ E_1^s(t) &= \max\{\kappa L\ ,\ L - E_2^d(t)\}, \\ E_2^s(t) &= \max\{(1-\kappa)L\ ,\ L - E_1^d(t)\}. \end{aligned}$$

In each economic position workers are supposed to act in accordance with the maximization of their interest function, as specified by (4.1). Given the assumption of a large number of identical workers (disregarding job preferences), workers may be supposed to expect that their individual actions (there are no coalitions) have no influence on $\tau(t)$, $p(t)$, $e_k(t)$, and $x_{sk}(t)$. The wage rate will, again, be assumed to be determined in the following way:

$$\text{(4.30)} \quad w_2(t) = \min\{\max[w_2^-(t),\ w_2^0(t)],\ w_2^+(t)\},$$

where $w_2^-(t) = p(t-1)x_b^{c-}/\{[1-\tau(t)]\psi\}$,

$$w_2^0(t) = w_2(t-1)\left[1 + g\left(\frac{E_1^d(t-1) + E_2^d(t-1) - L}{L}\right)\right],\ g(.) > -1,\ g(0) = 0,$$ [26]

$$w_2^+(t) = p(t)\alpha_b(t).$$ [27]

Product market

We reproduce the - slightly adjusted - equations of subsection 3.2.4,

(3.22) through (3.25).

Demand for consumption equals:

$$(4.31)\qquad X_b^{cd}(t) = \frac{1}{p(t)}\Big\{[1 - \tau(t)][\Sigma_{k\neq 3} w_k(t)E_k(t) + w_3^-(t)E_3] + $$
$$+ [1 - \tau(t-1)][w_3(t-1) - w_3^-(t-1)]E_3 + $$
$$+ p(t-1)[X_b^{cd}(t-1) - X_b^{ct}(t-1)]\Big\}.$$

Neglecting forced savings due to insufficient product supply, all the money that is available to households and firms is spent on private product [for investment demand, see (4.36)]. This total amount of money, to be denoted by MM(t), consists of a part M(t) that is transferred from the previous period, and a part that is generated within the current period (wage related income plus the minimum income of capitalists). For total product demand it is obtained that

$$(4.32)\qquad X_b^{d}(t) = MM(t)/p(t),$$

where:
$$MM(t) = M(t) + [1 - \tau(t)][\Sigma_{k\neq 3} w_k(t)E_k(t) + w_3^-(t)E_3],$$
$$M(t) = \max\{0, [1 - \tau(t-1)][1 - \sigma(t-1)]F(t-1)\} + $$
$$+ \sigma(t-1)F(t-1) + p(t-1)[X_b^{cd}(t-1) - X_b^{ct}(t-1)].$$

Total product supply $X_b^s(t)$ is shown by eq. (4.15).

With respect to transactions - see also eq. (4.14) - it is assumed that

$$(4.33)\qquad X_b^{it}(t) = \min\{X_b^{id}(t), X_b^{s}(t)\},$$

$$(4.34)\qquad X_b^{ct}(t) = \min\{X_b^{cd}(t), X_b^{s}(t) - X_b^{it}(t)\}.$$

The firms

Interests. The same general assumptions with respect to the firms are assumed to hold as enumerated at the beginning of Subsection 3.2.5. Instead of (3.26) we will now start from the following general complex interest function form for the firm (see 4.2):

$$P_f(t) = \Pi_k\, P_k(t)^{\lambda_{kf}} \qquad , \lambda_{kf} \geq 0,\ \Sigma_k \lambda_{kf} = 1.$$

As there are no multiple positions $\lambda_{kf} = 0$ for $k \neq 2,3$. Only capitalists and private sector workers need be considered. It will be assumed that the firms' actions are fully determined by the capitalists, i.e. $\lambda_{3f} = 1$; thus $P_f(t) = P_3(t)$. Capitalists are owner-entrepreneurs; the total number of firms equals E_3. Since the firms are assumed to be identical we will not further particularize the relevant elementary interest function $P_3(t)$. Because of the identity assumption real disposable profit income, w_3, and the consumption of state goods, x_{s3}, may equally well be considered on a class level (as an average) as on an individual level, while e_3 is fixed.

Capitalists are supposed to save for investment only, and act in accordance with the maximization of the expected value of their interest function which is specified as

(4.35) $\tilde{P}_3(t) = \Sigma_{n=0}^{2} \rho_n \tilde{P}_3^*(t+n)$, $\rho_n \geqq 0,\ \Sigma_n \rho_n = 1.$

Instruments. The firms' policy instruments are: product price $p(t,t+n)$, investment ratio $\sigma(t,t+n)$, and demand for labour $E_2^d(t,t+n)$.

Constraints. For the relationship between $\tilde{P}_3^*(t+n)$ and these instruments we first refer to the eqs. (4.8), (4.9), (4.11) through (4.17), and (4.21). In addition, the following relations will be used. We start again with some objective relationships where tildes should be thought added for future periods.

Investment demand is given by

(4.36) $x_b^{id}(t) = \sigma(t-1)F(t-1)/p(t).$

The capital stock equals:

(4.37) $K_b(t) = (1 - \delta)K_b(t-1) + x_b^{it}(t-1)$, $0 < \delta < 1.$

Eqs. (4.36) and (4.37) show the two-period time lag for the completion of investment projects that was also assumed to hold in the previous model.

The before-tax minimum income of capitalists is equal to

(4.38) $w_3^-(t) = w_2(t).$

The following equations, (4.39) and (4.40) do not necessarily hold when tildes are deleted.

As regards expectations assumptions 3 and 4 of Subsection 3.2.5 imply that

(4.39) $\tilde{E}_2(t+n) = E_2^d(t,t+n),\ \tilde{X}_b^{it}(t+n) = \tilde{X}_b^{id}(t+n),\ \tilde{X}_b^t(t+n) = \tilde{X}_b^s(t+n)$

$, \quad n = 1,2.$

Let, furthermore,

(4.40) $\tilde{w}_2(t+n) = w_2(t),\ \tilde{x}_{s3}(t+n) = x_{s3}(t),\ \tilde{\alpha}_b(t+n) = \alpha_b(t),\ \tilde{\tau}(t+n)$

$= \tau(t) \quad , \quad n = 1,2.$

Product price, demand for labour, investment ratio. As in the previous model the rate of change of the product price is taken to be a continuous monotonically increasing function h of excess demand, and labour demand is determined by the private capital stock [see eqs. (3.31) and (3.32)].

(4.41)[28]

$$p(t+1) = p(t)\left[1 + h\left(\frac{X_b^d(t) - X_b^s(t)}{X_b^s(t)}\right)\right] \quad , \ h(.) > -1,\ h(0) = 0,$$

$$p(t,t+2) = p(t+1).$$

(4.42) $E_2^d(t,t+n) = [\beta/\tilde{\alpha}_b(t+n)]\tilde{K}_b(t+n) \quad \text{if} \quad p(t,t+n)\tilde{\alpha}_b(t+n) \geqq \tilde{w}_2(t+n)$

$, \quad n = 0,1,2.$

Since $p(t)\alpha_b(t) \geqq w_2(t)$, due to (4.30), eq. (4.42) at least holds for period t (n = 0, tildes deleted)[29]. It follows, using (4.29), that $X_b(t) = \alpha_b(t)E_2(t) = \beta K_b^u(t)$.

For the determination of the investment ratio $\sigma(t)$ the following auxiliary equations are used to simplify notation, where $\rho_0 + \rho_2 > 0$ is assumed to hold:

$$B_1(t) \equiv \{[1 - \tau(t)]/[p(t+1)E_3]\}^{\varepsilon_{31}} . e_3^{\varepsilon_{32}} . X_s(t)^{\varepsilon_{33}},$$

$$B_2(t+2) \equiv [p(t+2)\alpha_b(t+2) - w_2(t+2)].[\beta/\alpha_b(t+2)],$$

$$\rho \equiv \rho_0/(\rho_0 + \rho_2),$$

$$\bar{\rho} \equiv 1/\{1 + [B_1(t)/\tilde{B}_1(t+2)][p(t+1)/\tilde{B}_2(t+2)]\},$$

$$(4.43)\quad \bar{\sigma}(t) \equiv p(t+1)[\tilde{w}_3^-(t+2)E_3 + \tilde{D}_b(t+2) - \tilde{B}_2(t+2)(1-\delta)K_b(t+1)]/[\tilde{B}_2(t+2)F(t)],$$

$$B_3(t) \equiv \left[\frac{1-\rho}{\rho}\cdot\frac{\tilde{B}_1(t+2)}{B_1(t)}\cdot\frac{\tilde{B}_2(t+2)}{p(t+1)}\right]^{\frac{1}{1-\varepsilon_{31}}},$$

$$s(t) \equiv \left[\frac{B_3(t)[F(t) + w_3^-(t)E_3] - \tilde{B}_2(t+2)(1-\delta)K_b(t+1) + \tilde{D}_b(t+2)}{\{B_3(t) + [\tilde{B}_2(t+2)/p(t+1)]\}F(t)}\right]$$

where $B_2(t)$ denotes the rate of return on capital, ρ the relative weight attached to the current period (with regard to period t+2), $\bar{\rho}$ the value of ρ for which capitalists would be indifferent between current and period t+2 profit income when $\varepsilon_{31} = 1$, $\bar{\sigma}(t)$ the value of $\sigma(t)$ for which $\tilde{F}(t+2) = 0$, and $s(t)$ the optimal value of $\sigma(t)$ that is obtained from the first-order condition for a maximum of (4.35) subject to eqs. (4.8), (4.9), (4.11) through (4.17), (4.21), and (4.36) through (4.42), if, for rather obvious reasons, $F(t) > 0$, $\tilde{B}_2(t+2) > 0$, $\bar{\sigma}(t) < 1$ and $1 \geqq s(t) > \max\{0, \bar{\sigma}(t)\}$ (the second-order sufficiency condition for a maximum is satisfied in that case).
Assuming that $\varepsilon_{31} > 0$ and using (4.43), it is obtained for $\sigma(t)$, depending on whether ε_{31} is less than or equal to one, that

$$(4.44)\quad \sigma(t)\begin{cases} = 0 \text{ if either } F(t) \leqq 0,\ \tilde{B}_2(t+2) \leqq 0,\ \bar{\sigma}(t) \geqq 1, \\ \quad\text{or } s(t) \leqq \max\{0, \bar{\sigma}(t)\}, \\ = \min\{s(t), 1\} \text{ otherwise,} \end{cases} \Bigg\}\ \varepsilon_{31} < 1,$$

$$\sigma(t)\begin{cases} = 0 & > \\ = \text{indeterminate if } \rho & = \ \bar{\rho}(t), \\ = 1 & < \end{cases} \Bigg\}\ \varepsilon_{31} = 1.$$

Note that $\tilde{B}_1(t+2) = B_1(t)$ holds, because of (4.40) and (4.41).

4.5. *Dynamical Aspects of the Model*

4.5.1. The Behaviour of the State

We start this section on the dynamical properties of the model with some remarks on the behaviour of the state.

1. First notice from (4.1), (4.5) and (4.6) that types of states can no

longer be defined as points on a unit square, as appeared to be possible for the previous model (see Fig. 3.2). A type of state is now represented as a point in the space spanned by ε_{kg} and λ_{ks} ($k = 1,2,3,4$; $g = 1,2,3$), and will be denoted by the ordered 16-tuple $(\underline{\varepsilon}_{kg}, \underline{\lambda}_{ks})$, where $\underline{\varepsilon}_{kg} = (\varepsilon_{11},..,\varepsilon_{13},..,\varepsilon_{41},..,\varepsilon_{43})$ and $\underline{\lambda}_{ks} = (\lambda_{1s},..,\lambda_{4s})$ are vectors of order (1×12) and (1×4), respectively. Again, an infinite number of types of states can be distinguished. However, there are 4 main classes of states, related to the four basic economic positions that were mentioned in Section 4.2: if $\lambda_{1s} = 1$ we have a *pure state sector worker state*, if $\lambda_{2s} = 1$ a *pure private sector worker state*, if $\lambda_{3s} = 1$ a *pure capitalist state*. The fourth class ($\lambda_{4s} = 1$), comprising states that exclusively further the interests of the unemployed, does not seem to be a very interesting class, empirically. In the sequel, this class of states will be neglected.

2. Before we go into the behaviour of our 'archetypes' of states first recall that - due to the budget constraint - the state can only freely vary its demand for labour $E_1^d(t)$ *or* the uniform income tax rate $\tau(t)$, and, second, that - due to the one-period future time-horizon of the state - the state does not take into account the future effects of its current period activities such as on labour productivity [30).]

3. Assuming that $\lambda_{4s} = 0$ and defining:

$$\omega_1 \equiv \varepsilon_{11}\lambda_{1s} + \varepsilon_{21}\lambda_{2s} + \varepsilon_{31}\lambda_{3s},$$

$$\omega_2 \equiv (\varepsilon_{12} + \varepsilon_{13})\lambda_{1s} + \varepsilon_{23}\lambda_{2s} + \varepsilon_{33}\lambda_{3s},$$

$$C_1 \equiv \tilde{w}_2(t)[(1 - \psi)\tilde{E}_2^d(t) + \psi L] + [(1 - \tilde{\sigma}(t))\max\{0, \tilde{F}(t)\} + \tilde{w}_3^-(t)E_3],$$

$$C_2 \equiv \tilde{w}_2(t)(\phi - \psi),$$

it is obtained from the first-order condition for program (4.28) that:

$$(4.45) \qquad E_1^d(t) = \max\{E_1^-, [\omega_2/(\omega_1 - \omega_2)](C_1/C_2)\},$$

if $0 \leqq [\omega_2/(\omega_1 - \omega_2)](C_1/C_2) \leqq L - \tilde{E}_2^d(t)$, and, of course, $\tau[E_1^d(t)] \leqq \tau^+(t)$; C_1 and C_2 are given because of (4.26) and (4.27) [31).]

The parameter ω_1 denotes the weight attached to real disposable income (which is dependent on taxation), and ω_2 the weight attached to state employment (either because of the numerical strength interest, for state sector workers, or because of the interest in state output) [32).]

If $\omega_2 \geqq \omega_1$ then $E_1^d(t) \geqq L - \tilde{E}_2^d(t)$; in that case the consequences of crowding out the firms in the labour market should be taken into account. For that situation, no easily tractable analytic expression for $E_1^d(t)$ can be derived, however. Notice that $E_1^d(t)$ only increases over time if C_1/C_2 increases over time (compare this with the employment growth rate target for bureaucrats in the model of Chapter 3). Note, furthermore, that $E_1^d(t)$ - *ceteris paribus* - increases if the difference between the state wage rate, $\phi w_2(t)$, and the dole rate, $\psi w_2(t)$, decreases (unless $\omega_2 = 0$).

4. *The behaviour of pure state sector worker states:* $\{(\underline{\varepsilon}_{kg}, \underline{\lambda}_{ks}) \mid \lambda_{1s} = 1\}$.
The interest function for these types of states can be written as:

$$(4.46) \qquad \tilde{P}_s(t) = C_3.[1 - \tau(t)]^{\varepsilon_{11}}.E_1^d(t)^{\varepsilon_{12} + \varepsilon_{13}},$$

where $C_3 = [\phi w_2(t-1)/p(t-1)]^{\varepsilon_{11}}.E^{-\varepsilon_{12}}.\alpha_s^{\varepsilon_{13}}$, while $\tau(t)$ and $E_1^d(t)$ are dependent on each other through the budget contraint (4.25).

If $\varepsilon_{11} = 0$, in which case no heed to taxes is paid, $E_1^d(t) = \min\{L, E_1^d[\tau^+(t)]\}$ will hold. State employment, and consequently, state output, is as large as possible. It makes no difference whether $\varepsilon_{12} = 0$ or $\varepsilon_{13} = 0$, as state production implies state employment, and conversely. Thus, for different reasons we may have to do with a '*bureau maximizing*' state sector worker state.
It is clear that types of states for which $\varepsilon_{11} = 0$ may easily run into financial trouble, in which case they would, by assumption, have to trim the state apparatus [see the text preceding (4.28)]. If $\varepsilon_{11} > 0$ then the state's demand for labour is checked by fiscal considerations. The higher ε_{11}, i.e. the more *tax-sensitive* the state is, the more this will be the case [see (4.45)]. If $\varepsilon_{11} = 1$ then $E_1^d(t) = E_1^-$ will even hold (in that case $\omega_1 = 1$ and $\omega_2 = 0$)[33].

5. *The behaviour of pure private sector worker states:* $\{(\underline{\varepsilon}_{kg}, \underline{\lambda}_{ks}) \mid \lambda_{2s} = 1\}$.
The interest function for these types of states can be written as:

$$(4.47) \qquad \tilde{P}_s(t) = C_4.[1 - \tau(t)]^{\varepsilon_{21}}.\tilde{E}_2(t)^{\varepsilon_{22}}.E_1^d(t)^{\varepsilon_{23}},$$

where $C_4 = [w_2(t-1)/p(t-1)]^{\varepsilon_{21}}.E^{-\varepsilon_{22}}.\alpha_s^{\varepsilon_{23}}$.

If $0 \leqq [\varepsilon_{23}/(\varepsilon_{21} - \varepsilon_{23})](C_1/C_2) \leqq L - \tilde{E}_2^d(t)$ then $\tilde{E}_2(t) = \min\{\tilde{E}_2^d(t), L$

$- E_1^-\}$ and $E_1^d(t) = \max\{E_1^-, [\varepsilon_{23}/(\varepsilon_{21} - \varepsilon_{23})](C_1/C_2)\}$; see 3. Otherwise, $L - E_1^d(t)$ should first be substituted for $\tilde{E}_2(t)$ in (4.47) before maximizing $\tilde{P}_s(t)$. If private sector workers are not interested in state goods, $\varepsilon_{23} = 0$, then $E_1^d(t) = E_1^-$ if $\varepsilon_{21} > 0$. When $\varepsilon_{21} = 0$ and $\varepsilon_{23} = 0$, then $E_1^d(t)$ is partially indetermined if $L - \tilde{E}_2^d(t) > E_1^-$; in that case we only know that $E_1^- \leqq E_1^d(t) \leqq L - \tilde{E}_2^d(t)$, as the workers are solely interested in private employment and do not mind to pay taxes. In case that private sector workers are interested in state goods ($\varepsilon_{23} > 0$) it is possible that $E_1^d(t) > E_1^-$, given no budgetary worries exist.

6. *The behaviour of pure capitalist states:* $\{(\underline{\varepsilon}_{kg}, \underline{\lambda}_{ks}) | \lambda_{3s} = 1\}$. The interest function for these types of states reads:

$$\tilde{P}_s(t) = C_5 \cdot \Big\{[1 - \tau(t)] \cdot [w_2(t-1)E_3 + (1 - \sigma(t-1))\max\{0, \tilde{F}(t)\}]\Big\}^{\varepsilon_{31}} \cdot E_1^d(t)^{\varepsilon_{33}}, \tag{4.48}$$

where $C_5 = p(t-1)^{-\varepsilon_{31}} \cdot (E_3/E)^{\varepsilon_{32}} \cdot \alpha_s^{\varepsilon_{33}}$, and $\tilde{F}(t)$ is related to $\tilde{E}_2(t)$ [see (4.12)].

First it should be remarked in passing that the time preference for capitalists governing the state is not equal to that for capitalists acting as entrepreneurs (see the previous section). And, secondly, note that the number of capitalists is not important for the behaviour of capitalist types of states as this number is supposed to be constant. Thus, if $\varepsilon_{32} = 1$ (and, consequently, $\varepsilon_{31} = \varepsilon_{33} = 0$) then the behaviour of these states will be indeterminate.

If $0 \leqq [\varepsilon_{33}/(\varepsilon_{31} - \varepsilon_{33})](C_1/C_2) \leqq L - \tilde{E}_2^d(t)$ then $\tilde{E}_2(t) = \min\{\tilde{E}_2^d(t), L - E_1^-\}$ and $E_1^d(t) = \max\{E_1^-, [\varepsilon_{33}/(\varepsilon_{31} - \varepsilon_{33})](C_1/C_2)\}$; see 3. Otherwise, $L - E_1^d(t)$ should again first be substituted for $\tilde{E}_2(t)$ in $\tilde{F}(t)$ before maximizing (4.48). The behaviour of pure capitalist states is similar to that of private sector worker states in that state sector expansion is only tolerated to the extent that extra consumption of state goods compensates for the concomitant rise in the tax burden.

7. The location of *pivot states* in the political space is still more difficult for the present model than for the one developed in Chapter 3 [see Section 3.3, point 5]. This is due to the fact that we cannot obtain tractable analytical expressions for $E_1^d(t)$ in case that $E_1^d(t) > L - \tilde{E}_2^d(t)$. We will not venture to locate such states for the present model. Only the following is noted. From (4.45) it can be derived that as along as a type of state from the class $\{(\underline{\varepsilon}_{kg}, \underline{\lambda}_{ks}) | \omega_2 = 0, \lambda_{4s} = 0\}$

governs, the state sector will be as small as possible and firms will never, on purpose, be crowded out by the state in the labour market (the state may be forced to do so because of the minimum state size constraint E_1^-). Moreover, as was established for the previous model, it can be demonstrated that - for any specified set of parameters - there exists a class of states for which, in equilibrium, $\tau(t) = \tau^+(t)$ necessarily holds (which makes them likely to produce economic cycles).

4.5.2. The Behaviour of the Firms.

Regarding the *investment behaviour* of the firm, the following holds if $\sigma(t) = s(t)$ [see (4.43) and (4.44)].

1. The investment ratio $\sigma(t)$ is positively related to $(1 - \rho)/\rho$ and, thus, negatively to ρ, the time preference parameter for capitalists-entrepreneurs;

2. Although $\tilde{B}_1(t+2)$ is assumed here to be equal to $B_1(t)$, it is noted that $\sigma(t)$ is positively related to $\tilde{B}_1(t+2)/B_1(t)$, which means, for example, that $\sigma(t)$ increases if the tax rate is expected to decrease (if $\varepsilon_{31} > 0$), if the consumption of state goods is expected to increase (if $\varepsilon_{33} > 0$), or if capitalists expect their position (indicated by $e_3 = E_3/E$) to be more secure in the future (if $\varepsilon_{32} > 0$). Note from the formula for $B_1(t)$ that capitalists - when considering their class interest, e.g. in case of political action - would be ambivalent with respect to changes in E_3, as a greater number of capitalists, for example, means - for given profits - a lower profit per capitalist. In this context, it is tempting to speculate about the effect of expected *nationalizations*. Our model suggests that it would lead to a lower investment level, as E_3/E diminishes while the profits of the remaining capitalists will probably not be expected to increase by this fact.

3. The relationship between $\sigma(t)$ and $\tilde{B}_2(t+2)/p(t+1)$ (the expected rate of return on capital; see the following section) is not immediately clear, due to $\tilde{D}_b(t+2)$; if we let the expected debt burden go to zero then a positive relationship shows up.

4. The rather awkward character of $s(t)$ is partly due to the minimum income level that capitalists demand for themselves $w_3^-(t)$, and partly to the way that ε_{31} appears in the expression for $s(t)$. If $w_3^-(t) \to 0$, and $\varepsilon_{31} \to 0$ the same expression follows as was obtained in the previous model, to wit: $s(t) = 1 - \rho[1 + (1 - \delta)K_b(t+1)p(t+1)/F(t)]$ [34].

4.5.3. Numerical Experiments

In order to acquire some additional knowledge on the dynamical properties of the model a number of computer simulations have been carried out. The same set of *parameter values* and *initial conditions* has been used as for the model in Chapter 3 (see Section 3.5), except that θ (the employment growth rate target for bureaucrats) was deleted, while the time preference for capitalists-entrepreneurs was put at $\rho = 0.25$ [35].

Tracing the behaviour of the model for different types of states, i.e. different $(\underline{\varepsilon}_{kg}, \underline{\lambda}_{ks})$, the same general *patterns of motion* appeared as were obtained for the previous model; that is,

1. equilibria,
2. regular cycles,
3. cycles marked by a periodic 'bankruptcy' of the state, forcing it to put $\tau(t) = \tau^{+}(t)$ and $E_1^d(t) = E_1^-$, and
4. shrinking private production accompanied by an accelerating inflation due to a chronic financial breakdown of the state.

Again, it appears that equilibria occur in case of types of states that are neither inclined to over-emphasize the expansion of the state sector in the short run, nor to restrict it too much. The more state production is restricted, the longer it takes before an equilibrium sets in; if it is restricted too much then regular cycles appear, which may pass into a situation of runaway inflation. For example the following was obtained for pure capitalist types of states:

	ε_{31}	ε_{32}	ε_{33}		*motion pattern*
	0.80	0.15	0.05	:	equilibrium (after 103 periods);
	0.85	0.10	0.05	:	equilibrium (after 249 periods);
$\lambda_{3s} = 1$	0.90	0.05	0.05	:	regular cycle;
	0.90	0.07	0.03	:	regular cycle (larger amplitude);
	0.90	0.09	0.01	:	runaway inflation.

If state production is pushed too hard - either for reasons of the employment that it brings or for the consumption of state goods - then financial problems for the state show up, leading to cycles with a periodic bankruptcy or even a chronic financial breakdown for the state. The reader is referred to the sensitivity analysis in Section 3.5, where the impact of parameter values and initial conditions is discussed. The general aspects of this analysis are also relevant in the present context.

What is *important* to stress here is that the patterns of motion are explicitly related to interests that make sense from an individual agent's point of view instead of the rather abstract and general statements, such as about 'left-wing' and 'right-wing' ideology, that were employed in the previous model. This approach makes it plausible, for example, that it is equally well possible to have a strongly expanding state sector when the interests of capitalists are exclusively furthered by the state, as when state sector workers' or private sector workers' interests are dominant. Crucial factors in this respect are the weight attached by agents to the consumption of state goods (relative to the consumption of private goods, for example), and - in case of a longer time horizon for the state - the importance of state activities for the technology with which the firms are confronted.

In principle, any of the four motion patterns can occur under any of the three 'archetypes' of states that we have discussed.

If we leave out the possibility of runaway inflation and follow what seems to be a rather general opinion by assuming that state sector workers are strongly in favour of state production (given their related interest in state employment), that private sector workers are moderately so, and capitalists are only slightly interested in it, then we can say - within the confines of our model - that state sector worker types of states are particularly likely to produce economic cycles with periodic financial problems for the state, that private sector worker states are most likely to produce equilibria, while capitalist states are prone to generate regular cycles.

4.6. *Equilibrium Analysis*

As in Chapter 3, an *equilibrium* is defined by the constancy of all variables over time [36]. The *necessary* and *sufficient conditions* for an equilibrium are given in Appendix 4A. Most of the equilibrium characteristics to be presented in this section are more or less similar to those derived for the previous model. A full exposition is convenient though as the characteristics will again be referred to in Chapter 6 when the political part of the model has been further elaborated. In order not to tire the reader the exposition will be kept as concise as possible. Proofs are given in Appendix 4B, if necessary. Proofs that are essentially the same as for the previous model will be omitted. The time index will be deleted, unless confusion may arise.

1. *An equilibrium need not exist; more than one equilibrium may exist* [cf. Section 3.4, characteristic 1].

2. *Money supply and product demand.* The relationship between type of state and labour demand as illustrated by Fig. 3.3 also holds for the

present model. Fig. 3.4, showing the relationship between money supply and product demand, should be adjusted, however, in the sense that the minimum income of capitalists, $w_3^- E_3$, is to be added to the money supply that is generated within a period (which involves disposable wage related income). Using (4A2), (4A3) and (4A6) it is obtained that

$$(4.49) \qquad pX_b = \left[\frac{\beta}{\delta[1 + (1 - \tau)(1 - \sigma)/\sigma]}\right].M.$$

It will be shown below (see 6) that σ is dependent on E_2 because of $w_3^- > 0$. If $w_3^- = 0$ then the expression for the previous model, (3.37), is again obtained, where apart from some parameters only τ played a role. Since $0 < \tau < 1$ and $\sigma > \delta/\beta$ - see (4A3) and recall that $X_b = \beta K_b$ - it also holds for this model that the velocity of circulation [the expression between large hooked brackets on the right-hand side of (4.49)] is greater than 1 and smaller than or equal to the ratio between the output-capital ratio and the depreciation rate of the private capital stock, $1 < [.] \leqq \beta/\delta$. Although this velocity of circulation again equals the reciprocal of $[(1 - \tau)(1 - \sigma)F + \sigma F]/pX_b$, it is not the reciprocal of the after-tax profit share, since the latter also involves the minimum income of capitalists; see further characteristic 2 of Section 3.4.

3. *All expectations are realized* [cf. Section 3.4, characteristic 3].

4. *Capital stock is fully utilized, but labour may be underemployed* [cf. Section 3.4, characteristic 4].

5. *Labour productivity in the private sector* [cf. Section 3.4, characteristic 5]. Equilibrium condition (4A2) shows that

$$(4.50) \qquad \alpha_b = v[(\alpha_s/\zeta)E_1]^{\eta}.$$

6. *Investment ratio and rate of return on capital.* The rate of return on capital r is defined as: $r \equiv (F + w_3^- E_3)/(pK_b)$, where $w_3^- = w_2$ by assumption. Using (4A3), if can be rewritten as: $r = \delta/\sigma + w_3 E_3/(pK_b)$, showing the impact of the minimum income that capitalists demand for themselves. If $w_3^- = 0$ then the familiar expression $r = \delta/\sigma$ is obtained. From conditions (4A2), (4A3) and (4A7) it follows that

either

$$(4.51a) \qquad \sigma = s \leqq 1,$$

$$\sigma = \frac{\delta E_2}{rE_2 - (\beta - r)E_3},$$

$$\rho = \left[1 + \frac{1}{r^{\varepsilon_{31}}(r - \delta)^{1 - \varepsilon_{31}}}\right]^{-1},$$

or

$$\text{(4.51b)} \qquad \sigma = \frac{\delta E_2}{rE_2 - (\beta - r)E_3} = 1,$$

$$r = \frac{\delta E_2 + \beta E_3}{E_2 + E_3},$$

$$\rho < \left[1 + \frac{1}{r^{\varepsilon_{31}}(r - \delta)^{1 - \varepsilon_{31}}}\right]^{-1}.$$

It appears that σ and r are related to E_2, and indirectly, therefore, to the type of state, given the labour force constraint. If $\bar{w_3} \to 0$ then $\sigma \to \delta/r$, in which case regime a) holds [37]. Whether we have to do with a) or b) now that $\bar{w_3} = w_2$ depends partly on the type of state considered, as σ is negatively related to E_2 in regime a). Regime a) will be called the *'normal'* case, as it allows for some positive dividend income above the minimum profit income level $\bar{w_3}$. Notice that in the normal case the equilibrium rate of return depends on the depreciation rate δ of the private capital stock and the time preference parameter ρ of capitalists-entrepreneurs (as was the case in the previous model), and on the capitalists' interest function parameter ε_{31}, which are all exogenously determined. If $\varepsilon_{31} \to 0$ then $r \to \delta + \rho/(1 - \rho)$ [cf. eq. (3.40)].

7. *Time preference condition for the firms*. As, obviously, $r < \beta$ should hold, it is required, using (4.51), that

$$\text{(4.52)} \qquad \rho < \left[1 + \frac{1}{\beta^{\varepsilon_{31}}(\beta - \delta)^{1 - \varepsilon_{31}}}\right]^{-1}.$$

If $\varepsilon_{31} \to 0$ then $\rho < (\beta - \delta)/(1 + \beta - \delta)$ [cf. eq. (3.41)].

8. *Wage rate and rate of return on capital.* Using (4A2) and (4A3), and putting $\bar{w}_2 \equiv w_2/p$, it is obtained that

$$\bar{w}_2 = (1 - r/\beta)\alpha_b. \tag{4.53}$$

In the normal case, (4.51a), this expression is similar to the corresponding expression for the previous model, (3.42), in that the real wage rate appears as a residual, for r is exogenously determined in that case [see also Section 3.4, characteristic 7]. Note, however, that, as there need not be a unique equilibrium (see below), it cannot altogether be ruled out that changes in r - and, consequently, in $\bar{w}_2$ - can be established by choosing a different level for E_2 [regime (4.51b)]. This means that we may have a, linear, 'wage-profit curve', given the type of state, instead of the single $\bar{w}_2$,r-combination that was obtained for the previous model [see also Fig. 3.5; here $\delta < r < \beta$ should hold, due to $\bar{w}_3 > 0$].

9. *Income distribution.* The share of the *before-tax* real private wage sum in private output, $\bar{w}_2/\alpha_b = 1 - r/\beta$ [see (4.53)], is uniquely determined in the normal case of (4.51a), as was obtained for the previous model. In case of regime (4.51b), however, this share and its complement, the before-tax profit share, depend on the level of E_2. Under both regimes the share of *total* real *disposable* wage-related income (excluding the minimum income for capitalists) is equal to: $(1 - r/\beta) + \tau(r - \delta)/\beta$. It appears that this share is always larger than the before-tax share. In contrast with the previous model, the value of σ does not matter in this respect. The reason is that, due to the minimum income level of capitalists and the uniform tax rate, part of the taxes is always paid by the capitalists. In the normal case, the disposable wage related income share is positively related to the state employment level through the effect of that level on τ. Under regime (4.51b) and if $E_2 = L - E_1$ then, using (4A5), a negative relationship between this share and the state employment level follows. Although private output should be maximized in order to maximize before-tax private wage income, this - clearly - need not be the case if one's interest is in diposable wage related income.

10. *Relative size of the production sectors.* With respect to the relative size of state and private sector, observe that

$$\frac{X_s}{X_b} = \left(\frac{\alpha_s}{\alpha_b}\right)\cdot\left(\frac{E_1}{E_2}\right). \tag{4.54}$$

As E_1 is related to the type of state, the relative size of the sectors in terms of employment (as well as the ratio of the wage costs, as $w_1 = \phi w_2$) is also dependent on it. The output ratio is related to the type of state too, but is crucially depends on the elasticity of private labour productivity with respect to state employment whether there is a positive or negative relationschip with state employment. Although it has not been mentioned in Chapter 3, this characteristic also holds for the previous model.

11. *An unemployment equilibrium implies that* $\tau = \tau^+$ [cf. Section 3.4, characteristic 11].

12. *There exists a (non-empty) class of states for which in equilibrium* $\tau = \tau^+$ *necessarily holds* [cf. Section 3.4, characteristic 13]; see (4B1).

Let $\bar{E}_1$ stand for an optimal state employment level that is obtained when taking $\tilde{E}_2(t) = L - E_1^d(t)$ for the solving of (4.28) - ignoring the employment constraint E_1^- and the maximum tax rate $\tau^+(t)$ - and $\bar{\bar{E}}_1(t)$ for an optimal level that results when taking $\tilde{E}_2(t) = \tilde{E}_2^d(t)$.

13. *If* $\tilde{P}_s(t)$ *is strictly quasi-concave in* $E_1^d(t)$ *for* $\tilde{E}_2(t) = L - E_1^d(t)$ *and for* $\tilde{E}_2(t) = \tilde{E}_2^d(t)$ (referred to in the sequel as the *sqc-assumption*) 38) - in which case $\bar{E}_1$ and $\bar{\bar{E}}_1$ are uniquely determined - *then equilibria with* $\tau < \tau^+$ - which are full employment equilibria; see 11 - *demand that* $\max\{E_1^-, \bar{\bar{E}}_1\} \geqq E_1 \geqq \bar{E}_1$.
    Observe that $\bar{E}_1$ is determined under the assumption that the least favourable circumstances for increases in $E_1^d(t)$ hold, when the tax constraint is not effective [as the private sector employment level is never negatively, but, generally, positively valued by the state; see (4.1), (4.5), and (4.6)], while $\bar{\bar{E}}_1$ is the optimal state employment level under the most favourable circumstances then. In the former case any increase of $E_1^d(t)$ is assumed to be at the cost of $\tilde{E}_2(t)$ 39). It is not difficult to see that $E_1 > \bar{E}_1$ may hold if $\tilde{E}_2^d < L - \bar{E}_1$, while $\bar{\bar{E}}_1 > E_1$; take, for instance, $\varepsilon_{22} >> \varepsilon_{23} = 1 - \varepsilon_{22}$, and $\lambda_{2s} = 1$.

Due to the more complicated nature of the function used to determine the behaviour of the state, it is impossible to derive a general, explicit expression for $\bar{E}_1$, as we were able to do for the previous model [see (3.43)]. As regards $\bar{\bar{E}}_1$, if $\lambda_{4s} = 0$ - in which case the interests of the unemployed have no influence on the behaviour of the state - it is obtained that:

$$(4.55) \qquad \bar{\bar{E}}_1 \begin{cases} = L \quad \textit{if} \quad \omega_1 - \omega_2 \leqq 0, \\ = \min\{[\omega_2/(\omega_1 - \omega_2)](C_1/C_2),\ L\} \quad \textit{if} \quad \omega_1 - \omega_2 > 0; \end{cases}$$

see Subsection 4.5.1, third remark [40].

For the previous model it holds that $\bar{\bar{E}}_1 \geq L - \tilde{E}_2^d$ for any type of state, excepting ($\lambda_s = 0$, $\varepsilon = 1$); see (3B2). This property is crucial for the equilibrium characteristics 14, 15, and 16 of the previous chapter. For the present model $\bar{\bar{E}}_1 < L - \tilde{E}_2^d$ may hold, namely for those types of states that are interested in the level of the income tax rate ($\omega_1 > 0$) [41]. This means that characteristics equivalent to the aforementioned cannot be obtained. Instead, the following two characteristics can be proved.

14. *If for an arbitrary type of state an equilibrium exists with* $\tau = \tau^+$ *and state employment level* E_1, *then it is an equilibrium for all those types of states for which the sqc-assumption is satisfied and* $\max\{E_1^-, \bar{\bar{E}}_1\} \geq E_1$ *in that situation. Types of states,* other than the aforementioned arbitrary type of state, *satisfying these conditions always exist;* see (4B2).

15. *If for an arbitrary type of state a full employment equilibrium exists with* $\tau < \tau^+$ *and state employment level* E_1, *then: (a) there exists another full employment equilibrium for this type of state if* $E_1 \neq E_1^-$, *the sqc-assumption is satisfied and* $\bar{E}_1 < E_1 < \bar{\bar{E}}_1$; *(b) there exists an unemployment equilibrium for this type of state if* $E_1 = E_1^-$; *(c) there are other types of states for which it is an equilibrium, although not for all those for which the sqc-assumption is satisfied and* $\bar{\bar{E}}_1 \geq E_1$ *in that situation;* see (4B3).

16. *If for an arbitrary type of state an unemployment equilibrium exists with state employment level* E_1, *then there exists a full employment equilibrium as well, although not necessarily for this type of state* [cf. Section 3.4, characteristic 17]; see (4B4). The latter part - which does not hold for the model of Chapter 3 - implies that for some types of states only an unemployment equilibrium may exist. This cannot hold for types of states for which $\varepsilon_{42} = 0$ and/or $\lambda_{4s} = 0$, in which case the unemployed are either not interested in the total employment level [see (4.5)] or have no influence on the state's activities [see (4B4)].

17. *More than one type of state can be associated with an equilibrium* [cf. Section 3.4, characteristic 18]; see characteristic 14 and characteristic 15c. This can also be seen by looking at the exponents in the interest function of the state. By appropriately changing these exponents - which implies changing the type of state - it is possible not to upset an equilibrium [42]. One reason is that some interests are shared by people of different economic positions (think of a low in-

come tax rate).

18. *More than one equilibrium may exist for a type of state;* see characteristics 15 and 16 [cf. Section 3.4, characteristic 19]. From a comparative static point of view this implies that changes in the economy need not necessarily demand another type of state in order to retain an equilibrium.

19. *A unique equilibrium (as defined in Section 3.4) exists iff for any type of state there exists at most only one* E_1,E_2*-combination that satisfies* (4A1)-(4A7). *In that case:* $E_1 + E_2 = L$ *and* $\tau = \tau^+$. *It is an equilibrium for those types of states for which the sqc-assumption is satisfied and* max $\{E_1^-, \bar{\bar{E}}_1\} \geq E_1$ *in that situation; if* $E_1 = E_1^-$ *happens to hold then it is a unique equilibrium for all types of states* [cf. Section 3.4, characteristic 20]. For the first part, see 17; the second part follows from characteristics 15 and 16 [there are always types of states for which $\bar{E}_1 < E_1 < \bar{\bar{E}}_1$; consider the class of states mentioned under (4B3)]; the third part follows from characteristic 14; the fourth part is rather obvious. By construction it can be shown that such an equilibrium may exist.

20. *The necessary and sufficient conditions for an equilibrium with maximum private output are given by:* (4A1)-(4A7) *and* $E_1 = \max \{E_1^-, [\eta/(1 + \eta)]L\}$ [cf. Section 3.4, characteristic 21] [43].

4.7. *Summary*

In order to get a more satisfactory treatment of the behaviour of the state and to clear the way for a natural incorporation of political phenomena into the model, an alternative approach to the study of the interaction between state and private sector was presented in this chapter. We started from the assumption that *activities* of individual agents and collectivities are related to *interests* of the agents involved, and that interests are again related to the *position* of an agent in the economic process. Distinguishing between three basic interests (the consumption of marketed goods, the consumption of non-marketed state goods, and the numerical strength of agents in a given position) the notion of an *elementary interest function* was introduced for the mediation between the interests and activities of agents in a certain position (social class). There are as many elementary interest functions as there are positions. More than one such function may be relevant for the determination of the behaviour of an agent, due to:

a. ideology,

b. social mobility,

c. multiple positions,

d. heterogeneous membership in case of collectivities.

Although the first three factors mentioned are very important for the coherence of the social class structure, attention was focused upon the behaviour of collectivities (such as the firm and the state). In that context the notion of a *complex interest function* was introduced. The behaviour of collective agents is seen as the result of complex processes of conflicts and compromises between agents with different basic interests on (possibly) more than one decision-making level within the collectivity. This prompted the use of the notions of a *nested* complex interest function and an *interest tree*. Further study along these lines seems to be promising.

Apart from the introduction of interest functions for the determination of the behaviour of agents, the general structure of the model developed in this chapter is the same as that of the previous one. As a result it appeared to be possible to re-establish quite a number of the results that were obtained for the previous model. For example, *numerical experiments* with different types of states brought out that the same patterns of motion can be generated (i.e., equilibria, regular cycles, cycles with a periodic financial breakdown of the state, and a situation of running inflation and permanent financial troubles for the state).

Most of the *equilibrium characteristics* could be retained too, although sometimes slightly adjusted. To these characteristics we added the observation that the size of the state sector relative to the size of the private sector, in terms of output, is not only dependent on the employment ratio of the sectors but also on the relationship between state production and technology.

But, of course, there are also *differences*. Peculiar to the new politico-economic model are the following results.

With respect to the *behaviour of the state* it was obtained that:

- the classic hypothesis of a bureau or output maximizing bureaucrat should be reconsidered when the quite natural assumption is made that a state sector worker also cares about marketed goods, and, thus, disposable income; not directly in contrast with that hypothesis but even, to some extent, adding a new motivation for it, is our assumption that state sector workers may intrinsically value state production;
- compared with the previous model, the set of states that may not be interested in stepping up state employment, even when an excess supply of labour is expected, is enlarged because of the account that is taken of the impact of consequent changes in the tax rate on disposable income;

recall that in the previous model it was only the pure private product biased state ($\lambda_s = 0$, $\varepsilon = 1$) that was not interested in that;

- the usual, well-known, statements about the spending behaviour of 'left-wing'/'socialist' and 'right-wing'/'conservative' governments seem to be too simplistic; in this respect, it is not only important to know what the relative power is of the remaining apparatuses within the state, it is also necessary to have information on the weights attached by capital owners, private sector workers, and so on, to their basic interests, as well as on the time-horizon of those agents making up the state organization; in principle, it is possible to have a capitalist state acting in exactly the same way as a bureaucratic (state sector worker) state, for example (even if the economy is not perfectly restrictive).

As regards the *behaviour of the firm* (assumed to be fully subservient to capitalist interests) it appeared that not only the time preference and the (expected) rate of return on capital, but also the expected consumption level of state goods, the expected tax rate, and the expected numerical strength of capitalists in the private sector (think of nationalizations) are important. It could be shown that the investment behaviour of the firms in the previous model is a special case of the present formulation.

Using the apparently generally accepted assumption that state sector workers are strongly in favour of state production (given their related interest in state employment), that private sector workers are less so, and capitalists are only slightly interested in it, *computer simulation* results showed that bureaucratic types of states are particularly likely to produce economic cycles with periodic financial troubles for the state, that private sector worker states are most likely to produce equilibria, while capitalist states are prone to generate regular cycles.

As for the *equilibrium* characteristics, the most notable difference with the previous model is that now an equilibrium may not be sustained by certain types of states because the state employment level would be too high for them, whereas in the previous model this could only be a problem for the pure private product biased state for which the state employment level had to be minimal. Another difference appeared to be that, under certain conditions, only an unemployment equilibrium can be obtained for some types of states.

APPENDIX 4A

NECESSARY AND SUFFICIENT CONDITIONS FOR AN EQUILIBRIUM

The necessary and sufficient conditions for an equilibrium are given by (4A1)-(4A7):

(4A1) $E_1 = E_1^d =$ solution of programme (4.28), implying that: $E_1^- \leqq E_1 \leqq L$, and $\tau \leqq \tau^+$;

(4A2) $E_2 = E_2^d = (\beta/\alpha_b)K_b > 0$, where $\alpha_b = v[(\alpha_s/\zeta)E_1]^\eta$;

(4A3) $K_b = \frac{\sigma F}{\delta p} > 0$, where $F = (p\alpha_b - w_2)E_2 - w_3^- E_3 > 0$, $w_3^- = w_2$;

(4A4) $w_2 \geqq \dfrac{px_b^{c-}}{(1 - \tau)\psi} > 0$, $w_2 = \dfrac{px_b^{c-}}{(1 - \tau)\psi} = w_2^-$ at any rate if $E_1^d + E_2^d < L$;

(4A5) $\tau = \left\{1 + \left[\dfrac{w_2(E_2 + E_3) + (1 - \sigma)F}{w_2[(\phi - \psi)E_1 + \psi(L - E_2)]}\right]\right\}^{-1}$, $\tau = \tau^+ = 1 - \dfrac{px_b^{c-}}{\psi w_2}$ iff $w_2 = w_2^-$;

(4A6) pX_b $(= p\alpha_b E_2) = M + (1 - \tau)w_2[(\phi - \psi)E_1 + (1 - \psi)E_2 + E_3 + \psi L]$,

$(1 - \tau)(1 - \sigma)F + \sigma F = M$,

(4A7) $\sigma = \min\{s, 1\}$ if $0 < \varepsilon_{31} < 1$, where, putting $\dot{\varepsilon} \equiv 1/(1 - \varepsilon_{31})$,

$$s = \frac{[(1 - \rho)/\rho]^{\dot{\varepsilon}} . [(\alpha_b - w_2/p)(\beta/\alpha_b)]^{\dot{\varepsilon}\varepsilon_{31}} . [1 + w_2E_3/F] - (1 - \delta)pK_b/F}{[(1 - \rho)/\rho]^{\dot{\varepsilon}} . [(\alpha_b - w_2/p)(\beta/\alpha_b)]^{\dot{\varepsilon}\varepsilon_{31}} + 1} > 0;$$

$\sigma = 1$ if $\varepsilon_{31} = 1$ [then $\rho < \bar{\rho} = r/(1 + r)$].

Condition (4A1) follows from (4.28)-(4.30), and $F > 0$ [see (4A3)]; the first part of (4A2) is obtained from (4.29), (4.30), (4.42), and $F > 0$, the second part from (4.18)-(4.20); the first part of (4A3) follows from (4.33), (4.36), (4.37), and (4.41), the second part from (4.12), (4.13), (4.14)-(4.17), (4.33), (4.41), and $F > 0$; (4A4) follows from (4.30), and $F > 0$; the first part of (4A5) is obtained from (4.25), the second part from (4.22) and (4A4); (4A6) is obtained from (4.14)-(4.17), (4.32), (4.36), and (4.41); (4A7) follows from (4.43), (4.44), and (4A3).

APPENDIX 4B

PROOFS OF SOME OF THE EQUILIBRIUM CHARACTERISTICS

(4B1) *Characteristic 12: There exists a (non-empty) class of states for which in equilibrium $\tau = \tau^+$ necessarily holds.*

Proof: Note that:

1. the restriction $\tau(t) \leqq \tau^+(t)$ prohibits, for an equilibrium, that $E_1^d(t) \to L$ (and, thus, $E_2(t) \to 0$; see below), and
2. for any $E_1^d(t)$, $E_1^- \leqq E_1^d(t) \leqq L$, there exists a type of state for which that $E_1^d(t)$ is the solution to (4.28) - neglecting the tax constraint - while $d\tilde{P}_s(t)/dE_1^d(t) > 0$ up to $\tau[E_1^d(t)] = \tau^+(t)$.

Take the class of states for which $\varepsilon_{12} = \varepsilon_{22} = 1$, $\varepsilon_{11} = \varepsilon_{13} = \varepsilon_{21} = \varepsilon_{23} = 0$, $\lambda_{1s} > 0$, $\lambda_{3s} = \lambda_{4s} = 0$; in that case $\tilde{P}_s(t) = E^{-1}$. $E_1^d(t)^{\lambda_{1s}}.\tilde{E}_2(t)^{1 - \lambda_{1s}}$ and $E_1^d(t) = \min \{E_1^d[\tau^+(t)], \max [L - \tilde{E}_2^d(t), \lambda_{1s}.L]\}$. Thus, if $\lambda_{1s} = 1$ for example, then $E_1 = E_1(\tau^+)$ and $\tau = \tau^+$ necessarily holds.

Because of $w_3^- > 0$, the condition $\tau - \tau^+ \leqq 0$ leads to a much more complicated expression in E_1 and E_2 than was obtained for the previous model [see (3A8) and recall from (4.51) that σ or r are now dependent on E_2].
Observe, however, from (4.51) that $r \to \beta$ if $E_2 \to 0$ ($\sigma = 1$), and from (4.53) that, consequently, $\bar{w}_2 \to 0$. It is then easily seen from (4A4) and (4A5) that $E_1 \to L$ is ruled out.

(4B2) *Characteristic 14: If for an arbitrary type of state an equilibrium exists with $\tau = \tau^+$ and state employment level E_1, then it is an equilibrium for all those types of states for which the sqc-assumption is satisfied and* max $\{E_1^-, \bar{\bar{E}}_1\} \geqq E_1$ *in that situation. Types of states,* other than the aforementioned arbitrary type of state, *satisfying these conditions always exist.*

Proof: Suppose max $\{E_1^-, \bar{\bar{E}}_1\} \geqq E_1$. For $E_1^d(t) > E_1$ it would be obtained that $\tau(t) > \tau^+(t)$, as can be observed from the formulas for τ and τ^+ in (4A5) that the state is confronted with (with time indices added), recalling that expected values of variables are equal to their previous period values [see (4.27)]. For $E_1^d(t) < E_1$, if $E_1 > E_1^-$, it would be obtained that $\tau(t) < \tau^+(t)$, $E_1^d(t) + \tilde{E}_2(t) < L$, and $E_1^d(t) < \bar{\bar{E}}_1$, which cannot be optimal as $\tilde{P}_s(t)$ is strictly quasi-concave in $E_1^d(t)$; if max $\{E_1^-, \bar{\bar{E}}_1\} < E_1$ then a decrease in $E_1^d(t)$ would clearly be preferred and feasible from the point of view of the state. As for the existence part of the characteristic, consider the class of states mentioned under (4B1).

(4B3) *Characteristic 15: If for an arbitrary type of state a full employment equilibrium exists with* $\tau < \tau^+$ *and state employment level* E_1*, then:*

a. *there exists another full employment equilibrium for this type of state if* $E_1 \neq E_1^-$*, the sqc-assumption is satisfied, and* $\bar{E}_1 < E_1 < \bar{\bar{E}}_1$*;*

b. *there exists an unemployment equilibrium for this type of state if* $E_1 = E_1^-$*;*

c. *there are other types of states for which it is an equilibrium, although not for all those for which the sqc-assumption is satisfied, and* $\bar{\bar{E}}_1 \geqq E_1$ *in that situation.*

Proof: a. $\bar{E}_1$ and $\bar{\bar{E}}_1$ are continuous functions of E_1 and E_2 (see note 39). Using $\bar{\bar{E}}_1 > E_1 > E_1^-$, it can be checked from (4A1)-(4A7) - where (4.51) and (4.53) may be used as auxiliary relations - that a new full employment equilibrium is obtainable, satisfying the necessary condition that max $\{\hat{E}_1^-, \hat{\bar{\bar{E}}}_1\} \geqq \hat{E}_1 \geqq \hat{\bar{E}}_1$, where ˆ is used to denote the new equilibrium values.

b. Using (4A1)-(4A7), it can be checked that such an unemployment equilibrium exists, by lowering E_2 while keeping E_1 constant.

c. From characteristic 13 it follows that it is an equilibrium for all those states for which max $\{E_1^-, \bar{\bar{E}}_1\} \geqq E_1 \geqq \bar{E}_1$. Recall that E_1 is bounded away from zero ($E_1^- > 0$) as well as from L. Take $\varepsilon_{12} = \varepsilon_{22} = 1$, $\varepsilon_{11} = \varepsilon_{13} = \varepsilon_{21} = \varepsilon_{23} = 0$, $\lambda_{1s} > 0$, and $\lambda_{3s} = \lambda_{4s} = 0$; in that case $\bar{E}_1 = \lambda_{1s}.L$ and $\bar{\bar{E}}_1 = L$. Observe that $\bar{E}_1 \in (0,L]$. The latter part of c also follows immediately from characteristic 12.

(4B4) *Characteristic 16: If for an arbitrary type of state an unemployment equilibrium exists with state employment level* E_1*, then there exists a full employment equilibrium as well, although not necessarily for this type of state.*

Proof: In case of a full employment equilibrium with $\tau < \tau^+$, E_1 is sustained by a state, for which the sqc-assumption is satisfied, iff max $\{E_1^-, \bar{\bar{E}}_1\} \geqq E_1 \geqq \bar{E}_1$. Using the class of states defined in the proof of (4B3), if can be checked from (4A1)-(4A7) that a full employment equilibrium with $\tau < \tau^+$ can be obtained by increasing the level of E_2, keeping the state employment level at E_1, until $E_1 + E_2 = L$. As regards the latter part of the characteristic, choose

1. $\omega_2 = 0$,
2. $\omega_3 < \omega_1$ $(\omega_3 = \varepsilon_{42}.\lambda_{4s})$,
3. ρ such that $\sigma = 1$ [see (4.51)], and
4. $\phi = 1$.

For given $\tilde{E}_2^d$, $\tilde{P}_s$ can be written as: $\tilde{P}_s = D_0'(1 - \tau)^{\omega_1}(E_1^d + \tilde{E}_2^d + E_3)^{\omega_3}$, where D_0' has a given expected value for the state, and $\tilde{E}_2^d = E_2$. Under these circumstances it is obtained that:

$$\bar{\bar{E}}_1 = - E_2 + \left[\frac{\omega_3[1/(1 - \psi)] - \omega_1}{\omega_1 - \omega_3}\right].E_3 + \left[\frac{\omega_3}{\omega_1 - \omega_3}\right].\left[\frac{\psi}{1 - \psi}\right].L.$$

By varying the dole rate parameter ψ it can be seen that $\bar{\bar{E}}_1 < L - E_2$ may hold, for all E_2. Now, although $E_1 > \bar{\bar{E}}_1$ may hold, in which case $E_1 = E_1^-$, E_1 may be bounded away from E_1^- [let $E_1^- \to 0$ and take $E_1 = E_1^-$, than $\alpha_b \to 0$, because of (4.50), causing $\bar{w}_2 \to 0$, because of (4.53), urging τ to become negative, because of (4A5)]. It follows that only an unemployment equilibrium may exist. It should be noted, however, that if $\omega_3 = 0$ for the type of state under consideration (i.e., $\varepsilon_{42} = 0$ or $\lambda_{4s} = 0$) then the change in $\bar{\bar{E}}_1$ due to a change in $\tilde{E}_2^d$ $(= E_2)$ is nonnegative (neglecting negative values for $\bar{\bar{E}}_1$); in that case a full employment equilibrium should be obtainable. To that purpose first increase E_2 until $E_1 + E_2 = L$ $(\tau < \tau^+)$; if $\bar{E}_1 > E_1$ in that situation (which is no equilibrium; see characteristic 13) then E_2 should be decreased keeping $E_1 + E_2 = L$ until either $E_1 \geqq \bar{E}_1$ or $\tau = \tau^+$ (see characteristics 13 and 14).

APPENDIX 4C

SOME COMMENTS ON THE MARXIST THEORY OF CLASSES

In the Marxist scheme there are two basic classes: the capitalist class (bourgeoisie) and the working class (proletariat). In addition, social groupings are distinguished that are more or less 'in between' and are most of the time labelled the middle classes (petty bourgeoisie), comprising the old middle class (traditional petty bourgeoisie, made up by small businessmen, craftsmen, and the like), and the new middle class (new petty bourgeoisie, typically made up by the middle ranks in the organizations of state and firms). Now, although there certainly is no consensus among Marxists with respect to the demarcation of classes, there seems to be a rather general agreement on three things. *Firstly*, that top managers in firms and the heads of the state apparatuses (top bureaucrats and politicians) should be considered as belonging to the capitalist class. *Secondly*, that people in the middle ranks in the organizations of state and firms belong to the middle class [44)]. *Thirdly*, that the unemployed do not constitute a separate class; there are working class unemployed and middle class unemployed.

Our main points of *critique* are the following. In the *first* place the fact that the state is not really distinguished from a firm. In our opinion there are important differences between the positions of people in state and private sector (see Section 4.2), which cause them to have different interests. This cannot be glossed over by saying that only their more immediate interests differ but not their fundamental, basic, interests which boil down to the establishment of socialism for the workers and the continuance of capitalism for the top ranks in state as well as private sector [as Wright does; Wright (1976, p. 41)]. Apart from the fact that such a statement is not very fruitful unless it is followed by a careful spelling out of the implications of such presumably common fundamental interests for the activities of the agents involved, it is hard to see why top rank bureaucrats - as well as lower rank bureaucrats for that matter - would not be more interested in the establishment of some other mode of production than the aforementioned, one in which bureaucrats would have a more dominant place (think of 'state capitalism').

Our *second*, related, point of critique concerns the treatment of managers and the heads of state apparatuses. According to Poulantzas - who's book on *Classes in Contemporary Capitalism* is seen as "the most systematic and thorough attempt to understand precisely the Marxist criteria for classes in capitalist society" [Wright (*op. cit.*, p. 4)] - these functionaries belong to the capitalist class not so much because of inter-personal relationships, social milieu, or the ownership of capital, but because of the fact that the former "fulfil the 'function of capital'" [Poulantzas (1978b, p. 180)] and occupy, therefore, the place of capital, while the latter "manage the state function in the service of capital" (*ibid.*, p. 187). In our view, there is a confusion here of phenomena that have to do with representation of interests related to a single position or to multiple positions due to a belonging to more than one class [45)], structural coercion, and pressure. Due to structural coercion and pressure these functionaries *may* behave as pure capitalists (think of the profit constraint for managers). Nevertheless, as state and private sector employees they have interests that differ from each other and should, therefore, not be put together [46)]. This is not a matter of academic interest only. For example, by focusing upon a capitalist class and a working class that are rooted in positions in the private sector the suggestion has in fact been made (and is still made) that the historical course of capitalism is basically determined by the struggle and increasing polarization between these two classes, which should eventually lead to the 'seizure' of state power by the working class and the expropriation of the expropriators, the bourgeoisie. As the heads of the state apparatuses are considered to manage the state functions in the service of capital one is inclined to conclude that they would be without 'employ' in such a situation, ready to put their activities - more or less grudgingly perhaps - at the service of their new masters, the proletariat. But this seems to be a rather naïve hypothesis with respect to the position and behaviour of state sector workers. And it is well-known that Marx, Engels and Lenin already stressed the important role that bureaucrats at times have had, and may have, in history [see, e.g., Engels (1847), Lenin (1918), Marx (1843, 1852, 1871)][47)]. Although Marx did not use the word class with respect to bureaucrats, Engels did from time to time [Engels (1846, 1847)]. Lenin emphasized the conclusion drawn by Marx in '*Der Bürgerkrieg in Frankreich*' that the state apparatuses would have to be smashed by the proletariat when taking over. Now why should the 'state machinery' be smashed in case of a bureaucracy that "has no power of its own" [Poulantzas (1978a, p. 351)[48]]. And how can the statement that "since the bureaucracy is neither a class nor a fraction of a class, it can in no way play a principal role in the constitution of a form of state [Poulantzas (1978a, p. 357)] be harmonized with the possible occurrence of a "state bourgeoisie, which can in fact constitute a distinct class or class fraction", "having real control of production", in which case "the exploitation and extraction of surplus-value is shifted towards the heads of the state apparatuses itself" [Poulantzas (1978b, p. 189)] [49)]. In our view it is better to consider state sector workers as constituting a separate class in a capitalist economy; a class whose power, i.e. potential to realize its (class) interests, may vary according to the structural coercion and pressure that it faces.

Our *last* point of critique concerns the unemployed. The unemployed are not considered as a separate class, and, apart from their function as an industrial reserve army, they do not receive much attention [see, however, Offe (1972, pp. 41-44)]. In general, the unemployed are indeed rather unimportant from a social power point of view as they have the weakest position with respect to production in the economy. Nevertheless, on the basis of this economic position they constitute a different class, with different class interests. This particularly applies to the chronically unemployed [50)]. The temporarily unemployed who still orientate themselves on participation in state or private production form a more complex case. They can best be compared with those having multiple positions (Wright's 'contradictory locations'). The power base of this class is located in its numerical strength which may be(come) substantial as Marxists will probably be the first to acknowledge.

CHAPTER 5

ON POLITICAL ACTIVITIES

5.1. Introduction

So far, our dealings with political phenomena concerned the sharpening of our conception of the state, and the study of the behaviour of different types of states under the neglect (outside Section 2.5) of political activities emanating from outside the state sector. Our interest was in the importance of structural coercion and representation (see Section 1.6) as determinants of state behaviour. We did not analyze the process by which a particular type of state comes into existence. The *genesis of a new type of state* will be studied in the present chapter. To that purpose attention is focused upon political activities. Political activities were defined as activities that affect or are intended to affect the behaviour of the state (see Section 1.6). In so far as deliberate influence attempts are involved we will now also be concerned with pressure as a determinant of state behaviour. The organization of the chapter is as follows. In Section 5.2 we start out with a distinction between different *forms of political action*, or instruments of political participation. One such instrument will particularly be considered in this chapter, namely voting and its consequences for the behaviour of political parties and the state. Since political activities - and, thus, voting - will be associated with interest functions, and as *economic conditions* (real disposable income, employment, state production) are important for the values that these functions take, a review is given of the literature on the impact of economic conditions on electoral behaviour. Section 5.3 presents a general *model of choice behaviour* that will be used in different contexts in the chapter. In Section 5.4 the model is applied to *voters*, their decisions to vote or not to vote, and - in case the former holds - their choice of political party. The analysis allows for the existence of more than two parties. Section 5.5 discusses the behaviour of *political parties*. Section 5.6 deals with *cabinet formation* in multi-party systems. A new approach to coalition formation in case of a multi-party system is suggested. In Section 5.7 we go into the importance of elections for changes in the *type of state*, and the *behaviour of politicians*. Using a nested complex interest function for the state, special attention is given to the position of bureaucrats, ministers, and members of parliament. Elected ministers occupy a peculiar place among politicians because they represent bureaucrats - as heads of the bureaucratic departments - as well as political parties. Bureaucrats and politicians are alike in so far as they are all state sector workers. The section also indicates that through the incorporation of political activities into the analysis a *complete politico-economic system* is obtained, characterized by feedback from the economic sphere on the political sphere, and conversely, which makes not only the behaviour of a state endogenous but also the type of state. Section 5.8 shortly addresses some *other forms* of political action, such as political strikes, the formation of new political parties, and revolutions. They will be approached with the help of a *measure of political support of the state*. Section 5.9 deals with the *empirical determination* of the values of some important parameters in the models used. Section 5.10 summarizes.

5.2. Political Activities: Voting Behaviour and Economic Conditions

5.2.1. Voting as a Political Activity

Political activities were defined as activities - by individuals or collectivities - that affect or are intended to affect the behaviour of the state (see Section 1.6). It is useful to distinguish between three categories of political activities:

- activities that do not purposely influence state behaviour;
- activities that are meant to affect state behaviour, although in an indirect way;
- activities that are directly aimed at influencing the behaviour of the state.

The first category comprises activities that exert structural coercion on the state, while the second and the third category cover activities involving *pressure* (see Section 1.6). Activities that do not purposely influence the behaviour of the state have already extensively been dealt with in the previous chapters; they structured the economic model used to determine the activities of the state. Examples of (potential) indirect influence attempts are: participation in riots, tax-evasion, tax-avoidance, letters to the editor of a newspaper, private provision of collective goods, migration to another jurisdiction ('voting-with-the-feet'), participation in party and political campaign activities. Examples of direct influence attempts are: pressure group activities (lobbying), individual actions to influence politicians or bureaucrats directly (e.g., corruption), voting, social movements [1].

Notice that *voting* is *just one* of many possible forms of political action or instruments of political participation. Moreover, it is an instrument that can only (effectively) be used in societies where ('non-manipulated') *elections* are held; it should be realized in this context that many, and perhaps even most, capitalist economies do not have real, free, elections [2]. Given the early state of the (more rigorous) analysis of the interaction between state and private sector one should be very careful in drawing conclusions from analyses that consider only one or a very limited set of political instruments. We will return to this later on.

With respect to the *choice* of political instrument, or instrument-mix, one may surmise that a political actor will somehow take into account the expected costs and benefits of the activities considered [3]. Restricting attention to the category of direct influence attempts, it seems to be clear, then, that - apart from activities directed at individual politicians or bureaucrats [bribery, blackmail, (threat of) violence] - it will most of the time only pay *collective* agents such as trade unions, political parties, big corporations, and so on, to choose this sort of activities as a political instrument [4].

It is not surprising, therefore, that as regards the political activity that we will particularly be concerned with in this chapter - voting - one has been puzzled by the fact that it at all occurs. As certain costs (energy, time, poll tax) have to be incurred, and the probability that one's vote is decisive in a large scale election may be expected to be infinitesimal (and so the expected benefit from voting, no matter what difference it makes to the voter which party or issue wins the election), no rational voter would seem to have an incentive to vote. Nevertheless, a turnout of 70 or 80 per cent in local and national elections is no exception. To account for this *voter's paradox* it has been advanced that people may derive satisfaction from the act of voting *per se*, because of the fulfilment of a sense of 'citizen duty' or social responsibility, for example [5]. But this explanation is still rather disconcerting for those who intuitively at least feel that voters react to what they perceive as the outcome of programmes and policies of parties and politicians. And in fact there are strong indications from empirical research that voters do react to such matters (see below), suggesting that voters do believe that their vote counts. To explain these results - which is also important for the understanding of other political activities by individual agents - one has pointed at:

- the subjectiveness of the probability estimate that one's vote is effective (it may be much higher than what is objectively justified);
- the positive relationship between the probability estimate and the closeness of an election (or the rate of abstention);
- the fact that voters may be interested in the number of votes that their party (issue, candidate) gets, and not just whether the election is won or not;
- instead of maximizing expected utility, a voter may use a different decision rule such as 'minimax regret', in which case little incentive is

needed for the voter to participate;
- the importance of the role played by (opinion) leaders, and propaganda [6].

As regards the last point, a voter may be persuaded of the closeness of an election, or, more generally, of the importance of a vote. It means that the reaction of a voter may be mediated by agents (Party, Church, Union) that are considered by the voter as promoters of the voter's interests; this may be regarded by the voter as the optimal way to act when confronted with the complexity of politics. It may also be hypothesized that voters use, more or less conscious, the conditional strategy 'as-long-as-you-vote-I-will-vote-as-well' because experience has taught that it leads to more satisfactory results in situations where a collective good (here the election result) is involved and the free-rider problem shows up [7]. Although there are still many questions to be answered, it is important that the existing empirical evidence indicates that voters react to situations that they have been, or expect to be, confronted with. The question then becomes which variables are to be included in an analysis of voting behaviour. Here we shall follow the direction taken by a by now already rather substantial amount of empirical research in this area, on a micro- as well as macro-level, in focusing on the relationship between economic conditions and electoral behaviour.

5.2.2. Voting Behaviour and Economic Conditions: Review of the Literature

Although the impact of other determining factors - such as religion, ethnic group, party membership, etc. [see, e.g., Campbell *et al.* (1965)] - will not be completely neglected, our primary concern will be with the influence of economic conditions on voting behaviour. According to the conventional wisdom, as worded for example by political commentators, election results reflect the way that the economy is developing at the time of an election.

Moreover, there are some empirical studies suggesting that politicians act on such beliefs, lowering taxes or stepping up state expenditures shortly before an election while postponing the less pleasant policy measures until the election is over [see Frey and Schneider (1978a,b), Nordhaus (1975), Wright (1974)].

The results of scientific analysis seem, on the whole, to corroborate the conventional wisdom, although there is still much dispute about the importance and nature of the aforementioned relationship. The more sophisticated systematic (empirical) analysis of economic influences on electoral behaviour is of the last decennium, and was started off by Kramer (1971). A related strand of research deals with the impact of economic conditions on polls such as Gallup's [8]. The vote-share of a party (or its popularity, or the popularity of a political candidate) generally serves as the dependent variable. As variables representing economic conditions are mainly used: inflation, unemployment, and per capita income (nominal, real, disposable). To account for non-economic influences (wars, personality factors, party identification, and so on) dummy and proxy variables are employed. Initially, the analysis has mainly been performed on a macro-level but more recently a number of micro-level studies, using survey data, have appeared. Since rather extensive reviews of the early and more recent literature are presented elsewhere [see Kramer (1971), Monroe (1979), Schneider (1978)], a *synopsis* will be given of the critique and suggestions that have been put forward in them, and of the more general issues involved.

1. Although the empirical results are sensitive to changes in, for example, the specifications of variables (levels, change-in-levels, rates of change) or the time period covered, it can be concluded that there are at least strong indications that short-term fluctuations in *inflation*, *unemployment*, and *per capita income* do affect election outcomes and government popularity ratings [9]. These findings have been interpreted as lending support to the view that voters (1) hold incumbent parties *responsible* for economic events, (2) that they take these events - more particularly, the record of the aforementioned aggregate variables: inflation, unemployment, and per capita income - as an indication of how their interests will be promoted by these parties in the future, and (3) that voters have a rather short time horizon which probably mainly covers the election year only.

2. Evidence put forward by Bloom and Price (1975) seems to suggest that a government is much less rewarded for good times than it is punished for bad times [see also Tufte (1978, p. 126)]. Accordingly, a distinction should be made between elections preceded by economic downturns and those during times of relative prosperity. Others, however, have found little evidence for the existence of such an *asymmetry* in evaluation [see Fair (1978), Goodman and Kramer (1975)]. In this context, it is interesting to note that Tufte not only seems to find that voters may punish more than reward, but that degrees of prosperity may take a great difference in the electoral support for the incumbents, with very good times being considerably more rewarded by the electorate than moderately good times. Relevant to this question of non-linearity also is the suggestion made by some students of political participation that stimuli, such as changes in economic conditions, must exceed a certain *threshold* before an agent changes his or her behaviour, i.e. votes for another party or changes his or her popularity rating [see Breton

(1974, p. 76), Downs (1957, pp. 46, 86-87), Frey and Garbers (1971, p. 320)][10].

3. An important point of critique of the present studies is that *distributional aspects* are neglected. People are clearly differently affected by economic events. To give an example, blue collar workers are much more likely to become unemployed in case of a recession than white collar workers. There are some hints in the literature that it is important to distinguish between different *socio-economic groups* or *classes* [11].

4. Although it is often assumed that voters are short-sighted - and, indeed, there is some evidence that voters are myopic; see Fair (1978) - it is also argued - and, again, there is some evidence; see Kiewiet (1980) - that the voter's *time horizon* extends much further in the past. It is pointed out, for example, that *dramatic events* (involving so-called critical elections) such as the Great Depression may have long-lasting effects on the attitude of a voter with respect to a party; according to this line of reasoning the Democratic party in the U.S., for example, would still benefit from worsening economic conditions in which unemployment becomes an important issue [see Okun (1973, p. 175)]. Related to this is the supposition that voters are influenced by the perception of more deeply rooted differences between political parties [see Kiewiet (1980), Monroe (1979), Okun (1973), Weatherford (1978)]. This evokes the concept of *party identification*. An interesting suggestion in this context has been made by Fiorina (1977). In an otherwise abstract theoretical study of party choice in a two-party system he defines party identification as a (stock-) variable indicating the difference between the discounted accumulated political experiences of voters with respect to the promotion of their interests by the parties, adjusted for an initial party bias. In this way economic conditions not only affect the decision of the voter in the short run but also in the longer run through their contribution to the voter's party identification.

5. Not only are there objective differences between the policies of political parties [see, e.g., Hibbs (1977)], voters also appear to perceive such differences, and seem to act on such *perceptions*. Micro-level empirical studies are, however, less conclusive on the impact of individual economic conditions on voting [see Monroe (1979)]. One reason may be that there are no *'pocket-book voters'* in the strict sense, i.e. voters that are only interested in how they are personally affected by economic conditions. Kinder and Kiewiet (1979) conclude from their study based on survey data that personal experiences seem to be poli-

tically unimportant.
The voter's judgement of the more general economic situation appears to be more influential for the vote decision, as personal economic fortunes can usually readily be imputed to very local, situation specific, factors. In this respect Weatherford's suggestion is important, that the political response to economic conditions is mediated through *class* identification, which should imply that "financial worries are seen as worries which other class members have, and not as 'bad luck' which is limited to the individual" [Weatherford (1978, p. 924)].

6. A satisfactory micro-foundation of the alleged relationships between economic conditions and political response is lacking [12]. For example, Monroe observes that "very little of the literature gets into the question of *trade-offs* within the voter's preference for certain policies" [Monroe (1979, p. 161); emphasis ours]. Another shortcoming is that the consumption and distribution of services and goods provided by the *state* is not explicitly taken into account. Generally, disposable income is the only variable to capture the influence of state activities [13].

7. A rather neglected but probably important area of research is the question of voter *turnout*; the question of whether people will vote or not, as opposed to how their vote choice is made.
Arcelus and Meltzer, for example, hypothesize that the principal fluctuations in the percentage of the votes received by parties in congressional elections in the U.S. arose from changes in the participation rate and not from shifts between parties [Arcelus and Meltzer (1975a, p. 1238)].

8. There is no satisfactory treatment of multi-party systems. Attention is focused upon *two-party* systems; in case there are more than two parties, the parties are clustered into a government and an opposition [14].

9. Finally, as was already referred to earlier, there are no doubt many *other factors* that have an influence on the electoral behaviour of people.

It should not be surprising after the aforegoing that it is not at all clear what exactly the relative importance of economic factors is.

In the following two sections of this chapter a model of voting behaviour will be developed that - theoretically at least - largely seems to meet the critique and suggestions summarized above.

5.3. *Choice Behaviour*

Until now we have either focused upon the behaviour of a single (collective) agent, the state, or on the behaviour of identical agents, such as the firms. An exception was made for workers; as regards job preferences, it was assumed that one part (κ) of the labour force prefers to be employed by the state, the other part by business (see Subsection 3.2.3). The reason for this distinction is not far to seek, as the assumption of completely uniform behaviour might have entailed that *all* of the employed are either employed by the state or the firms. Such a distribution problem is also bound to occur when we start to consider the party choice of voters. If voters behave identically then, always, one of the political parties will receive all of the votes. This would be a highly uncomfortable result, of course. Now instead of, again, assuming a rather arbitrarily fixed split up among the agents involved (here, voters), a model will be presented that seems to be satisfactory from a theoretical and empirical research point of view. The model can also be used for the study of labour mobility (although this will not be done in this book), as well as for other purposes where a choice among some alternatives is present.

Suppose there are I_k options (alternatives) available to the members of a set of agents indicated by k. Let the options be denoted by o_i, $i = 1,2,...,I_k$. Let furthermore,

$V_{ko_i}(T)$ = valuation of option o_i by a k-agent at time T;

$f_{ko_i}(T)$ = fraction of k-agents that opts for o_i at time T.

The following logistic relationship is suggested for the determination of $f_{ko_i}(T)$:

$$f_{ko_i}(T) = \frac{\exp\,[V_{ko_i}(T)]}{\Sigma_{j=1}^{I_k} \exp\,[V_{ko_j}(T)]}, \quad i = 1,..,I_k;\ \Sigma_i\, f_{ko_i}(T) = 1. \tag{5.1}$$

In very general terms eq. (5.1) says that if the valuation of a certain option relatively increases (decreases) it will more (less) frequently be chosen. The attractiveness of this particular formulation is related to:

1. its theoretically satisfactory properties; under certain conditions, for example, it is consistent with a model of utility maximizing agents, where a random utility component is introduced to take account of agent specific effects and unobserved attributes of the options [see Domencich and McFadden (1975), Hensher and Johnson (1981)] [15];

2. its computational simplicity;
3. its belonging to the more standard functional forms in empirical research - the logit model - on which a lot of work has been done [see, e.g., Hanushek and Jackson (1977, Ch. 7), Theil (1971, 1972), and the aforementioned literature].

There are two problems to be faced: first, the *determination of* $V_{ko_i}(T)$; second, the possible existence of a *previous choice effect*. As regards the first problem we propose - for such choice settings as the labour market or general elections - to use the interest functions introduced in Chapter 4 [see eq. (4.1)]. Let,

$\tilde{Z}_{ko_i}(T)$ = the expected extent to which the interest realization of agents in economic position k will be improved upon in the future when option o_i is chosen at time T.

It is postulated that $V_{ko_i}(T)$ is a function of $\tilde{Z}_{ko_i}(T)$:

$$V_{ko_i}(T) = V_{ko_i}[\tilde{Z}_{ko_i}(T)]. \qquad (5.2)$$

The function may be specified such that option specific effects are taken into account (see Subsection 5.4.2). The second problem has to do with the fact that (5.1) does not seem to allow for a previous choice effect. Such a choice independence is often not very plausible. Due to habit formation, social norms ('one should not waver'), or finite sensibility for changes in the attractiveness of the available options, people will be inclined to repeat their choice (think of voting). Using (5.2), we, therefore, prefer the following adjusted specification to (5.1) for recurrent choice settings:

$$f_{ko_ho_i}(T) = \frac{\exp\{V_{ko_ho_i}[\tilde{Z}_{ko_i}(T)]\}}{\Sigma_{j=1}^{I_k} \exp\{V_{ko_ho_j}[\tilde{Z}_{ko_j}(T)]\}}, \qquad (5.3)$$

$$h,i = 1,..,I_k, \quad \Sigma_i\, f_{ko_ho_i}(T) = 1,$$

where the first option index, o_h, indicates the previous choice, conditional upon which the valuation concerning o_i is determined; $f_{ko_ho_i}(T)$ will be called the *floating rate* or *transition rate*.

In the following section eq. (5.3) will be applied to the special choice setting of an election. This application will enable us to give a clearer view of the properties of the choice model.

5.4. The Behaviour of Voters: Party Choice and Voter Turnout

5.4.1. Introduction

Voting will be considered here as a two-stage decision-making process, consisting of a decision to vote or to abstain, and a decision about the preferred political candidate or party [cf. Arcelus and Meltzer (1975a, p. 1233)].

We first go into the second stage: the choice of political party (for convenience, we will only speak of parties). The decision to participate - voter turnout - will be considered next.

5.4.2. Choice of Political Party

Suppose there are I parties. In order to determine the number of people that vote for party o_i $(i = 1,..,I)$ at election date T $(T = 1,2,..)$ - or, shortly, election T - the following information is needed in addition to the floating rate expression (5.3): (a) the economic position of the voters, (b) a full specification of their interest function, (c) their party choice at the previous election, and (d) their *party valuation* $V_{ko_h o_i}(T)$, given their previous choice o_h, say.

Position, interest function, previous party choice

In our model a voter is either a worker in the state sector, a worker in the private sector, a capital-owner (owner-entrepreneur), or unemployed; multiple positions are neglected.
Observe that, by using the interest functions, we do not only allow for the influence of inflation, unemployment, and per capita (disposable) income, but also for distributional aspects, and the impact of the consumption of state goods (see points 1, 3, and 6 of the synopsis in Subsection 5.2.2). Observe, furthermore, that these functions, that are specified for different economic positions, suggest a class interest oriented instead of a pocket-book voter (see point 5 of the aforementioned synopsis).
The position of a voter at election date T need not be the same as it was at T-1. Thus, the class status and, consequently, the interests of people

that voted for party o_i at the previous election may have been changed. The number of people in a given position that voted for o_i at the last election should be determined, therefore, just before every election date.

The determination of the party valuation

Basically, a voter has two sources of information on the performance of a party o_i:

1. the factual outcomes with respect to the voter's interests that can be imputed to the activities of o_i;
2. the hypothetical, or promised outcomes regarding these interests as stored in o_i's platforms, propaganda, and so on.

Now, it stands to reason to suppose that a voter prefers to rely upon the first source of information; after all, it is the hardest bit of information the voter can get. And, 'normally', the most plausible case in which the facts are imputed to the activities of o_i will be when o_i is incumbent, and particularly when o_i is the sole incumbent party (i.e., no part of a coalition government). We, therefore, make the following assumptions:

- factual outcomes with respect to interests are taken as an indication of o_i's performance when o_i is the sole incumbent party (the *responsibility hypothesis*);
- hypothetical outcomes with respect to interests on the basis of party platforms, and so on, are taken as an indication of o_i's performance when o_i is in the opposition or when the future is concerned;
- in case of a coalition government, factual as well as hypothetical outcomes with respect to interests are used to determine o_i's performance; the outcomes will be weighted by a factor indicating the relative power of o_i within the coalition, as that party cannot be held responsible for the factual outcomes alone. Let the voter, furthermore, be endowed with a finite time horizon, extending from some period in the past towards (at most) the next election [16]. Elections are assumed to take place at the very end of a time period.

Before becoming more specific concerning the determination of the party valuation variable $V_{ko_h o_i}(T)$, we introduce some notation.

m = incumbency considered, counted backwards ($m = 1,2,\dots$; $m = 1$ stands for the coming incumbency); an *incumbency* (of a party or coalition) may survive more than one *election term*, which covers the time - *periods* - between two elections;

n_m = number of periods that incumbency m consists of;

t_m = last period of incumbency m [17];

$z_{ko_i}(t_m)$, $\hat{z}_{ko_i}(t_m)$ = performance of party o_i during incumbency m as perceived by a voter in position k, and determined at time t_m on the basis of, respectively, factual (z) and hypothetical, promised, ($\hat{z}$) outcomes; $z_{ko_i}(t_m) = 0$ if $m = 1$;

$y_{ko_i}(t)$ = the degree of responsibility of party o_i for factual outcomes, in period t, as perceived by a voter in position k; it is zero if o_i is in the opposition or if a future incumbency is considered (in which case only hypothetical outcomes count), it equals one if o_i is the sole incumbent party, it is between zero and one if o_i participates in a coalition;

$\bar{m}_k$ = earliest incumbency of which the performance is taken into account by a voter in position k, given the voter's time horizon with respect to the past;

$P_k(t)$, $\hat{P}_{ko_i}(t)$ = the value of the interest function of a voter in position k at time t as determined by, respectively, the factual outcomes, and the hypothetical outcomes imputed to party o_i;

$\tilde{Z}_{ko_i}(T)$ = the - at election date T - expected extent to which the interest realization for a voter in position k will be improved upon as a result of a (single party) incumbency of party o_i;

$a_{ko_h o_i}$, $b_{ko_h o_i}$ = parameters to catch party and economic position specific effects;

$c_{ko_i}(t)$, $\bar{c}_{ko_i}(t_m)$

$\hat{c}_{ko_i}(t)$, $\hat{\bar{c}}_{ko_i}(t_m)$ = non-negative weights (not necessarily summing up to one).

The following specifications are suggested. The specifications will be commented upon after their full presentation. Let, at election T,

(5.4) $$\tilde{Z}_{ko_i}(T) = \sum_{m=1}^{\bar{m}_k} [\bar{c}_{ko_i}(t_m).z_{ko_i}(t_m) + \hat{\bar{c}}_{ko_i}(t_m).\hat{z}_{ko_i}(t_m)],$$

where,

(5.5) $$z_{ko_i}(t_m) = \sum_{f=1}^{n_m} y_{ko_i}(t_m-f+1).c_{ko_i}(t_m-f+1).ln[P_k(t_m-f+1)/P_k(t_m-f)]$$

(5.6)

$$\hat{z}_{ko_i}(t_m) = \sum_{f=1}^{n_m} [1 - y_{ko_i}(t_m-f+1)].\hat{c}_{ko_i}(t_m-f+1).ln[\hat{P}_{ko_i}(t_m-f+1)/\hat{P}_{ko_i}(t_m-f)]$$

$$, \hat{P}_{ko_i}(t_m-f) \begin{cases} = P_k(t_m-f) & if \quad t_m-f \leqq t_2, \\ = \hat{P}_{ko_i}(t_m-f) & if \quad t_m-f > t_2. \end{cases}$$

Let, furthermore, using eq. (5.2),

(5.7) $$V_{ko_ho_i}(T) = [\tilde{Z}_{ko_i}(T) - a_{ko_ho_i}]/b_{ko_ho_i}.$$

Given the necessary data, the floating rate for different k can be determined from eq. (5.3). Let,

$E'_{ko_i}(T)$ = the number of people in position k that voted for o_i at the *previous* election, as measured *just before* election T;

$E_{ko_i}(T)$ = the number of people in position k that voted for o_i at election T.

In case of *no vote abstention*, the total number of votes for party o_i at election T, to be denoted by $E_{o_i}(T)$, then results from

(5.8) $$E_{o_i}(T) = \sum_{k=1}^{4} E_{ko_i}(T),$$

where

(5.9) $$E_{ko_i}(T) = \sum_{j=1}^{I} f_{ko_jo_i}(T).E'_{ko_j}(T).$$

Eqs. (5.4) through (5.6) suggest that $\tilde{Z}(T)$ - omitting the subscripts k and o_i for notational convenience - is determined as a sum of the weighted relative changes in the value of the interest function that are imputed to party o_i. The weights are supposed to reflect:

1. the importance attached to incumbencies ($\bar{c},\hat{\bar{c}}$), and to periods within incumbencies ($c,\hat{c}$);

2. the reliability of hypothetical outcomes stored in $\hat{z}(t_m)$ ($\hat{\bar{c}}$).

Thus, for example, the supposedly lasting effects of the Republican - Great Depression - incumbency and the Democratic - New Deal - incumbency in the U.S. should show up through a relatively large, although probably diminishing (due to memory decay) value for $\bar{c}$ for those incumbencies (see point 4 of the synopsis in 5.2.2). The reliability of hypothetical outcomes may be influenced by, for example, the discrepancy between such outcomes and the factual outcomes when o_i is incumbent, or by extra-parliamentary activities of o_i. In so far as reliability is concerned it may be expected that the weight attached to hypothetical outcomes is smaller than that for factual outcomes.

The difference between the valuation of two parties, o_i and o_j, labelled the *party valuation differential*, is equal to

$$V_{ko_h o_i}(T) - V_{ko_h o_j}(T), \qquad h,i,j, = 1,..,I.$$

Fig. 5.1 shows the relationship between the floating rate and the party valuation differential for a two-party system with parties o_h and o_i according to eq. (5.3); the density of the logistic distribution which it displays is symmetric around zero.

The larger the differential measured along the abscissa the higher the percentage of people from social class k that 'floats' from o_h (their previous choice) to o_i. It is 50% if the differential is zero. In that case people are indifferent between o_h and o_i. In case of more than two parties the floating rate concerning any two parties would be negatively related to the valuation of the remaining parties, as is easily seen from eq. (5.3). Indifference - which means that the party valuation differentials are all zero - would then imply that the floating rates are all equal to 1/I, in which case 1/I of the *total* number of voters in position k will vote for a given party. Consequently, in order to maintain its relative size (vote share) it is not sufficient for a party whose electoral support at the previous election exceeded 1/(I - 1) times the aggregate support of the other parties, to score a valuation equal to that of the other parties, for example. We shall return to this later on.

It is interesting now to look at the underlying relationship between the floating rate and the *expected interest realization ratings* $\tilde{z}(T)$, and to focus upon the significance of the parameters a and b. Consider the following equation, obtained from eqs. (5.3) and (5.7):

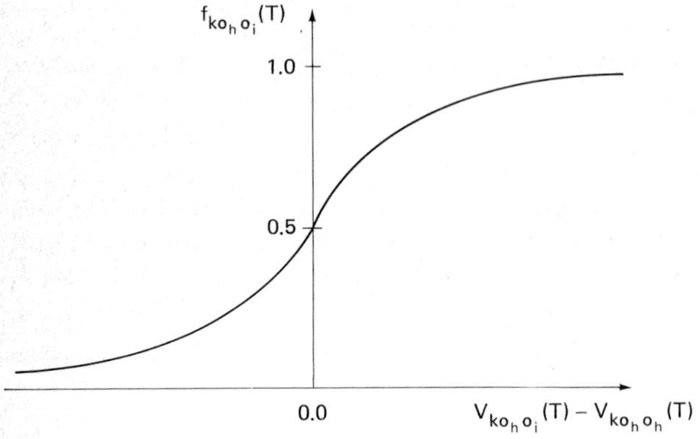

Fig. 5.1. Floating rate and party valuation differential.

(5.10)

$$f_{ko_h o_i}(T) = \frac{1}{\Sigma_{j=1}^{I} \exp \{[\tilde{Z}_{ko_j}(T) - a_{ko_h o_j}]/b_{ko_h o_j} - [\tilde{Z}_{ko_i}(T) - a_{ko_h o_i}]/b_{ko_h o_i}}$$

The parameters a and b determine the *sensitivity* of the floating rate with respect to the expected interest realization ratings. Without loss of generality it is assumed that

(5.11) $a_{ko_h o_h} = 0$, for all h.

From eq. (5.10) the following simple expressions are obtained for the effect on the floating rate of changes in the expected interest realization ratings:

(5.12) $$\frac{\partial f_{ko_h o_i}(T)}{\partial \tilde{Z}_{ko_i}(T)} = \frac{1}{b_{ko_h o_i}} . f_{ko_h o_i}(T).[1 - f_{ko_h o_i}(T)],$$

and

(5.13) $$\frac{\partial f_{ko_h o_i}(T)}{\partial \tilde{Z}_{ko_j}(T)} = - \frac{1}{b_{ko_h o_j}} . f_{ko_h o_i}(T) . f_{ko_h o_j}(T) \qquad , j \neq i.$$

As the parameters b are allowed to differ for different parties, the

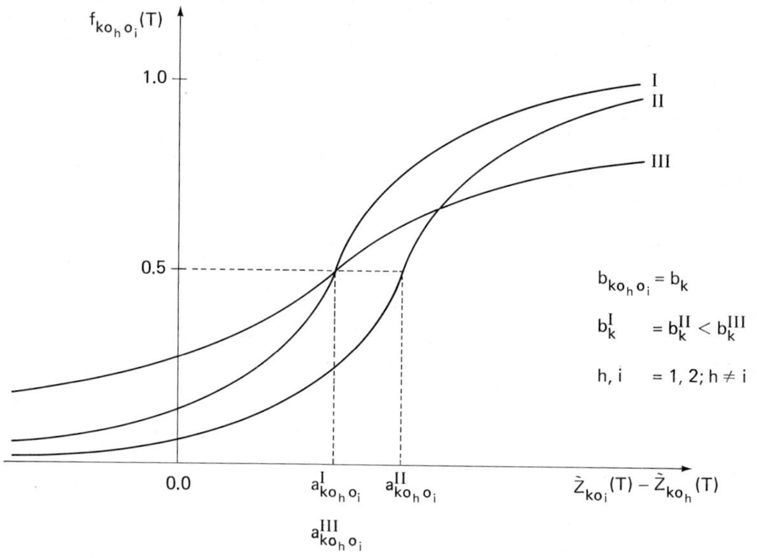

Fig. 5.2. Floating rate and expected interest realization differential.

floating rate cannot, in general, explicitly be related to the *expected interest realization differentials*:

$$\tilde{Z}_{ko_i}(T) - \tilde{Z}_{ko_j}(T);$$

see eq. (5.10). For reasons of exposition, it may be useful, however, to picture the relationship in question when the parameters b are identical; see Fig. 5.2, where, again, a two-party system is referred to. It shows that 50% of the voters from social class k that voted for o_h at the previous election now chooses for o_i when the expected interest realization differential equals the value of the parameter a.

It also illustrates how the parameters a and b affect the shape and position of the function. By means of these parameters it is possible to allow for party and voter specific effects; that is, effects that are not already accounted for by the consideration of the class interests that we have focused upon. For example, it cannot *a priori* be taken for granted that voters from different classes will react in the same way when confronted with the same expected interest realization ratings (on the basis

of different interests). Moreover, to give another example, it may be surmised that there, generally, will be a world of difference for a communist between voting for a conservative party and voting for a social-democratic party, even though he or she has come to expect that his or her interests - as comprised by the interest realization ratings - are better served under the incumbency of either party. In short, the realization of the particular interests that we explicitly deal with is not all that matters (see point 9 of the synopsis in 5.2.2). Other factors - think of ideology - create barriers or obstacles to floating, which may be translated into terms of *political distances* between parties.
Although we will not belabour this subject here, it stands to reason to expect that a greater political distance will be reflected by a larger value of the relevant parameter a, which implies that for any given floating rate a larger expected interest realization differential will be needed in that case (see Fig. 5.2) [18]. Notice from Fig. 5.2, furthermore, that a smaller value of the parameter b causes the floating rate function to adopt a more step-like shape. For sufficiently small values of b a critical region for the expected interest realization differential can be obtained where the floating rate is highly sensitive to changes in the differential.

5.4.3. Some Additional Remarks

We conclude our analysis of party choice with a few remarks.

1. Observe that the expected interest realization ratings $\tilde{Z}(T)$ [see eqs. (5.4)-(5.6)] can be considered as (stock-) variables reflecting *party identification* in so far as the class interests are concerned that are taken into account by these variables (see point 4 of the synopsis in 5.2.2).

2. As Fig. 5.2 clearly shows, floating *thresholds* are accounted for in our model. In that case the value of the relevant sensitivity parameter a (relevant with respect to the parties considered) should be sufficiently large, and/or the value of the relevant parameter b should be sufficiently small (see point 2 of the synopsis in 5.2.2).

3. An *asymmetric effect* of economic prosperity and depression on the electoral support received by the incumbent party (or parties; see point 2 of the synopsis in 5.2.2) may not only result because "in bad times the economy becomes a salient issue, whereas in good times it diminishes in importance relative to other determinants of voting behaviour", as Bloom and Price (1975, p. 1244) suggest, following

Campbell *et al.* (1965, pp. 554-555) - which should be reflected in the weights $c(t)$, $\hat{c}(t)$, $\bar{c}(t_m)$, $\hat{\bar{c}}(t_m)$; it may also result from the 'bigger party effect' that was earlier referred to. To see this, consider eq. (5.9) and Fig. 5.2, and assume that there are only two parties, o_1 and o_2, that the parameters a and b are identical for h,i = 1,2 (implying that the floating rate function for each voter category has the same shape and position), and that periods of prosperity, economic standstill, and economic downturn, correspond with, respectively, a positive, zero, and a negative expected interest realization differential, where the governing party is labelled o_i. In that case the bigger (governing) party will be "'punished' by the voters for economic downturns" but is "not 'rewarded' accordingly for prosperity" [Bloom and Price (*ibid.*)], while the reverse holds for the smaller party. In fact the bigger party is even 'punished' for an economic standstill which keeps the interest realization differential at zero, or a slight prosperity.

4. Changes in the *sensitivity parameters* a and b of the floating rate functions may come about in a number of ways. Due to new information on current and past political issues, demographic changes in the composition of the voter categories (e.g., because of changes in the size of the electorate) or class mobility (see also below) the values of these parameters may rise or fall, changing the *political mobility* of the voters. Class mobility, for instance, which may be due to the mobility of labour between state and private sector, for example, may not only affect the extent of party identification, expressed by $\tilde{Z}(T)$, because newcomers will probably have to rely on rather recent political events that have become relevant to them in their new position and with which they have been able to build up some experience, it may - for the same reasons - also affect the sensitivity parameters.
Another possible reason for changes in these parameters may be the appearance of *new political parties*. One of the nice properties of the logistic floating rate function exposed by eq. (5.2) is that the effect of a new party is easily accounted for; one should only expand the denominator with the valuation of the new party. Note, however, that eq. (5.3) implies that

$$f_{ko_ho_i}(T)/f_{ko_ho_g}(T) = \exp\,[V_{ko_ho_i}(T) - V_{ko_ho_g}(T)], \qquad (5.14)$$

which means that the floating rate ratio for the parties o_i and o_g is independent of the presence or absence of a new party. But, this is only realistic if the new party is a really different, 'independent', alternative. Consider, for example, a two-party system with a 'left-wing' party o_h and a 'right-wing' party o_i, and suppose that $f_{ko_ho_i}(T) = 1/4$, and, thus, $f_{ko_ho_h}(T) = 3/4$, then

$$f_{ko_ho_h}(T)/f_{ko_ho_i}(T) = 3 .$$

Now, suppose that a new 'right-wing' party o_g had presented itself during the election campaign, and that

$$a_{ko_ho_i} = a_{ko_ho_g}, \quad b_{ko_ho_i} = b_{ko_ho_g}, \quad V_{ko_ho_i}(T) = V_{ko_ho_g}(T).$$

Then,

$$f_{ko_ho_i}(T) = f_{ko_ho_g}(T) = 1/5 \quad \text{and} \quad f_{ko_ho_h}(T) = 3/5$$

would have been obtained, which means that the fraction of voters in position k that now prefers a 'right-wing' party has increased from 1/4 to 2/5. This result does not seem to be realistic in view of the fact that the right-wing parties are equally valuated. One would have expected, instead, that

$$f_{ko_ho_h}(T) = 3/4 \quad \text{and, thus,} \quad f_{ko_ho_i}(T) = f_{ko_ho_g}(T) = 1/8.$$

In other words, one would expect that, loosely spoken, the floating rate regarding o_i is split up between o_i and o_g in the new situation; or, put differently, that the old floating rate with respect to o_i is twice the new floating rate. In order to allow for this effect the parameter $a_{ko_ho_i}$ (= $a_{ko_ho_g}$) should be changed into

$$a'_{ko_ho_i} = a_{ko_ho_i} - b_{ko_ho_i} \ln(1/2).$$

5. Reasons for *large shifts* in party choice (landslides, or so-called critical elections) are easily found by considering the constituent parts of the party valuation variable V(T); see eqs. (5.4)-(5.7). The following factors may be mentioned:
   a. salient current issues;
   b. dramatic experiences during the most recent incumbency (possibly involving large shifts in class status);
   c. a widely occurring re-evaluation of past incumbencies involving significant changes in $\bar{c}$, for example;
   d. important changes in the party structure (in particular, the establishment of new parties;
   e. important changes in the electorate (through enfranchising, for

example).

5.4.4. Voter Turnout

We now turn to the first stage of the voting process: the decision to vote. We will approach this issue in a negative way by focusing upon its counterpart, the decision to abstain from voting. Fluctuations in the participation rate of voters can be substantial [19)], and may be important for the vote shares obtained by parties. Recall, in this context, the hypothesis of Arcelus and Meltzer that changes in the participation rate, and not the shifts between parties, are the cause of the principal fluctuations in the vote shares obtained in U.S. Congressional elections (see point 7 of the synopsis in Subsection 5.2.2). Although abstention may have numerous causes [see Milbrath and Goel (1977)], the following two have in particular attracted attention in the literature:

a. *indifference*, and
b. *alienation* [see, e.g., Davis, Hinich, and Ordeshook (1970, p. 437), Mueller (1979, p. 100), Riker and Ordeshook (1973, pp. 323-330)].

Indifference occurs when voters perceive no real difference between parties; that is, when the party valuation differential vanishes:

$$[V_{ko_h o_h}(T) - V_{ko_h o_i}(T)] \to 0 \qquad \text{for all } i.$$

Alienation is said to occur if the political system - including the most preferred party - is perceived to be unresponsive to the voter's interests; in our terminology, alienation in this view arises when

$$V_{ko_h o_i}(T) \ll 0 \qquad \text{for all } i.$$

To these causes we would like to add the following form of alienation, which occurs when all parties are performing exceedingly well; in that case,

$$V_{ko_h o_i}(T) \gg 0 \qquad \text{for all } i.$$

In the first case the voters can be said to be *negatively alienated*, in the second case they are *positively alienated*. In our view abstention because of positive alienation is a very plausible reaction to a situation in which even the worst performing party lives up to the voter's desires. Of the three causes of abstention considered, the first one - indifference - seems to be the most important in the sense that the rate of abstention may be surmised to be highest in case of complete indifference, whatever the degree of alienation.

It appears to be possible to incorporate these thoughts into a single formula for the determination of the rate of abstention and, consequently, the rate of voter turnout. The following relationship is suggested [20].

$$(5.15)\qquad \Gamma_{ko_h}(T) = \frac{\Gamma^{+}_{ko_h}(T)}{1 + \gamma_{ko_h}\cdot\sigma_{ko_h}(T)^{2\bar{\gamma}_{ko_h}}\cdot\exp\{-\,[\mu_{ko_h}(T) - \bar{\bar{\gamma}}_{ko_h}]^2/\bar{\bar{\bar{\gamma}}}_{ko_h}\}},$$

where

$\Gamma_{ko_h}(T)$ = rate of abstention among people in economic position k who opted for o_h at the previous election;

$\Gamma^{+}_{ko_h}(T)$ = the maximum rate of abstention; $\Gamma^{+}_{ko_h}(T) = 0$, for all T, in case of compulsory voting;

$\mu_{ko_h}(T)$ = average of $V_{ko_ho_i}(T)$, $i = 1,..,I$;

$\sigma_{ko_h}(T)^2$ = variance of $V_{ko_ho_i}(T)$, $i = 1,..,I$;

γ_{ko_h}, $\bar{\gamma}_{ko_h}$, $\bar{\bar{\gamma}}_{ko_h}$, $\bar{\bar{\bar{\gamma}}}_{ko_h}$ = parameters; $\gamma_{ko_h}, \bar{\gamma}_{ko_h} \geqq 0$, $\bar{\bar{\bar{\gamma}}}_{ko_h} > 0$.

Fig. 5.3 illustrates the relation between $\Gamma_{ko_h}(T)$ and $\mu_{ko_h}(T)$ for different $\sigma_{ko_h}(T)^2$ when $\gamma_{ko_h}, \bar{\gamma}_{ko_h}, \bar{\bar{\bar{\gamma}}}_{ko_h} > 0$ and $\bar{\bar{\gamma}}_{ko_h} = 0$.

The variable $\mu(T)$ - omitting subscripts for convenience - measures the degree of alienation, $\sigma(T)^2$ the lack of indifference. If $\sigma(T)^2 = 0$ then all parties are equally valuated and $\Gamma(T) = \Gamma^{+}(T)$ whatever the level of valuation. If, moreover, $\Gamma^{+}(T) = 1$ then nobody would vote in that situation. For a given value of $\sigma(T)^2$, the rate of abstention is lowest if $\mu(T) = \bar{\bar{\gamma}}$, where $\bar{\bar{\gamma}}$ may be labelled the *positive-alienation threshold*. If people are used to improvements in their lot then $\bar{\bar{\gamma}} > 0$ may hold, for example. The higher the variance of the party valuations is, the lower the rate of abstention becomes; if $\sigma(T)^2 \to \infty$ then $\Gamma(T) \to 0$, in which case we have a 100% voter turnout. Relation (5.15) is symmetric around $\bar{\bar{\gamma}}$, for given $\sigma(T)^2$; the variance of the party valuations determines the 'shallowness' of curve II in Fig. 5.3. The parameter γ controls the combined effect of alienation and indifference on the rate of abstention; $\bar{\gamma}$ (in the exponent of σ) controls the impact of indifference (it is defined that $0^0 = 1$); $\bar{\bar{\bar{\gamma}}}$

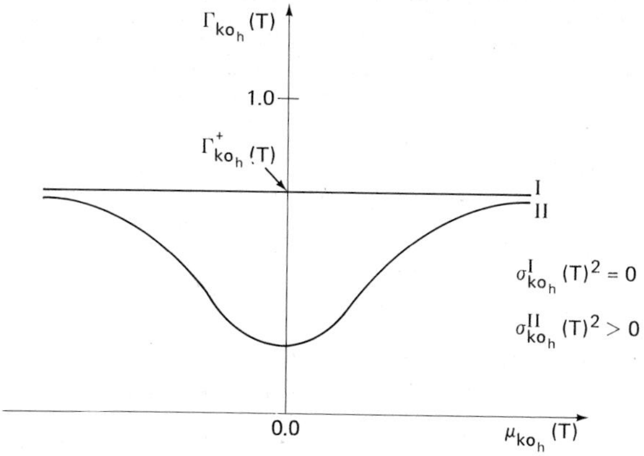

Fig. 5.3. Abstention due to indifference and alienation.

controls the impact of alienation on the rate of abstention.

Denoting the choice of non-voting by o_0, total abstention is determined by

$$(5.16) \qquad E_{o_0}(T) = \sum_{k=1}^{4} E_{ko_0}(T),$$

where

$$(5.17) \qquad E_{ko_0}(T) = \sum_{h=0}^{I} \Gamma_{ko_h}(T).E'_{ko_h}(T).$$

Letting E(T) stand for the size of the total electorate, the overall rate of abstention $\bar{\Gamma}(T)$ equals

$$(5.18) \qquad \bar{\Gamma}(T) = E_{o_0}(T)/E(T).$$

The floating rate for those who abstained at the previous election but who now participate is given by

$$(5.19) \qquad f_{ko_0o_i}(T) = \frac{\exp\,[V_{ko_0o_i}(T)]}{\Sigma_{j=1}^{I} \exp\,[V_{ko_0o_j}(T)]}, \quad i = 1,..,I,$$

where $\Sigma_i\, f_{ko_0o_i}(T) = 1$.

In case of abstention, the total number of votes for party o_i then follows from eq. (5.8)

$$E_{o_i}(T) = \sum_{k=1}^{4} E_{ko_i}(T),$$

and, instead of eq. (5.9),

$$(5.20) \qquad E_{ko_i}(T) = \sum_{j=0}^{I} f_{ko_j o_i}(T).[1 - \Gamma_{ko_j}(T)].E'_{ko_j}(T) \qquad , i = 1,..,I.$$

5.5. The Behaviour of Political Parties

5.5.1. Introduction

In the previous section we presented a model of voting behaviour. It gives an example of how political pressure can be related to the - imputed - behaviour of parties and the state, and it shows that, in principle, such pressure can be incorporated into a more formal kind of analysis. It remains to be analyzed what the impact of this sort of pressure is on the behaviour of parties and the state. The present and the following section are reserved for that purpose. There are three problems to be tackled. *First*, how do political parties behave? *Second*, what type of government (legislature plus cabinet) results from an electoral outcome? Given the composition of the legislature after an election, this problem boils down to the question which party or coalition of parties will form the cabinet. *Third*, what type of state results, given a new government and the bureaucracy that this government will be confronted with [21])? In this section attention will be restricted to the first problem.

5.5.2. Party Behaviour: Evaluation of the Literature

Of the aforementioned problems, the first problem - how do political parties behave? - has most frequently been subject to a more formal kind of analysis. Downs presented the first large-scale approach to it in his prolific work *An Economic Theory of Democracy* [Downs (1957)], where he based himself on the idea of spatial competition among parties put forward in Hotelling (1929), and on Schumpeter's proposition that we must start from the competitive struggle for power and office - and, consequently, in democracies for votes - in order to understand how democratic policies may serve social ends [Schumpeter (1947, p. 282)].
Since then, the study of party behaviour has typically been cast in the form of *spatial models* "wherein candidates affect citizens' choices by offering proposed policies to the citizens" [Riker and Ordeshook (1973, p. 307)]. The policies are represented by points in a one- or more-dimen-

sional issue space. Citizens have given preferences with respect to the political issues. Candidates (parties) aim at winning elections, which keeps them preoccupied with their electoral support (number of votes, vote share). However, spatial models of party behaviour are, as yet, seriously *deficient* in a number of respects:

a. political parties are typically considered as teams, the members of which are characterized by having the same motivation, namely the acquisition of as much electoral support as possible at the coming election; parties are not allowed to have a preference for going into the opposition;
b. there exists a 'perfect' spatial mobility for the parties;
d. in order to reach their goal of obtaining electoral support parties passively adjust their policies to the voters' preference structure;
d. there is no distinction between state and government.

As regards the first point, it has been put forward that, instead of maximizing the expected number of votes or vote share at the coming election, parties may rather be interested in: the winning of as many elections as possible in the future [Barry (1970, p. 105)]; the maximization of the present value of all future legislation [Stigler (1972, p. 103)]; the realization of ideological preferences whenever electoral success seems secure [Frey (1977a, pp. 129-130)]. The last two suggestions direct attention to the role played by the interests of the constituencies of parties, and, as these interests are typically diverse, they, consequently, question the adequacy of the conception of a party as a team [22]. Related to this is the question of whether winning the election or becoming incumbent is really that important to parties as to justify the exclusive attention that it has received in the literature [23]. The usual motivation for assuming such a goal is that "once in the opposition, the party will have no opportunity to change the 'world' according to its own ideology" [Frey and Lau (1968, p. 359)]. We, however, are more inclined to take Stigler's point of view that "political effectiveness is a more or less smooothly increasing function of the size of a party" [Stigler (1972, pp. 99-100)]. Stigler mentions three reasons for it: firstly, the larger an opposing party becomes, the easier it will be for it to persuade sub-coalitions of the 'majority' - using vote-trading - to join it on its desired issues (that constituencies of parties are generally heterogeneous is obviously important here in case of a two-party system); secondly political systems contain some element of division of power, with parties holding a share of offices according to their relative size; thirdly, the larger an opposing party is the more costs it can inflict upon the majority in enforcing policies which the opposition disapproves of [24]. In order to explain the fact that minority parties often persist for long periods, Stigler suggests that a minority is more effective in achieving its ends as a homogeneous minority than as a part of a more heterogeneous majority. Consider here the way that we approached collectivities. Collectivities, such as political parties, are regarded as - in general - being composed of different interest blocs with different degrees of power. Now, clearly, (random) winning of votes (or party members) may be interesting for an interest bloc in a party from an external power point of view (for example, with an eye to its influence in parliament), but it may at the same time endanger the position of that bloc within the collectivity, depending on the interests of the newcomers. In short, there will most likely be a trade-off between internal and external power for the interest blocs in a collectivity, so that it is - in principle - quite possible that a party goes into the opposition and does not try to become a majority party [25].

We can be short on the remaining points of critique on spatial models of party behaviour. Perfect spatial mobility - even when parties are not allowed to pass each other in an ideological dimension - is of course out of the question as soon as one conceives of a party as a carrier of interests. Moreover, it requires that voters cannot be predisposed to favour one of the parties prior to the start of the election campaign [Zechman (1979)]. The voter is limited to that information that can be completely controlled by a party; there are no consequences of past performances. Instead of assuming that a party passively adjusts its policies to the existing preference structure of the voters, our approach would suggest a more active party which tries to persuade voters - no doubt by means of attractively designed party platforms - to back its naked or (disguised) interests. As we have to do with a collectivity and not with an individual decision maker, party activities will generally be the results of compromises and are, therefore, not straightforwardly deducible to the interests of one of its interest blocs (cf. our notion of a complex interest function). Regarding the final point of critique, it should be remarked that by focusing on party platforms (proposed policies) in a situation of 'no recall', attention has been withdrawn from the state and concentrated on the government. Consequently, the potential influence of bureaucrats on the behaviour of (the representatives of) parties - so much stressed by other scholars within the Public Choice tradition - has been neglected [see Subsection 5.7.2].

5.5.3. An Alternative Approach to Party Behaviour

In our view it is better to start with the class structure of a party's constituency (which comprises all who voted for the party), and the class interests represented by that constituency. In accordance with Subsection 4.3.2 we would assume that parties act as if they maximize the following complex interest function:

$$(5.21) \quad P_{o_i}(t) = \Pi_k \, P_k(t)^{\lambda_{ko_i}(t)} \quad , \lambda_{ko_i}(t) \geq 0, \; \Sigma_k \, \lambda_{ko_i}(t) = 1, \; i = 1,..,I.$$

The power weights may be supposed to be, *inter alia*, determined by the class structure of the party, i.e., the fractional breakdown of the class status of its constituency (see further Section 5.9) [26]. The maximization of (5.21) is restricted by economic and political constraints. The actual behaviour and policy proposals (platforms) of a political party may be expected to be dependent on the perceived structure of the economy, and the (expected) behaviour of other political parties, voters, and bureaucrats. It is obvious that huge informational problems are met here, for the political party in question and for the researcher who wants to model such behaviour. Due to the typical heterogeneous class structure (implying different class interests) and large size of political parties alone, subtle strategic behaviour *vis-à-vis* other parties and voters is not to be expected (see Subsection 5.7.4 on the manipulation of voters by politicians).

With respect to *party platforms* (which determine the $\hat{P}$ in Subsection 5.4.2) we would speculate that, in general, the maximization of (5.21) under a time horizon extending not further than the next election, and subject to some model representing the perceived structure of the economy, might be a good, first, approach (see also Subsection 5.7.4). The platform would then be based on the optimal values of the instrument variables that are expected by the party to be available when it is incumbent, and the resulting values of the dependent variables. In regard to the *actual behaviour* of a party, we propose to take a more indirect approach by looking at the outcomes that can be surmised to result from the behaviour of parties, rather then exactly specifying the activities of each. After all, it is the behaviour of the state that we are interested in, and not so much the activities of parties per se. Now, more than one political party is, generally, represented by the state; and, at any rate, it comprises a bureaucracy that should be taken into account. The behaviour (policies) of the state should, therefore, not simply be identified with the behaviour of a particular political party (see Section 5.7).

In the following section we go into the problem of what type of cabinet may be expected to result after an election; in that context we will have to face the problem of coalition formation. In the section after that we discuss the influence of parties on the policies of the state.

5.6. Cabinet Formation

5.6.1. Introduction

In case of a two-party system we may safely assume that the cabinet will be formed by the majority party. The interest function of the cabinet will in that case be identical to the interest function of that party; that is, if the representatives of the party fully adhere to the party line (see Section 5.7.2). Although two-party systems, such as the U.S., are often the subject of analysis, it would be unsatisfactory - especially for someone with a European background - to ignore the complications that arise from the existence of more than two parties (after all, multi-party systems are the more common). The central problem to be tackled here is that of coalition formation. As it is quite normal for multi-party systems that no single party is endowed with a majority of the votes or parliamentary seats, parties are frequently confronted with the situation that a coalition has to be formed in order to get a majority. It is no surprise, given the analytical difficulties in this area of politics, that theory has not very far advanced as yet. In this section we do not intend to present an exhaustive treatment of the problem, nor to give a detailed account of the relevant theoretical and empirical studies. We only want to outline some ideas that are inspired by our interest function approach and our treatment of voting behaviour. Subsection 5.6.2 discusses some existing theories of coalition formation. An alternative approach is presented in Subsection 5.6.3.

5.6.2. Existing Theories of Coalition Formation

According to De Swaan (1973, pp. 8-9) - on whose review of coalition theories we will base ourselves - there are some six *main theories* of political coalition formation. There are three theories which only take *resources* (size, weight, votes) into account [27]: the theory of the 'Minimal Winning Set' [due to Von Neumann and Morgenstern (1944)], which leads to the prediction that only those coalitions will form that exclude actors whose weight is unnecessary for the coalition to be *winning*, i.e., to satisfy a majority criterion, so that it can form the cabinet; the 'Minimum Size Principle' [based on Gamson (1961) and Riker (1962)], which predicts coalitions that are both winning and of smallest weight (a subset of the Minimal Winning Set); the 'Bargaining Proposition' [Leiserson (1968)], which says that those coalitions will form that are both winning and consist of the smallest number of actors (parties), irrespective of the total weight involved (again, a subset of the Minimal Winning Set). The first two theories refer to the plausible idea that the participating parties in a coalition are interested in the spoils (cabinet posts) of forming a cabinet and are unwilling to share those with unnecessary actors. The third theory uses the argument that smaller coalitions can more easily be held together and that bargaining and negotiations are easier to complete in them.

Consider the following *example*. Suppose there are 5 parties: A, B, C, D and E, with, respectively: 15, 5, 40, 30 and 10 per cent of the total vote. Suppose, furthermore, that the majority criterion demands that more than 50% of the vote is required in order for a coalition to be winning. Then, according to these theories one of the following coalitions will form:

Minimal Winning set : AC, ADE, BCE, CD;
Minimum Size Principle: AC, ADE, BCE;
Bargaining Proposition: AC, CD.

The following two theories do not only take resources into account but also the *policy preferences* of the actors. The first, 'Minimal Range Theory' [Leiserson (1966)], uses the concept of the 'range of a coalition', defined as the 'distance' between the two actors in the coalition whose positions on a policy scale are furthest apart. It predicts that only those coalitions will result that do not consist of actors that are unnecessary for them to be winning, while they increase their range (and thereby 'ideological diversity'). Moreover, the range of these coalitions should not be larger than that of any other winning coalition (in view of the spoils). The second theory, labelled 'Closed Coalitions of Minimal Range' [or 'Minimal Connected Winning Coalitions'; Axelrod (1979)], predicts minimal range coalitions that contain all actors whose policy positions are within that minimal range. The underlying argument is that conflict of interest in a coalition would be mitigated this way.

Suppose that the parties in our *example* given above can be ordered in the following way from left to right along a 'Left-Right' socio-economic scale (a scale that is typically used): A, B, C, D, E.
Then, according to the last mentioned theories one of the following coalitions will form:

Minimal Range Theory : ABC, AC, CD;
Closed Coalitions of Minimal Range: ABC, CD.

Note that all of the preceding theories predict coalitions that are minimal in some sense, either with respect to their weight, their number of members, or their range on a policy scale. Non-minimal coalitions occur quite frequently, however. The reasons for such coalitions may be various. To name a few: the attachment of a high value to consensus, the requirement of qualified majorities, the fact that the parliamentary system of cabinet and legislature is not isolated from outside factors to an extent that justifies its investigation from a closed-system point of view (recall, in this context, our discussion of the position of minority parties). De Swaan adds another reason in the form of a third (policy preference) theory of coalition formation: 'Policy Distance Minimization' [De Swaan (1973, Ch. V)], predicting that only those winning coalitions will emerge of which the members expect that it will adopt a policy that is as close as possible, on a policy scale, to their own most preferred policies. Special attention is paid in this theory to the differential opportunity for parties in a coalition to steer the coalition's policy in a preferred direction. A crucial role is played by the 'pivot actor' who, on the basis of the weight distribution in the coalition, may 'swing the vote' (see note 31). Parties prefer coalitions in which they are pivotal. To the extent that the combined weight of the numbers on the one side of the pivot actor exceeds that of the other side the expected policy will be drawn in that direction, away from the pivot actor's most preferred policy.

All of the aforementioned theories assume that each party has a preference ordering over all possible coalitions, and that those coalitions are most likely to form, in any given situation, which are *undominated* - a coalition r being undominated if there is no other coalition which is strictly preferred by all of its members to r. The set of undominated coalitions is called the *equilibrium set* [see Taylor and Laver (1973, p. 206)]. The coalitions in this set are - theoretically - equally likely to form.

The main conclusion from empirical tests of these theories - which involve a statistical comparison of the predicted sets with the set of coalitions that actually have formed - is that, in 'normal' times, coalitions tend to be of closed minimal range (minimal connected winning); see De Swaan and Mokken (1980). This conclusion would suggest that ideology plays a relatively more important role than sheer size or the pivotal position of a party in a coalition as such. Coalition members tend to look for partners that are adjacent on the policy scale. Only parties that add to the ideological range of a (winning) coalition are fenced off.

Remarks

Although this outcome should be welcomed as an important and certainly interesting first result, there seems to be a number of omissions and weaknesses in these theories that should be questioned.

First, the 'theory' that comes out as superior (Minimal Connected Winning) does not have a satisfactory theoretical underpinning [see De Swaan (1973, pp. 98-100, p. 145), Taylor (1972, p. 372)].

Second, it is assumed that parties are indifferent between coalitions that are non-winning or from which they are excluded, and - or at least - that they prefer to such coalitions any winning coalition of which they are a member. Taylor and Laver (1973, p. 235) regard this assumption as unrealistic in two respects. First, certain parties (such as communist parties) may sometimes prefer to stay out of a coalition (even when invited to join); and, second, they argue that the assumption implies that minority coalitions will never form (of which Taylor and Laver counted 45 in their study of 132 West European governments). The treatment of minority coalitions, and also of non-minimal coalitions (with the exception of De Swaan's theory), is *ad hoc*.

Third, the policy scales that are used to differentiate between the ideologies of parties (often the conventional one-dimensional socio-economic 'Left-Right' scale [28)]) are also of a rather *ad hoc* nature, and - together with the ordering of the parties along the scales - are generally assumed to remain constant over time (see our fifth remark). Remarkably, on the whole, multi-dimensional models do not appear to be more successful than those based on a one-dimensional (socio-economic) continuum; see Taylor and Laver (1973, p. 228).

Fourth, political parties are treated as unitary actors: "all the individual parliamentary members of a party are assumed to have the same preferences amongst coalitions, and there is no 'overlapping' of parties in any of the ideological dimensions (so that one may speak of an ordering of the parties in each dimension)" [Taylor and Laver (1973, p. 233)] [29)].

Fifth, the theories are all static in the sense that: "Dynamical and historical considerations do not explicitly play a part. Each time a government leaves office, it is as if the slate were wiped clean: equilibrium coalitions are once again predicted to form, regardless of which governments had been in office previously" [Taylor and Laver (1973, p. 234)]. Neglected are the accumulated experiences of former collaborations, successful and unsuccessful.

Sixth, the fact that parties are organizations of voters, or people eligible to vote, is neglected. No reference is made to models of voting behaviour, which should - granted the previous statement - somewhere come into the picture. Cabinet formation and voting behaviour appear to have been totally separate research subjects up till now.

Finally, none of the theories explains which coalition will actually form the cabinet in case that the predicted set contains more than one coalition.

5.6.3. An Alternative Approach

We will now outline an alternative approach to political coalition formation. The following procedure will be followed:
First we determine the *attractiveness of a party* for another party. Then we determine the *attractiveness of a coalition* for a party. This is followed by the determination of the set of undominated coalitions that are equally likely to form: the *equilibrium set*. Finally, we compare our approach with the earlier mentioned theories of coalition formation.

The attractiveness of a party

Our approach to the determination of the attractiveness of a party for another party starts from the idea that, as voters can be considered to be the constituent parts of parties, this attractiveness should be related to their valuation of parties. More specifically, we speculate that the floating rate of voters from category k that float from party o_h to party o_i [see eq. (5.10)] indicates the attractiveness of o_i for this voter category k of party o_h, and that the attractiveness of o_i for o_h can be identified with a weighted average of the floating rates for different k, where the weights - denoted by λ_{ko_h} - indicate the relative strength with which the classes get their interests promoted by party o_h.
Formally, letting:

$Q_{ko_ho_i}(T)$ = attractiveness of party o_i for voters from social class k of party o_h at election date T,

$Q_{o_ho_i}(T)$ = attractiveness of party o_i for party o_h at T,

it is assumed that

$$(5.22) \quad Q_{ko_ho_i}(T) = \frac{\exp\,[V_{ko_ho_i}(T)]}{\Sigma_{j=1}^{I} \exp\,[V_{ko_ho_j}(T)]} \quad , \; 0 < Q_{ko_ho_i}(T) < 1,$$

and

$$(5.23) \quad Q_{o_ho_i}(T) = \Pi_k \, Q_{ko_ho_i}(T)^{\lambda_{ko_h}(T)} \quad , \; 0 < Q_{o_ho_i}(T) < 1$$

$$, \; \Sigma_{i=1}^{I} Q_{o_ho_i}(T) \leqq 1.$$

Recall that $V_k(T)$ - deleting party indices for notational convenience - denotes the party valuation of voters from category k, see eq. (5.7).

Further refinements may be obtained by allowing for the existence of party factions, of unequal power, which comprise voters from different categories [30].

The attractiveness of a coalition

The attractiveness of a coalition is assumed to depend on two factors:

a. the attractiveness of the parties that form the coalition;
b. the relative power of the parties within the coalition (based, e.g., on their share of parliamentary seats).

Let,

r = suffix to denote coalitions, $r = 1,..,R$; in total there are $2^I - 1$ non-empty coalitions (including single party coalitions) possible;

Δ_r = the set of parties in coalition r;

$Q_{ko_hr}(T)$ = attractiveness of coalition r for voter category k of party o_h at T;

$Q_{o_hr}(T)$ = attractiveness of coalition r for party o_h at T;

$y^r_{ko_i}(T)$ = relative importance (weight, power) imputed to party o_i in r by a voter of class k at T.

The following specifications are proposed, using eq. (5.22):

$$(5.24) \qquad Q_{ko_hr}(T) = \prod_{o_i \in \Delta_r} Q_{ko_ho_i}(T)^{y^r_{ko_i}(T)} \quad , \; 0 < Q_{ko_hr}(T) < 1,$$

$$(5.25) \qquad Q_{o_hr}(T) = \Pi_k\, Q_{ko_hr}(T)^{\lambda_{ko_h}(T)} \quad , \; 0 < Q_{o_hr}(T) < 1.$$

If $y^r_{ko_i}(T)$ is equal for all k then it also holds, using (5.23), that

$$(5.26) \qquad Q_{o_hr}(T) = \prod_{o_i \in \Delta_r} Q_{o_ho_i}(T)^{y^r_{ko_i}(T)}$$

By means of eq. (5.25) it is possible to determine a coalition attractiveness matrix with as typical element $Q_{o_h r}(T)$. The transpose of this matrix, labelled Q^r, reads:

$$(5.27) \qquad Q_r = \begin{bmatrix} Q_{o_1 1}(T) & \cdots & Q_{o_I 1}(T) \\ \vdots & & \vdots \\ Q_{o_1 R}(T) & \cdots & Q_{o_I R}(T) \end{bmatrix}.$$

The rows of this matrix show the attractiveness that is imputed by the parties to the coalitions which are represented by the row numbers.

The equilibrium set; an example

The equilibrium set was defined as the set of undominated coalitions. Recall that a coalition r is said to be undominated if there is no other coalition which is strictly preferred by all of its members to r. For the moment we make the usual assumption (see the second remark in the previous subsection) that parties are indifferent between coalitions that are non-winning or from which they are excluded, and - or at least - that they prefer to such coalitions any winning coalition of which they are a member. A coalition is winning if it satisfies a given majority criterion. The equilibrium set is found by selecting those row vectors of Q^r which represent coalitions that satisfy the majority criterion *and* for which there exists no other such vector with components that are all larger in value, neglecting the components that refer to parties that are not participating in the coalition considered.

Consider the following *example*. Suppose there are three parties: o_1, o_2 and o_3 (thus, $I = 3$). Let the distribution of the parliamentary seats be as follows: 20 for o_1, 40 for o_2 and 40 for o_3. In total there are 7 non-empty coalitions possible $(2^I - 1)$. By making the usual assumption that a simple majority enables a coalition to form the cabinet, the number of interesting coalitions is restricted to four (2^{I-1}); thus $r = 1,2,3,4$. The sets of parties that make up these coalitions are indicated by: $\Delta_1 = \{o_1, o_2\}$, $\Delta_2 = \{o_1, o_3\}$, $\Delta_3 = \{o_2, o_3\}$, $\Delta_4 = \{o_1, o_2, o_3\}$.
Let, furthermore, the relative power imputed by a voter to a party in a coalition be equal to the fraction of the total number of seats (represented by the coalition) that it controls, irrespective of the class that

the voter belongs to. Thus, for example, in coalition 2, in which the parties o_1 and o_3 participate,

$$y^2_{ko_1}(T) = 1/3 \qquad \text{and} \qquad y^2_{ko_3}(T) = 2/3 \quad , \text{ for all } k.$$

The assumption allows us to use eq. (5.26) for the determination of the elements of the matrix Q^r. As regards the attractiveness of the parties - appearing on the right-hand side of eq. (5.26) - it is assumed that

$$Q_{o_1o_1}(T) = 0.6, \qquad Q_{o_2o_1}(T) = 0.3, \qquad Q_{o_3o_1}(T) = 0.1,$$

$$Q_{o_1o_2}(T) = 0.3, \qquad Q_{o_2o_2}(T) = 0.5, \qquad Q_{o_3o_2}(T) = 0.1,$$

$$Q_{o_1o_3}(T) = 0.1, \qquad Q_{o_2o_3}(T) = 0.2, \qquad Q_{o_3o_3}(T) = 0.8.$$

Using eq. (5.26), the coalition attractiveness matrix is then easily determined:

$$Q^r = \begin{bmatrix} 0.38 & 0.42 & - \\ 0.18 & - & 0.40 \\ - & 0.32 & 0.28 \\ 0.22 & 0.31 & 0.23 \end{bmatrix} \begin{array}{l} \textit{Parties} \\ : \; o_1, o_2 \\ : \; o_1, o_3 \\ : \; o_2, o_3 \\ : \; o_1, o_2, o_3 \; . \end{array}$$

The empty cells of the matrix refer to non-participating parties, the attractiveness ratings of which can be neglected. For convenience, we have indicated the parties in each coalition behind the relevant rows of the matrix.

In this example, the equilibrium set appears to contain one coalition only, namely coalition 1, represented by the first row vector; it is the only undominated coalition. Thus, our prediction would be that the coalition made up by the parties o_1 and o_2 will form the cabinet.

Remarks

Comparing our approach with the earlier mentioned theories of coalition formation, we note the following.

1. By allowing for the possibility that parties do not only base their preferences for coalitions on size or (fixed) ideological considerations but also on the achievements of parties with respect to issues

that they are interested in and on their relative power within a coalition, our approach seems to contribute to a more general and more satisfactory explanatory theory of coalition formation. The equilibrium set need not differ from the one obtained from Closed Minimal Range theory. If there are substantial political distances (thresholds) between parties (see Subsections 5.4.2 and 5.4.3), such that the effects of these distances dominate the performance effect on the attractiveness of the parties - which, corrected for the power of parties within a coalition determines the attractiveness of coalitions - then it is quite possible that closed minimal range coalitions result (unless the power effect is important).

2. Although the approach is traditional in so far as it does not allow for minority coalitions to be predicted, it differs from other theories (with the exception of De Swaan's Policy Distance Minimization theory [31)]) in that there is nothing in the way of non-minimal coalitions to come out. As regards minority coalitions we would, furthermore, like to add the suggestion that the assumption that winning coalitions of which parties are a part are preferred to non-winning coalitions need not necessarily imply that minority coalitions will never form, as Taylor and Laver argue (see the second remark in the previous subsection). In our view, a quite plausible prediction would be that such a coalition will form in case of an empty equilibrium set, in which case there are no undominated majority coalitions. Under the aforementioned assumption the alternative prediction would seem to be that - in case of an empty equilibrium set - no coalitions will be formed [and not that the theory cannot make a prediction, as Taylor suggests; see Taylor (1972, p. 365)]. We will not further speculate here about the composition of minority coalitions.

3. In the light of our approach it is also interesting to reconsider the assumption that parties prefer coalitions of which they are a member to coalitions of which they are excluded. Once one admits that the political record of parties co-determines their attractiveness it cannot be ruled out - theoretically, at least - that a party comes to expect another party to be more successful in promoting its interests in a given situation than itself.
   For example, a conservative party might acknowledge the superiority of a labour party in handling situations of great social unrest. It is clear that the predicted set of coalitions may be altered if one allows for this change in assumptions. Consider again the example given in the previous subsection. When all the coalition attractiveness ratings are taken into account, the matrix Q^r reads:

$$Q^r = \begin{bmatrix} 0.38 & 0.42 & (0.10) \\ 0.18 & (0.23) & 0.40 \\ (0.17) & 0.32 & 0.28 \\ 0.22 & 0.31 & 0.23 \end{bmatrix},$$

where the figures between parentheses refer to parties excluded from the coalition considered. In this case parties do indeed prefer coalitions of which they are a member.

Suppose, however, that in our example:

$$Q_{o_2 o_2}(T) = 0.2 \qquad \text{and} \qquad Q_{o_2 o_3}(T) = 0.5;$$

then, the first two figures in the second column of Q^r change places, i.e., $Q_{o_2 1}(T) = 0.23$ and $Q_{o_2 2}(T) = (0.42)$. The new matrix reads:

$$Q^r = \begin{bmatrix} 0.38 & 0.23 & (0.10) \\ 0.18 & (0.42) & 0.40 \\ (0.17) & 0.32 & 0.28 \\ 0.22 & 0.31 & 0.23 \end{bmatrix}.$$

Now if we would make the usual assumption that membership of a coalition is preferred, we would neglect the attractiveness to party o_2 of the second coalition. In that case - as there is no undominated majority coalition - no coalition would be predicted to form. However, if the assumption is changed and we do permit that party o_2 has a positive valuation (equal to 0.42) of coalition 2, it seems that this coalition should be predicted to form. Although party o_1 would prefer coalition 1, it will not be able to persuade party o_2 - under the present assumptions at least - to join it (note that o_2 and o_3 prefer coalition 3 to 1).

4. Our approach is based on a radically different conception of parties. A party is not treated as a unitary actor but as an amalgam of different interests (although it allows for homogeneous parties as a special case). The presence of different interests typically leads to a divergent appreciation of coalitions by the factions of a party. Moreover, there may be an overlapping of parties in the sense that people with the same interests (belonging to the same class) may support different parties.

5. The approach is clearly dynamic; accumulated experience as well as changes in party constituences may play a crucial role.

6. Cabinet formation is no longer strictly seperated from voting behaviour. Recognizing that parties are organizations of voters, we dovetailed our model of coalition formation with the model of voting behaviour proposed in Section 5.4.

7. The approach shares the shortcoming of the other theories that it does not explain which coalition will actually form the cabinet in case that the equilibrium set contains more than one coalition. Additional assumptions would be required to narrow the set down. In the context of a politico-economic model, a non-unique prediction will imply that multiple, equally likely, time paths are predicted for the economy, dependent on the type of state that will turn up.

5.7. *The Behaviour of the State*

5.7.1. Introduction

By assumption, the state behaves in accordance with the constrained maximization of the complex interest function that is supposed for it to hold. Given the constraints and the instruments that are available to the state, the behaviour of the state directly follows from the specification of this function. The specification used in the previous chapter [see eq. (4.6)] was based on eq. (4.2); it reads,

$$P_s(t) = \Pi_k \, P_k(t)^{\lambda_{ks}(t)} \quad , \ \lambda_{ks}(t) \geq 0, \ \Sigma_k \, \lambda_{ks}(t) = 1,$$

where $P_k(t)$ indicates an elementary interest function (incorporating the interests of social class k), and $\lambda_{ks}(t)$ denotes the weight attached to $P_k(t)$ within the state organization. At that time we did not explicitly refer to the organizational structure of the state, and the position of bureaucrats and politicians (ministers and members of parliament) in it. However, as we are interested in this chapter in the impact of parties on the behaviour of the state, we should consider the particular position that the party representatives (the politicians) occupy within that organization. This will be done in Subsection 5.7.2. Suggestions are made for a more sophisticated state interest function. Subsection 5.7.3 shortly addresses the interrelationship between the political and economic sphere in an economy. The question is raised whether state sector workers take the effects into account of their policies on the political activities of private sector agents; and if so, in what way. A tentative answer to this question is given in Subsection 5.7.4. The discussion there will be centered around an important topic in the Public Choice Approach: the manipulation of voters by elected politicians.

5.7.2. The Interest Function of the State Revisited

The state comprises *government* and *bureaucracy*. Thus, notwithstanding all the difficulties we have already met in predicting what the government will look like *qua* party composition in case of a capitalist economy with elections, we have to proceed beyond that and face the problematic of the bureaucracy. In this context, a fruitful use can be made of the notion of a nested complex interest function (see Section 4.3.2). The decision-making structure of the state may be pictured by the interest tree shown in Fig. 5.4 (cf. Fig. 4.4).

There are two decision-making levels: the governmental level and the bureaucratic level. On the bureaucratic level (the second level) $P_{21}(t)..P_{2n}(t)$ denote the interest functions of the level specific interest blocs of the bureaucrats (think of the departments, for example). Each of these functions may, of course, in itself be a complex interest function, as further distinctions in interest blocs may have to be made and as, moreover, bureaucrats may have multiple positions (think of the so-called 'fifth power' of all sorts of committees of experts, etc.). On the governmental level (the top level) we find three interest functions. The first, indicated by $P_{11}(t)$, belongs to the representative interest bloc of the bureaucrats. This bloc is made up by the ministers as formal heads of the bureaucratic apparatuses. The second, $P_{12}(t)$, expresses the interests of ministers and members of parliament as politicians. Politi-

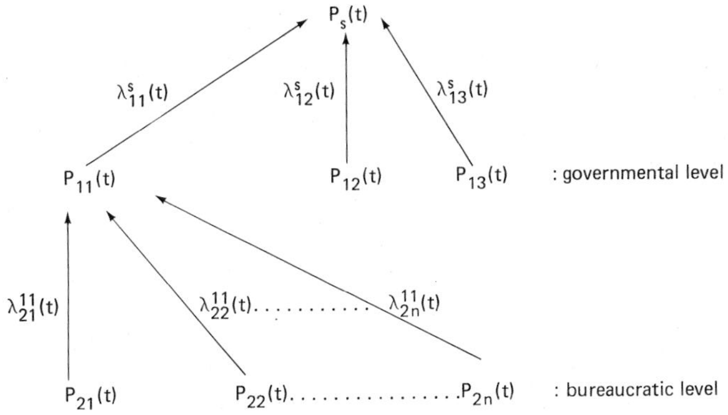

Fig. 5.4. A state interest tree.

cians are state sector workers just like bureaucrats; the main difference is that the position of politicians is politically, generally, less secure than that of bureaucrats, which is particularly apparent in political systems with elected politicians. Elected politicians do not only represent their own interests (shaped by their position in the state sector) and, in case of ministers, the interests of bureaucrats, they also represent the interests of political parties. To account for the latter aspect of their position, we inserted the interest function $P_{13}(t)$, which stands for the interests of the level specific interest bloc of the politicians as party representatives.
The functions $P_{12}(t)$ and $P_{13}(t)$ may be specified as nested interest functions comprising the complex interest functions of cabinet and parliament, if so desired.

Using the notation introduced in Subsection 4.3.2 in particular the eqs. (4.3) and (4.4), and assuming that there are no multiple positions, the following interest function for the state is obtained:

$$(5.28) \qquad P_s(t) = P_{11}(t)^{\lambda^s_{11}(t)} . P_{12}(t)^{\lambda^s_{12}(t)} . P_{13}(t)^{\lambda^s_{13}(t)}$$

$$, \lambda^s_{1i}(t) \geqq 0, \; i = 1,2,3, \; \Sigma_i \lambda^s_{1i}(t) = 1,$$

where:
$$P_{11}(t) = \Pi^n_{j=1} P_{2j}(t)^{\lambda^{11}_{2j}(t)} = \Pi^n_{j=1} P_{1,2j}(t)^{\lambda^{11}_{2j}(t)}$$

$$, \lambda^{11}_{2j} \geqq 0, \; \Sigma_j \lambda^{11}_{2j} = 1,$$

$$P_{12}(t) = P_{1,12}(t),$$

$$P_{13}(t) = \Pi^4_{k=1} P_{k,13}(t)^{\lambda_{k,13}(t)} \quad , \lambda_{k,13}(t) \geqq 0, \; \Sigma_k \lambda_{k,13}(t) = 1.$$

Recall that $\lambda^{h'i'}_{hi}$ denotes the relative strength with which the interests of interest bloc i on decision-making level h are represented by bloc i' on level h'; $P_{k,hi}$ denotes the elementary interest function for economic position k, as particularized for bloc i on level h, while $\lambda_{k,hi}$ denotes the weight attached to P_k within that bloc. Note that only if the particularized elementary interest functions $P_{k,hi}(t)$ - see Subsection 4.3.1 - are identical for all the interest blocs, and can be denoted by the elementary interest functions $P_k(t)$ (which means that class interests are represented, so that no particularization is needed), eq. (5.28) can be written in the simple form of eq. (4.2), i.e.,

$$P_s(t) = \Pi_k \; P_k(t)^{\lambda_{ks}(t)} ,$$

where, for example, $\lambda_{1s}(t) = \lambda^s_{11}(t) + \lambda^s_{12}(t) + \lambda_{1,13}(t).\lambda^s_{13}(t)$.

From eq. (5.28) it can be inferred that for the analysis of the impact of parties on the behaviour of the state one should not only know the type of government - i.e., the character and relative power of incumbent and opposing parties - in order to determine $P_{13}(t)$, but that one also should have knowledge of the room that party representatives (politicians) have to promote their own specific interests as state sector workers, represented by $P_{12}(t)$. That is, one should know the weights $\lambda^s_{12}(t)$ and $\lambda^s_{13}(t)$. Once that is settled, there remains the problem of what the relative power of the bureaucrats is *vis-à-vis* the politicians, as indicated by $\lambda^s_{11}(t)$. A very crude measure would be the ratio between the number of bureaucrats and the total number of state sector workers (bureaucrats and politicians), which - under the present circumstances - would generally imply that the bureaucrats control the state organization, i.e. $\lambda^s_{11} \approx 1$. An important factor here is also the frequency of government changes, as it is beyond doubt that the possession of information adds to the power of the bureaucrats. And recall in that context that bureaucrats are the monopolistic suppliers of quite a number of goods. Whatever one's judgement in these matters, to impute all the power to the politicians - although they may be formally vested with it - seems to be grossly wrong for most capitalist economies. We will return to the question of the estimation of the power weights in Section 5.9.

It may be noted here that the relative power of the bureaucrats *vis-à-vis* the politicians (the government) is something different than the relative power with which the interests of the bureaucrats are promoted within the state organization. Bureaucrats (as well as politicians, for that matter, but they are numerically much less important) generally have two entries in the state organizaton for their interests: one direct, namely their position within the state organization; and one indirect, to wit their representatives (politicians) in the government. Given the political participation rate of bureaucrats - some evidence suggests that state employees have the highest election turnout of any occupational group; see Bush and Denzau (1977) - this indirect way of getting their interests promoted increases in importance the larger the state size becomes. This opens up an interesting vista of a self-reinforcing process when combined with the hypothesis that bureaucrats are (primarily) interested in the growth of the state sector.

Given all the problems involved in the prediction of coalitions in case of

a multi-party system, and, on top of that, the fact that, with the present theories at least, one cannot be sure that the predicted set will contain only one coalition, it may be worthwile to consider alternative ways for the determination of the strength with which the different interests of parties are represented within the government. Here too, a crude measure would be the numerical strength (share of seats) of the parties.
It would be in line with Stigler's proposition that a party's political effectiveness is a more or less smoothly increasing function of its size [Stigler (1972, p. 99)]. Since there seems to be no equally simple alternative, such a measure should certainly deserve the attention of researchers.

5.7.3. A Complete Politico-Economic System

In this chapter we have been concerned with the relationship between economic conditions and voting behaviour, the relationship between voting behaviour and the size and class composition (structure) of parties, the relationship between the size and class composition of parties and the type of government, and the relation between type of government, bureaucracy and type of state.
If we add to these the earlier noticed relationship between type of state and bureaucracy (e.g., its size), and between type of state and economic conditions, then it follows that we have in fact gone through the following politico-economic system; see Fig. 5.5.
This circuit shows the contours of a complete politico-economic system. Such systems involve, of course, many more relationships. For example, economic conditions may be directly influenced through political participation (think of strikes; see Subsection 5.2.1); there may be a direct

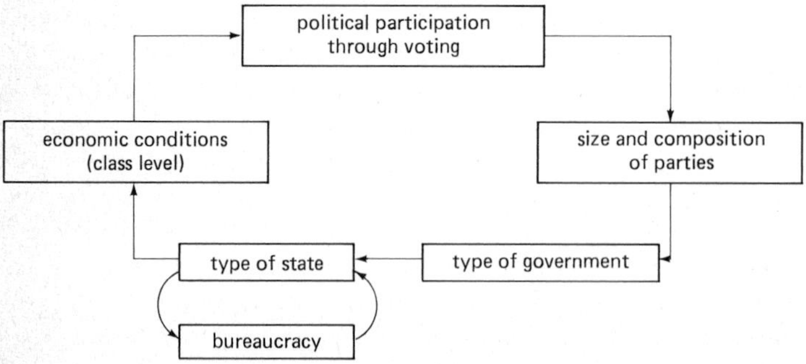

Fig. 5.5. A complete politico-economic system.

relationship between political participation and the type of state (e.g., if there are no parties, or in case of a *coup d'état*); the size of political parties may directly influence the forms and intensity of political participation (think of activist parties such as the communist); if we direct attention to the behaviour of the state, economic conditions clearly directly influence this behaviour; the type of state and its behaviour may directly influence the degree and nature of political participation (think of the suppression of political parties in dictatorial regimes). In short, there may be all sorts of loops and short-cuts in the circuit.

In the model that we developed in the previous chapter only the economic part of the politico-economic system was taken into account in the determination of the state's behaviour. We will now face the question whether state sector workers take the effects of their policies on the political activities of private sector agents into account as well; and if so, in what way.

5.7.4. On the Manipulation of Voters by Politicians

Although attention will be focused again on elections and voting in this subsection the discussion will, in our view, also be relevant for other forms of political participation.

The discussion will be centered around an important topic in the Public Choice Approach: the *manipulation of voters by politicians*, i.e. the deliberate playing upon the behaviour of voters by politicians for the furtherance of the interests represented by the latter. The reason why we did not go into this subject in Section 5.5 when we discussed the behaviour of political parties is that we preferred to elaborate upon the structure of the state organization first, and to indicate the position of politicians in it. Recall that politicians do not only represent the interests of their parties but also their own interests as state sector workers. Thus, politicians may not only want to manipulate voters for the benefit of the parties (voters) that they represent but also for their own benefit. Let us investigate the conditions for such manipulation within our theoretical framework.

From our point of view politicians will only manipulate voters if it contributes to the value of the interest function that is supposed for them to hold. We *first* concentrate on the case where politicians are under so much pressure from their party that they are unable to promote their own particular interests. Now recall that a party interest function - that politicians representing the party are supposed to maximize - is a weighted representation of the interests of the interest blocs in its constituency. Thus, in fact, we should focus upon the interest functions of these interest blocs. Consider the party interest function given by eq. (5.21):

$$P_{o_i}(t) = \Pi_k \, P_k(t)^{\lambda_{ko_i}(t)} ,$$

where, assuming an n-period time horizon [see eq. (4.1)],

$$P_k(t) = P_k[P_k^*(t), \ldots\ldots, P_k^*(t+n)],$$

$$P_k^*(t) = \bar{\bar{w}}_k(t)^{\varepsilon_{k1}} . e_k(t)^{\varepsilon_{k2}} . x_{sk}(t)^{\varepsilon_{k3}}$$

(recall that $\bar{\bar{w}}_k$ stands for average real disposable income, e_k for the fraction of the politically relevant population in economic position k, and x_{sk} for the average bundle of state goods available to agents in position k). In this case four interest blocs are distinguished, denoted by k. The question then becomes, how does the manipulation of voters by politicians representing o_i fit into the maximization of the interest function $P_k(t)$ of the interest bloc denoted by k?

Before answering this question we reproduce the nested state interest function given by eq. (5.28):

$$P_s(t) = P_{11}(t)^{\lambda^s_{11}(t)} . P_{12}(t)^{\lambda^s_{12}(t)} . P_{13}(t)^{\lambda^s_{13}(t)} .$$

In our case $\lambda^s_{12}(t) = 0$ as the politicians, by assumption, fully adhere to the party line [recall that $P_{11}(t)$ indicates the interest function of the representative interest bloc of the bureaucrats, $P_{12}(t)$ the interest function of the interest bloc of the politicians as state sector workers, and $P_{13}(t)$ the interest function of the interest bloc of the politicians as party representatives]. For $P_{13}(t)$ we may write

$$(5.29) \qquad P_{13}(t) = \Pi^I_{i=1} \, P_{o_i}(t)^{\lambda_{o_ig}(t)} , \quad \lambda_{o_ig}(t) \geq 0, \; \Sigma_i \, \lambda_{o_ig}(t) = 1,$$

where the suffix g stands for government; thus, $P_{13}(t)$ is a weighted representation of the party interest functions, the weights reflecting the relative strength with which the interests of the parties are represented within the government (cabinet and parliament).

Now, to return to our question, the manipulation of voters is, potentially, interesting as one may expect that some positive relationship exists between on the one hand,

$$\lambda_{ko_i}(t) \qquad \text{and} \qquad E_{ko_i}(T_t)/E_{o_i}(T_t)$$

- where T_t indicates the election date starting the election term in which period t occurs, and the right-hand expression denotes the number of voters from class k that voted for o_i at T_t as a fraction of o_i's constituency - and, on the other hand

$$\lambda_{o_ig}(t) \qquad \text{and} \qquad E_{o_i}(T_t)/\Sigma_i E_{o_i}(T_t)$$

(see also Section 5.9, point 5). These relationships entail that by winning voters of its own kind the interest bloc in o_i representing the interests of social class k, simultaneously, enhances, *ceteris paribus*, its internal and external power, the latter with respect to the government. An increase in the vote for party o_i coming from other social classes is interesting for that bloc in so far as its external power is considered, but detrimental to its internal power (see Subsection 5.5.2). In considering support for the winning of such votes the interest bloc would, consequently, have to face a trade-off in this respect.

Our conclusion is that an interest bloc of a party should have some - at least, intuitive - notion of the nature of the state interest function and of the aforementioned relationships between power weights and votes. The latter will be much more difficult to figure out in case of a multi-party system; that is, if the strength of parties is not supposed to be proportional to their relative size and a substantial difference in strength between incumbent and opposing parties is assumed to exist.

Given such notions the interest bloc might consider a change in the presentation of its interests in the party so that the importance that it attaches to the relative size of its own constituency within the party and the relative size of its party within the government will manifest itself in the interest functions of the party and the state. It might turn out that we would have to substitute a new function, indicated by $P_k'(t)$, for $P_k(t)$, so that

$$(5.30) \qquad P_{o_i}(t) = \Pi_k \, P_k'(t)^{\lambda_{ko_i}(t)} ,$$

where, for example,

$$(5.31)\quad P_k'(t) = P_k'\Big[e_{ko_i}(T_t)^{\lambda_{1ko_i}(t)} . e_{o_i}(T_t)^{\lambda_{2ko_i}(t)} . P_k^*(t)^{\lambda_{3ko_i}(t)}, \ldots,$$

$$e_{ko_i}(T_{t+n})^{\lambda_{1ko_i}(t+n)} . e_{o_i}(T_{t+n})^{\lambda_{2ko_i}(t+n)} . P_k^*(t+n)^{\lambda_{3ko_i}(t+n)}\Big]$$

$$, \lambda_{jko_i}(t) \geqq 0, \; j = 1,2,3, \; \Sigma_j \lambda_{jko_i}(t) = 1,$$

with,

$$e_{ko_i}(T_t) = E_{ko_i}(T_t)/E_{o_i}(T_t) \quad \text{and} \quad e_{o_i}(T_t) = E_{o_i}(T_t)/\Sigma_i E_{o_i}(T_t).$$

The weights in eq. (5.31) should be such that the interest function $P_k(t)$ of our interest bloc is maximized by the policies of the state, taking into account the relative strength with which $P_k'(t)$ will be represented within the state organization [see eqs. (5.28)-(5.30)]. They will be dependent on the time horizon of the interest bloc, and on its expectations with respect to the way that voters will react on the policies of the state. They should be zero, for example, if no systematic influence of state policies is expected by the interest bloc. They should also be zero for the periods extending up to the next election, as the vote shares are fixed from the last election onwards until the next election.

Within our theoretical framework, the interest bloc - given a sufficiently long time horizon - should have some (intuitive) notion of the constituent elements of eq. (5.20) which shows the total vote for party o_i coming from social class k at election T; it reads,

$$E_{ko_i}(T) = \Sigma_{j=0}^{I} f_{ko_j o_i}(T).[1 - \Gamma_{ko_j}(T)].E_{ko_j}'(T),$$

where f(T) - omitting subscripts for notational convenience - indicates the floating rate function given by eq. (5.10), $\Gamma(T)$ the abstention rate function given by eq. (5.15), and $E'(T)$ denotes the economic position (at T) and the previous party choice of voters. It should be clear from the specification of f(T) and $\Gamma(T)$ that party platforms would also be affected in case of manipulation of voters by politicians.

Now, even neglecting the additional complications that arise from the consideration of the relationship between votes and parliamentary seats (the latter are more important for the relative power of parties within the government), and from the consideration of the behaviour of other parties as well as other interest blocs within the party itself, it appears to us that the level of sophistication demanded from interest blocs and their representatives (the politicians) to behave in the indicated strategic way *vis-à-vis* other parties and voters is *unrealistic* (given also the lack of well-established theories in this field). In our view, the neglect of such strategic behaviour in politico-economic models is permitted, *in general*. At any rate, the fine tuning policies of the kind employed by the Nordhaus and MacRae models on political business cycles seem to be too simplistic [see Nordhaus (1975), MacRae (1977)].

Two cases in which politicians may reckon with the reaction of voters will be considered. Both cases involve a two-party system.
The *first* case occurs when an incumbent party in a two-party system - with politicians fully adhering to the party line and a subservient bureaucracy - expects a substantial loss of power within the government by loosing the election (which occurs when a party's strength within the government would not be proportional to its relative size but largely dependent on being incumbent or not). In that case it may be expected that state policies will be adjusted *when* a party's incumbency becomes endangered.
The *second* case occurs when the incumbent politicians of a party occupy a very strong position within their party as well as within the state organization, so that they can almost be sure of being renominated by their party, and are able to substantially influence the policies of the state. Since politicians as state sector workers (recall that multiple positions are neglected) are interested in political survival, it can then be anticipated that they will keep an eye on the expected vote share of their party, and that they will try to improve it when their party's victory (and, consequently, their re-election) is thought to be in danger.
In those cases the party interest function (see above) might be substituted by

(5.32)

$$P'_{o_i}(t) = \{\exp [-(\tilde{e}_{o_i}(T_t+1) - e^*_{o_i}(T_t+1))^2]\}^{\lambda_{1o_i}(t)} . \{P_{o_i}(t)\}^{1 - \lambda_{1o_i}(t)}$$

$$, \ 0 \leqq \lambda_{1o_i}(t) \leqq 1,$$

where T_t+1 denotes the first election date after period t (recall that T = 1,2,...), and e^* denotes a target vote share. The value of the weight λ can be expected to depend on the nearness of an election and on $e \gtreqless e^*$. Note that through the trade-off with the party interest function (unless λ = 1) the interests of the interest blocs within the incumbent party will have an impact on the policies chosen to secure re-election; re-election is desired, but not at all costs, where the costs to the different interest blocs may be differentially weighted dependent on the relative power

of those blocs within the party [32].
As regards the platforms of the parties we would speculate, in line with our discussion in Subsection 5.5.3, that they follow from the constrained maximization of (5.32), where now not only a party's perception of the structure of the economy but also its perception of the relationship determining the expected vote share will play a part.
In the present context it should, finally, be noted that some evidence exists suggesting that politicians indeed try to raise their popularity when it drops below some critical level, but are otherwise interested in other goals [see Frey and Schneider (1978a,b)].

5.8. Other Forms of Political Action, A Measure of Political Support of the State

In so far as political activities originating from the private sector are concerned our main interest up to now has been in the different aspects of voting. As we stated before, however, voting is just one form of political action, that, moreover, need not be possible in a capitalist economy. In this subsection some other forms of political action - political strikes, political demonstrations, the formation of new political parties, and revolutions - are broadly discussed (see further, Chapter 7). The discussion will be centred around a measure of political support of the state.

We will first make some remarks, however, on an important topic in political science: *political stability*. Political activities were defined as activities - by individual or collective agents - that affect or are intended to affect the behaviour of the state. Note that the absence of changes in state behaviour and the type of state - in which case one might speak of political stability - does not imply the absence of political activities. On the contrary, a type of state and its behaviour are the complex outcome of the political activities of the agents (citizens) that make up the polity. Some activities may counteract others. Activities may support a type of state (behaviour). The state may be able to counteract any assault on its existence by means of repression and coercion. The study of political stability is much more difficult, therefore, than the analysis of a single political activity or category of activities. It is not surprising to find that its causes are still subject to much dispute in political science [see Castles (1974)]. The more promising research direction seems to be to trace out first the causes and consequences - *ceteris paribus* - of separate (categories) of political activities, in the way that has been done with respect to electoral behaviour (voting, voter turnout, party behaviour in the context of elections, coalition formation). What we plan to do in this subsection is to present some ideas that might be useful in that context, and which are inspired by the way we have approached political phenomena so far. Our starting point is eq. (5.20). This equation shows the total number of votes from people in position k for party o_i as a function of the floating rates, the abstention rates, and the previous vote choice. We will now adapt it to a more general political context. Suppose there are I ($\geqq$ 1) identifiable political groups (cliques, parties, or whatever) in the economy, of which there are J, $1 \leqq J \leqq I$, incumbent. Without loss of generality these incumbent groups can be denoted by $o_1, \ldots, o_J$. Suppose, furthermore, that the incumbent groups are held responsible for the extent to which the interests of people are realized (the responsibility hypothesis). The following *measures of political support* can then be specified. As a measure of political support of the incumbent group o_j by people in economic position k may serve the following variable $\Omega_{ko_j}(t)$, specified as

$$(5.33) \qquad \Omega_{ko_j}(t) = \sum_{h=0}^{I} f_{ko_h o_j}(t).[1 - \Gamma_{ko_h}(t)].E'_{ko_h}(t)/E_k(t)$$

$$, \quad 0 \leqq \Omega_{ko_j}(t) \leqq 1.$$

The floating rates and abstention rates may be considered to indicate what people would do in case of (non-manipulated) elections in period t, irrespective of whether there are indeed elections or not in the economy considered. With some adjustments of the terminology, the procedure developed in Section 5.4 to determine these rates for elections can be applied in case of no elections as well. For example,

$E'_{ko_h}(t)$ = the number of people in economic position k, as measured just before the determination of the degree of political support in period t, that backed the political group o_h at the time of the previous determination.

The size of the, politically relevant, population is again taken to equal the size of the total labour force E. The overall support of the incumbent group o_j is specified as

$$(5.34) \qquad \Omega_{o_j}(t) = \Sigma_k\, \Omega_{ko_j}(t).E_k(t)/E(t) \qquad , \quad 0 \leqq \Omega_{o_j}(t) \leqq 1,$$

based on the support given by the different classes in the economy, weighted by the numerical shares of the classes in the population. The class specific support of the state is given by

$$(5.35) \qquad \Omega_{ks}(t) = \sum_{j=1}^{J} \Omega_{ko_j}(t) \qquad , \quad 0 \leqq \Omega_{ks}(t) \leqq 1.$$

Total support for the state equals

$$(5.36) \quad \Omega_s(t) = \sum_{j=1}^{J} \Omega_{o_j}(t) \qquad , \ 0 \leqq \Omega_s(t) \leqq 1.$$

Remarks

1. First note with respect to the total support measures, eqs. (5.34) and (5.36), that apart from numerical strength all the political groups are equally *weighted*. This may be realistic in case of one-man-one-vote elections, but even then some (groups) of people will generally be considered by the political groups to be more important than others because of wealth or control of (or share in) production [33]. Moreover, in case of more than one incumbent group it may be necessary to introduce some weighting factor to express the importance (power) of the different groups in order to arrive at a satisfactory overall measure $\Omega_s(t)$; to that purpose one might use the relative number of ministries held, or the seat share, for example. Note, furthermore, that the measures, which are defined here on a macro-level, may also be useful for subcentral levels, provided that the appropriate particularizations are made [34].

2. The measures refer to the behaviour of *two sorts of people*: the floating rates f(t) - deleting subscripts for convenience - refer to people who do care about what the different existing political groups do, the abstention rates $\Gamma(t)$ refer to people that do not (or no longer) care about what these groups do. From eq. (5.15) it can be observed that the latter category no longer bothers either because all groups are rated equally good or bad as regards the promotion of its interests [$\sigma(t)^2 = 0$; indifference], or because the average achievement of the groups is so satisfactory that one looses interest [$\mu(t)$ has a large positive value; positive alienation], or because the achievements are so bad that people do not consider their interests to be properly represented [$\mu(t)$ has a large negative value; negative alienation].

3. A *100 percent support* can only be obtained by the state when there is no opposition (and no abstention); which may only be conceived of in a situation of national emergency in which case all political groups share in the government. In that case

$$\Omega_s(t) = 1, \qquad \text{while} \qquad \Omega_{o_j}(t) = 1 \quad \text{if} \quad J = I = 1.$$

Otherwise, as $f(t) < 1$ [see (5.3)], there are always people opting for the opposition, although this may be a negligible number in extreme cases. A situation of *no political support* at all can only occur if $\Gamma(t) = 1$ for all k, which means that no one is interested in what political groups are doing. If, moreover, $\Gamma(t) = 1$ for all groups, then there is absolutely no support for the state. In that case

$$\Omega_{ko_j}(t) = \Omega_{o_j}(t) = \Omega_{ks}(t) = \Omega_s(t) = 0.$$

This can only happen if there is complete indifference $[\sigma(t)^2 = 0$ for all k; see eq. (5.15)]; alienation is not sufficient. Both of these extreme situations are highly unlikely, of course. Even in political systems with one (official) party there are other collectivities, like unions, that may function as political groups to which people refer.

4. Let us focus upon low as well as high values of $\Omega_s(t)$, and consider such political phenomena as revolutions, the formation of new political groups, riots (against the government), political demonstrations, and political strikes.

It seems that voting in elections is the only political activity of the aforementioned that is compatible with *large values of* $\Omega_s(t)$. It is quite possible that people are neither indifferent nor alienated [i.e., $\Gamma(t)$ is small; see eq. (5.15)] as regards the performance of the existing political groups and massively support the incumbents because of their - relative - success in the promotion of interests. The other political activities are unlikely to occur under such circumstances, except for the formation of new parties (see 6).

Small values of $\Omega_s(t)$ are more likely to produce those activities. However, one has to be careful here. Consider the following situations.
- $\Gamma(t)$ *is small*, for all k,h. In that case people are neither strongly alienated nor indifferent with respect to the existing political system. In response to the relatively bad performance of the incumbents they choose sides with opposing political groups. Typical forms of political activity in this case should be demonstrations, strikes, and voting if there are elections. Demonstrations and strikes are probably rather easily organized since one can fall back on the organizational apparatuses of the political groups.
- $\Gamma(t)$ *is large*, $\mu(t) >> \bar{\bar{y}}$, for all k,h. Under these circumstances of positive alienation - and the more so the higher the value of $\mu(t)$ - political activities are least to be expected. A lack of support does not per se lead to uprisings, therefore, and need not be disquieting to the incumbents. However, under certain conditions such a situation may, nevertheless, be politically unstable, and new political groups may be formed (see 6) [35].

- $\Gamma(t)$ *is large*, $\mu(t) \ll \bar{\bar{\gamma}}$, for all k,h. In this case of negative alienation, activities are to be expected. However, as people have turned their backs to the existing political groups, organized political manifestations such as large scale demonstrations and strikes are less likely to occur whenever the degree of alienation is small. Riots, spontaneous protest meetings, and so on, are the most probable (initially). The larger the absolute value of $\mu(t)$ grows, the easier it will be to overcome the usual problems of organization that may be aggravated by the use of coercion from the side of the state, or even from the side of the opposition as both sides have a stake in the existing political system. Under those circumstances the formation of new political groups, large scale demonstrations and strikes, and even revolutions may happen.

Notice that as the party valuation variable V(t) - see eqs. (5.4) through (5.7) - and, thus, $\mu(t)$ is related to *changes* in the values of the variables representing the interests of people, and not to the *levels* of these variables, a state of poverty as such need not be sufficient for political action, according to our model. On the other hand, in case of prosperity, a decline in the growth rate of income or employment may be sufficient.

5. It is clear that the political support measure may differ in value for different *economic positions* k. It follows that some activities may be restricted so some k at a particular time. For example, capitalists may fully support a type of state that is perceived to promote their interests, and may, therefore, stick to voting at regular intervals, while workers may judge that their interests are completely neglected by the existing political groups, and may, consequently, abstain from voting and rely on protest meetings, strikes, or the formation of a new party, in order to get their interests represented. Whenever such activities directed against the state become influential, they may evoke counteractions in support of the state from those that gain from the present situation. In this context, it may be speculated that compulsory voting will particulary be espoused by political parties that expect to be favoured by voter categories that abstain not because they are indifferent, but because they are alienated.

6. Let us now take a closer view of the political phenomena of revolutions and the formation of new political groups. To start with *new political groups*, we would suggest that - taking the problem of organization into account - such groups are likely to arise: (1) if all existing groups are perceived to perform highly unsatisfactory, $\mu(t) \ll \bar{\bar{\gamma}}$; (2) in case of a more or less stationary situation when the expected interest real-

ization ratings, $\tilde{Z}(t)$, are approximately zero; people are then probably easily inclined to give new groups (e.g., parties) with promising platforms the benefit of the doubt (reliability); (3) when the achievements of some group(s) are strongly negatively valuated while the political distance to the other group(s) is too large (in case of parties, this is when 'transition parties' occur) [36]. The third case is compatible with high as well as low values of the political support measures, depending on who the incumbents are. The character, or ideology, of the new group of course depends on the category and number of people that are ready for a new choice, and on the category of people that have the resources available to get a new group organized. Notice that when new political groups get no opportunity - through participation in an incumbency or identifiable action - to actually show what their platforms and propaganda are worth, the reliability of their proposed policies may be expected to dwindle (i.e., the weight $\hat{c}$ will probably decline, see Subsection 5.4.2), and so their attractiveness to voters. This may be an important reason for the observed *withering away* of third parties [see Mazmanian (1974, p. 143)]. The demise of such parties is also to be expected in case they function as transition parties.

7. A *revolution* may be defined as an overthrow of the type of state which is initiated or actively supported by people from outside the state sector, and which is accompanied by (threat of) violence. There seems to be no generally accepted definition; see Freeman (1972). In our view revolutions are relatively most likely to occur if $\mu(t) \ll \bar{\bar{\gamma}}$, where it is, again, important to recall that the average valuation of the achievements of the existing political groups is based on changes in interest function values and not on the levels of these values. Whereas new political groups may be formed in prosperous times, revolutions seem to be typically tied to (strongly) worsening conditions [37]. Theories of revolution commonly employ a basic 'fed up' concept [38], as well as some notion that the government must be blamed for this [cf. our responsibility hypothesis; see Freeman (1972, p. 356)]. However, these conditions are not sufficient for a revolution to take place. A serious problem may be to find people willing to actively support the cause with all its inherent risks of injury. Since the contribution of an ordinary revolutionary to the course of the revolution is typically infinitesimal (objectively), we meet the same (free-rider) problem here as was encountered in the explanation of voting behaviour (see Subsection 5.2.1). This problem will be all the more serious if the existing political groups are all rejected by the discontented, so that the organization of the revolution cannot be facilitated by the use of the apparatuses of already existing political organizations. Nevertheless, history shows that this problem can be overcome. Arguments similar to

those used to explain the voter's paradox can be employed here to explain the revolutionary's paradox; the reader is referred to Subsection 5.2.1 for those arguments [39].

We would like to add here, finally, that - although necessary - the 'seizure of state power' through a revolution (or via electoral success, for that matter) is not in itself sufficient for the carrying through of such *far-reaching changes in the economy* as the change from basically private ownership to basically collective or state ownership of the means of production.
First, the realization of such changes takes time, which means that the time horizon of the new politicians as well as of their supporters should be long enough in order to persevere and to accept some delay in the improvement of their situation; in addition, future results should not be discounted too much [see eqs. (5.4)-(5.7)]. Some direct improvements - e.g., the distribution of land, or wage rate increases - will be expedient, but have to be repeated as (according to our approach) one-time improvements may be expected to loose their effect, even if the improvement is permanent.
Second, activities, such as the withdrawal of bank accounts or the slowdown of investment, by those that are (or anticipate to be) negatively affected may seriously increase the degree of structural coercion and pressure on the state, so that even one-time improvements are out of the question; important in this respect is, of course, the position of the revolutionaries with respect to production in the economy.
Third, the new politicians will have to deal with the bureaucracy (judiciary, army, police, etc.). If the interests of the politicians run counter to the interests of the bureaucrats then it may be necessary to follow Marx' and Engels' advice to 'smash the state-apparatus' in order to get the planned policies carried out. However, the necessity (given the aforementioned points) to keep the economy going may force the politicians to refrain from this, as Lenin's experience has shown [see Emmanuel (1979, pp. 126-129)]. All in all, the conditions for the success of a revolution and the effectuation of a revolutionary political platform make it less surprising why the rise of democracy with (more or less) universal suffrage in capitalist economies has not led to the establishment of socialist planned economies. Far-reaching changes in the relations of production by means of political action demand an extraordinary situation [40].

5.9. *On the Empirical Determination of the Values of Some Important Parameters*

Central to the previous and present chapter has been the view that the actions of individual as well as collective agents in both the political and the economic sphere of an economy are related to interests of those agents, and that these interests are themselves related to the agents' positions with respect to production in the economy. The three types of interests that were attached to each of the four basic positions distinguished were incorporated into so-called elementary interest functions P_k for the determination of the actions of individual agents [see eq. (4.1)]. In these functions the parameters ε_{kg} ($k = 1,2,3,4$; $g = 1,2,3$) expressed the relative importance of interest g for an agent in position k. For the determination of the behaviour of collective agents (collectivities), which may, in principle, be made up by individual agents from any of the four basic positions, the elementary interest functions were incorporated into so-called complex interest functions [see eq. (4.2)]. In these functions the weight λ_{kc} denoted the relative importance of the elementary interest function P_k. The interest functions have been applied to determine the actions of firms and workers, and of political agents such as voters, political parties, and the state. Apart from ε_{kg} and λ_{kc} some other symbols played an important role in the political sphere, namely the weights c, $\bar{c}$, $\hat{c}$, $\hat{\bar{c}}$ (where subscripts and time indices are omitted, for ease of notation) and the sensitivity parameters a,b in the party valuation V and the so-called floating rate functions f, and the parameters γ, $\bar{\gamma}$, $\bar{\bar{\gamma}}$, $\bar{\bar{\bar{\gamma}}}$ - together with the aforementioned parameters - in the function determining the abstention rate Γ.

Now, although it is not the right place here to go into the very details of an empirical determination of the values of these parameters, we think it important to roughly indicate some ways along which one might go.

1. Let us first consider the interest function parameters ε_{kg}, the party valuation parameters a,b, and the weights c, $\bar{c}$, $\hat{c}$, $\hat{\bar{c}}$, as they appear in the eqs. (5.4)-(5.7), which were used to determine the behaviour of voters. Assume the following:
   a. there are two parties: o_1 and o_2;
   b. the perceived political distance between the parties and the party performance sensitivity show no variance over parties:

$$a_{ko_ho_i} = a_k \; (a_{ko_ho_h} = a_{ko_io_i} = 0), \; b_{ko_ho_i} = b_k, \quad h,i = 1,2;$$

   c. only the last two incumbencies (where an incumbency may cover more than one election term) are maximally considered by voters: $m = 2,3$;

d. party o_i (i equals 1 or 2) is dominant when m = 2 and opposing when m = 3;

e. the weights attached to incumbencies equal:

$$\bar{c}_{ko_i}(t_2) = 1, \qquad \hat{\bar{c}}_{ko_h}(t_2) = \hat{o}, \qquad \bar{c}_{ko_h}(t_3) = (1 + o)^{-n_2},$$

$$\hat{\bar{c}}_{ko_i}(t_3) = \hat{o}(1 + o)^{-n_2},$$

where o and $\hat{o}$ are discount rates and n_2 denotes the number of periods covered by incumbency 2 (the present incumbency);

f. the weight attached to a given period of an incumbency (the first, second, and so on) is equal for both parties and for both incumbencies; only some finite number n of such periods attain a positive weight, where n does not exceed the length of the incumbency of shortest duration (recall that n_m denotes the total number of periods of incumbency m):

$$c_{ko_h}(t) = c_{ko_i}(t) = \hat{c}_{ko_h}(t) = \hat{c}_{ko_i}(t), \text{ to be denoted by } c_k(t),$$

$$c_k(t_m\text{-}f+1) = 0 \text{ for } f > n,\ n \leq \min_m n_m,$$

$$c_k(t_m\text{-}f+1) = (1 + o)^{1 - f}/\Sigma_{f=1}^{n}(1 + o)^{1 - f} \qquad , f = 1,..n;$$

g. the interest function of each voter category covers one period, so that $P_k(t) = P_k^*(t)$.

Putting a random disturbance term, $\bar{\zeta}(T)$, in eq. (5.10), the following logit form of regression equation is obtained:

$$(5.37) \qquad ln\left[\frac{f_{ko_ho_i}(T)}{1 - f_{ko_ho_i}(T)}\right] = \underline{u}(T).\underline{v} + \bar{\zeta}(T) \ ,$$

where $\underline{u}(T)$ is a $1 \times (1 + 12n)$ vector comprising a constant term variable and variables representing for given k the (actual and promised) relative changes in average real disposable income, the fraction of the population in position k, and the average bundle of state goods that is available during the two incumbencies considered; $\underline{v}$ is a $(1 + 12n) \times 1$ vector comprising the coefficients to be estimated [41]. The regression coefficients contain 7 parameters which are to be identified: a_k, b_k, ε_{k1}, ε_{k2}, ε_{k3}, o and $\hat{o}$ (for the latter two, see assumptions e and f). Using election data the values of these parameters can be estimated if a restriction is laid on a_k, b_k or ε_{kg} (e.g., $\Sigma_g \varepsilon_{kg} = 1$).

The requirement of a sufficient number of observations may be an important constraint on the estimability of the parameters. Troublesome in this respect is probably not so much the fact that we need information on the economic position and vote decision of the voters - with present day election polls this seems to be feasible - as well the number of elections on which information is available, the imputation of the consumption of state goods and the application of party platforms [42]. It should be noticed in this context that observations on the floating rates

$$f_{ko_h o_i}(T) \quad \text{and} \quad f_{ko_i o_h}(T)$$

can be pooled if the perceptions of the voters of both parties regarding the values of the parameters and variables can be assumed to be the same. This was in fact assumed for the regression example given above. It is easily checked that in order to obtain the regression equation for the remaining floating rates one should only adjust the signs of the components of the vector $\underline{v}$.

Estimation is not restricted to two-party systems. The values of the parameters can, in principle, also be determined in case of more than two parties.

2. Although the parameters discussed under the previous point also appear in the abstention rate function [see eq. (5.15)] through the mean and variance of the party valuations, it is clear from the way that these parameters appear in that function that their estimation from that equation would be much more complicated. The estimation of the values of the remaining parameters in (5.15) - γ_k, $\bar{\gamma}_k$, $\bar{\bar{\gamma}}_k$, and $\bar{\bar{\bar{\gamma}}}_k$ (omitting the party index) - becomes straightforward if we use the estimates from the floating rate function to obtain estimates of $\mu_k(T)$ and $\sigma_k(T)$, which will be denoted bij $\overset{o}{\mu}_k(T)$ and $\overset{o}{\sigma}_k(T)$, respectively. Define:

$$\beta_0 \equiv - \ln \gamma_{ko_h} + \bar{\bar{\gamma}}^2_{ko_h}/\bar{\bar{\bar{\gamma}}}_{ko_h} \quad , \quad \beta_2 \equiv - 2\bar{\bar{\gamma}}_{ko_h}/\bar{\bar{\bar{\gamma}}}_{ko_h} ,$$

$$\beta_1 \equiv - \bar{\gamma}_{ko_h} \quad , \quad \beta_3 \equiv 1/\bar{\bar{\bar{\gamma}}}_{ko_h} .$$

From eq. (5.15) - adding a disturbance term $\xi(T)$ - the following logit form of regression equation is then obtained:

(5.38)

$$ln\left[\frac{\Gamma_{ko_h}(T)}{\Gamma^{+}_{ko_h}(T) - \Gamma_{ko_h}(T)}\right] = \beta_0 + \beta_1 ln\overset{o}{\sigma}_{ko_h}(T)^2 + \beta_2\overset{o}{\mu}_{ko_h}(T) + \beta_3\overset{o}{\mu}_{ko_h}(T)^2 + \bar{\xi}(T$$

where, given the maximum abstention rate, all the parameters can be identified.

3. Having estimates of the parameters appearing in the floating rate functions and abstention rate functions, it would be possible to obtain estimates of the variables indicating for a party the attractiveness of other parties and of party coalitions [given estimates of the weights λ (see 5) and y^r in eqs. (5.22)-(5.26)], by means of which the equilibrium set of coalitions - comprising party coalitions that are equally likely to form - can be determined. It would, in addition, be possible to obtain estimates of the measures of political support [see eqs. (5.33)-(5.36)].

4. What to do if there are no elections? In that case one should look for other forms of expression of political attitudes, such as changes in the membership of political organizations, the attendance of political meetings, the frequency and scale of political strikes. Interviews might be useful for the determination of the parameters ε_{kg} in the elementary interest functions.
   It may be expected that the more a political regime is based on coercion the more difficult it will be to determine political attitudes. It will be hard then for a government under such a regime to get reliable estimates of its political support, for example.

5. We conclude this section with some remarks on the empirical determination of the values λ_{kc}, denoting the relative strength or power with which the interests of people in economic position k are represented by collectivity c. Some knowledge of the literature on the concept and measurement of social power suffices to know that intricate, as well as ideologically delicate, problems are involved her [43].

   Sociologists and political scientists have, roughly, followed four methodological approaches to the measurement problem [see Mokken and Stokman (1976)]:
   a. the *reputational method*, which is based on the asking of 'experts' to rate the power of agents;
   b. the *positional method*, which is based on the detection of critical or central (formal) positions in decision-making structures (under this approach one is, e.g., interested in the existence of inter-

locking directorates);

c. the *decision method*, which is based on the detection of the extent to which agents actively participate in the realization of particular, concrete, decisions:

d. the *method of policy analysis*, which consists in the analysis of policy outcomes in order to find out to what different extent agents benefit from the policies considered.

Econometricians employ some methods for the determination of the value of preference function parameters which also deserve our attention; two methods are particularly used:

e. the *(imaginary) interview method* [see Johansen (1974) ,Van der Geest (1977); for applications to governments and political parties, see Van Eijk and Sandee (1959), Merkies and Nijman (1980)];

f. the *revealed preference method*, in which case one tries to determine the values of the parameters of the (assumed) preference function of an agent from actual policy outcomes, where the latter are supposed to coincide with the optimal outcomes assumedly aimed at by the agents [see, e.g., Phlips (1974) for applications to consumption analysis; for applications to government decision making, see Friedlaender (1973), Hordijk, Mastenbroek, and Paelinck (1976), Nijkamp and Somermeyer (1971), Reuber (1964)].

Although studies employing these last two methods for the determination of the values of the preference function parameters of collectivities, such as governments or political parties, do not explicitly refer to power differences between agents making up these collectivities, these methods may nevertheless be useful in case one wants to explicitly take into account such differences (see below). The aforementioned methods can be categorized according to the kind of information that thay use: opinions (a, e), actual (non-verbal) behaviour (c, d, f), non-behavioural aspects of decision-making structures (b).

Each of these methods has its special advantages and disadvantages under given circumstances, and each may be expected to lead to results that are peculiar to it [see, e.g., Mokken and Stokman (1976, p. 41)] However, for the empirical determination of the power weights λ_{kc} in the complex interest functions of collectivities the positional method and the revealed preference (or policy analysis) method are probably the most promising - particularly, in case of such a complex collectivity as the state. The interview method applied to individual agents may be helpful in determining the values of the parameters ε_{kg} [44].

The *positional method* should be adapted to the type of collectivity that one is interested in. For example, if the life of a collectivity critically depends on financial contributions of its members, then the share of members in economic position k in these contributions may be a good estimate for their relative power λ_{kc}. If sheer numbers are important - as might be the case in voting bodies - then the numerical share of a category of agents becomes relevant [45]. Together with hierarchical positions, these two factors - numerical shares and shares in contributions - may, for example, be assumed to determine the power weights in the interest function of political parties. Estimates of these weights so obtained could, e.g., be employed in the estimation of the party and coalition attractiveness measures [see eqs. (5.23) and (5.25)].

The *revealed preference method* would involve the determination of the values of the λ_{kc} from actual outcomes by using the first-order conditions for the constrained maximization of the collectivity's interest function.

To give an *example*, suppose we have a type of state in which the interests of bureaucrats (as obedient servants of the state) and unemployed may be assumed to be completely uninfluential ($\lambda_{1s} = \lambda_{4s} = 0$). Suppose further that $P_k(t) = P_k^*(t)$, that there is a proportional income tax rate $\tau(t)$, that state expenditure $O(t)$ consists of the state wage sum, and that a balanced budget is aimed at; the expected level of total taxable income, denoted bij $\tilde{W}(t)$, of private employment $\tilde{E}_2(t)$, of real income $\tilde{\bar{w}}_k(t)$, and of the state wage rate $\tilde{w}_1(t)$ are taken as given. Let, finally, the state expect that its demand for labour will be satisfied. Using eqs. (4.1) and (4.2), the following maximization problem results, where time indices are deleted for notational convenience:

$$\max_{\tau, E_1^d} P_s = P_2^{\lambda_{2s}} . P_3^{\lambda_{3s}} \qquad , \lambda_{2s} + \lambda_{3s} = 1,$$

$$= A(1 - \tau)^{[\varepsilon_{21}\lambda_{2s} + \varepsilon_{31}(1 - \lambda_{2s})]} . {E_1^d}^{[\varepsilon_{23}\lambda_{2s} + \varepsilon_{33}(1 - \lambda_{2s})]}$$

subject to

$$\tilde{T} = \tau \tilde{W} \quad ,$$

$$\tilde{O} = \tilde{w}_1 E_1^d \, ,$$

$$\tilde{T} - \tilde{O} = 0 \quad .$$

where A has a given expected value, and T denotes the total tax sum. From the first-order condition for an interior solution it is obtained that

$$E_1^d = \left[\frac{\varepsilon_{23}\lambda_{2s} + \varepsilon_{33}(1 - \lambda_{2s})}{(\varepsilon_{21} + \varepsilon_{23})\lambda_{2s} + (\varepsilon_{31} + \varepsilon_{33})(1 - \lambda_{2s})}\right] \cdot \left(\frac{\tilde{w}}{\tilde{w}_1}\right) .$$

Given estimates of ε_{kg}, this equation could then be used to estimate the relative strength with which the interests of private sector workers and capitalists are represented by the state (denoted, respectively, by λ_{2s} and $\lambda_{3s} = 1 - \lambda_{2s}$) using observations on $\tilde{w}$, $\tilde{w}_1$, and E_1^d. That is, if indeed an interior solution may be assumed to hold. If inequality constraints should be taken into account then the approach exemplified above becomes less attractive as it would involve a specification error in case that boundary solutions occur. Moreover, it is not always possible to get explicit expressions for the instrument variables such as E_1^d above. And, in addition, the problem of underidentification is likely to be met if one wants to determine the values of more power weights, such as those appearing in the parties' interest functions which may be expected to be reflected by the weights λ_{ks} in the state's interest function.

Consider for example, the nested state interest function represented by eq. (5.28)

$$P_s = P_{11}^{\lambda_{11}^s} . P_{12}^{\lambda_{12}^s} . P_{13}^{\lambda_{13}^s} \quad , \lambda_{1i}^s \geq 0,\ i = 1,2,3,\ \Sigma_i\ \lambda_{1i}^s = 1,$$

where P_{11} is the interest function of the representative interest bloc of the bureaucrats on the top - governmental - level of the decision-making structure of the state, P_{12} is the interest function of the top level specific bloc of the politicians as state sector workers, and P_{13} is the interest function of the top level specific bloc of politicians as party representatives; time indices are again deleted, for convenience. Let politicians fully adhere to the party line, so that $\lambda_{12}^s = 0$ and $\lambda_{13}^s = 1 - \lambda_{11}^s$.

Suppose, there are two parties, o_1 and o_2. For P_{13} we write, using eq. (5.29),

$$P_{13} = P_{o_1}^{\lambda_{o_1 g}} . P_{o_2}^{\lambda_{o_2 g}} \quad , \lambda_{o_h g} \geq 0,\ h = 1,2,\ \Sigma_h\ \lambda_{o_h g} = 1,$$

where the subscript g stands for government. For P_{o_h} $(h = 1,2)$ it is written, using eq. (5.21),

$$P_{o_h} = \Pi_k\ P_k^{\lambda_{ko_h}},$$

where P_k $(k = 1,2,3,4)$ is the elementary interest function given by eq. (4.1). Let, finally, $P_{11} = P_1$; it then follows for P_s that

$$P_s = P_1^{\lambda_{1s}} . P_2^{\lambda_{2s}} . P_3^{\lambda_{3s}} . P_4^{\lambda_{4s}},$$

$$\text{with } \lambda_{1s} = \lambda^s_{11} + [\lambda_{1o_1}\lambda_{o_1g} + \lambda_{1o_2}(1 - \lambda_{o_1g})].(1 - \lambda^s_{11}),$$

$$\lambda_{ks} = [\lambda_{ko_1}\lambda_{o_1g} + \lambda_{ko_2}(1 - \lambda_{o_1g})].(1 - \lambda^s_{11}) \quad \text{for } k = 2,3,4.$$

One needs only to consider the previous example to see that underidentification of parameters may occur if there is no additional information on the power weights. However, such information can be obtained by applying the positional method to parties and government.
For example, it would be possible to let

$$\lambda_{ko_h} = E_{ko_h}/E_{o_h} \quad \text{and} \quad \lambda_{o_hg} = \text{share of parliamentary seats},$$

where the former indicates the fraction of party o_h's constituency that belongs to social class k. Given knowledge of the politico-economic model (implicitly) employed by the state, and the appropriate data, one could then use an iterative procedure for the determination of λ^s_{11} in case that the use of first-order conditions is ruled out.

5.10. *Summary*

From our analysis it appears that is is possible to model political activities using the Interest Function Approach introduced in the previous chapter. By means of a rather simple model of choice behaviour we were able to formalize the *behaviour of voters* (including abstention from voting), as well as the coalition formation behaviour of *political parties*, meeting to a large extent the critique that can be raised against theories in this area. The *core* of our approach to voting behaviour is based on the following two considerations:

1. the attractiveness of a party to an agent will depend on the extent to which that agent expects that the realization of its interests will be improved upon under an incumbency of that party; such expectations will be based on the proposed policies and past actual achievements of political parties;
2. an agent will loose interest in supporting political parties if the least attractive party is still highly attractive (positive alienation), if the most attractive party is still highly unattractive (negative alienation), or if there is no difference in attractiveness between parties (indifference).

The first consideration forms, in addition, the core of our approach to the coalition formation behaviour of parties. Here we have to do with collective agents for which complex interest functions hold, reflecting the interest structure of the parties. The approach allows for the fact that parties may have an attractiveness that varies over the *interest blocs* within the parties.

As regards *other forms of political action*, some suggestive remarks on the occurrence of new political parties, political demonstrations, political strikes, and revolutions were made using a *measure of political support of the state*.
The measure may be useful for the study of political activities in economies with *or* without elections. In an economy with no elections the measure indicates what people would do in case that (non-manipulated) elections were held.

Although our main interest has been theoretical, a number of suggestions were made regarding the *empirical determination* of the values of the parameters that were used in the modelling.

Given the complexity of this field of research it should not be surprising that we had to leave the reader with unanswered questions. For example, it proved to be very difficult to deal, in a realistic way, with the leeway that politicians may have to *manipulate* voters in order to improve the election prospects of themselves and/or of the parties that they represent. Whatever the value of the suggestions that we have made in this respect, it appears that those Public Choice models which assume that state policies are directed at the maximization of the number of votes - or, for that matter, the vote share, or vote plurality - and which put everything else in some easily manipulable constraints, are too simplistic.

Using the model of voting behaviour presented in this chapter it is possible to develop *complete politico-economic models* in which not only the behaviour of the state is endogenous, but the type of state as well. Examples of such models will be investigated in the following chapter.

CHAPTER 6

A COMPLETE POLITICO-ECONOMIC MODEL

6.1. Introduction

In this chapter we present and analyze a complete politico-economic model. The model is a politically extended version of the model developed in Chapter 4. In that model a type of state was defined as a point in the space spanned by the weights ε_{kg} and λ_{ks} $(k = 1,..,4;\ g = 1,2,3)$, where the former - appearing in the elementary interest functions P_k [see eq. (4.1)] - indicate the importance that agents of social class k attach to their different class interests (for example, their average real disposable income), while the latter - appearing in the complex interest function of the state, P_s [see eq. (4.6)] - denote the relative strength with which the interests of class k are promoted by the state. Each ordered 16-tuple $(\underline{\varepsilon}_{kg},\underline{\lambda}_{ks})$ represented a type of state. For *given* $(\underline{\varepsilon}_{kg},\underline{\lambda}_{ks})$ we studied the behaviour of the state as determined by the structure of the model; that is, we endogenized the *behaviour* of an exogenously determined type of state.

In the model to be presented below the *type of state* will be made *endogenous* as well through the introduction of political parties and elections which will determine the values of the λ_{ks} in the vector $(\underline{\varepsilon}_{kg},\underline{\lambda}_{ks})$; the value of $\underline{\varepsilon}_k$ remains fixed.

The model is specified in Section 6.2. Section 6.3 deals with the characteristics of equilibria. A number of numerical experiments are reported on in Section 6.4. Section 6.5 summarizes. The reader is referred to the List of Symbols in case the meaning of symbols that were earlier introduced is lost.

6.2. The Model

We start from the *previous model* represented by the eqs. (4.1), and (4.5) through (4.44). *In addition* we will now use eqs. (5.4)-(5.10) and (5.15) -(5.20) for the political representation process. This process causes the weights λ_{ks} in eq. (4.6) to be no longer fixed. To avoid duplication the aforementioned equations will not be reproduced here. *Voting* will be the only form of political participation that is explicitly considered. For simplicity, it is assumed that there are only *two parties*, o_1 and o_2.

In order *to complete* the model the following remains to be specified, apart from parameter values and initial conditions:

a. the exact nature of the voters' interest functions [see eq. (4.1)];
b. the economic position of the voters at the time of an election as well as their previous election choice;
c. the determination of the party platforms, if voters are supposed to take interest in them;
d. the determination of $\underline{\lambda}_{ks}$ in the vector denoting the type of state, $(\underline{\varepsilon}_{kg}, \underline{\lambda}_{ks})$;
e. a political dominance criterion indicating the vote share that a party should at least obtain in order to become incumbent; the dominant party will be the incumbent party, which furnishes the politicians that make up the cabinet;
f. the nature of the weights attached to outcomes of incumbencies $(\bar{c}, \hat{\bar{c}})$ and periods within incumbencies $(c, \hat{c})$; see eqs. (5.4)-(5.6) [recall that the hat (ˆ) indicates that promised outcomes (party platforms) and not factual outcomes are weighted].

Ad a. With respect to the *voters' interest functions* it is assumed that

$$(6.1) \quad \begin{aligned} P_k(t) &= P_k^*(t) && , k = 1,2,4, \\ P_3(t) &= \Sigma_{n=0}^{2} \rho_n P_3^*(t+n) && , \rho_n > 0, \Sigma_n \rho_n = 1; \end{aligned}$$

for $P_k^*(t)$, see eqs. (4.1) and (4.5). Workers and unemployed are supposed to have a time horizon that does not extend into the future. For capitalists the same specification is taken as was assumed for them to hold in their quality of entrepreneurs [see eq. (4.35)]. The investment process forces them to look into the future.

Ad b. Excepting the capitalists, which are postulated to comprise a fixed number (E_3) of people, the *economic position* of a voter at election date T need not be the same as it was at T-1. Thus, the class status and, consequently, the interests of people that voted for party o_i (i = 1,2) at the previous election may have changed. The number of people in position k = 1,2,4 that voted for o_i at the last election should be known, therefore, just before an election date (see Subsection 5.4.2). The following approximation is used, where, e.g., $\Delta E_k(t-1) = E_k'(T) - E_k(T-1)$ (recall that the prime indicates that the number is determined just before the election):

(6.2) (i) for k = 3 we have:

$$E_{3o_i}'(T) = E_{3o_i}(T-1),$$

(ii) for k = 1,2, let:

$$E'_{ko_i}(T) \begin{cases} = [E_{ko_i}(T-1)/E_k(T-1)]E'_k(t) \\ \qquad , \ if\ \Delta E_k(T-1) \leqq 0, \\ = E_{ko_i}(T-1) + \{[E_{4o_i}(T-1) - \Delta E_{3-ko_i}(T-1)]/ \\ \quad /[E_4(T-1) - \Delta E_{3-k}(T-1)]\}\Delta E_k(T-1) \\ \qquad , \ if\ \Delta E_k(T-1) > 0\ and\ \Delta E_{3-k}(T-1) \leqq 0, \\ = E_{ko_i}(T-1) + [E_{4o_i}(T-1)/E_4(T-1)]\Delta E_k(T-1) \\ \qquad , \ if\ \Delta E_k(T-1) > 0\ and\ \Delta E_{3-k}(T-1) > 0, \end{cases}$$ [1)]

(iii) for k = 4 it holds that:

$$E'_{4o_i}(T) = E_{4o_i}(T-1) - \Delta E_{1o_i}(T-1) - \Delta E_{2o_i}(T-1).$$

For the determination of $E'(T)$ - omitting subscripts for convenience - when k = 1,2, use hase been made of the assumptions that the chance of getting a job in the labour market does not depend on electoral behaviour and that people retain their economic position when employment levels are maintained.

Ad c. A party platform is defined here as an ordered n-tuple comprising - for a number ($\geqq$ 1) of future periods - the values of the variables representing the class interests of the electorate, that a party asserts to realize in case that it would be incumbent. Platforms are supposed to be made (revised) every period. Although it will be assumed for the numerical experiments that voters do not attach any importance to such platforms, our analysis of equilibria will allow for the possible influence of them, in which case voters are supposed to rely on the most up-dated versions of the platforms. In line with what we suggested in Subsection 5.5.3 it is assumed that a party's platform can be obtained by maximizing the party interest function given by eq. (5.21),

$$P_{o_i}(t) = \Pi_k P_k(t)^{\lambda_{ko_i}(t)}$$

- where $P_k(t)$ is given by eq. (6.1) - subject to some economic model (which may be the same as the one employed for the maximization of the state interest function), while using as instruments those that are supposed to be available to the state (that is, an income tax rate τ, and demand for labour E_1^d). The party platform can then be determined by using

the optimal values for the instruments and the economic model (which should specify the perceived relationships between the variables representing the class interests and the instruments.
For our purposes these assumptions will do.

Ad d. With respect to the *power weights* λ_{ks} in the state interest function it is assumed that with each party a vector $\underline{\lambda}_{ks}$ is associated that determines the type of state when the party becomes incumbent [since a type of state is characterized by $(\underline{\varepsilon}_{kg}, \underline{\lambda}_{ks})$]. The values of the components of these vectors are assumed to be exogenously determined. In this way the behaviour of the state *and* changes in the type of state are made endogenous; the kind of change remains exogenous (only in one of the numerical experiments we will endogenize the sort of change as well).

Ad e. Regarding the *political dominance criterion*, it is assumed - taking into account the possibility of a tie - that the dominant (incumbent party) stays dominant as long as it obtains 50% or more of the votes; otherwise, the other party takes over. Thus, if the dominant party (prior to the election) is indicated by o_d, then, to stay dominant, it is required for that party that

(6.3) $$E_{o_d}(T) \geqq E_{o_i}(T) \qquad , \; i = 1,2.$$

Ad f. The *weights* attached to incumbencies, and periods within incumbencies, in eqs. (5.4)-(5.6) are specified in the following way:

(6.4) *for* m = 1 (*coming incumbency*):

$$c_{ko_i}(t_m-f+1) = \hat{c}_{ko_i}(t_m-f+1) = (1+o)^{f-n_m} / \sum_{f=1}^{n_m} (1+o)^{f-n_m} ,$$

$$\bar{c}_{ko_i}(t_m) = \hat{\bar{c}}_{ko_i}(t_m) = \hat{o} ,$$

for m ≧ 2 (*past incumbencies*):

$$c_{ko_i}(t_m-f+1) = \hat{c}_{ko_i}(t_m-f+1) = (1+o)^{1-f} / \sum_{f=1}^{n_m} (1+o)^{1-f} ,$$

$$\bar{c}_{ko_i}(t_m) = (1+o)^{t_m - t} ,$$

$$\hat{\bar{c}}_{ko_i}(t_m) = \hat{o}(1+o)^{t_m - t} ,$$

where it is assumed that election T occurs in period t; o and $\hat{o}$ are exogenously determined.

The *general structure* of the model is illustrated by Fig. 6.1. For the *sequence of events* per time period the reader is referred to Table 3.1.

6.3. *Equilibrium Analysis*

Definition. An *equilibrium* is defined by the constancy of all variables (in the economic as well as political sphere) over time and the existence of a dominant party.

This definition differs from the definition used in Chapters 4 and 5 only with respect to the now added requirement that a dominant party exists.

From (6.2) it can be checked that the constancy of all variables implies that

$$(6.5) \qquad E_{ko_i}(T) = E'_{ko_i}(T) \qquad , \text{ for all } i,k,T.$$

The *necessary* and *sufficient* conditions for an equilibrium are given by eqs. (4A1)-(4A7), (6.3) and (6.5). The assumption concerning the power weights λ_{ks} (see above under *ad* e) should be taken into account when considering condition (4A1).

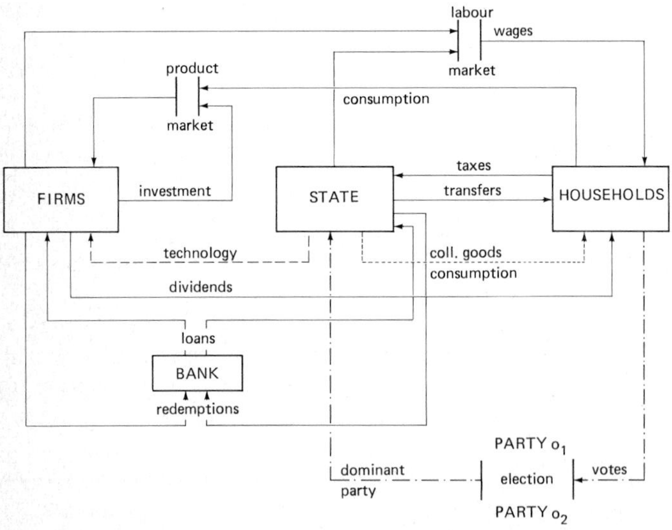

Fig. 6.1. Structure of the complete politico-economic model (⟶ = money flows).

In the sequel, equilibrium values of variables will be denoted by deleting the time index, unless confusion may arise.

From the constancy of all variables it follows that there can be no change in dominant party in an equilibrium, as the vote share of the parties will be constant as well.
The voter's valuation of the parties, indicated by V [see eq. (5.7)], will be solely dependent on the appreciation of the party platforms, in so far as the class interests that we have distinguished are concerned, and, on other factors that may be important to voters (such as a party's stand on religion); recall that these other factors are represented by parameters (a and b) in V.
Note, furthermore, as regards the platforms of the parties, that in so far as the dominant party is concerned only this party's platform for the future will be taken into account by voters, and not its previous platforms, as voters base their valuation of that party on factual outcomes in so far as the past is concerned (the responsibility hypothesis).

Using eqs. (5.17), (5.20), and condition (6.5), the *equilibrium constituencies* of the parties can be determined from the following three equations:

$$(6.6) \qquad (1 - \Gamma_{ko_0})E_{ko_0} = \Gamma_{ko_1}E_{ko_1} + \Gamma_{ko_2}E_{ko_2} \qquad , \text{ for all } k ,$$

$$(6.7) \qquad E_{ko_1} = \left[\frac{f_{ko_0o_1}\Gamma_{ko_2} + f_{ko_2o_1}(1 - \Gamma_{ko_2})}{f_{ko_0o_2}\Gamma_{ko_1} + f_{ko_1o_2}(1 - \Gamma_{ko_1})}\right].E_{ko_2} \qquad , \text{ for all } k ,$$

$$(6.8) \qquad E_{ko_0} + E_{ko_1} + E_{ko_2} = E_k \qquad , \text{ for all } k .$$

The solution of this equation system - which gives the parties' constituencies from social class k as a function of the floating rates, abstention rates, and size of that class - is not particularly illuminating, and will, therefore, be omitted. The numerator and denominator of the fraction in (6.7) denote, on the one hand, that part of the parties' constituencies that will vote again but that will choose for the other party (the second term), and, on the other hand, the fraction of the parties' abstention rates that will not be compensated by the winning of voters who did not vote at the last election.
Note, here, that against the number of agents that previously voted but now - at the election considered - decides to abstain there stands an equal number of agents that did not vote at the last election but now decides to vote [eq. (6.6)]; however, only a fraction of it will go to

either party. The number of agents from class k that did not vote at the last election but will vote for party o_i at the coming election equals [see eq. (6.6)]:

$$f_{ko_0o_i}(1 - \Gamma_{ko_0})E_{ko_0} = f_{ko_0o_i}(\Gamma_{ko_1}E_{ko_1} + \Gamma_{ko_2}E_{ko_2});$$

thus, only part of party o_i's contribution to the number of non-voters is compensated, the other part goes to the other party.

In case of compulsory voting $\Gamma_{ko_h} = 0$, for all h, and thus,

$$E_{ko_0} = 0, \quad E_{ko_i} = [f_{ko_ho_i}/(f_{ko_1o_2} + f_{ko_2o_1})].E_k \quad , h,i = 1,2;\ h \neq i.$$

In case of complete vote abstention $\Gamma_{ko_h} = 1$, and, thus,

$$E_{ko_0} = E_k, \quad E_{ko_1} = E_{ko_2} = 0 \quad , \text{for all } k .$$

In order for the parties to have the same class structure (i.e., the same number of voters from a particular social class) - in which case the sizes of the parties will be equal as well - it is demanded that

$$f_{ko_0o_1}\Gamma_{ko_2} + f_{ko_2o_1}(1 - \Gamma_{ko_2}) = f_{ko_0o_2}\Gamma_{ko_1} + f_{ko_1o_2}(1 - \Gamma_{ko_1}) \quad , \text{for all } k;$$

see eq. (6.7). Of course, an equal size does not necessarily imply an equal class structure (this is easily seen in case of compulsory voting; see above).

Although most of the *equilibrium characteristics* derived from the model in Chapter 4 carry over to the present model, some of them have to be revised due to the further endogenization of political phenomena. The characteristics that remain valid were numbered: 1, 2, 4 through 13, 15(a), and 18. Regarding the first characteristic and those that need to be adjusted the following is remarked.

1. *Characteristic* 1 - which says that an equilibrium need not exist - also holds for the present model. Notice that the political dominance criterion as specified in (6.3) cannot in itself be an obstacle to an equilibrium, since there always exists a party with a constituency that is as large as, or larger than, that of the other party. This criterion may only be an obstacle in itself if more than 50% of the vote is re-

quired; from eq. (6.7) it is easily seen that it is possible, for example, that an equilibrium demands that parties have the same size. In the context of characteristic 1 it should also be remarked that, since each party, on becoming incumbent, causes the power weights λ_{ks} in the state interest function to change in an *a priori* (exogenously) determined way, we can no longer arbitrarily choose types of states - i.e., vectors $(\underline{\varepsilon}_{kg}, \underline{\lambda}_{ks})$ - to see whether they are compatible with an equilibrium. Only those types of states are of interest that can be sustained by a dominant party. Thus, given the $\underline{\lambda}_{ks}$ associated with our two parties, only changes in $\underline{\varepsilon}_{kg}$ remain to be considered.

2. *Characteristic* 3 - which says that all expectations are realized - does not completely carry over as the expected performance of the opposition party can never be realized in an equilibrium. What remains true is that no expectations are violated.

3. *Characteristics* 14, 15(c), and (17) - which assert that more than one type of state can be associated with an equilibrium - do no longer hold as such. A change in the vector $\underline{\lambda}_{ks}$ would require the dominance of the other party (and, would, consequently, upset the equilibrium), while a change in the vector $\underline{\varepsilon}_{kg}$, is not always feasible [2)].

4. *Characteristic* 15(b) - which says that an unemployment equilibrium exists for any type of state for which a full employment equilibrium exists with $\tau < \tau^+$ (maximum tax rate) and $E_1 = E_1^-$ (minimum state size) - cannot be maintained in its general form, as a decrease of E_2 may not be feasible due to the political dominance criterion.

5. *Characteristic* 16 - which asserts that a full employment equilibrium exists if an unemployment equilibrium exists, although not necessarily for the type of state for which the unemployment equilibrium holds - can also no longer be maintained in its general form. If a full employment equilibrium demands another type of state, then it would have to be sustained by the party that is opposing in case of the unemployment equilibrium. However, this may not be feasible, for the type of state that results from the dominance of that party need not be compatible with an equilibrium (its demand for labour, and, consequently, the level of labour productivity in the private sector, may be too low for the production of the minimum consumption basket x_b^{c-}).

6. *Characteristic* 19 needs to be adjusted as well. It says that:
   a. a unique equilibrium (i.e., at most one equilibrium per type of state, and identity of equilibria over types of states) exists if for any type of state there exists at most only one E_1,E_2-combina-

tion that satisfies (4A1)-(4A7);

b. that in that case $E_1 + E_2 = L$ (full employment) and $\tau = \tau^+$;

c. that such an equilibrium will also be an equilibrium for those types of states for which the strict quasi-concavity assumption holds and $\max \{E_1^-, \bar{\bar{E}}_1\} \geqq E_1$ in that situation (where $\bar{\bar{E}}_1$ is the optimal state employment level in case that crowding out of private labour demand in the labour market is neglected);

d. that such an equilibrium is a unique equilibrium for all types of states if $E_1 = E_1^-$, happens to hold.

Ad a: In addition to (4A1)-(4A7) the conditions (6.3) and (6.5) should now be met.

Ad b: It can be shown that a unique equilibrium need no longer be a full employment equilibrium, nor an equilibrium with $\tau = \tau^+$ [3].

Ad c and d: these assertions do no longer hold in their general form; see 3.

There even need not be any other type of state at all for which it is an equilibrium. In that case, there is only *one* E_1,E_2*-combination* and *one type of state* satisfying the equilibrium conditions; such an equilibrium may be called a *strictly unique politico-economic equilibrium.*

7. *Characteristic* 20 - which says that the necessary and sufficient conditions for an equilibrium with maximum private output are given by (4A1) -(4A7) and $E_1 = \max \{E_1^-, [\eta/(1+\eta)]L\}$ - is incomplete under the present model. The eqs. (6.3) and (6.5) should be added to the conditions already mentioned

6.4. Numerical Experiments

In this section we report on a number of numerical experiments that have been carried out with the complete politico-economic model specified by eqs. (4.1), (4.5)-(4.44), (5.4)-(5.10), (5.15)-(5.20) and (6.1)-(6.3). The experiments are, again, based on the set of *parameter values* and *initial conditions* presented in Section 3.5 (with θ omitted, $E_3 = 10$, and $\rho = 0.25$), as were the experiments in Chapter 4. They will not be reproduced here. Some parameter values and initial conditions have to be added, however.

In addition to the previously stated parameter values it is assumed, for all k and h,i = 1,2, that

$$\hat{\bar{c}}_{ko_i}(t_m) = 0, \quad \bar{c}_{ko_i}(t_m) = (1 + o)^{t_m - t}, \quad a_{ko_ho_i} = a, \quad b_{ko_ho_i} = b,$$

$$c_{ko}(t_m-f+1) = (1+o)^{1-f} / \sum_{f=1}^{n_m} (1+o)^{1-f}, \quad \Gamma^+_{ko_h}(T) = 0$$

, for all T, m = 2,3;

see eqs. (5.4)-(5.7), (5.15), and recall that $a_{ko_h o_h} = 0$ [4].

The assumptions imply that voters attach no importance to party platforms and only rely on the fact [$\hat{\bar{c}}(t_m) = 0$; m > 1, and eq. (5.6) can be neglected, therefore]; the imputed past performance of the parties is discounted (see c and $\bar{c}$, $o > 0$); the sensitivity parameters a and b (appearing in the party valuation variable V) show no variation over social classes and parties; voting is compulsory [$\Gamma^+(T) = 0$, for all T, so that eqs. (5.15)-(5.20) can be neglected]; only two incumbencies are considered, the present one and the previous one (m = 2,3). As regards the last assumption, the past time horizon ($\bar{m}_k$) of the voters is supposed to be long enough to allow the time discount rate o to 'fully' decay the values of the variables affected in case that the total length of the two incumbencies would exceed it; recall that an incumbency may involve more than one election term - the time between two successive elections - which is here supposed to take 4 time periods. The parameters o, a, b, and the parameters determining the type of state, ε_{kg} and λ_{ks}, remain to be specified.
Recall with respect to λ_{ks} that with each party a particular vector $\underline{\lambda}_{ks}$ is associated which determines the type of state - represented by ($\underline{\varepsilon}_{kg}$, $\underline{\lambda}_{ks}$) - when the party becomes incumbent. The values of the components of these two vectors and of $\underline{\varepsilon}_{kg}$ are exogenously determined. Changes in the constituencies of the parties will have no impact on them, therefore.
To the initial conditions presented in Section 3.5 the following are added concerning the expected interest realization ratings ($\tilde{Z}$) and the constituencies of the parties; election T = 0 - which is the first election to be considered - is supposed to take place at the end of period t = 0:

$$\tilde{Z}_{ko_i}(0) = 0 \qquad \text{for all } i,k,$$

$$E'_{1o_1}(0) = 5, \quad E'_{2o_1}(0) = 40, \quad E'_{3o_1}(0) = 0, \quad E'_{4o_1}(0) = 5,$$

$$E'_{1o_2}(0) = 5, \quad E'_{2o_2}(0) = 45, \quad E'_{3o_2}(0) = 10, \quad E'_{4o_2}(0) = 0.$$

The prime indicates that the constituencies are determined just before the election. The constituency of party o_2 is somewhat more rooted in the private sector than that of party o_1. The expected interest realization ratings are all put equal to zero for T = 0. Party o_2 is assumed to be dominant, initially.

The following results have been obtained with the model. We will first present some more general outcomes which refer to experiments with various value assignments to the components of the vectors $\underline{\lambda}_{ks}$ associated with the two parties. This will be followed by a more detailed discussion of a number of experiments. The last experiment reported on involves a *fully* endogenous type of state; in that experiment it is not only the change in the type of state but also the character of that change which has been made endogenous.

1. Overlooking the outcomes for different value assignments to the vectors $\underline{\lambda}_{ks}$ associated with the parties, it appears that the model generates the same *patterns of motion* as did the truncated politico-economic model of Chapter 4, to wit:
   1. equilibria;
   2. regular cycles;
   3. cycles marked by a periodic 'bankruptcy' of the state, forcing it to put the income tax rate at its maximum, $\tau(t) = \tau^{+}(t)$, and to trim the state organization, $E_1^d(t) = E_1^-$;
   4. shrinking private production accompanied by an accelerating inflation due to a chronic financial breakdown of the state.

   For a discussion of the causes of these motion patterns, see Subsection 4.5.3.

2. Interests that do not lead to an equilibrium when undistortedly (exclusively) represented by the state - given the initial conditions specified above, or even irrespective of the particular initial conditions chosen - may lead to an equilibrium if they are *confronted* with other types of influential interests within more or less 'broad-spectrum' parties and/or with the interests of an influential bureaucracy within the state organization. The reason, of course, is that the confrontation will negatively affect the strength with which the interests are promoted by the state. Dependent on the character of the other interests this may open up a path towards an equilibrium.

   Elections resulting in a change in the type of state may inflict shocks upon the economy as a change in the type of state may lead to a (substantial) change in state behaviour. Although we did not find as yet such cases under our experiments, it can be speculated that interests that lead to an equilibrium when exclusively represented by a state in case of no elections - given the set of initial conditions - need not lead to an equilibrium if elections occur so that the representations of these interests by the state may alternate (and conversely).

3. An increase in the time discount rate ρ - implying a more *myopic* voter

- steps up the amplitude of the fluctuations in the party votes and the frequency of government changes.

4. *An experiment with a capitalist party and a labour party.* Fig. 6.2 shows the time profile of some variables for the following additional parameter values: a = 0.5; b = 0.17; o = 100; $\varepsilon_{11} = \varepsilon_{12} = \varepsilon_{21} = \varepsilon_{22} = \varepsilon_{41} = \varepsilon_{42} = 0.4$, $\varepsilon_{13} = \varepsilon_{23} = \varepsilon_{43} = 0.2$; $\varepsilon_{31} = 0.9$, $\varepsilon_{32} = \varepsilon_{33} = 0.05$; $\lambda_{1s} = 0.2$ and $\lambda_{2s} = 0.8$ if o_1 is the incumbent party (in that case $\lambda_{3s} = \lambda_{4s} = 0$), $\lambda_{3s} = 1$ if o_2 is the incumbent party (in which case $\lambda_{1s} = \lambda_{2s} = \lambda_{4s} = 0$). Party o_1 will be labelled the *labour party*, as it causes the state to further the interests of workers exclusively, when it is incumbent; party o_2 is called the *capitalist party*. The ratio of a and b has been chosen such that the floating rate - for all k - equals 5% if the expected interest realization differential (see Subsection 5.4.2) equals zero. The discount rate o is sufficiently high to ensure that only economic conditions in the period at the end of which the election is held (the election 'year') are taken into account by voters [as suggested by the findings of Fair (1978), and Bloom and Price (1975)]. As, by assumption, voters do not rely on party platforms, this means that the expected interest realization rating of the opposing party will be zero. Consequently, the value of the parameter a implies that 50% of the supporters of the incumbent party will vote for the opposition party if they experience a deterioration in their situation (indicated by a decrease in the value of their interest function) of 50% over the election year; see eqs. (5.4)-(5.7) and (5.10).
We note the following.

- Regarding the *upper part* of the figure, observe from the values for ε_{ks} that, under the incumbency of both parties, the state intrinsically values the production of state goods. As the difference between the wage rate for state employees and the dole rate is rather small [$w_4(t) = 8/9\ w_1(t)$], state production is increased under both types of governments if private demand for labour is expected to decrease (and the tax constraint is not binding); however, the adjustment to the expected situation on the labour market is less pronounced if the capitalist party is dominant, for this party is much less strongly inclined towards state production ($\varepsilon_{33} = 0.05$, while $\varepsilon_{13} = \varepsilon_{23} = 0.2$). After some initial financial problems for the state under the dominance of the capitalist party - set in by a substantial fall in the private wage rate due to the depression that is started with, and urging the state to put $\tau(t) = \tau^+(t)$ and $E_1^d(t) = E_1^-$ - a relatively large state sector emerges that is sustained by both parties. Labour productivity in the private sector attains a level of around 6 times its initial value thereby increasing the capital-labour ratio which simultaneously causes

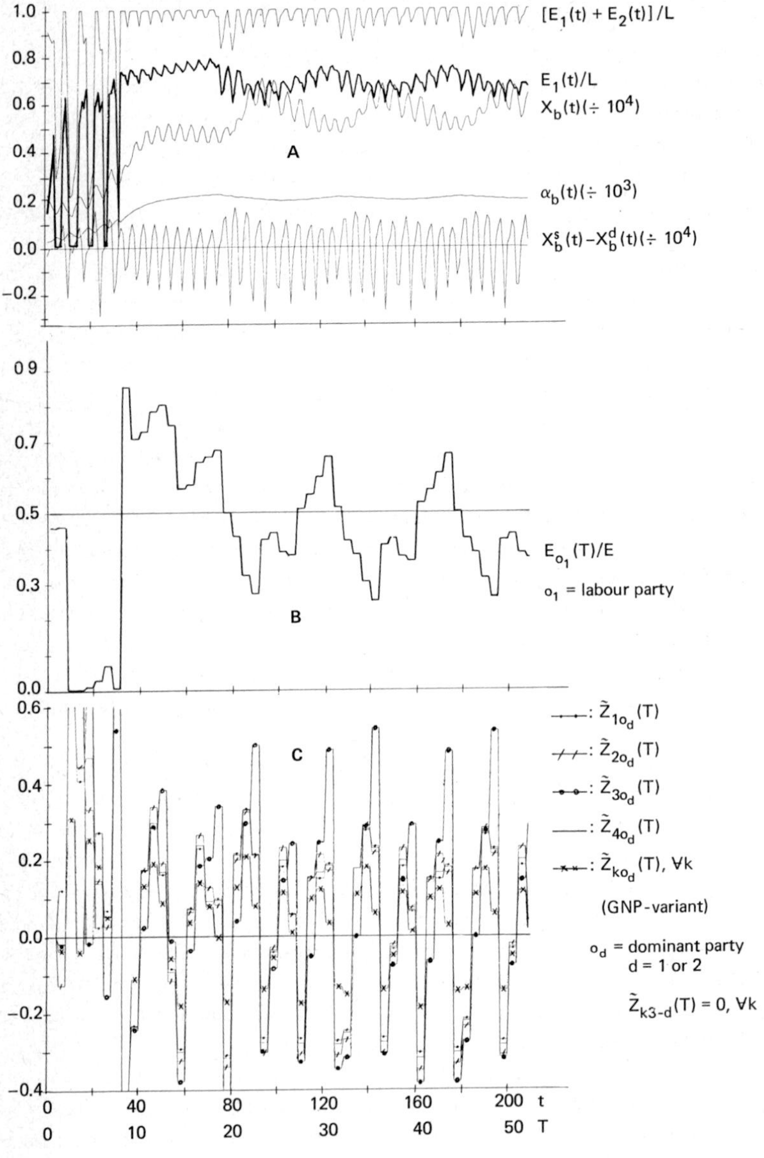

Fig. 6.2. Outcome of the complete politico-economic model with a capitalist party and a labour party.

private demand for labour to fall.

- The figure reveals a *cyclical pattern*. The main cycles are a short cycle with a period of 5 and a long cycle with a period of 50. An interesting outcome is that the troughs in the long private output cycle coincide with a change in government from labour party to capitalist party (see the upper and middle part of the figure). Total employment consistently remains on a somewhat higher level when the labour party governs; the troughs in the long cycle occur when the capitalist party governs. The cycles are truly politico-economic cycles because changing the values of the parameters determining the type of state alone suffices to generate an equilibrium. The state clearly puts its own mark on the outcome of the economic process. The long cycles are co-determined by the changes in government, the short cycle by the behaviour of the state during the incumbency of a particular party.

- The *downturn* in the long private output cycle sets in during the second half of the incumbency of the capitalist party. It is influenced by the following developments during an incumbency of that party which negatively affect the investment level in the private sector:

a. the price level is relatively low, on average, in particular halfway the incumbency;
b. the wage level is relatively low too, but especially at the beginning of the incumbency when the trough in the total employment cycle occurs;
c. apart from the start the level of private labour productivity gradually diminishes throughout the incumbency of that party (it is built up again when the labour party governs).

- Although not completely visualized in the figure, it appears from the results that a *change in government* (incumbency) is, generally, preceded by a strong increase in the tax rate in reaction to a high level of state debts, as well as a low level of private output; both factors negatively affect real disposable income, although not for all economic positions to the same extent.

- The *middle* and *bottom* part of the figure, respectively, show the time profiles of the vote share of the labour party and the expected interest realization ratings. The latter also shows the profile for a variant on the specification of the model. In this alternative specification the rate of change of real per capita GNP - where real per capita GNP is defined as $[X_b(t) + \bar{w}_1(t)E_1(t)]/E$ - has been substituted for the rate of change of the interest function value in eq. (5.5); we will speak of the *GNP-variant*. This GNP-variant is taken into consideration as per capita GNP is probably the most important single variable of the three (macro-) variables that are usually taken to reflect economic conditions [to wit: per capita income, aggregate unemployment, inflation; see, e.g., Fair (1978, p. 171)]. The different outcomes to which these two cases lead are quite striking (see also below). Looking at the sign and value of the expected interest realization ratings ($\tilde{Z}$) of the incumbent party it shows that the sign is not the same for some k in 9 out of 50 elections (opposite signs for all k in 2 cases), and that the differences in value between the rating according to the GNP-variant and the other ratings are often quite substantial, as is reflected by the fluctuations in the vote shares (see, in particular, the rating of the capitalists, $\tilde{Z}_3$). Notice, furthermore, that the time profiles of the interest realization ratings for k = 1,2,4 are almost alike. This is due to the fixed wage and dole rate structure [$w_1(t) = \phi w_2(t)$, $w_4(t) = \psi w_2(t)$], the uniform tax rate, and the identity of the ε_{kg} for these positions. All the difference comes from the diverging interest in state and private sector employment.

5. *A capitalist party that is less interested in state goods.* The potentially differential impact of political parties on the economy is even better exposed by the following case. Fig. 6.3 shows what happens when $\varepsilon_{33} = 0.03$ is substituted for $\varepsilon_{33} = 0.05$ in the previous example. The result is a capitalist party that is less interested in state goods, and, consequently, in state employment.

The change in value appears to have significant consequences for the time profiles of the variables; this is partly so, because the weight attached to state goods was already very small. The effect of the second change in incumbency is striking. Employment in the state sector is immediately strongly diminished under the dominance of the capitalist party, which leads to a fall in the wage rate, followed by a boom in investment and production. The boom ends, and a depression follows, through an erosion of labour productivity and a fall in the price level (the wage rate remains rather low). Although the private production level under the dominance of the capitalist party is comparable with that in the previous example, the private sector employment level is higher due to a lower capital-labour ratio resulting from a lower level of labour productivity.

The lower part of Fig. 6.3 shows the vote share of the labour party. Although not shown in the picture, it appears, furthermore, that this time the signs of the interest realization ratings are unequal in 20 elections under the two specifications. These outcomes suggest that, if the basic model is the 'true' model, changes in per capita GNP are an unreliable predictor of changes in party vote shares.

6. *Changed political mobility*. To show the effect of a change in political mobility, a = 0.2 and b = 0.07 have been substituted for a = 0.5 and b = 0.17 in the first example. The change implies a more step-like floating rate function, while now 50% of the supporters of a party votes for the other party if the expected interest realization differential of the parties equals -0.2, instead of -0.5. The floating rate remains the same for a zero differential (f = 0.05) as a/b has been kept constant.

The result is an increase in the number of government changes, as shown in the lower part of Fig. 6.4. The upper part shows that the long cycle has a shorter period now, and is less pronounced as the different types of states do not long get the opportunity to put their mark on the economic process. The even development of labour productivity reflects this state of affairs.

The changes in party size are of the 'land-slide' type at almost every fourth election, resulting in a change in incumbency. These changes are preceded by a relatively large increase in the tax rate and the price level. Both increases are related to a substantial rise in the state's debt burden one period earlier - effectuated by an unexpected decrease in dividend income taxes - which led to an excess demand in the product market. Although these events appear to follow a cyclical pattern, with a period of 5 (most of the time), the aforementioned increases occur during the election year only every fourth election. This result suggests the importance of the particular type of expectations adjustment mechanism that is assumed to hold for the state (and of the voters' time horizon, of course). In this model the state's expectations in a particular period are based on the economic outcomes of the immediately preceding period only [see eqs. (4.26) and (4.27)].

7. *Fully endogenous power weights* λ_{ks}. We have assumed that a change in incumbency leads to a change in the type of state - a type of state being indicated by $(\underline{\varepsilon}_{kg}, \underline{\lambda}_{ks})$ - through a change in the power weights λ_{ks}, which indicate the relative strength with which the interests of the different social classes are represented by the state. With each party we associated a particular vector $\underline{\lambda}_{ks}$, the values of the components of which were exogenously determined. In our final example these values will be made endogenous as well by assuming that the weights are based on the *numerical strength* with which the social classes are represented in the parties and the state.

Let T_t denote the election date starting the election term (the time

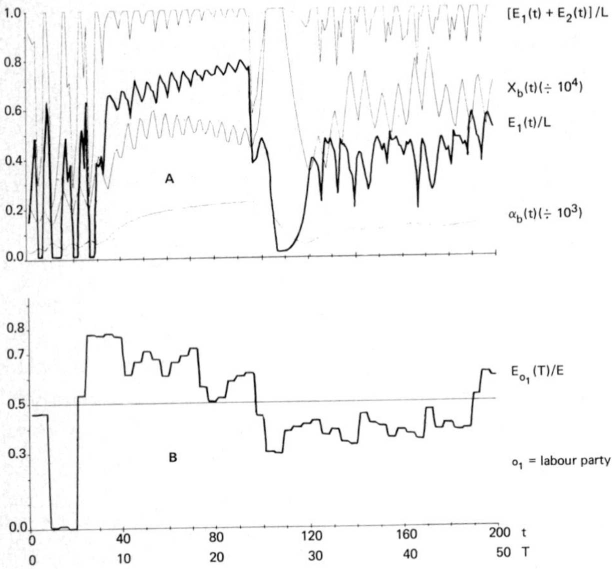

Fig. 6.3. Capitalist party that is less interested in state goods.

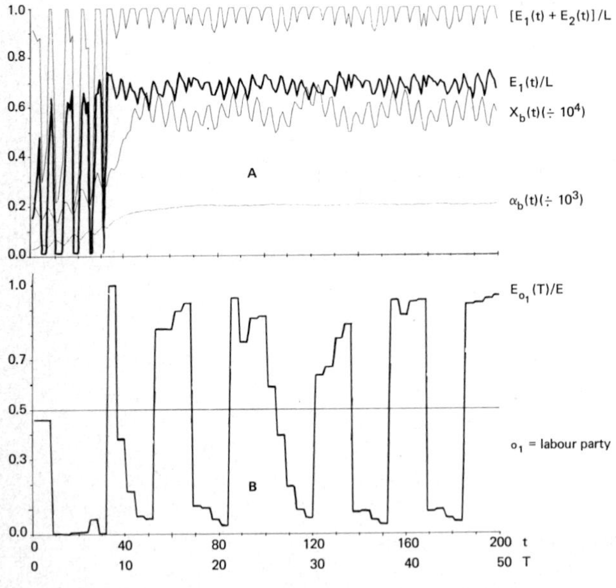

Fig. 6.4. Effect of changed political mobility.

between elections) in which period t occurs, and assume that changes in λ_{ks} only occur at elections. The dominant party is supposed to have full control over the government. Politicians have no leeway to pursue their interests as state sector workers; the opposing party is powerless [see eqs. (5.28), (5.29)]. The interest function of the state [eq. (4.6)] is based on the following disaggregated specification:

$$(6.9) \qquad P_s(t) = P_1^*(t)^{\lambda_1^s(T_t)} \cdot \left[P_1^*(t)^{\lambda_{1o_d}(T_t)} \cdot P_2^*(t)^{\lambda_{2o_d}(T_t)} \cdot P_3^*(t)^{\lambda_{3o_d}(T_t)} \cdot P_4^*(t)^{\lambda_{4o_d}(T_t)} \right]^{1 - \lambda_1^s(T_t)},$$

where $\lambda_1^s(T_t)$ indicates the relative power of the bureaucrats *vis-à-vis* the politicians as party representatives within the state organization, and $\lambda_{ko_d}(T_t)$ the strength with which the interests of people in economic position (social class) k are represented within the dominant party o_d, as determined at the last election. The expression between hooked brackets is the complex interest function of the dominant party.

Under these assumptions it follows for the weights λ_{ks}, attached to the elementary interest function P_k^* in the state interest function, that

$$\lambda_{1s}(T_t) = \lambda_1^s(T_t) + \lambda_{1o_d}(T_t)[1 - \lambda_1^s(T_t)], \quad \text{and}$$

$$\lambda_{ks}(T_t) = \lambda_{ko_d}(T_t)[1 - \lambda_1^s(T_t)] \qquad \text{for } k = 2,3,4.$$

With respect to $\lambda_1^s(T_t)$ and $\lambda_{ko_i}(T_t)$ - as o_d stands for either o_1 or o_2 - it is assumed that

$$(6.10) \qquad \begin{aligned} \lambda_1^s(T_t) &= \omega\lambda_1^s(T_t-1) + (1 - \omega)[E_1(T_t) - E_p]/E_1(T_t), \\ \lambda_{ko_i}(T_t) &= \omega\lambda_{ko_i}(T_t-1) + (1 - \omega)E'_{ko_i}(T_t)/E'_{o_i}(T_t), \quad \text{for all } k \end{aligned}$$

$$, \ 0 < \omega < 1,$$

where E_p denotes the number of politicians, which is taken to be constant over time. Eqs. (6.10) show that the relative strength with which the interests of agents of a particular social class k are represented within the parties and the state adjusts itself to the numerical strength of that class within these collectivities. For the state, only the power weight of the bureaucrats is shown; the power weight of the dominant party follows from it, as it is equal to $1 - \lambda_1^s(T_t)$. The latter indicates the weight attached within the state interest function to the complex interest function of the dominant party, which is a weighted representation of the interests of the different social classes.

Let, finally,

$$E_p = E_1^-, \quad \omega = 0.9, \quad \lambda_1^s(0) = 0.01,$$

$$\lambda_{1o_1}(0) = 0.2, \quad \lambda_{2o_1} = 0.8, \quad \lambda_{3o_1}(0) = 0, \quad \lambda_{4o_1}(0) = 0,$$

$$\lambda_{1o_2}(0) = 0, \quad \lambda_{2o_2} = 0, \quad \lambda_{3o_2}(0) = 1, \quad \lambda_{4o_2}(0) = 0.$$

The number of politicians is put equal to the minimum number of state sector workers (which determines the minimum state size).
The value of the power adjustment parameter, $\omega = 0.9$, implies that the adjustment to the numerical strengths of the social classes within the parties and the state is only very gradual.
Party o_1 starts as a labour party in which the interests of the private sector workers are especially influential; party o_2 starts as a capitalist party that exclusively promotes the interests of the capitalists. The weight attached to the interest function of the bureaucrats within the state interest function is small, at the start [$\lambda_{1s}(0) = \lambda_1^s(0) = 0.01$; recall that party o_2 is dominant, initially].

Note from (6.10) that a persistent minimum state size implies that $\lambda_1^s \to 0$. Whether the weights λ_{1s} will also go to zero depends on the position of the state sector workers (the politicians in that case) within the parties. However, as then $E_1(t) = E_p = E_1^- = 1$, this weight will, generally be close to zero as well. A minimum state size need not per se conflict with the interests of state sector workers as they may be strongly tax sensitive (see Subsection 4.5.1, point 4). The position of the state sector workers (and, consequently, that of the bureaucrats, as E_p is fixed) within the parties and the state will be strengthened when the state size is increased. If the bureaucrats are tax sensitive then this process will sooner or later be stopped under the influence of the bureaucrats themselves. In our example the bureaucrats are not strongly tax sensitive; the weight attached to real disposable income in their elementary interest function equals 0.4 ($\varepsilon_{11} = 0.4$), while the total weight attached to state employment (directly, or indirectly through the importance that they attach to state goods) equals 0.6 ($\varepsilon_{12} + \varepsilon_{13} = 0.6$).

Fig. 6.5 shows results of the full endogenization of λ_{ks}. The bottom two pictures clearly show a gradual take-over by bureaucrats of the

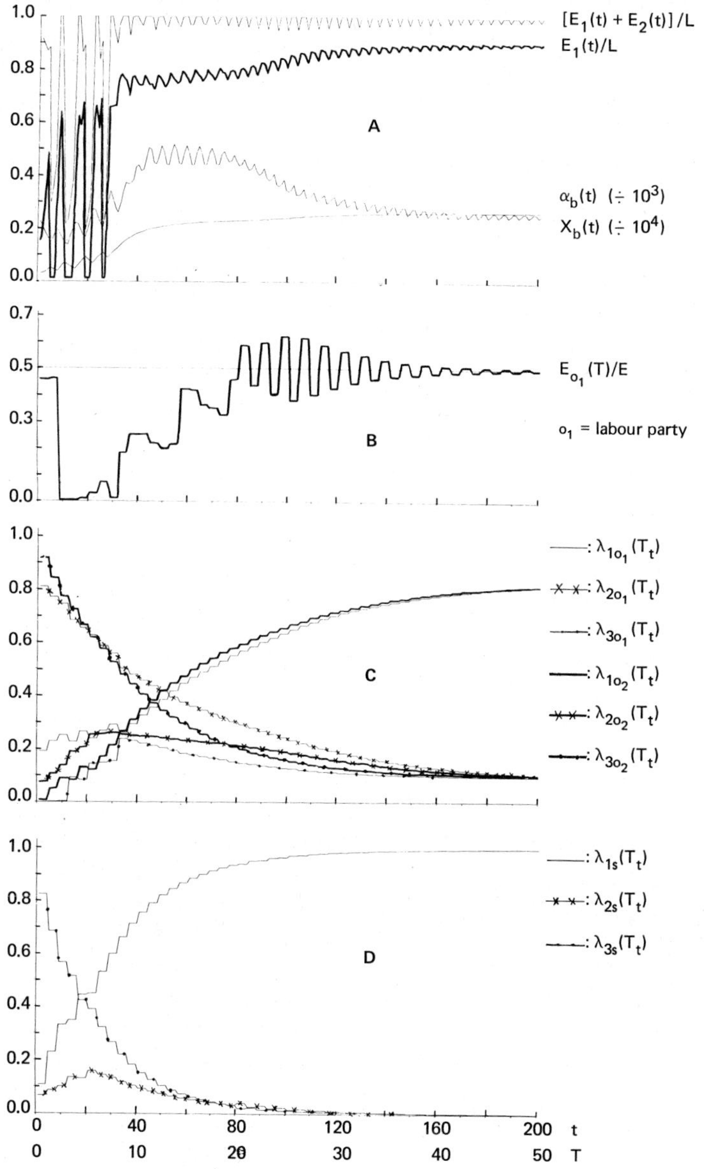

Fig. 6.5. Effect of fully endogenous power weights.

control over the activities of the (eventually identically composed) parties and the state ($\lambda_{1o} \rightarrow 0.81$, $\lambda_{1s} \rightarrow 0.99$); a complete harmony between the interests of parties, government, and bureaucracy results. Because of this, the numerous changes in party dominance - from period 80 onwards at every election - do, eventually, no longer have an effect. The politico-economic process is heading for a full-employment equilibrium, characterized by a very large state sector; 90% of the total labour force is, ultimately, employed by the state.

6.5. Summary

In this chapter we presented and analyzed a complete politico-economic model, characterized by an *endogenous type of state*. Through *elections* in which two political parties appeared, citizens were enabled to influence the power weights λ_{ks} in the interest function of the state - which indicate the relative strength with which the interests of social class k are represented by the state. In order to become incumbent (dominant) a political party's vote share had to satisfy a political dominance criterion. The dominant party determined the value of the λ_{ks}.
The model is an extended version of the model analyzed in Chapter 4.

An *equilibrium analysis* of the model yielded, *inter alia*, the following results, where an equilibrium is now defined by the constancy of all variables over time *and* the existence of a dominant party.
- Given the constancy of all variables in an equilibrium, the expected interest realization ratings of parties ($\tilde{Z}$) - which indicate the extent to which voters expect that the realization of their interests will be improved upon under the incumbency of a party - will be all equal to zero in so far as they are based on factual outcomes [see eqs. (5.4)-(5.6)]. A possibly different appreciation of party platforms is the only reason why, in an equilibrium situation, voters need not be indifferent between parties concerning the promotion of the basic class interests that we have distinguished (real disposable income, numerical strength, availability of state goods). The overall valuation of the parties [V, see eq. (5.7)] may, furthermore, be different in case of an equilibrium due to the presence of other factors that voters attach importance to (such as a party's stand on religion). If voters are completely free to abstain from voting then the presence of such other factors and/or a different appreciation of the party platforms concerning the aforementioned class interests are the reasons why voters would vote in an equilibrium. The floating, and abstention from voting, that results for these reasons determines the equilibrium size and composition (class structure) of the parties.
- Most of the equilibrium characteristics established for the model in

Chapter 4 carry over to the present model. Some adjustments have to be made, however, because of the political dominance criterion and the fact that vectors $(\underline{\varepsilon}_{kg}, \underline{\lambda}_{ks})$, characterizing types of states, can no longer arbitrarily be chosen from the set of these vectors. Given the vectors $\underline{\lambda}_{ks}$ that are associated with the two political parties in the model, only the values of the parameters ε_{kg} (the weights attached to the basic class interests in the elementary interest functions) remain to be manipulated. The main consequence is that an equilibrium need no longer be an equilibrium for more than one type of state. There may now exist a strictly unique politico-economic equilibrium, in which case there is only one type of state satisfying the equilibrium conditions. Such an equilibrium may involve less than full employment, and the tax rate need not be maximal.

From *numerical experiments* with the model the following results were obtained.

- The model generates the same patterns of motion as did the truncated politico-economic model of Chapter 4 (i.e., equilibria, regular cycles, cycles with a periodic financial breakdown of the state, and a situation of running inflation and permanent financial troubles for the state).
- As may be expected, equilibria are more likely when extreme interests are confronted with each other in 'broad spectrum' parties (so that they may have to give in to each other), then when they are promoted by interest-specific parties. A confrontation with the interests of an influential bureaucracy within the state organization may (but, of course, need not) also have this effect.
- An increase in the time discount rate of voters - implying a more myopic voter - steps up the amplitude of the fluctuations in the vote shares of the parties and the frequency of government changes.
- The experiments that were discussed in greater detail indicated the potential effect of government changes and changes in political mobility on the politico-economic process. One of these experiments dealt with the consequences of a full endogenization of the power weights λ_{ks}, which was obtained by basing them on the numerical strength with which social classes are represented in the parties and the state. It showed a gradual take-over by bureaucrats of the control over the activities of the - eventually identically composed - parties and the state, resulting in a complete harmony between the interests of parties, government, and bureaucracy. The experiments also suggested the importance of a disaggregation towards social classes.

CHAPTER 7

PRESSURE GROUPS

7.1. Introduction

In the previous chapters we have studied the interaction between state and private sector by means of a series of models. As regards the behaviour of the state we analyzed the impact of the representation of interests by state sector workers (bureaucrats and politicians) - who, after all, decide on the activities of the state - and of structural coercion and pressure emanating from the private sector. The latter two concepts refer to constraints on the activity set of - in this case - the state from which state sector workers choose activities for the realization of their interests (see Subsection 1.6.2). Pressure here refers to constraints that arise from deliberate attempts by agents in the private sector to influence the state, any other constraint is subsumed under structural coercion. The state was supposed to behave in accordance with the maximization of an interest function - a weighted representation of the interests of bureaucrats and politicians - subject to a number of (in)equality constraints. In the models developed in Chapters 3, 4, and 6, all these constraints had to do with structural coercion only. The two forms of pressure introduced in Chapter 6 - voting and the activities of political parties - were incorporated by assuming, on the one hand, that politicians fully adhere to the party line, and, on the other hand, that the state (as well as a political party) does not directly interact with a single voter (one-sided interaction). Consequently, we did not have to face the analytically difficult problems of bargaining and threats that are closely associated with pressure. In Chapter 2, where pressure originating from co-operative behaviour of a large number of relatively small firms was considered (see Subsection 2.5.2), the problem was avoided by simply assuming that no bargaining would occur, the state taking the firms' activities as given. It was then suggested that the state might be forced to do so in case of implicitly co-operative behaviour, as it would be hard to get the firms into a bargain when there is no organization that can be called upon [1].

Although the neglect of threats and bargaining seems to be acceptable in case that pressure is exerted by an insignificant agent (i.e., an agent who cannot noticeably affect the value of the interest function of - in this context - the state), or if the pressure originates from the implicitly co-operative behaviour of insignificant agents, it would be unsatisfactory to leave the analysis at that. In our view, at least any rather comprehensive analysis of the interaction between state and private sector of advanced capitalist economies should pay attention to the fact that huge organizations have developed that cannot be considered as insignificant and anonymous to the state. Of collectivities - including the state - that have the capacity to threaten and to bargain it can be expected that they will use this capacity whenever this is perceived to further the realization of the interests that they represent.

The analysis of the behaviour of such collectivities and of its consequences for the interaction between state and private sector, is not only empirically relevant, and interesting in itself, it is also clearly important for democracies, as pressure from the side of collectivities other than political parties may restrict the opportunities for voters to affect the behaviour of the state.

The analysis is all the more important as the trend towards organization and concentration appears to continue (see Section 1.1).

Collectivities - which might also be called *interest groups* - that try to influence the behaviour of another collectivity will be labelled *pressure groups*, in line with our use of the word pressure.

The common, more restricted, definition of a pressure group demands that the collectivity subject to influence is the state [2)].

In *this chapter* we will indeed, particularly, be concerned with the *interaction* between a *pressure group* and the *state* (which may function as a pressure group too, according to our definition).

However, the analysis will also be relevant for the study of the interaction between pressure groups in the wide sense, such as between a consumer organization and a firm, or a labour union and a firm.

There are *two problems* to be considered: *first*, the determination of the impact of pressure on the behaviour of a collectivity; *second*, the determination of the pressure activities of a collectivity. After some remarks on the relevant literature in Section 7.2, we present our approach to the first problem in Section 7.3. Central to this approach is the concept of an *augmented interest function*, which is a weighted representation of the interest functions of pressure groups. Attention will be restricted to the interaction between two pressure groups only, which accentuates the exploratory character of our study. Section 7.4 mentions some implications of our approach for the behaviour of such groups. Section 7.5 goes into the second of the aforementioned problems; it reflects on the use of pressure directed at the state by a labour union and a firm. Section 7.6 summarizes.

7.2. Some Remarks on the Literature

Notwithstanding the apparent importance of studying the interaction between state and pressure groups in the private sector - witness also the existence of corporate government relations departments and of firms specializing in government relations and public affairs counseling [see Haley and Kiss (1974)] - one cannot speak of an abundance of formal models, here, even though the subject has often been discussed in the literature [3]. This is not surprising if one realizes that there are, on the one hand, many ways to put pressure on the state, and, on the other hand, many targets for which it may be attractive to use pressure. As regards the former, one may think of all sorts of market an non-market activities - in market an non-market social relationships with the state (see Subsection 1.6.2 on those concepts) - such as bargaining or "making one's case clear" in informal contacts with state sector workers, formal (open) bargaining, political campaign contributions, investment or production stops, strikes, interlocking directorships (multiple positions). Targets may, *inter alia*, be: tariffs, subsidies, price controls, military procurements, tax credits, employment, exchange rates. Moreover, the state is a complicated organization.

The few (empirical) models that we know of in this area are all concerned with one type of state activity (policy instrument): e.g., Braam (1973) with state supply of 'wet' infrastructure (locks, bridges, etc.), Pincus (1975) with the structure of tariffs, Salamon and Siegfried (1977) with U.S. federal corporate income tax rates and state excise tax rates. This also holds for the empirical part in Zusman (1976), which is concerned with consumer and producer subsidies for a particular product; its analytical part - a co-operative game model - in principle allows for the incorporation of various instruments.

These studies clearly suggest the effectiveness and importance of pressure [4]. However, as Pincus remarks, in estimating pressure group successes one should be aware of the fact that more than one type of state activity may be relevant; against the failure of pressure in one area may stand its success in another one [Pincus (1975, pp. 775-776)].

A major shortcoming specific to Zusman's model is that the agents (players) involved are assumed to have all the information that is relevant to the game, which seems to be too unrealistic for most cases.

Characteristic of all the aforementioned models is that the treatment of the interests and behaviour of state sector workers - from which the benefits should come - is rather *ad hoc* and unsatisfactory from a theoretical point of view [5]. This is important, for, to give an example, a large corporation, with relatively many employees, that is structurally incurring financial losses, may have a bargaining position with respect to a labour government that is very different from that with respect to a government run by capitalists. Another characteristic is that they do not deal with the actual conduct of (or bargaining processes between) state and pressure groups. In this respect, they follow the 'structure-performance' approach that is often used in industrial economics, in which case a causal relationship is assumed to hold between the characteristics of an industry and the results of the behaviour of firms in that industry, neglecting the activities that have led to these results [6].

In the *following section* we will work out the contours of a model of the interaction between a pressure group and the state that fits into our approach to the behaviour of the state and other collectivities as developed in the Chapters 4 and 5. It is not only theoretically interesting but, in principle, also implementable for empirical research. The model should be regarded as tentative and exploratory. It puts no restriction on the state's use of its instruments as the aforementioned models typically do. As these models, however, it does not explicitly deal with bargaining processes as such [that is, processes of concession; see Cross (1969, p. 8)], but with the consequences that can be expected to arise from the characteristics underlying the many-sided interaction - inclusive of bargaining and threats - between state and pressure group. For the development of general politico-economic models, the direct inclusion of bargaining processes, instead of treating them as a 'black box', would seem to lead to a too great complexity.

7.3. The Augmented Interest Function

The question that we have to face is how to model the often 'many-ways-many-targets' interaction between the state and a pressure group.
For our tentative answer to this question we first reproduce eq. (4.2), showing the complex interest function that is assumed to hold for a collectivity:

$$P_c(t) = \Pi_k \, P_k(t)^{\lambda_{kc}(t)} \qquad , \; \lambda_{kc}(t) \geqq 0, \; \Sigma_k \, \lambda_{kc}(t) = 1,$$

where P_k represents the interests of agents belonging to social class k [see eq. (4.1)]. Recall that collectivities were supposed to act in accordance with the constrained maximization of the interest function that is assumed to hold for them.
Now, in case of a pressure group that is able to noticeably and structurally (enduringly) affect the interests of a collectivity subject to its pressure we would suggest that a fair approximation of the behaviour of that collectivity can be arrived at by substituting for the collectivity's interest function a so-called *augmented interest function*, which is a

weighted representation of the interests functions of that collectivity and the pressure group. More specifically, denoting the two pressure groups that we will focus upon by c_1 and c_2, and indicating an augmented interest function by $\bar{P}$, it is assumed that c_1 and c_2 act in accordance with the constrained maximization of the following function:

$$(7.1) \qquad \bar{P}_{c_h}(t) = P_{c_h}(t)^{1-\lambda_{c_i}^{c_h}(t)} . P_{c_i}(t)^{\lambda_{c_i}^{c_h}(t)} ,$$

$$\lambda_{c_i}^{c_h}(t) \geqq 0, \; h,i = 1,2, \; h \neq i.$$

where λ indicates the strength with which the interests of c_i are furthered by c_h; if $\lambda = 0$ then (7.1) reduces to the expression of a complex interest function for a collectivity, if $\lambda = 1$ then (7.1) shows that c_h will exclusively further the interests of c_i (c_h has become fully 'altruistic' in appearance). The weight λ is supposed to reflect the 'acknowledged power' of c_i, or, one might say, the extent to which the interests of c_i are 'vested'. The way that its value is thought to be determined will be worked out below. In the formulation of (7.1) it has implicitly been assumed that c_h is fully acquainted with the interest function of c_i. This, obviously, need not be the case; c_h may only have a vague idea of what the interests of c_i are. In fact it is c_h's perception of c_i's interest function that counts.

In continuance of the aforegoing argumentation, it stands to reason to base the *constraints*, subject to which (7.1) is supposed to be maximized, on the assumption that the activities of the pressure group in question, c_h, will be taken as given by the other group, c_i; after all, c_h is assumed to pay heed to the 'acknowledged power' of c_i.

Thus, *for the sake of modelling*, the approach roughly suggests to augment c_h's interests with the interests of c_i and to specify the constraints *as if* there is no pressure.

As an intuitively clear *example* of a situation in which (7.1) would be relevant we mention the *company town*, where c_1 stands for the local government, for example, and c_2 for the company. It can be expected that both collectivities will deliberately try to influence the activities of the other and, thus, act as pressure groups; e.g., the local government will push for employment, the company for infrastructural facilities.

According to our approach the behaviour of both groups would approximately be in accordance with the constrained maximization of (7.1) - where the weight λ may be substantially larger for $c_h = c_1$ than for $c_h = c_2$ if the company's activities can be transferred to locations outside the jurisdiction of the local government. The use of (7.1) would seem to be more fruitful than trying to capture by means of constraints alone the intricate relationship between the two pressure groups.

In fact we have already employed the construct of an augmented interest function when we analyzed the decision structure of a collectivity in Subsection 4.3.2. It was then suggested that because of the, generally, intimate and structural relationship between representatives and represented in a collectivity the interest function(s) of the latter should be incorporated in a multiplicative way into the interest function of the former.

Even though we do not explicitly deal in this section with pressure activities, it should be clear that the existence of 'vested interests' is not at variance with the persistence of such activities in reality. On the contrary, a 'vested interest' can be thought of as being produced by accumulated pressure, a capital good that is subject to decay - just like the 'goodwill' produced by accumulated advertising [see Nerlove and Arrow (1962)].
Because of the neglect of such activities, the suggested approach may at best offer a fair approximation of pressure group behaviour.

The value of λ in (7.1) - which in principle lends itself for empirical estimation (see Section 5.9) - can be taken to depend on the following factors that we will first mention and then explain:

a. the *objective threat potential* of c_i for c_h, denoted by $\chi_{c_i}^{c_h}(t)$;

b. the *group cohesiveness* of c_i in its relationship with c_h, denoted by $\bar{\chi}_{c_i}^{c_h}(t)$;

c. an *information factor*, denoted by $\bar{\bar{\chi}}_{c_i}^{c_h}(t)$.

Ad a. The *objective threat potential* variable should measure the extent to which c_i can maximally hurt the interests of c_h, objectively, i.e. for an outside observer having the best available information. A plausible specification would seem to be:

$$\chi_{c_i}^{c_h}(t) = [P_{c_h}^{+}(t) - \bar{\bar{P}}_{c_h}(t)]/P_{c_h}^{+}(t) \qquad , \; 0 \leq \chi_{c_i}^{c_h}(t) \leq 1, \tag{7.2}$$

where:

$P_{c_h}^{+}(t)$ = maximum value of the complex interest function (P) for c_h at time t, in case that the activities of c_h are taken as given by c_i (no pressure by c_i);

$\bar{\bar{P}}_{c_h}(t)$ = maximum value of the complex interest function (P) for c_h in case that c_i maximally hurts the interests of c_i; denoting an activity from c_h's activity set A_h by a_h and from c_i's activity set A_i by a_i:

$$\bar{\bar{P}}_{c_h}(t) = \max_{a_h} [\min_{a_i} P_{c_h}(a_h, a_i; t)];$$

it can be called the *maximum security level* of c_h [cf. Luce and Raiffa (1957, p. 66)].

Ad b. *Group cohesiveness* is another factor that is important in this context. The concept of group cohesiveness has a central place in theories of group dynamics [see Cartwright (1968, p. 91)]. A definition advanced by Festinger states that the "Cohesiveness of a group is (...) the resultant of all the forces acting on the members to remain in the group" [Festinger (1968, p. 185)]. The homogeneity of activity patterns of a group and its readiness for action are supposed to depend on it. The resultant force is though to have at least two types of components:

a. forces that derive from the group's attractiveness, and
b. forces whose source is the attractiveness of alternative memberships [Cartwright (1968, p. 92)].

The size of a group, its geographical dispersion, and the homogeneity of its members' interests, are important elements determining the attractiveness of the group and, thus, its cohesiveness (think of communication, and the coordination of activities).

As regards the attractiveness of alternative memberships - where we include non-membership - one may think of the 'free-rider', for example; if people expect that they will be able to enjoy the benefits of a group's activities without contributing a 'fair share', they will be inclined not to join.

The construction of a satisfactory single index of group cohesiveness is not easy [see Cartwright (1968, p. 106)]. However, it does not seem to be impossible that such an index, ranging from zero to one, can be constructed [7]. This index of group cohesiveness, denoted by $\bar{\chi}$ $(0 \leqq \bar{\chi} \leqq 1)$, and the objective threat potential χ $(0 \leqq \chi \leqq 1)$ determine the so-called *objective threat intensity* of a collectivity; it is indicated by π. The value of π is supposed to be a function H of χ and $\bar{\chi}$, and should be restricted to the zero-one interval, as a threat intensity cannot exceed 100%. Formally, denoting the first partial derivative of H with respect to χ and $\bar{\chi}$, respectively, by H_1 and H_2, it is assumed that

$$(7.3) \qquad \pi_{c_i}^{c_h}(t) = H[\chi_{c_i}^{c_h}(t), \bar{\chi}_{c_i}^{c_h}(t)] \qquad , H_1, H_2 > 0, \ 0 \leqq H[.] \leqq 1.$$

Ad c. The threat intensity perceived by c_h need not be equal to the aforementioned objective threat intensity π which an outsider with the best available information would calculate. What is perceived will be labeled the *effective threat intensity*. It is determined by the information that c_h has on π and on c_i's inclination to bring π into play. Important in this respect is the way that c_i 'sells' or 'advertises' its objective threat intensity [8].

The effective threat intensity is indicated by Π. Its value - which is also restricted to the zero-one interval - is taken to be a function J of π and $\bar{\bar{\chi}}$, where $\bar{\bar{\chi}}$ - the information factor - should respresent the information on π. Formally, denoting the first partial derivative of J with respect to π and $\bar{\bar{\chi}}$ by J_1 and J_2, respectively, it is assumed that

$$(7.4) \qquad {}_{c_j}\Pi_{c_i}^{c_h}(t) = J[\pi_{c_i}^{c_h}(t),\ {}_{c_j}\bar{\bar{\chi}}_{c_i}^{c_h}(t)] \qquad , J_1, J_2 > 0,\ 0 \leqq J[.] \leqq 1,$$

where the prefix c_j indicates the pressure group whose perception of the information and of the effective threat intensity is involved.
The value of $\bar{\bar{\chi}}$ may be supposed to be non-negative.

Fig. 7.1 illustrates the conceptual structure of our approach, so far, where, for notational convenience, group indices have been deleted.

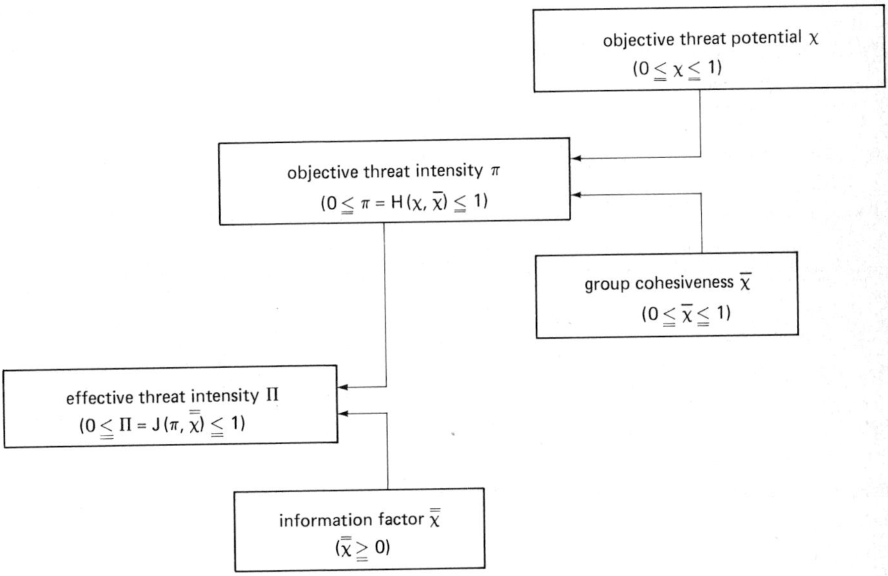

Fig. 7.1. From the objective threat potential to the effective threat intensity of a pressure group (group indices deleted).

We now turn to the relationship between the weight λ attached to the interest function of pressure group c_i in the augmented interest function of c_h - see eq. (7.1) - and the effective threat intensity of c_i.
It seems to be reasonable to demand that a functional specification of this relationship should satisfy the following properties:

1. $\lambda_{c_i}^{c_h}(t)$ is monotonically strictly increasing in ${}_{c_h}\Pi_{c_i}^{c_h}(t)$;

2. $\lambda_{c_i}^{c_h}(t)$ is monotonically strictly decreasing in ${}_{c_h}\Pi_{c_h}^{c_i}(t)$;

3. $\lambda_{c_i}^{c_h}(t)$ is monotonically strictly increasing in ${}_{c_h}\Pi_{c_i}^{c_h}(t)$ and ${}_{c_h}\Pi_{c_h}^{c_i}(t)$,

   when keeping ${}_{c_h}\Pi_{c_i}^{c_h}(t) = {}_{c_h}\Pi_{c_h}^{c_i}(t)$;

4. $\lambda_{c_i}^{c_h}(t) = 0$ if ${}_{c_h}\Pi_{c_i}^{c_h}(t) = 0$;

5. $\lambda_{c_i}^{c_h}(t) = 1$ if ${}_{c_h}\Pi_{c_i}^{c_h}(t) = 1$ and ${}_{c_h}\Pi_{c_h}^{c_i}(t) = 0$;

6. $\lambda_{c_i}^{c_h}(t) = 1/2$ if ${}_{c_h}\Pi_{c_i}^{c_h}(t) = {}_{c_h}\Pi_{c_h}^{c_i}(t) = 1$.

Most of the properties speak for themselves, and need not be commented upon. With respect to property 3 it is remarked that it is based on the idea that collectivities will become less co-operative, i.e. less concerned with each other's interests, the more insignificant these collectivities become to each other. As, in reality, c_i would typically be one out of many collectivities that c_h is confronted with, it is plausible - and it is also common - to assume that non-co-operative behaviour will increasingly prevail the more insignificant collectivities become to each other [9].
A specification that satisfies the properties 1 through 6 is:

$$(7.5) \qquad \lambda_{c_i}^{c_h}(t) = \frac{{}_{c_h}\Pi_{c_i}^{c_h}(t)}{1 + {}_{c_h}\Pi_{c_h}^{c_i}(t)} \text{ .}$$ [10]

It is of course possible to attach a prefix c_j to λ (in which case Π

should be prefixed with c_j as well), so that one can distinguish between the weight that the interest function of c_i gets in the augmented interest function of c_h ($c_j = c_h$), and c_i's perception of what that weight - indicating its 'acknowledged power' - should be ($c_j = c_i$).

7.4. Implications

In this section we mention a number of implications that follow from the Interest Function Approach to the interaction between collectivities where pressure is involved.

1. An augmented interest function for a collectivity implies that this collectivity is supposed to simultaneously further its own interests and the interests of another collectivity (a pressure group). This 'altruistic' behaviour need not be mutual, of course. It depends on the effective threat intensities of the collectivities. If the effective threat intensity of a collectivity c_i for another collectivity c_h is zero, and, thus $\lambda = 0$ in (7.1), then the interests of c_i will be neglected and it may only have an indirect influence on c_h either because it has joined a pressure group that has a positive effective threat intensity for c_h, or because it is part of a larger social grouping whose activities are taken care of in the constraint set of c_h [which case is commonly considered in general (politico-) economic models; think of the activities of firms, for example].

2. As regards the interaction between state and private sector our approach not only suggests that the state might further the interests of pressure groups - such as a large corporation, a labour union, or a trade association - it also suggests that a collectivity in the private sector might further the interests of the state.
   Note, in this context, that although the state's objective threat potential may be very large (think of the possibility of nationalization), its effective threat intensity may be much smaller as it depends on the cohesiveness of the state - which is influenced by its size and the diversity of the interests of bureaucrats and politicians - and the information that it gives on its threat intensity. It will also be important what perception the private sector collectivity has of the state's interests. Moreover, even if the state has a strong 'vested interest' with a private sector collectivity, it depends on the instruments at the collectivity's disposal what the benefits for the state will be. Finally, notice the significance of the time horizon. Nationalization, for example, may loose its threatening character if a collectivity's time horizon is very short.

3. Regarding the promotion by the state of interests of pressure groups in the private sector, it may, furthermore, be useful to point at the importance of changes in the type of state (through changes in party dominance, for example) and of changes in the production structure, or in technology. Such changes may strongly affect the effective threat intensity of a pressure group. As was already hinted at in Section 7.2, a large corporation, with relatively many employees, that is structurally incurring losses, may have a much larger effective threat intensity for a labour government interested in private sector employment than for a government run by capitalists who are interested in profits.

4. For the interaction between collectivities in the private sector the approach suggests that collectivities that have a positive effective threat intensity for each other (as may hold in case of a duopoly, or a bilateral monopoly) will show implicit collusion.
Recognizing their interdependence they will come to the sort of behaviour that was envisaged by Chamberlin in his influential book on monopolistic competition for a small number of sellers [see Chamberlin (1962 [1933], in particular pp. 46-51)].
We would like to stress, however, that the augmented interest function presupposes the existence of pressure activity. The 'vested interests' that these collectivities will have with each other are based upon it. If a collectivity c_i, having a positive objective threat intensity for another collectivity c_h, would not exert any pressure at all upon c_h - and, thus, would not act as a pressure group - then its interests will not be represented by c_h, although its behaviour may still influence c_h as c_i may react - although not retaliate - upon the activities of c_h. Thus, in case of a duopoly, if one firm would never retaliate ('show its teeth') then the other firm should not be expected to further its interests.
Implicit collusion may, therefore - and, in our view, typically will - be accompanied by pressure activity. In case of firms, implicit collusion and overt competition can occur at the same time which will make it even more difficult for antitrust laws to be applied than implicit collusion alone would. Note, furthermore, that a collectivity (such as a firm) may have an indirect 'grip' on another collectivity (which need not per se be a firm) if it appears in an augmented interest function of another collectivity (such as the state, for example).

5. In evaluating the working of a democracy one should realize that the behaviour of the state is only partly determined by the pressure exerted by voters and political parties.
To repeat, the behaviour of the state is determined by:
a. the representation by bureaucrats and politicians of their own in-

terests;

b. the structural coercion originating from the private sector;

c. the pressure exerted by agents in the private sector (pressure groups), *among which* voters and political parties.

Note that in so far as costs incurred in pressure activities can be deducted from taxable income, (non-participating) voters will have to pay for their loss in influence.

6. An augmented interest function can be said to reflect a degree of 'organization' or 'socialization' of the activities of the collectivities considered, which may even culminate into a new collectivity with one decision-making centre as a formal confirmation of a strong mutual interdependence.

7. As mentioned above, the value of the weight λ in (7.1) - denoting the relative strength with which the interests of a pressure group are furthered by a collectivity - can in principle be estimated, empirically. One might use the revealed preference method to that purpose (see Section 5.9).

As regards the determinants of λ - the objective threat potential χ, the group cohesiveness $\bar{\chi}$, and the information factor $\bar{\bar{\chi}}$ - it seems that the estimation of $\bar{\bar{\chi}}$ will be relatively the most difficult. At least a rough numerical indication of χ and $\bar{\chi}$ should be possible.

For the determination of $\bar{\bar{\chi}}$ one might at first instance think of using the funds allocated to pressure purposes by a pressure group. However, what is missing is an indication of the effect of such funds on the weight λ. It can be seen from eqs. (7.2)-(7.4) that even if estimates were available on λ, χ, and $\bar{\chi}$, $\bar{\bar{\chi}}$ would not be identifiable, in general; for each pressure group, namely, there are two such $\bar{\bar{\chi}}$'s, one standing for a pressure group's perception of the information that the other group is giving, and one for a pressure group's perception of the information that itself transmits. Only by making assumptions with respect to these perceptions, estimates can be obtained.

7.5. *Some Reflections on the Use of Pressure Directed at the State by a Labour Union and a Firm*

7.5.1. Introduction

In the previous section we were concerned with the behaviour of a collectivity that is subject to pressure. The approach that we suggested in that section abstracted from the actual activities involved in that pressure.
In this section we want to explore some aspects of such activities for two

collectivities in the private sector, a labour union and a firm, in so far as these activities are aimed at influencing the state.
This will be done by working out an example. It is meant to give an indication of the sort of research that can be done.

7.5.2. Pressure by a Labour Union

Suppose we have a union of private sector workers with the following interest function:

$$(7.6) \qquad P_u = \bar{\bar{w}}_2^{\varepsilon_{21}} . e_2^{\varepsilon_{22}} . x_{s2}^{\varepsilon_{23}} \qquad , \varepsilon_{2g} \geqq 0,\ g = 1,2,3,\ \Sigma_g\, \varepsilon_{2g} \leqq 1,$$

which is the elementary interest function of private sector workers, having as arguments their real disposable wage income, their numerical strength, and the bundle of state goods at their disposal [see eq. (4.1)]; the subscript u stands for union. Only one time-period is considered; time indices are deleted, for convenience. It is assumed that the effective threat intensity of collectivities that the union is confronted with (among which the state) is zero, so that the augmented interest function shown by eq. (7.1) reduces to the complex interest function for a collectivity, here P_u.

The union is supposed to recognize that the strength with which its interests are represented by the state are dependent on the factors mentioned in the previous section:

1. its objective threat potential, which will be assumed to be positively related to the number of its members, and its strike-fund;
2. the cohesiveness of the union;
3. the information that it communicates to the state as regards its objective threat intensity (the latter depends on the first two factors).

Consequently, there are in principle three ways open to the union in which to build up a 'vested interest' with the state in order to bring state behaviour more into accordance with its interest.

Let us focus upon the goods provided by the state that are (collectively) consumed by private sector workers; they are denoted by x_{s2}. In specifying a relationship between x_{s2} and the union's activities - in so far as those are relevant to the aforementioned factors - we will follow an approach taken in studies of the advertising behaviour of firms. These studies typically postulate a direct relationship between sales and advertising (-messages, -spending), leaving out of account the intermediate effects of the latter on the 'utility function' of the consumer [see, e.g., Schmalensee (1972)]. In the same way we will assume that x_{s2} is a function of some

union activities, leaving out of account the intermediate effect of, for example, a change in the cohesiveness of the union on the weight λ representing the relative strength with which the union's interests are represented in the augmented interest function of the state, and its consequent effect on the behaviour of the state. This seems to be the most fruitful approach to begin with, given the complexity of the way that state behaviour depends on the activities of the union.
It is assumed that

$$(7.7) \qquad x_{s2} = B_1^{\iota_1}.B_2^{\iota_2}.B_3^{\iota_3} \qquad , \iota_i > 0,\ i = 1,2,3,\ \Sigma_i \iota_i < 1,$$

where, B_1 = outlays on the union's objective threat potential;
B_2 = outlays on the union's cohesiveness;
B_3 = outlays on the information transmitted by the union.

The elasticity parameter ι_i denotes the relative change in the bundle of state goods at the disposal of private sector workers which is due to a given relative change in the outlays on political pressure activity i. Time-lags and cross-effects of expenditures are neglected.

Expenditures are supposed to be solely financed out of contributions made by unionists. Let f_i stand for the fraction of disposable wage income that is contributed to the union for pressure activity i. Then,

$$(7.8) \qquad B_i = f_i \bar{\bar{w}}_2 E_2^n \qquad , i = 1,2,3,$$

where E_2^n denotes the number of unionists; furthermore, using (7.6) and (7.7), P_u can now be written as

$$(7.9) \qquad P_u = [(1 - \Sigma_i f_i)\bar{\bar{w}}_2]^{\varepsilon_{21}}.e_2^{\varepsilon_{22}}.[B_1^{\iota_1}.B_2^{\iota_2}.B_3^{\iota_3}]^{\varepsilon_{23}},$$

where $\Sigma_i f_i$ denotes the fraction of disposable wage income paid as contribution to the union by a private sector worker. Taking $\bar{\bar{w}}_2$, E_2^n, and e_2 $(= E_2/E)$ as given, a maximum of P_u requires that

$$(7.10) \qquad f_i = \frac{\varepsilon_{23}\iota_i}{\varepsilon_{21} + \varepsilon_{23}\Sigma_i\iota_i},$$

and, thus,

$$(7.11) \qquad \Sigma_i f_i = \frac{\varepsilon_{23}\Sigma_i\iota_i}{\varepsilon_{21} + \varepsilon_{23}\Sigma_i\iota_i}.$$

If $\varepsilon_{21} = 1$, which means that private sector workers are only interested in

their real disposable income ($\varepsilon_{22} = \varepsilon_{23} = 0$), then it follows from (7.10) and (7.11) that $f_i = \Sigma_i f_i = 0$, implying that no contribution is paid for the pressure activities considered.
If $\varepsilon_{21} = 0$ and $\varepsilon_{23} > 0$, then all disposable wage income will be transferred to the union, $\Sigma_i f_i = 1$; see eq. (7.11). From (7.10) and (7.11) it, furthermore, follows that

$$(7.12) \qquad \frac{f_i}{\Sigma_i f_i} = \frac{\iota_i}{\Sigma_i \iota_i},$$

which says that the relative size of the budget allocated to pressure activity i will be equal to the (perceived) relative size of the elasticity of state goods supply with respect to expenditures on that activity, ι_i.
As regards the elasticity ι_i, it is clear from eqs. (7.8) and (7.10) that, *ceteris paribus*, the money spent on activity i will be positively related to ι_i.
In view of the lags that will be involved in changing the behaviour of the state through a change in cohesiveness or the objective threat potential, it can be expected that ι_3, referring to informational activities of the union, will relatively have the largest value. Given the assumed one-period time horizon of the union the largest budget will be allocated to this sort of activities, which may comprise strikes, propaganda, and so on.
The parameters ι_i can empirically be estimated when data on x_{s2} and B_i are available. Given the simple nature of eq. (7.7) and the complexity that is in fact involved, one should not expect too much of such estimates [11)]. One should, at any rate, have to pay heed to changes in the type of state, and changes in economic conditions, which affect the behaviour of the state.

Of course, a more general model of union behaviour would, simultaneously, have to deal with the union's activities with respect to firms.

7.5.3. Pressure by a Firm

Fig. 7.2 shows along which ways a firm may exert pressure upon the state. There is a choice between:

a. direct pressure and pressure via a mediating collectivity (such as a trade association, or political party);
b. central and local state apparatuses;
c. government (politicians) and bureaucracy (bureaucrats).

In general, one may hypothesize, that a firm will, successively, show the following types of pressure activity directed at the state, when it sees its effective threat intensity going up (e.g., because of a sustained growth of the firm's size):

1. no activity at all ('free-riding');
2. pressure via trade association on local and central government and bureaucracy;
3. pressure on local government and bureaucracy; pressure via trade association on local and central government and bureaucracy;
4. pressure on local and central government and bureaucracy; diminishing activity via trade association; pressure via other mediating collectivities (such as a political party).

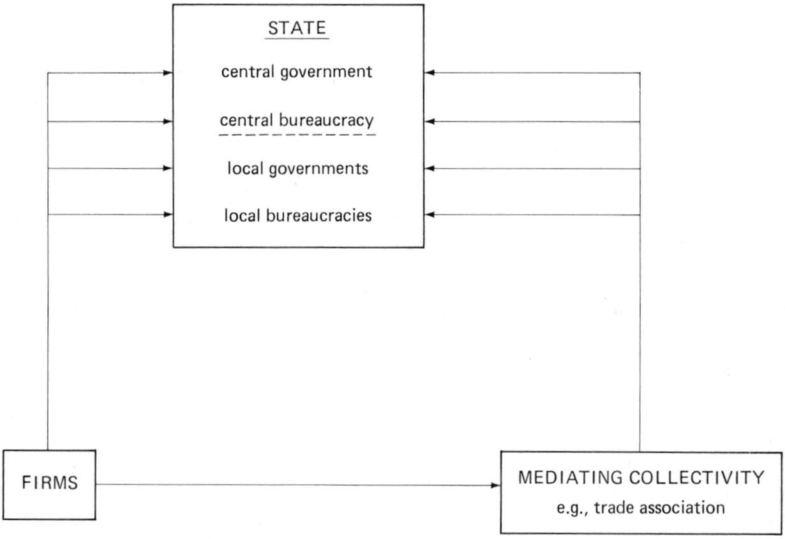

Fig. 7.2. Different ways for a firm to put pressure upon the state.

As regards stage 4 it is noted that firms may diminish their use of a trade association for several reasons when they consider themselves to be strong enough to build up their own direct pressure; for example, one may think of the lower degree of cohesiveness of an association, or of the higher degree of visibility of the activities of an association (were it for the simple fact alone that other firms are involved) [12]. Note, furthermore, that firms may have an influence on the central government and bureaucracy through their influence on a local government and/or bureaucracy. The strength of this influence depends on the weight attached to the augmented interest function of the local government and/or bureaucracy in the nested interest function reflecting the decision-making structure of the state organization (see Subsection 4.3.2).

The following example is presented to give an idea of the sort of studies to which the acknowledgement of the aforementioned activities as options to the firm to further its interests may lead.

Consider a firm in an industry where the product price is determined through bargaining with the state. The firm considered has the option to bargain with the state directly (face to face) or via a trade association [13]. The industry is, furthermore, characterized by a concentration process, whereby the market share of our firm gradually increases relative to the shares of the other firms. For simplicity, total market demand is assumed to be constant, and production costs are neglected. The firm is supposed to maximize profits, given by

$$(7.13) \qquad P_f(t) = p_f(t)X_f(t) - B_{f1}(t) - B_{f2}(t),$$

where $p_f(t)$ denotes the product price for the firm at time t, $X_f(t)$ stands for the firm's sales, and

$B_{f1}(t)$ = outlays at time t for the support of the pressure (bargaining) activities of the trade association (contributions);

$B_{f2}(t)$ = outlays at time t for direct pressure.

As regards the concentration process, it is simply assumed that

$$(7.14) \qquad \frac{X_f(t)}{X_b} = \frac{1}{1 + e^{-t}},$$

where X_b stands for (fixed) total market sales in the industry, and t ranges from $-\infty$ to $+\infty$.
Assuming that at least some direct pressure as well as some pressure through the trade association is required [14], let, furthermore,

$$(7.15) \qquad p_f(t) = B_{f1}(t)^{\iota_{f1}(t)} . B_{f2}(t)^{\iota_{f2}(t)}$$

$$, \iota_{fi}(t) > 0, \ i = 1,2, \ \Sigma_i \ \iota_{fi}(t) < 1.$$

No lags or cross-effects of the activities are considered. With respect to the firm's price flexibility parameters $\iota_{fi}(t)$ it seems to be plausible to assume that they are a strictly quasi-concave function of the firm's market share of the form pictured in Fig. 7.3. These functions will not further be specified.

In Fig. 7.3, x_{fi}, i = 1,2, denotes the market share at which $\iota_{fi}(t)$ at-

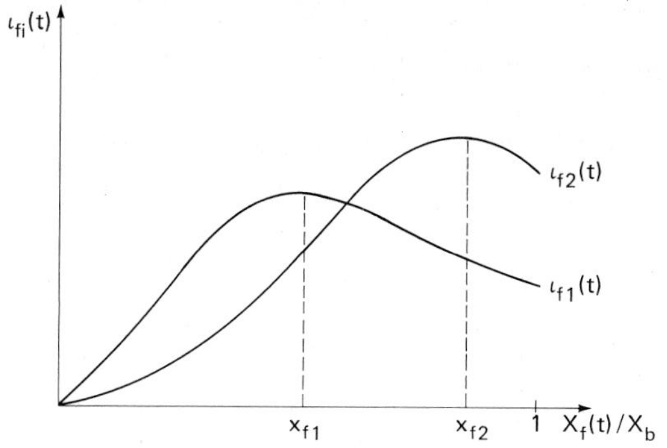

Fig. 7.3. Price flexibility as a function of the firm's market share.

tains its maximum. Because of the cohesiveness advantage of the firm it has been assumed that the maximum of $\iota_{f2}(t)$ exceeds the maximum of $\iota_{f1}(t)$. For both types of pressure activities it has, moreover, been assumed that over a certain range of market shares the firm will get a better price out of a given budget the larger its market share is. Beyond the market share x_{fi}, however, the value of $\iota_{fi}(t)$ is taken to fall, which means, in so far as activity i is concerned, a lower price for a given budget the larger the market share grows. This fall can be thought to be due, for example, to the adverse reactions of other collectivities (such as consumer organizations), evoked by the increasing visibility of the firm, which accompanies its increasing market share [15]. As the firm's direct pressure activity can, presumably, better be covered than its pressure through the trade association, it is assumed in Fig. 7.3 that once $\iota_{f2} > \iota_{f1}$ this inequality is continued.
Another reason for the fall in $\iota_{f2}(t)$ may be the loss of cohesiveness that can be expected to accompany the firm's growth.

Maximization of the profit function (7.13) demands, given eqs. (7.14) and (7.15), that

(7.16)

$$B_{f1}(t) = \left\{ [\iota_{f1}(t)]^{1 - \iota_{f2}(t)} \cdot [\iota_{f2}(t)]^{\iota_{f2}(t)} \cdot \left[\frac{X_b}{1 + e^{-t}}\right] \right\}^{\frac{1}{1 - \iota_{fi}(t) - \iota_{f2}(t)}},$$

$$B_{f2}(t) = \left\{ [\iota_{f1}(t)]^{\iota_{f1}(t)} \cdot [\iota_{f2}(t)]^{1 - \iota_{f1}(t)} \cdot \left[\frac{X_b}{1 + e^{-t}}\right] \right\}^{\frac{1}{1 - \iota_{fi}(t) - \iota_{f2}(t)}} .$$

Eqs. (7.16) clearly show the stimulating effect that the increasing market share in itself - neglecting its effect on $\iota_{fi}(t)$ - has on the budgets $B_{f1}(t)$ and $B_{f2}(t)$. It can also be seen that $B_{fi}(t)$ is positively related to $\iota_{fi}(t)$, *ceteris paribus*.

What exactly the effect of the increasing market share on the size of the budgets will be, depends, of course, on the specification of the relationship between $\iota_{fi}(t)$ and the market share.

From (7.16) the following expression for the relative size of the budgets is obtained:

$$(7.17) \qquad \frac{B_{f1}(t)}{B_{f2}(t)} = \frac{\iota_{f1}(t)}{\iota_{f2}(t)} .$$

It follows that the firm will concentrate its outlays for pressure on the trade association until the market share is reached (somewhere between x_{f1} and x_{f2}) at which the elasticities have become equal. After that point, the firm will mainly rely on its direct pressure.

Using eqs. (7.15) and (7.16), it is obtained with respect to the product price of the firm that

$$(7.18) \qquad p_f(t) = \left\{ [\iota_{f1}(t)]^{\iota_{f1}(t)} \cdot [\iota_{f2}(t)]^{\iota_{f2}(t)} \cdot \left[\frac{X_b}{1 + e^{-t}}\right]^{\iota_{f1}(t) + \iota_{f2}(t)} \right\}^{\frac{1}{1 - \iota_{f1}(t) - \iota_{f2}(t)}} .$$

Again, the specification of the relationships between $\iota_{fi}(t)$ and the firm's market share are needed in order to indicate the path that $p_f(t)$ will follow. However, that much is certain, that $p_f(t)$ need not be an increasing function of time, which would normally be expected to hold for a firm with an increasing market share.

For the budget to sales ratios it is obtained:

$$(7.19) \qquad \frac{B_{f1}(t)}{p_f(t)X_f(t)} = \iota_{f1}(t) \quad \text{and} \quad \frac{B_{f2}(t)}{p_f(t)X_f(t)} = \iota_{f2}(t),$$

and thus,

$$(7.20) \qquad \frac{B_{f1}(t) + B_{f2}(t)}{p_f(t)X_f(t)} = \iota_{f1}(t) + \iota_{f2}(t).$$

From (7.19) it can be concluded, conversely, that if the model is descrip-

tive, then observations on such ratios would indicate the firm's perception of the price flexibility with respect to its political activities.
From (7.20) it follows that the path followed by the total budget to sales ratio can be pictured in Fig. 7.3 by summing the curves of $\iota_{f1}(t)$ and $\iota_{f2}(t)$ vertically. Obviously, this ratio need not be an increasing function of the firm's market share either.
Using eqs. (7.13), (7.14), (7.16) and (7.18) it follows for the firm's profits that

$$(7.21)\qquad P_f(t) = [1 - \iota_{f1}(t) - \iota_{f2}(t)]\left\{[\iota_{f1}(t)]^{\iota_{f1}(t)} \cdot [\iota_{f2}(t)]^{\iota_{f2}(t)} \cdot \left[\frac{X_b}{1 + e^{-t}}\right]\right\}^{\frac{1}{1 - \iota_{f1}(t) - \iota_{f2}(t)}} .$$

As these profits are dependent on the price flexibilities $\iota_{fi}(t)$, which are dependent on the firm's market share, the question arises what the firm's optimal market share would have been. Now, without having to specify the relationships between $\iota_{f1}(t)$ and the firm's market share it is easily seen that this share may be less than 100%.
If follows that if, for whatever reasons, a firm's market share exceeds its optimal share it may wish to *demarket*, i.e. "attempt to reduce, temporarily or permanently, the level of customer demand" [Bloom and Kotler (1975, p. 63)].

7.6. *Summary*

In this chapter we have been concerned with the behaviour of *pressure groups*, i.e. collectivities (interest groups) that try to influence the behaviour of other collectivities. Special attention has been given to the interaction between a pressure group and the state.
As indicated in the introduction to this chapter the modelling of such behaviour is complex because of the analytically complicating phenomena of bargaining and threats that are closely associated with pressure.

The *tentative* approach that we suggested in this chapter is based on the idea that a pressure group that is able to noticeably and structurally (enduringly) affect the interests of a collectivity which is subject to its pressure, that such a pressure group builds up a *'vested interest'* with that collectivity, which forces the latter to simultaneously further the interests of the pressure group along with its own interests. It was suggested that, in order to arrive at a fair approximation of the behaviour of that collectivity, its complex interest function - as defined by eq. (4.2) - should be substituted by an *augmented interest function*, a weighted representation of the interest functions of that collectivity and the pressure group. In this context the reader is reminded that a complex interest function only represents the interests of the agents that make up a collectivity.

As regards the constraints subject to which the augmented interest function of the collectivity is supposed to be maximized it was suggested that they should be based on the assumption that the activities of the collectivity will be taken as given by the pressure group. After all, the latter's 'vested interest' has already been taken account of in the collectivity's augmented interest function.

The weight attached to the pressure group's interests in the augmented interest function was supposed to depend on three factors:

a. the objective threat potential of the pressure group for the collectivity subject to its pressure (indicated by the extent to which the former can maximally hurt the interests of the latter);
b. the cohesiveness of the pressure group;
c. the information that the collectivity reaches on the so-called objective threat intensity of the pressure group - which is determined by the first two factors - and its inclination to put it into play.

Together, these three factors determine the so-called effective threat intensity of the pressure group.
A functional relationship between the aforementioned weight and the effective threat intensity satisfying certain desirable properties was proposed.

For the development of general (politico-) economic models the suggestions summarized above seem to add up to a useful first approach, although it is acknowledged that only two pressure groups have been considered, and that the application of the approach in empirical research may be hampered by serious measurement problems. In cases where 'vested interests' are surmised to play an important role it could at least serve the purpose of tracing out the consequences of different assumptions with respect to the importance of such interests.
The - unattractive - alternative would seem to be to completely neglect the existence of pressure, or to try to capture by means of constraints alone the intricate relationships between pressure groups.
Even if we disregard any measurement problems, it should be clear, however, that the suggested approach may at best only offer a fair approximation of pressure group behaviour as it neglects the actual pressure activities (such as strikes, and lobbying) that sustain a 'vested interest'.

By treating actual conduct as a 'black box' it resembles the 'structure-performance' approach in industrial economics.

As *implications* of the augmented interest function approach we mentioned, *inter alia*, the following.

- The larger the weight that is attached to the interests of a pressure group by a collectivity, the more 'altruistic' the collectivity's behaviour will be in appearance.
In case of firms this will manifest itself as implicit collusion, which will be sustained by pressure, however. This means that implicit collusion and overt competition may simultaneously occur.
It was remarked that this combination would make it even more difficult for antitrust laws to be applied as implicit collusion alone already would make it.
- The state may further the (perceived) interests of a pressure group in the private sector (such as a trade association, or a labour union); conversely, a private sector collectivity may also further the (perceived) interests of the state. As an example that may be intuitively clear we mentioned the 'company town'.
- The promotion by the state of the interests of a pressure group further restricts the opportunity for voters to influence state behaviour. Other (possible) restrictions, that we paid attention to in earlier chapters, are the representation by bureaucrats and politicians of their own interests, and the structural coercion that originates from the private sector.
These restrictions should be taken into account when evaluating the working of a democracy in a capitalist economy.
- Changes in the type of state (through a change in party dominance, for example) or changes in the production structure of the economy, or in technology, may strongly affect the effective threat intensity of a pressure group and, consequently, the strength with which its interests are represented by another collectivity, such as the state. This may be an important reason for a pressure group to foster multiple positions (interlocking directorates).
- An augmented interest function reflects a degree of 'organization' or 'socialization' of the activities of the collectivities considered, which may even culminate into a new collectivity with one decision-making centre as a formal confirmation of a strong mutual interdependence.

Although we neglected actual pressure activities in the augmented interest function approach, special attention was given to such activities in a final section. By means of relatively simple examples concerning the pressure activity directed at the state by a labour union and a firm we tried to indicate some potentially interesting research areas.

The results that were obtained, such as that a labour union with a short time horizon will prefer to exploit its threat potential for the state by giving information on it (through strikes, and so on.), instead of building up its 'vested interest' through an expansion of its size or an increase in the cohesiveness of the union, or that a firm may deliberately wish to demarket (i.e., to diminish its market share) because of its 'visibility' or in order to increase the firm's cohesiveness, these results are particularly meant to stimulate further research and the development of realistic models. For, although pressure activity directed at the state appears to be a matter of great empirical relevance - witness also the existence of corporate government relations departments and of firms specializing in government relations counseling - models are almost completely lacking.

CHAPTER 8

EPILOGUE

In this book we have presented a non-normative, explanatory, analysis of the interaction between state and private sector in a capitalist economy, a field of research that was denoted as *political economics*. In carrying out the analysis, we paid heed to a number of analytical requirements that we think a study in political economics should satisfy. These requirements are, that account should be taken of: the existence of social classes; the dynamics of social class (power) structures; the relative autonomy of political processes and its consequences for, and dependence on, economic processes; individual motivations; and, finally, the possibility of mathematical formalization. The last requirement has to do with the fact that the thrust of an argument in this research area often depends on the exact specification of the relations involved.
Of particular usefulness for the study of politico-economic phenomena appeared to be the *Interest Function Approach* that we developed in the chapters 4 and 7. It enabled us to model in a uniform and natural way the activities of agents in the political sphere and in the - for an economist - traditional economic sphere. It also enabled us to deal explicitly with the fact that collective agents - collectivities, such as the state, or a firm - are typically made up by individual agents with diverging interests (forming interest blocs). In this context, it is noted that the applicability of the instruments constructed for the Interest Function Approach - to wit, the *elementary interest function*, the *(nested) complex interest function*, and the *augmented interest function* - is not restricted to the field of political economics. In our view, these instruments may prove to be valuable constructs for a general theory of organization.
From the many (empirical) research suggestions that we have made in this book we may conclude that the analysis has opened up a rich mine for further exploitation.

In the remainder of this chapter we would like to mention two important traditional practices in economics that we have broken with in this book, and then point at a number of issues regarding the state that are of interest in the context of our analysis.

The first important tradition that we rejected is to view the state as an extraneous body to the economy (the 'benevolent dictator'). We, furthermore, deemed as too simplistic here the conception of the state as the executive committee of the interests of capitalists, on the one hand, and the more modern conceptions of the bureau maximizing bureaucrat and the vote maximizing politician, on the other hand. Instead, we have worked on a theory of the *state as an organization that forms an integral part of the economy* considered, whose behaviour - like that of a collectivity in the private sector - is determined by the particularized class interests of the agents comprising it (the state sector workers: bureaucrats and politicians) and the behavioural constraints originating from the environment in which it acts.

Another important traditional practice in economics that we broke with is to assume that people confine themselves to the market for the furtherance of their interests. As we have shown in the aforegoing chapters, *non-market activities* in the political sphere - such as voting and lobbying - may have a substantial influence on the production and distribution of goods in an economy. We have also shown that the modelling of such activities is possible.

Our conception of the state conflicts with the idea of *'voter-sovereignty'* that is often associated with democracies. It is not only of importance here that state sector workers are considered as agents trying to further their own interests, it is also necessary to stress that voting is only one - admittedly important - form of pressure that is brought to bear upon the state. The influence of pressure groups other than voters and political parties should not be ignored. It should also be realized in this context that the state in a capitalist economy is confronted with outcomes of decisions taken in the private sector, that do not - at least, explicitly - have the consent of voters.

The interest function approach developed in this book also suggests that *laws* should be expected to reflect the influence of class interests, formally and in their implementation. As state sector workers are supposed to have their own particular class interests, it will depend on the constraints on their behaviour whether, and to what extent, class interests other than the state sector workers' will be served. However, the means required for the establishment of such constraints will generally be unevenly distributed over the social classes in an economy (think of the unemployed). Paraphrasing Adam Smith's famous fundamental idea we would say: it is not from the benevolence of the butcher, the brewer, the baker, *and the lawgiver*, that we expect our dinner *and legal rights*, but from their regard to their own interests [see Smith (1970 [1776], p. 13); italicized words added].

This brings us to the role played by *economic policy advisors* in this context. From the analysis it follows that policy advices will only have an effect if the agent which is being advised perceives them as beneficial to the furtherance of its interests. Useful advices demand, therefore, that the policy advisor occupies her/himself with the intersection of economics

and politics, i.e. political economics. For example, an economist might be asked by the state to give advice on how to better the prospects of an underdeveloped region in the country, or on how to strengthen a weak industry. An adherent to the conception of the state as a 'benevolent dictator' ('social welfare maximizer') might indicate with respect to the former that the infrastructure of the region should be improved, and with respect to the latter that the tariffs for imported competing goods should be scaled up. A political economist, on the other hand, would take along in her/his advice an evaluation of the interests represented by state sector workers, and of the relative strength with which they are promoted by them in the state organization. Elsewhere we have shown how important the interests represented by state sector workers may be for the (un)even development of private production sectors [see Van Winden (1979b)]. As a consequence, the possibility arises that such an economist might turn down a request because he/she observes a factual (not formal) lack of interest in solving the problems involved. As soon as one accepts the conception of the state as an organization representing particular interests, the functioning of the economic policy advisor also gets a deeper significance for agents in the private sector. For such an agent it then becomes important to know to what extent its interests are (really) furthered by the state, and, also, in which way it can have its interests better promoted by the state.
For example, for a region confronted with a stagnant economy the advice of a political economist might be to rely on its own forces because no support from the state can be expected given the prevailing interest and power structure. The advice might also point at ways (pressure activities) to change that structure.
In this whole context, the interests represented by the advisor retain, of course, a significance of their own. Advising becomes less 'innocent' when particular interests - not necessarily one's own - instead of the 'public interest' are served by it.

It may, furthermore, be useful to note that the *ad hoc* character that *state policies* often seem to have, is probably less the result of deficient information than the outcome of conflicts of interests within the state organization and between the state and pressure groups in the private sector. Moreover, such policies may have their own logic, in so far as they are the outcome of compromises that are produced in a systematic way, as we in fact assumed in the Interest Function Approach.

NOTES TO CHAPTER 1

1. This definition is based on Engels (1892, pp. 165-166) and Weber (1972 [1922], p. 29).

2. See Bacon and Eltis (1978, 1979), De Vries (1978), Friedman (1976), Goode (1979), Hadjimatheou and Skouras (1979), OECD (1978), O'Connor (1973), Vermaat (1979).

3. The literature referred to should only serve the purpose of giving an idea of the work that has been done in these areas.

4. To have the adjective 'political' refer to the behaviour of the state is in accordance with the rather common interpretation that politics has to do with the causes, nature, and consequences of state policies; see, e.g., Hoogerwerf (1979).

5. The consequent risk of a serious specification error in econometric estimation is discussed in Crotty (1973); see also Blinder and Solow (1974, p. 71) where it is argued that this may explain the poor policy predictions of some of the econometric models despite impressive 'goodness-of-fit' statistics.

6. For a discussion of various possible allocation systems, see, e.g., Shubik (1970a).

7. "The modern state is but a committee for managing the common affairs of the whole bourgeoisie".

8. Notice, that even Marx's and Engels' aforementioned statement can be interpreted as implying some relative autonomy for the state, as the *common* affairs of the *whole* bourgeoisie - comprising different fractions - is taken care of [see Miliband (1973, p. 85)].

9. See, e.g., Alavi (1972), Altvater (1972, 1976), Boddy and Crotty (1975), Dallemagne *et al.* (1974), Gerstenberger (1976), Gough (1975), Magdoff (1969), Mandel (1973), O'Connor (1973), Offe (1972), Stuurman (1978), Sweezy and Magdoff (1972), Yaffe (1976); surveys of the literature are given by Esser (1976), Gold, Lo and Wright (1975), Guggenberger (1974), Jessop (1977), Koch (1979); see also the somewhat older works by Baran (1973), Baran and Sweezy (1968), Sweezy (1968).

10. The synopsis is largely based on Poulantzas (1978b, pp. 14-35).

11. The figure is based on Stuurman (1978, p. 146).

12. With respect to Poulantzas' emphasis on structural analysis Gold, Lo and Wright remark: "Although there is a fairly rich discussion of *how* the relative autonomy of the state protects the class interests of the dominant class, and of the functional *necessity* for such a state structure, there is no explanation of the social mechanisms which guarantee that the state will in fact function in this way" [Gold, Lo and Wright (1975, p. 38)]. Observe the correspondence with mainstream economics where it is also too easily concluded that the state will step in where the private sector 'fails' (state activities *because of* externalities, technical indivisibilities, etc.).

13. Baumol (1965), Buchanan and Tullock (1962), Olson (1965), Taylor (1976).

14. Arrow (1963), Black (1958), Buchanan and Tullock (1962), Farquharson (1969), Sen (1970). Forerunners are Wicksell and Lindahl; see Musgrave and Peacock (1967).

15. Comanor (1976), Davis, Hinich and Ordeshook (1970), Downs (1957), Pommerehne (1978), Romer and Rosenthal (1979), Selten (1971), Taylor (1972). A classic contribution to the theory of party competition is Hotelling (1929).

16. Downs (1957), Frey (1971), Riker and Ordeshook (1968).

17. Brennan and Buchanan (1978), Downs (1957), Frey and Lau (1968), Lindbeck (1976). A forerunner is Schumpeter (1947).

18. Blankart (1975), Downs (1967), Niskanen (1974), Orzechowski (1977), Tullock (1974a).

19. Breton (1974), Davis, Dempster and Wildavsky (1966), Miller (1977), Niskanen (1974).

20. Bartlett (1973), Frey (1968, 1974a), Galbraith (1967).

21. Frey (1974b, 1977b), MacRae (1977), Nordhaus (1975); for a game-theoretical model, see Aumann and Kurz (1978).

22. Arcelus and Meltzer (1975a,b), Bloom and Price (1975), Goodhart and Bhansali (1970), Goodman and Kramer (1975), Fair (1978), Kramer (1971), Lepper (1974), Stigler (1973); see, however, Gevers and Proost (1978), Hibbs (1977), and, in particular, Frey and Schneider (1978a,b) where also the activities of the state are part of the analysis.

23. See in this context Buchanan (1967) on 'fiscal illusion'.

24. See Frey (1977a, Ch. 11; 1978).

25. It has been shown, for example, that economic (business) cycles can deliberately be created by politicians acting under a re-election constraint.

26. There are some hints in the literature, however, of the (possible) importance of making such a distinction; see Arcelus and Meltzer (1975a, p. 1268), Kramer (1971, p. 133), Stigler (1973, p. 167), Wagner (1977); see also Myrdal (1953, Ch. 8) in this context. In addition, we should refer to the works of the students of pressure/interest groups; see, e.g., Egozi (1973), Helleiner (1977), Pincus (1975). In this perspective the frequently used adjective 'public' in the literature is somewhat odd; see O'Connor (1972).

27. An exception is Bernholz (1966).

28. See, however, Bartlett (1973, Part 4), Breton (1974, Ch. 5). According to Foley (1978, p. 224): "State policy itself is decided in elections only in rare and marginal instances. Whatever group or fraction holds State power, the great mass of State policy is determined within the administrative apparatus of the State, a bureaucracy in which an intense struggle for influence among emergent interests constantly manifests itself". Although this may not be true under all circumstances it gives at least a warning against too high expectations.

29. The older notion of political economy - although advocated by some critics of contemporary economic theory [see Jessop (1977, p. 371), Morgenstern (1972, p. 1175), Shubik (1970b, p. 407)] - is too ambiguous. With the passage of time it has taken such divergent meanings as 'economics applied to the state', 'economics' in the ordinary sense, 'value loaded economics', as well as what we just called 'political economics', see., e.g., Schumpeter (1972, pp. 21-22). See also Gurley (1971).
In contrast with such labels as the 'theory of the collective/public sector' or the 'theory of public economics' the proposed term does not suggest that attention should be restricted to the state. After all, it is also the 'theory of the firm', for example, that is involved here.
It is also noted in this context that the label 'theory of non-market decision making' addresses in fact a much larger research area than what is referred to here.

30. We realize that it is hazardous to study phenomena where different sciences are involved, with their own traditions and approaches [see, in the context of our subject, Barry (1970), Hirschman (1970, pp. 15-20)]. However, as the alternative of not studying them is worse in our opinion, we cannot do otherwise than to try to make some contact.

31. See Miliband (1973a, Ch. 3). As we will not study the nature of ideology in this book we need not go into the discussion regarding the question of what the ideological apparatuses of the state are; see Laclau (1975), Miliband (1970, 1977), Poulantzas (1969, 1978a).

32. The term bureaucracy will not be used to identify a form of government ruled by officials [cf. Niskanen (1974, p. 23)].

33. For The Netherlands, see WRR (1979, p. 19); for the United States, see Musgrave and Musgrave (1973, p. 111). Moreover, state employment appears to be a fairly good proxy for the state's total direct spending, i.e. total state expenditure excluding transfers [see Borcherding (1977, p. 33)].

34. In order to be specific, simplifications cannot be avoided. Especially in the field of political economics, an all-embracing theory cannot be aimed at [compare Downs (1957, p. 290), Jessop (1977, p. 369), Shubik (1970b, pp. 406-407)]. Research outcomes will always be conditional on the specific institutional assumptions that have to be made. What is important, however, is that institutions are at all considered. Moreover, the development of particular institutions will, of course, still be amenable to analysis. A politico-economic model with a heterogeneous bureaucracy is developed in Van Winden (1979b).

35. In Marxist terms, only the capitalist model of production is studied with no remnants of other modes of production.

36. See, e.g., Cameron (1978). After a study of data for 18 nations Cameron concludes that "the openness of the economy is the best single predictor of the growth of public revenues relative to the economic product of a nation" (*op. cit.*, p. 1254). Second-best is the partisanship of government, with leftist domination going together with large increases. The impact of partisanship is more pronounced in larger nations with more closed economies than in smaller ones with open economies. Cameron's tentative explanation for this points at the positive effect of greater openness on the degree of industrial concentration, the degree of unionization, the scope of collective bargaining, strength of labour confederations, and the chance of enduring leftist governments.

37. A model with two private production sectors is presented in Van Winden (1979b). In this model, the state comprises two bureaucratic departments whose production is allowed to have a differential impact on the technology of the private production sectors.

38. Particularly in case of elections, discrete time instead of continuous time is an appropriate choice.

39. Similar assumptions are, e.g., made in Barro and Grossman (1976). 'Rational expectations' models employ very strong assumptions with respect to the availability of information; see Friedman (1979). The incorporation of more sophisticated expectations adjustment processes, involving more information, would demand the explicit consideration of information costs.

40. In this section we draw on Van Winden (1976, 1980).

41. Bannock, Baxter and Rees (1979, p. 273): "A market exists when buyers wishing to exchange money for a good or service are in contact with sellers wishing to exchange goods or services for money. Thus, a market is defined in terms of the fundamental forces of supply and demand, and is not necessarily confined to any particular geographical location"; Stigler (1966, p. 85): "A market (...) is the area within which the price of a commodity tends to uniformity, allowance being made for transportation costs"; Lipsey and Steiner (1975, p. 62): "a market is defined as an area over which buyers and sellers negotiate the exchange of a well-defined commodity"; Lancaster (1973, p. 67): "Markets are social institutions in which goods and services can be freely exchanged for other goods and services. In all modern economies the exchange is indirect - one good is exchanged for money, which is then exchanged for other goods". The index to Samuelson (1976) does not even mention the concept as such.

42. Thus, according to our definition, state policies cannot be considered as the results of (political) market processes in so far as they are coercive (citizens cannot opt out).

43. It may be clear that even for modern money economies attention should not *a priori* be restricted to markets with indirect exchange when studying the interaction between state and private sector.

44. See Walker (1943, Ch. 6) for an early contribution to the incorporation into economic theory of activities that take place outside the market.

45. A borderline case is advertising, it may be part of an exchange process (in which case it is a MA), but it also plays a part in establishing such processes (in which case it should be considered as a NMA). Observe that concepts like selling, buying, borrowing, hiring, do not denote MA in themselves, but the result of such activities by agents.

46. NMA may involve MA, such as in case of public relations activities. Also note, that NMA may develop into MA, for example in case of lobbying.

47. Compare Max Weber's definition of a social relationship: "Soziale Beziehung soll ein seinem Sinngehalt nach aufeinander gegenseitig eingestelltes und dadurch orientiertes Sichverhalten mehrerer heiszen. Die soziale Beziehung besteht also durchaus und ganz ausschlieszlich: in der Chance, dasz in einer (sinnhaft) angebbaren Art sozial gehandelt

wird, einerlei zunächts: worauf diese Chance beruht" [Weber (1972 [1922], p. 13)].

NOTES TO CHAPTER 2

1. This chapter is based on Van Winden (1976, 1980).

2. A collective good is a good "which all enjoy in common in the sense that each individual's consumption of such a good leads to no subtraction from any other individual's consumption of that good"; Samuelson (1954, p. 387). The usual example is national defense. Other examples are: the maintenance of internal order, the law, protection against floods, the infrastructure of a country in terms of health. Goods may also be collective with respect to a subset of agents in the economy [so-called 'local public goods'; see, e.g., Ruys (1974, Ch. 4)]; see Chapter 4.

3. See, e.g., Galbraith (1967), Niskanen (1974), Peabody and Rourke (1965).

4. A classic work on the socio-political importance of the total employment level (high levels as well as low levels) is Kalecki (1971).

5. We disregard the possibility of bribing individual state sector workers; see Rose-Ackerman (1975) on this subject.

6. Think of the prisoner's dilemma and the free-rider problem. As regards the prisoner's dilemma, see Luce and Raiffa (1957, pp. 94-97), Taylor (1976); the free-rider problem is exposed in Olson (1965), Stigler (1974).

7. As the firms are tax-price takers and capital costs are deductible, the profit tax has no effect on the behaviour of the firms. If capital costs are not deductible then the firms' behaviour is influenced by τ_2 as the first half of (2.8) then reads: $(1 - \tau_2)(1 - \tau_1)\partial G/\partial K_b = r$.

8. See Intriligator (1971, p. 191).

9. Throughout this chapter liquidity problems are supposed to be absent. The non-negativity of P_b is ensured by (2.12).

10. A game is called a supergame if it is repeated. The strategies for these games are called supergame strategies [see Friedman (1977)]. The game presented here may be seen as the constituent game of a particular supergame for which the equilibrium supergame strategy of the firms is assumed to be given.

11. See Kydland (1975). Alternatively, it can be said that the state uses a Stackelberg strategy; see Simaan and Cruz (1973). The appropriateness of this terminology from a Marxist point of view is discussed in Appendix 2A.

12. Movements along the strictly convex isoquants are dominated by τ_3 [$dK_b/dE_2 = -(1 + \tau_3)w/r$], movements along expansion paths by τ_1.

13. Note that this constraint is violated if $E_2 = 0$ and/or $K_b = 0$.

14. See, e.g., Intriligator (1971, pp. 16-19).

15. The strict convexity follows from the properties of the production function.

16. Putting $\partial P_s/\partial E_2 = f_E$, $\partial P_s/\partial K_b = f_K$, $\partial^2 P_s/\partial E_2^2 = f_{EE}$ and so on for other partial derivatives of P_s, one obtains with respect to the curvature of the contours of P_s that: $dE_2/dK_b = - f_K/f_E$, and $d^2E_2/dK_b^2 = - f_E^{-3}$ $[f_{KK} \cdot f_E^2 - 2f_{EK} \cdot f_E \cdot f_K + f_{EE} \cdot f_K^2]$, where $f_E = w + \partial G/\partial E_2 - \varepsilon(2w + \partial G/\partial E_2)$ and $f_K = (1 - \varepsilon)\partial G/\partial K_b$. The expression between square brackets is a negative definite quadratic form [see, e.g., Takayama (1974)], due to the properties of the production function. It follows that $d^2E_2/dK_b^2 > 0$ (strict convexity) if $f_E > 0$ and, thus, $\varepsilon < (w + \partial G/\partial E_2)/(2w + \partial G/\partial E_2)$; in that case $dE_2/dK_b < 0$. If $f_E < 0$ [$\varepsilon > (w + \partial G/\partial E_2)/(2w + \partial G/\partial E_2)$] then $d^2E_2/dK_b^2 < 0$ (strict concavity), while $dE_2/dK_b > 0$. If $f_E \to 0$ then $|dE_2/dK_b| \to \infty$. Observe that $1 > (w + \partial G/\partial E_2)/(2w + \partial G/\partial E_2) > 0.5$, and that $\partial G/\partial E_2$ can be chosen such that $(w + \partial G/\partial E_2)/(2w + \partial G/\partial E_2)$ will be arbitrarily close to its lower or upper bound.

17. The conditions are sufficient for a unique global maximum as $P_s(E_2,K_b) = (2\varepsilon - 1)w(E^* - E_2) + (1 - \varepsilon)G(E_2,K_b)$ is strictly (quasi) concave, and the constraint functions [the left-hand sides of the inequality constraints in (2.14a)] are all concave in E_2 and K_b. The conditions are necessary for such an equilibrium because there exists a E_2,K_b-combination for which the inequality constraints are satisfied as strict inequalities (the constraint qualification condition). See, e.g., Intriligator (1971), Takayama (1974).

18. For the rising part of the surplus constraint curve it holds that $\partial N/\partial K_b < 0$ (see Fig. 2.2), where $\partial N/\partial K_b = (1 - q)\partial G/\partial K_b - r$.

19. It should be noted that the abrupt change in the behaviour of the state would probably be mitigated if one allowed for positive effects of state production (e.g., education, research) on private production. As observed by Bacon and Eltis (1978, pp. 189-191), however, in their analysis of the economic impact of a changing size of the non-market sector (the sector that does not market its products), the size of the non-market sector may also have unfavourable consequences because of the existence of 'Verdoorn effects' [see Verdoorn (1952)] or 'learning by doing' [see Arrow (1962)].
For this reason, they assume, like we have done in the present model, that the production function is not altered by a reallocation of labour from the market sector to the non-market sector.

20. $\partial N/\partial k_b < 0$ will at least hold if ε approaches ε^{p2}, see c.

21. Assuming positive cross-partial derivatives for the production function, $\partial N/\partial K_b > 0$ should hold at intersections of the capital constraint curve with contours of the surplus constraint function.

22. In passing it should be noted that, since labour always positively contributes to state production as well as private production, the most important effect of a flexible total employment target or a downward adjustment of the dole rate (ψw) will probably be that through an

enlargement of the opportunity set more economies will have an equilibrium and that economies become less restrictive.

23. The figures for A are rounded off.

24. Using (2.8), one obtains as input demand functions:
$$E_2 = (1 - \tau_1)^{1/\iota} \cdot (1 + \tau_3)^{(\mu - 1)/\iota} \cdot (\mu/r)^{\mu/\iota} \cdot (v/w)^{(1 - \mu)/\iota} \cdot A^{1/\iota},$$
$$K_b = (1 - \tau_1)^{1/\iota} \cdot (1 + \tau_3)^{-v/\iota} \cdot (\mu/r)^{(1 - v)/\iota} \cdot (v/w)^{v/\iota} \cdot A^{1/\iota},$$
where $\iota = 1 - \mu - v$.

The following sufficient conditions for a perfectly restrictive econo-
my have been used: $E_1 = E_1^-$, $K_b = \bar{K}_b$, $N = 0$ and $\tau_1 \geq q$, which demands
that

1. $\tau_1 = 1 - r(\bar{K}_b)^{1 - \mu} \cdot [\mu A(E^* - E_1^-)^v]^{-1}$;

2. $\tau_3 = vr\bar{K}_b [\mu w(E^* - E_1^-)]^{-1} - 1$;

3. $A(1 - q)(E^* - E_1^-)^v (\bar{K}_b)^\mu \{r\bar{K}_b + w[E^* + \psi(L - E^*)]\}^{-1} = 1$;

4. $\tau_1 \geq q$.

The necessary and sufficient conditions for a permissive economy: $E_1 = E_1^-$, $K_b = \bar{K}_b$ and $N > 0$ for $0 \leq \varepsilon \leq 0.5$, lead to the same relations 1
and 2 for τ_1 and τ_3, but the equality sign in 3 has to be substi-
tuted by a 'larger than' sign ($>$), and 4 should be discarded.

25. To solve the non-linear constrained optimization problem we used the
subroutine E04HAF developed by the Numerical Algorithms Group of Not-
tingham University, NAG-Library Manual, January 1974. Apart from the
interval $0.6 \leq \varepsilon \leq 0.7$, only first decimal values have been used for
ε.

26. For the N-person supergame it has been shown that under certain conditions even implicit co-operative behaviour (that is co-operative behaviour not backed up by binding agreements) may occur; see Friedman
(1977), Taylor (1976).

27. Obviously, $E_1 = E_1^-$, $K_b \leq \bar{K}_b$ and $N = 0$ need not hold in this case.

28. See Luce and Raiffa (1957, pp. 110-111).

29. These effects may, of course, also occur in case of significant
changes in structural coercion [cf. Peacock and Wiseman (op.cit.)] or
pressure.

30. See Domhoff (1967, 1979), Galbraith (1967), Mills (1956), Miliband
(1973a); for The Netherlands, see Helmers et al. (1975).

31. According to Poulantzas, the Communist parties underestimated the danger of fascism in the inter-war period just because of their reliance
on the predominant role of the productive forces and the economism to
which it lead; see Poulantzas (1974, p. 47).

32. See Laclau (1975), Miliband (1973b).

33. It should be noticed that in that case (competitive capitalism)

Poulantzas assigns the dominant role to the economic; at the stage of state monopoly capitalism the dominant role is held by the political [Poulantzas (1978a, pp. 55,211)]. Once again, however, it is not clear what he exactly means with the notion 'dominant role'.

NOTES TO CHAPTER 3

1. The content of this chapter is based on Van Winden and Van Praag (1981).

2. The latter assumption rests on the common view that productivity in the state sector can hardly be changed. A constant private labour productivity is not excluded, however.

3. See, e.g., Anderson (1961), Dougherty (1974), Jorgenson and Griliches (1967), Rees (1980).

4. See, e.g., Gough (1975, p. 80), OECD (1978, p. 8). Instructive are also the governmental reports on innovation [for The Netherlands, see Tweede Kamer (1979)]. In addition to the activities indicated in the text we could further mention the maintenance of internal and external order (through defense, police): "The existence of state monopolies of violence made it possible for a process of purely *economic* (market) competition to take place. If entrepreneurs would have had to maintain private armies to protect their factories from attempts at destruction by competitors and to safeguard the roads, railways and canals over which their products were transported, the process of industrialization could hardly have proceeded - certainly not as quickly as it did", Van Benthem van de Berg (1976, p. 301).

5. See, however, Aarrestad (1978), Johnston (1975), McMillan (1978), Ritzen (1977). For empirical studies, see Denison (1967), Griliches (1964). As stated in the previous chapter (see note 19), one justification might be that the size of the state may also have unfavourable consequences for labour productivity because of the possible impact of private production and investment through so-called 'Verdoorn effects' and 'learning by doing'. However, although this matter cannot be settled without much more empirical research, it should be noticed that these effects may also occur in the state sector. Moreover, private production and investment need not decline if there is a positive impact of state activities on labour productivity [see the critique of Hadjimatheou and Skouras (1979, p. 399) on Bacon and Eltis (1978)].

6. See Anderson (1961), Arrow (1962, p. 159), Bacon and Eltis (1978, p. 109), Den Hartog *et al.* (1975, p. 53).

7. In the seminal article by Nordhaus (1975) vote plurality maximizing politicians make use of a Phillips-curve like trade-off between unemployment and inflation under the assumption that unemployment and inflation appear as arguments in a preference function for voters, which are assumed to be myopic as regards the evaluation of past events. The optimal policy for politicians gives a sawtoothed path for unemployment, and a slightly smoothed path for inflation, with unemployment (inflation) attaining its highest (lowest) level just after an election in order to combat inflation, and its lowest (highest) level just before an election [see also MacRae (1977), Frey (1974b), and Chapter 5].

8. Nevertheless, it will be shown that the phenomenon of a political

business cycle may also occur when no re-election constraint exists.

9. See McMillan (1978). In McMillan (1978), and also in Aarrestad (1978), optimal control models are developed, focusing upon the maximization of a social welfare function, in which a similar non-negative relationship appears between productivity and (the stock of) a public intermediate good. The concept of a public intermediate good dates back to, at least, Meade's discussion of the 'creation of atmosphere' [Meade (1952)].

10. For the state as well as for the firms (see Subsection 3.2.5) 'hard budget constraints' [Kornai (1979)] are assumed, being only mitigated in the sense that debts are allowed to accumulate when state or firms do not find it possible to avoid them.

11. The symbol E_3, denoting the number of capitalists, will be introduced in the next chapter. Note that only distributed profits are taxed.

12. As wages in the state sector typically seem to follow wages in the private sector [in The Netherlands, e.g., the wage rate for state employees has officially been tied to the private wage rate for about 20 years now; for the United States, see Quinn (1979)], and unemployment benefits are often legally tied to the wage rate in social security systems [see, for the European Communities, Commissie van de Europese Gemeenschappen (1976)], it seems acceptable at this stage of the analysis to take their relationship as a political fact for bureaucrats and politicians. A more refined model would have to consider these payments as outcomes of politico-economic processes. The symbol w_3, denoting the income of capitalists, will be introduced in the next chapter.

13. A statutory, absolute minimum income level exists, for example, in Germany, Belgium and Luxembourg; see Kapteyn and Halberstadt (1979).

14. A less rigorous assumption would be that the trimming of the state apparatus is related to the state's debt burden.

15. More attention will be paid to this parameter κ in Chapter 5.

16. Assuming that $w_2(0) > 0$ it follows that $w_2(t) > 0$. Assuming that $X_b(0) > 0$ it follows from (3.4), (3.21), (3.28) and (3.32) that $E_2^d(t) > 0$.

17. Only the firms definitely know what price they are going to charge for their products; see Subsection 3.2.5.

18. Otherwise, we cannot have a situation in which there are positive transfers, from one period to another, of disposable income and/or money reserved for investment, while $D_b(t) = D_s(t) = 0$; all the money, generated by loans for wages and unemployment benefits, would have flown back to the bank by the end of a period. It may be assumed that M has also been supplied by the bank.

19. In the numerical experiments reported in Section 3.5 investment demand never exceeded total supply.

20. Note that the expectation of dividends implies that positive excess funds are expected.

21. See Fisher (1970, 1972). For a different point of view, see Hey (1974).

22. Recall that the decisions on p(t+1) and $\sigma(t)$ are made at the end of period t. Assuming that $X_b(0) > 0$ it follows from (3.4), (3.5), (3.21), (3.28) and (3.32) that $X_b^s(t) > 0$. Assuming that $p(0) > 0$ it then follows from (3.31) that $p(t) > 0$. If $p(t) > 0$, $w_2(t) > 0$ and $E_2^d(t) > 0$ it follows from (3.14), (3.22) and (3.23) that $X_b^d(t) > 0$.

23. Later periods are only of interest in so far as investments are considered, and in that case $p(t,t+n)\tilde{\alpha}_b(t+n) > \tilde{w}_2(t+n)$ should hold; see the ensuing text.

24. It is easily shown that $\tilde{F}(t+1) > 0$ if $\tilde{F}(t+2) > 0$, so that (3.26) is well defined in this case.

25. In passing it should be noted that although only a relatively few formal political economic models exist, there is a large number of economic policy models [see Fox, Sengupta and Thorbecke (1973)]. The social welfare functions or preference functions used in these models are usually specified in a linear, log-linear or quadratic way. Quite often a quadratic formulation is preferred [see Fox, Sengupta and Thorbecke (1973), Friedlaender (1973), Holt (1962), Nijkamp and Somermeyer (1971), Theil (1964)]. Although its nice mathematical properties are an important point in its favour, it also has some serious shortcomings. Positive and negative deviations from the optimum are equally negatively valued; moreover, it often is not clear what the optimum value (the target) should be [see Wood (1965)].

26. In the following chapter we will have to make some critical remarks with respect to these assumptions.

27. Maximization of $\varepsilon \ln X_b(t) + (1 - \varepsilon)\ln X_s(t)$ subject to $E_1(t) + E_2(t) = L$, demands that $E_2(t) = \varepsilon L$; see eqs. (3.3) and (3.4).

28. As is easily seen from eqs. (3.8) and (3.9), labour productivity is bounded from above by the size of the total labour force.

29. In general, the first-order condition for an interior solution to (3.19) demands that: $2\lambda[\ln E_1^d(t) - \ln E_1(t-1) - \theta] - (1 - \varepsilon)(1 - \lambda) = 0$, provided that $E_1^d(t) \leq L - \tilde{E}_2^d(t)$, and: $2\lambda\{E_1^d(t) - [L + S(t)/\tilde{\alpha}_b(t)]\}[\ln E_1^d(t) - \ln E_1(t-1) - \theta] - (1 - \lambda)\{E_1^d(t) - (1 - \varepsilon)[L + S(t)/\tilde{\alpha}_b(t)]\} = 0$, provided that $E_1^d(t) > L - \tilde{E}_2^d(t)$ and, thus, $\tilde{E}_2(t) = L - E_1^d(t)$.

30. For $\tilde{P}_b(t) = \sum_{n=o}^{2} \rho_n[1 - \sigma(t,t+n)]\tilde{F}(t+n)$ it is obtained that:

$$\sigma(t) \begin{array}{l} = 0 \\ = \text{indeterminate} \\ = 1 \end{array} \quad \text{if} \quad \rho \begin{array}{c} > \\ = \\ < \end{array} \tilde{r}(t+2),$$

where $\tilde{r}(t+2) = [p(t,t+2)\tilde{\alpha}_b(t+2) - \tilde{w}_2(t+2)][\beta/\tilde{\alpha}_b(t+2)]/p(t,t+1)$.

31. If $n = 0,\ldots,N$ $(N > 2)$ and $\sigma(t,t+n) = 0$ for $n > 0$, so that only the effect of investment in period t is considered, the same solution for $\sigma(t)$ is obtained, with $\rho = \rho_0/(\rho_0 + \rho_2 + \ldots + \rho_N)$. Using dynamic pro-

gramming techniques to determine $\sigma(t,t+n)$, future investments can be allowed for as well [see, e.g., Intriligator (1971)].

32. Recall that the firm does not expect to have any influence on the behaviour of the state (assumption 2 in Subsection 3.2.5).

33. Due to the fixed size of the labour force the model cannot generate non-zero steady state growth. Moreover, it can be shown that an equilibrium marked by stationarity for quantity variables (excluding the stock of money) and a constant rate of change for price level and wage rate can only exist if that rate of change is equal for both of them and $D_s(t) \neq 0$ [as $\sigma(t) > 0$ should hold because of replacement investments, $D_b(t) = 0$, see (3.11) and (3.36); see also Fig. 3.4 in this context]. However, an equilibrium concept that allows for $D_s(t) \neq 0$ is hard to accept, given the assumption that priority is given to a balanced budget. Also note that the assumptions exclude an equilibrium with no production at all (see note 22; in addition, recall that $x_b^{c-} > 0$).

34. The possibility that the state's demand for labour is indeterminate [see Section 3.3, point 4] is neglected.

35. The labour market is the only market in the model where a crowding-out effect may occur. The labour market rationing parameter κ and the expectations of state and firm with respect to its value are important in this respect. In passing it should be noted that the real value of κ has no impact on equilibria since state and firms expect their demand for labour to be realized and there is no excess demand in equilibrium.

36. In equilibrium, M equals the amount of money that is available in the economy on a long term base (see Subsection 3.2.4). Notice from (3A5) and (3A6) that condition (3A6) may be dropped if M is adjusted - just like wage related money supply - to whatever is demanded for transactions (which is the sole reason for people to hold money in our model); in that case, the supply of money will always be equal to the total demand for money. As, moreover, the market value of private product supply equals that of demand for any product price (since all income is spent), it would then be appropriate to take private product as *numéraire*. It should be remarked, however, that the equilibrium results obtained below will not change whether M is fixed or not.

37. This is not to say that nothing can be done about it. The crucial question becomes how ρ is determined. Class struggle may be one of its determinants. Observe, however, that the consequences could be different from what might be expected. As it seems plausible that an inverse relationship exists between the strength of the position of capitalists and ρ, it is likely that capitalists demand a high rate of return when in a weak position, which leaves a low equilibrium value for the real wage rate. The conclusion may be that an equilibrium tendency is not very likely in that case. See, in this context, also Dobb (1973, pp. 267 *seq.*), Sraffa (1960, pp. 33).

38. This share equals: $(1 - r/\beta) + \tau(1 - \sigma)r/\beta$. Using (3.39) and (3.40), one minus this share (which renders the after-tax profit share) can be written as the reciprocal of the expression between brackets in (3.37) (the velocity of circulation of money).

39. We have neglected here the type of state characterized by $(\lambda_s = 0, \varepsilon = 1)$, which is the only type of state for which $\tau(t) = \tau^+(t)$ may necessarily hold because it does not sustain an equilibrium with $E_1 > E_1^-$.

40. For $\eta = 1$, it is obtained from (3A8) that, in case of a unique equilibrium, $E_1 = \max\{E_1^-, [0.5L - (1 + A_2)/(2A_1)]\}$ should hold, where $1 + A_2 = -\{1 - \phi + (1 - \sigma)[(1 - r/\beta)^{-1} - 1]\}/(\phi - \psi)$. Maximum feasible private output demands that: $E_1 = \max\{E_1^-, 0.5L\}$. Thus, if $\eta = 1$, a unique equilibrium implies maximum private output only if $\max\{E_1^-, 0.5L\} = \max\{E_1^-, [0.5L - (1 + A_2)/(2A_1)]\}$.

41. A unique equilibrium with $\phi = 1$ and $\sigma = 1$ demands that: $(1 - \tau)\psi w_2(E_1 + E_2) = px_b^{c-}(E_1 + E_2) = px_b^{c-}L$ (since $\tau = \tau^+$, and $E_1 + E_2 = L$), while $(1 - \tau)w_2E_1 = \tau w_2E_2$ (balanced budget); it follows that $\bar{w}_2E_2 = x_b^{c-}L/\psi$ should hold.

Using (3A8) it is straightforwardly shown that a unique equilibrium with $\phi = \sigma = 1$ implies that $E_1 = \max\{E_1^-, [\eta/(1 + \eta)].L\}$.

42. The rate of return on utilized capital equals: $\beta[1 - (w_2/p)/\alpha_b]$.

43. It may be interesting to note that for the 15 types of states composed from the same values λ_s but from the middle three only for ε the same patterns of motion were obtained with a model in which an 'auctioneer' operated in the product market to balance supply and demand per period, except that the numbers for ($\lambda_s = 0$, $\varepsilon = 0.01$) and ($\lambda_s = 0.75$, $\varepsilon = 0.01$) changed places.

44. In passing, note that the motion pattern for a pure and simple 'bureau-maximizing' bureaucratic type of state ($\theta \to \infty$) will be similar to that for ($\lambda_s = 0$, $\varepsilon = 0$). In both cases state employment is maximized.

45. Compare, in this context, Bacon and Eltis (1978, p. 191): "a minimum wage in terms of market sector outputs, and minimum required profits net of tax, may both set upper limits to the proportion of marketed output that can be diverted to the non-market sector in the very long run".

46. The consequences of such an assumption are explored in Van Winden (1979b).

47. In addition, a deeper understanding of the economic need not significantly affect the results. Substituting $\tilde{E}_2^d(t) = [\beta/\alpha_b(t-1)]K_b(t)$ for $\tilde{E}_2^d(t) = \max\{0, [X_b^t(t-1) - S(t)]/\alpha_b(t-1)\}$ in (3.17) for the types of states represented by the Figs. 3.7, 3.8 and 3.9, did not basically change the results, for example.

48. Using 0.9 instead of 0.1 for κ, the motion pattern for all types of states in the last two rows of Table 3.2 changed into equilibria, except for ($\lambda_s = 1$, $\varepsilon = 0.99$), ($\lambda_s = 1$, $\varepsilon = 1$), and ($\lambda_s = 0$, $\varepsilon = 1$), for which now pattern number 4 was obtained,. Using a proportional rationing scheme based on demand in the labour market instead of (3.20) for the states represented by the Figs. 3.7, 3.8 and 3.9, changed the pattern number for the bureaucratic state from 2 into 4.

NOTES TO CHAPTER 4

1. See, in this context, Courant *et al.* (1979), Tullock (1974a).

2. The number of top-bureaucrats that are in real control of the state's bureaucracy may be sufficiently small to circumvent the free-rider problem, at least to some extent [see Olson (1965)].

3. We partly draw on Van Winden (1979a).

4. It is not the right place here to present a critical examination of the many theories of classes, elites, conflict groups, and so on, that have been proposed in the course of time, and of the criticism that they received [see, e.g., Bottomore (1970), Carchedi (1977), Dahrendorf (1976), Poulantzas (1973, 1978b), Wright (1976)]. As our approach is clearly related to the Marxist theory of social classes but differs from it in some important respects, some comments on this theory will be made in an appendix to this chapter; see Appendix 4C.

5. In general, given vectors $\underline{x} \in R^n$, with components x_k $(k = 1,..,n)$, the set S_n defined as: $S_n = \{\underline{x} \mid \underline{x} \geq 0, \Sigma_{k=1}^n x_k = 1\}$ is called a $(n - 1)$-dimensional unit simplex [see, e.g., Arrow and Hahn (1971, p.403)].

6. Think of the importance of the number in the context of elections, political movements, etc.

7. Compared with the assumed basic interest in control over private goods, $\bar{w}_k$, and state goods, x_{sk}, there is clearly more room for a different point of view as regards the relevance of numerical strength, e_k. However, one should not point at restriction of competition by capitalists, for example, as evidence to the contrary, for then one overlooks the importance of $\bar{w}_k$ as a basic interest.

8. Otherwise, one would make the mistake - successfully attacked by Olson (1965) - to suppose that groupings of agents with common interests will always attempt to further those common interests.

9. Note that this means that they need not consciously do so; i.e., they may act 'as if'.

10. The difficulties of allocation encountered here clearly show up in Wright's cited study on the class boundaries in advanced capitalist societies.

11. This definition suffices for our purposes. It is noted that the classification of social groupings is subject to dispute in sociology; see, e.g., Merton (1968, in particular pp. 353-354).

12. In his discussion of the firm, Kornai distinguishes between two types of conflicts. The first type is based on the division of labour between control processes in the institution, which leads to different interests as agents have the propensity to identify themselves with tasks and roles; this type of conflict appears in essentially the same form in all modern economies, according to Kornai. The second type of conflict is related to the forms of ownership of the society: "there remains a fundamental conflict of interest between the employees, the managers, and the owners. In everyday life this conflict of interest becomes manifest in disputes about wages, income and social benefits which are rooted in the deep class conflicts revolving around the question of power and ownership" [Kornai (*ibid.*, p. 93)].

13. As interest functions are not defined on a purely individual level, and, in case of collectivities, will typically represent processes of power and conflict between interests, we prefer not to speak of 'util-

ity functions', 'objective functions', or 'social welfare functions'.

14. Recall that we are only concerned with representation in this section, and not with structural coercion or pressure. Although the interests of the unemployed and private sector workers do not count within the state, the promotion of their interests may be enforced through pressure (strikes, political movements), for example.

15. The slope of the straight line through the origin and D equals $-\lambda_{1s}/(1 - \lambda_{1s})$ times the slope of C_2 at D.

16. The procedure resembles the Nash Bargaining Solution for co-operative games [see Nash (1950, 1953) for two-person co-operative games; for generalizations to n-person games, see Luce and Raiffa (1957, pp. 349-350), Harsanyi (1963); these models are also presented in Friedman (1977, Ch. 11)]. If the threat-payoffs are at the origin and $\lambda_{kc} = \lambda_{k'c}$ with $k,k' \in \{1,2,3,4,\}$ and $k \neq k'$, then the same solution is arrived at. One reason why we prefer our model is that the direct empirical determination of threat-payoffs for collectivities such as the state will be very difficult, if not impossible. The empirical content of the weights λ_{kc} may be sought, for example, in such things as numerical shares in the membership of a collectivity, income shares, share in contributions etc. (see Section 5.9). Besides, notice that given the values of λ_{kc} it is possible to say something about the threat-payoffs that would lead to the same result along the lines of the Nash model, since we know that the slope of the straight line through the threat-point and the solution point (which is unique in case of a convex feasible set) is of opposite sign to the slope of the relevant contour at the solution point [cf. Friedman (1977, pp. 243-245)].

17. These notions are the analogues of the 'nested utility/production function' and 'utility/production tree' concepts used in demand and production theory; see Strotz (1957), Sato (1967), Keller (1976).

18. On the analogy of the branch utility function in demand theory [see Strotz (1957, p. 270)] the P_{hi} may be called *branch interest functions*.

19. Note that, whereas in case of agents in multiple positions there is a confrontation between different internal interests, there is a confrontation between internal and external interests in case of representative agents. In passing, it may be noted here that for agents with multiple positions an additive form of complex interest function seems to be more appropriate.

20. It should be remarked that the total labour force E is not a satisfactory reference variable for numerical strength on this social structural level of analysis, and has therefore been deleted.

21. See, in this context, Pejovich (1978); in particular, Furubotn's contribution (*ibid.*, Ch. 7). See also Dunning and Stilwell (1978).

22. In Chapters 5 and 7 we will return to that subject.

23. Other unemployed people, such as housewives or pensioners, are neglected. For chronically unemployed workers (4.1) seems to be appropriate.

24. Think of the econometric models that are currently used in many coun-

tries.

25. For the extreme case that $\tilde{E}_2^d(t) = 0$ and, thus, $\tilde{e}_2(t) = 0$, $\tilde{e}_2(t)$ is deleted from $\tilde{P}_s(t)$.

26. Assuming that $w_2(0) > 0$ it follows that $w_2(t) > 0$. Assuming that $X_b(0) > 0$ it is obtained from (4.16), (4.30), (4.37), and (4.42), that $E_2^d(t) > 0$.

27. Recall from Subsection 3.2.5 that only the firms definitely know what price they are going to charge for their products.

28. Assuming that $X_b(0) > 0$ it follows from (4.16), (4.17), (4.30), (4.37) and (4.42) that $X_b^s(t) > 0$. Assuming that $p(0) > 0$ it then follows from (4.41) that $p(t) > 0$. If $p(t) > 0$, $w_2(t) > 0$ and $E_2^d(t) > 0$, it is obtained from (4.22), (4.31) and (4.32), that $X_b^d(t) > 0$.

29. Periods for which $n > 0$ are only of interest in so far as investments are concerned, and in that case $p(t,t+n)\tilde{\alpha}_b(t+n) > \tilde{w}_2(t+n)$ should hold; see the ensuing text.

30. The consequences of a longer time horizon are explored in Van Winden (1979b).

31. For $E_1^d(t) \leqq L - \tilde{E}_2^d(t)$ it is obtained that $P_s(t) = C_0[1 - \tau(t)]^{\omega_1} . E_1^d(t)^{\omega_2}$, where C_0 is given.

32. For convenience, it will be assumed in the sequel that $\omega_1 > 0$ and/or $\omega_2 > 0$. When $\omega_1 = \omega_2 = 0$, then $E_1^d(t) = E_1^-$ if $L - \tilde{E}_2^d(t) \leqq E_1^-$, while $E_1^d(t)$ is indeterminate in the interval $[E_1^-, L - \tilde{E}_2^d(t)]$ if $L - \tilde{E}_2^d(t) > E_1^-$.

33. A perverse case in which the budget surplus of the state - due to expectational errors - is so large that $d\tau(t)/dE_1^d(t) < 0$, cannot completely be ruled out. As this case is not very likely to occur, however, no attention will be paid to it.

34. It may be interesting to note that in case of a multiplicative specification of $\tilde{P}_3(t)$, i.e. $\tilde{P}_3(t) = \Pi_n \tilde{P}_3^*(t+n)^{\rho_n}$, instead of (4.35), it is obtained that $s(t) = 1 - \rho\{1 + (1 - \delta)K_b(t+1)p(t+1)/F(t) - [p(t+1)\tilde{D}_b(t+2) - \tilde{B}_2(t+2)w_3^-(t)E_3]/[\tilde{B}_2(t+2)F(t)]\} + w_3^-(t)E_3/F(t)$. Notice that ε_{31} has disappeared from the expression for $s(t)$. If $w_3^-(t) = 0$ the expression from Chapter 3 is again obtained [$\tilde{D}_b(t+2) = 0$ in that case].

35. Its original value, $\rho = 0.1$, caused the time pattern for the investment ratio to be rather volatile, with $\sigma(t)$ alternating between 1 and 0. It should further be noted here that the funds initially available to the firms for investment and/or distribution (dividends) - which equalled 800 in the previous model - have been left at that for the present model. This implies a monetary injection of 200 as these funds would (ceteris paribus) now equal 600, given the adjustment made for

the minimum income of capitalists [cf. eq. (4.12)].

36. The content of note 33 of Chapter 3 is also relevant for the present model.

37. If, moreover, $\varepsilon_{31} \to 0$ then it can be derived, using (4A3) and (4A7), that $\sigma \to (1 - \rho)/[1 + \rho(1 - \delta)/\delta]$; cf. eq. (3.39).

38. A real-valued function $f(x)$ defined over a convex set X in R^n is called strictly quasi-concave if for every distinct $x,y \in X$: $f[ax + (1 - a)y] > \min \{f(x), f(y)\}$, for all a, $0 < a < 1$ [Intriligator (1971, p. 464)].

39. In an equilibrium the interest function for the state, eq. (4.6), can be written as: $\tilde{P}_s(t) = D_0(t)[1 - \tau(t)]^{\omega_1}.E_1^d(t)^{\omega_2}.[E_1^d(t) + \tilde{E}_2(t) + E_3]^{\omega_3}.\tilde{E}_2(t)^{\omega_4}.[(1 - \tilde{\sigma}(t))\max\{0, \tilde{\bar{F}}(t)\}+ \tilde{\bar{w}}_2(t)E_3]^{\omega_5}$, where $\omega_1 = \Sigma_{k=1}^4 \varepsilon_{k1}\lambda_{ks}$, $\omega_2 = \Sigma_{k=1}^4 \varepsilon_{k3}\lambda_{ks} + \varepsilon_{12}\lambda_{1s}$, $\omega_3 = \varepsilon_{42}\lambda_{4s}$, $\omega_4 = \varepsilon_{22}\lambda_{2s}$, $\omega_5 = \varepsilon_{31}\lambda_{3s}$, $D_0(t)$ has a given expected value for the state, $\bar{F}(t)$ is given by (4A3) divided by p, and $\tau(t)$ is given by (4A5) using $(1 - \sigma(t)) \max\{0, F(t)\}$ instead of $(1 - \sigma(t))F(t)$; $p(t)$, $w_2(t)$, $\alpha_b(t)$ and $\sigma(t)$ are expected by the state to have their previous period value [see (4.27)]. As $\tilde{P}_s(t)$ is a continuous function of $E_1^d(t) \in [0,L]$, taking either $\tilde{E}_2(t) = L - E_1^d(t)$ or $\tilde{E}_2(t) = \tilde{E}_2^d(t)$, $\bar{E}_1$ and $\bar{\bar{E}}_1$ exist. For every choice of E_1 and E_2 the equilibrium values of $\tilde{E}_2^d(t)$ (= E_2) and $\alpha_b(t)$, $\sigma(t)$, and $\bar{w}_2(t)$ [see (4.50), (4.51), (4.53)] are determined, and, consequently, the equilibrium values of $\bar{E}_1$ and $\bar{\bar{E}}_1$; $\bar{E}_1$ and $\bar{\bar{E}}_1$ appear in this way as continuous functions of the E_1,E_2-combination chosen.

40. Note that $\bar{\bar{E}}_1 > L - \tilde{E}_2^d(t)$ may hold. Putting: $C_1 = w_2[(1 - \psi)E_2 + \psi L] + (1 + \sigma)[(p\alpha_b - w_2)E_2 - w_2E_3] + w_2E_3$, $C_2 = w_2(\phi - \psi)$, $D_1 = (- \omega_1 + \omega_2 + \omega_3)C_2$, $D_2 = (\omega_2 + \omega_3)C_1 + (\omega_2 - \omega_1)C_2(E_2 + E_3)$, $D_3 = \omega_2C_1(E_2 + E_3)$, where ω_1, ω_2 and ω_3 are defined in the previous note, it is obtained for $\bar{\bar{E}}_1$ if $\phi \leqq 1$:

$$\bar{\bar{E}}_1 \begin{cases} = L \quad \textit{if} \quad -\omega_1+\omega_2+\omega_3 \geqq 0, \\ = \min \{- D_2/(2D_1) - \sqrt{[(D_2/(2D_1))^2 - D_3/D_1]}, L\} \quad \textit{if} \quad -\omega_1+\omega_2+\omega_3 < 0. \end{cases}$$

If $\phi > 1$, the determination of $\bar{\bar{E}}_1$ becomes more complicated; in that case $\bar{\bar{E}}_1$ may be equal to zero if $-\omega_1+\omega_2+\omega_3 \geqq 0$, for example [it can be shown that if $\phi \leqq 1$, or $\omega_3 = 0$, $\tilde{P}_s(t)$ is strictly quasi-concave in $E_1^d(t)$, in equilibrium, given $\tilde{E}_2(t)$; this need no longer be true if $\phi > 1$ and $\omega_3 > 0$]. When $\varepsilon_{42} = 0$ or $\lambda_{4s} = 0$ (i.e., $\omega_3 = 0$) then the expression for $\bar{\bar{E}}_1$ in the text is obtained.

41. See note 39.

42. Consider the interest function for the state as written in note 39. It is easily shown that ε_{kg} can be changed in ω_1 and ω_2, for example,

while keeping ω_1 and ω_2 constant.

43. Maximum private output will again be implied by a unique equilibrium if $\phi = 1$ and $\sigma = 1$, in which case no redistribution of dividend income or savings on total wage costs are feasible. If $\phi = 1$ and $\sigma = 1$ then $\bar{w}_2(E_2 + E_3) = x_b^{c-} E/\psi$ should hold ($\tau = \tau^+$), cf. note 41 of Chapter 3; observe, furthermore, using eqs. (4.51) and (4.53), that $\bar{w}_2(E_2 + E_3) = [(\beta - \delta)/\beta]X_b$, in case that $\sigma = 1$.

44. As regards the lower ranks (in so far as 'unproductive' workers are concerned) there is less consensus. Employees in these positions are by some subsumed under the working class [see Carchedi (1977), Wright (1976)], by others under the petty bourgeoisie [Poulantzas (1978b)].

45. Cf. Wright's 'contradictory class locations'.

46. This is not to say that in as much as top-executives in state or private sector have real control, although not legally, they should not also be considered as capitalists [cf. Wright (*op. cit.*, pp. 25 and 33)].

47. In his most outspoken discussion on bureaucracy Marx even stated: "Die Bürokratie gilt sich selbst als der letzte Endzweck des Staats" [Marx (1843, p. 248)], and "Die Staatszwecke verwandeln sich in Bürozwecke oder die Bürozwecke in Staatszwecke" (*ibid.*, p. 249); see, in this context, Albrow (1970, Ch. 4).

48. "Since the bureaucracy has no power of its own, its relative autonomy is none other than which devolves on this state in the power relations of the class struggle; state power is held by classes, since the state is in fact only a power centre" [Poulantzas (1978a, p. 351)]. But where are the bureaucrats as bureaucrats, disregarding their impact due to the fact that they have class affiliations because of social milieu, multiple positions etc., which are not the question here.

49. Poulantzas clearly did not want to pay much attention to this - for his class theory rather disturbing - phenomenon of a state bourgeoisie. In (1978b, p. 188) he speaks of the 'quite unique case' of the state bourgeoisie. Elsewhere, however, he locates the phenomenon in 'certain developing countries' (1978a, p. 334) and, if we understand him right, in the USSR (1973, p. 29); an already classic work on the existence of a dominant bureaucratic class in the USSR is Djilas (1971). [We will not go into the discussion here whether the USSR economy can be considered as a type of capitalist economy - state capitalism - or not; see Miliband (1977, pp. 30-31)].

50. In Marxist theory the chronically unemployed are subsumed under the so-called 'Lumpenproletariat' which comprises 'declassed elements' [Stuurman (1978, p. 135)].

NOTES TO CHAPTER 5

1. See, in this context, Breton (1974, Ch. 5), Milbrath and Goel (1977, Ch. 1).

2. As regards the establishment of democracy in seventeen major OECD countries, see Therborn (1977). A rough calculation from a table presented by Dahl (1971, pp. 232-234), in which 114 countries are ranked by opportunities to participate in national elections and to oppose

the government, circa 1969 [in that year there were 140 nominally independent countries; see Dahl (*op.cit.* p. 11)], shows that - as regards the participation in elections only - in around 50% of the 'capitalist economies' over 90% of adult citizens were eligible to vote, while in around 59% of these countries there was at least some positive percentage of adult citizens eligible to vote.

3. Observe that an election term of positive length implies that the cost of influencing state behaviour is infinite during that period. According to Breton (1974, p. 49) "this is one of the reasons why citizens engage in other political activities (...) besides voting and accounts for the fact that voting is far from being the only influential (or even the most important) factor in the determination of the composition and level of public output".

4. Recall our discussion in Chapter 2 regarding the opportunities of small firms to particularize the tax structure. See, further, Chapter 7.

5. See Downs (1957, Ch. 14), Riker and Ordeshook (1968). The voter's calculus is quite often formalized as follows: $R = PB - C + D$, where R stands for the expected utility of voting less the expected utility of abstaining, B for the potential benefit that the voter receives from the electoral success of his more preferred party (candidate, issue), P denotes the probability that the voter will, by voting, bring about the benefit B, C the cost of voting, and D the utility obtained from voting independent of the voter's contribution to the election outcome. Only if $R > 0$, it would be reasonable to vote. See Riker and Ordeshook (*op. cit.*).

6. See Ferejohn and Fiorina (1974), Riker and Ordeshook (1973, pp. 67-69), Stigler (1972, pp. 103-104).

7. According to Taylor (1976) such a conditional strategy may under certain conditions (e.g., the future should not be discounted too much) lead to a voluntary co-operative solution in a Prisoner's Dilemma supergame.

8. See, e.g., Goodhart and Bhansali (1970), Frey and Schneider (1978a,b,c,). There is some evidence that election results are closely related to popularity ratings; see Schneider (1978, p. 26).

9. As for election studies, which are largely based on U.S. data, see Bloom and Price (1975), Fair (1978), Kramer (1971), Lepper (1974), Meltzer and Vellrath (1975); for critical discussions, see Arcelus and Meltzer (1975a,b), Goodman and Kramer (1975), Okun (1973), Stigler (1973). As regards popularity studies, see Frey and Schneider (1978a, b,c). The indications seem to be stronger for popularity ratings than for election results. One reason may be that popularity ratings can be obtained on a much more frequent basis, so that it is less likely that the hypothesized relationship is thwarted by structural shifts [cf. Frey (1979, p. 314)].

10. For a more general discussion of the importance of thresholds in economic problems, see Devletoglou (1968).

11. See Arcelus and Meltzer (1975b, p. 1268), Kramer (1971, p. 133), Schneider (1978, p. 60 *seq.*), Stigler (1973, p. 167), Weatherford (1978).

12. It may be useful to note that there need not be one such foundation;

different descriptions may be consistent with the observed overall relationship [cf. Tufte (1978, p. 127)].

13. See, however, Meltzer and Vellrath (1975) where some government tax and expenditure measures are explicitly considered.

14. For an attempt to deal with a three-party system (with two parties in the opposition) in the context of the assessment of the popularity of parties, see Kirchgässner (1979).

15. This is the case if the stochastic components of utility are independently Weibull distributed [Domencich and McFadden (*op. cit.*, pp. 61-69)]; the variable f_{ko_i} can be read as the probability that a k-agent opts for o_i.

16. Given the information problems already involved, it does not seem to be worthwhile to include more future elections. Moreover, strategic voting - for example voting for a less preferred party because one expects it to have a better chance of winning - will not be considered anyway.

17. If preferred, every election term can be considered to involve a new incumbency.

18. To go somewhat further, it may be speculated that this political distance is closely related to the class structure of the parties, which can be indicated - on the analogy of our approach to the social class structure in Section 4.2 - by a fractional breakdown of the class status of the voters of o_h and o_i. Let these breakdowns be denoted by the vectors

$$\underline{e}_{o_h} = [E_{1o_h}(T)/E_{o_h}(T), \ldots, E_{4o_h}(T)/E_{o_h}(T)] \quad \text{and}$$

$$\underline{e}_{o_i} = [E_{1o_i}(T)/E_{o_i}(T), \ldots, E_{4o_i}(T)/E_{o_i}(T)]$$

which represent points in the 4-dimensional class space. As a first approach it may then be suggested that the political distance, denoted by $\bar{d}$, is some (increasing) function of the Euclidean distance between $\underline{e}_{o_h}$ and $\underline{e}_{o_i}$, denoted by $d = d(\underline{e}_{o_h}, \underline{e}_{o_i})$; thus,

$$\bar{d}_{o_h o_i}(T) = \bar{d}_{o_h o_i}[d(\underline{e}_{o_h}, \underline{e}_{o_i})] \qquad , \ \bar{d}'_{o_h o_i}(T) > 0,$$

where $\bar{d}'$ denotes the first derivative of $\bar{d}$ with respect to d, and

$$d(\underline{e}_{o_h}, \underline{e}_{o_i}) = \{\Sigma_k [E_{ko_h}(T)/E_{o_h}(T) - E_{ko_i}(T)/E_{o_i}(T)]^2\}^{1/2} \qquad , \ 0 \leqq d \leqq \sqrt{2}.$$

It is not difficult to see that the maximum distance is given by: $d = \sqrt{2}$, in which case the parties have different but homogeneous constituencies (i.e., members from one class only). An alternative approach would be to use, instead of numerical shares, the relative strength or power - measured on a [0,1]-interval - of people with different economic positions in the parties.

19. See, e.g., Figure 1 in Goodman and Kramer (1975, p. 1256), showing the aggregate participation rate in congressional elections in the U.S. over the period 1896-1970.

20. *A priori*, there is no reason to exclude other types of - symmetric or skewed - relationships [think of upside-down density functions, or a different parameter specification according to the sign of $\mu(T)$]. What the most useful specification is, is an empirical question.

21. the analysis is cast in general terms; we do not go into the peculiarities of any existing type of political system, such as that of the U.S. or U.K.

22. It should be noted that ideology does play a role in spatial models of coalition formation; see below. A spatial model of party competition that takes account of conflicting interests within the parties is presented in Coleman (1971).

23. Compare - in a somewhat similar context - the ambivalent attitude of labour unions with respect to co-determination.

24. Mark, in this context, Hirschman's suggestion that it was not the assumption of inelastic demand that was wrong or unrealistic in Hotelling's model, "but the inference that the 'captive' consumer (or voter) who has 'nowhere else to go' is the epitome of powerlessness" [Hirschman (1970, p. 70)]. It may also be noted here that for some governmental decisions, such as constitutional amendments, a single majority is often not sufficient, as a qualified majority, such as two-third of the parliamentary votes is required.

25. Stigler (1972, p. 102) postulates an influence function I(s) for a party (indicating its probability of determining public policy), where I is a monotonically increasing function of the share of legislative seats s, and a gain function G(s) (indicating the opportunity to use the state machinery for the benefit of the party members), which decreases monotonically in s. The objective of the party is then to maximize, for given cost, the expected gain of its members: I(s)G(s). Stigler does not consider different interest blocs within a party, though, but uses Riker's proposition that parties seek to attain the minimum size necessary to electoral victory, so that the beneficiaries of political power be as few as possible, and its victims as numerous as possible. In this conception a deliberate choice for going into the opposition is irrational as the benefits for the party members are thought to be conditional on the attainment of an incumbency.

26. Note, however, that if the class structure is defined by the fractional breakdown of the class status of the party members (as we suggest), one should not overlook the fact that this may be a poor indicator for the distribution of power within a party, especially in the short run. We need only think of Robert Michels' 'iron law of oligarchy' in order to realize this [Michels (1962)]. If one wants to consider party fractions beyond the four basic classes (for example, because of the powerful position of elected party members) a nested complex interest function should be used [see eqs. (4.3) and (4.4)].

27. We use De Swaan's labelling.

28. Apart from socio-economic progressiveness, clericalism is, for example, taken into account; see Taylor and Laver (1973).

29. Factions are explicitly considered in Leiserson (1968). However, in that case coalition formation within a party (a mammoth party in Japan) is studied. Moreover, these factions are deemed to be atypical by Leiserson.

30. A measure of party attractiveness that is more adjustable to the theories mentioned in the previous subsection would be:

$$Q_{o_h o_i}(T) = \xi \Sigma_k \{\lambda_{ko_h}(T)[\tilde{Z}_{ko_i}(T) - \tilde{Z}_{ko_h}(T)]\} - (1 - \xi)\bar{d}_{o_h o_i}(T)$$

$$, \; 0 \leq \xi \leq 1,$$

where $\tilde{Z}(T)$ - omitting subscripts - is the expected interest realization rating [see eq. (4.4)], and $\bar{d}(T)$ denotes, say, the political distance between (or the ideological diversity of) the parties considered, which refers to other factors important to voters than the interests covered by $Z(T)$. In this way one can keep the option open to return to the aforementioned theories of coalition formation which use policy scales and do not take the performance record of parties into account (in that case $\xi = 0$). From a theoretical point of view we prefer the specification in eq. (5.22) as it better dovetails with our approach to voting behaviour.

31. De Swaan's theory appeared to be rather unsuccessful when confronted with empirical data [see De Swaan (1973)]. Disregarding some simplifications that this theory shares with the other theories and which may account for its failure, we would like to mention here the particular way in which he determines the expected policy of a coalition. As was noticed above, a crucial role in this respect is played by the 'pivot actor' in a coalition. An actor is said to be pivotal "when the absolute difference between the combined votes (weights) of members on his right (on the political scale: the author) and of members on his left is not greater than his own weight: the actor may 'swing the vote', or he 'holds the balance'" [De Swaan (1973, p. 113)]. To the extent that the combined weight of the members on the one side of the pivot actor exceeds that of the other side the expected policy will be drawn in that direction, away from the pivot actor's most preferred policy. In our view, this procedure will, generally, greatly overestimate the power of such a pivot actor. For example, it does not differentiate a situation in which there are, equally sized, big parties on the sides of that actor from a situation in which the pivot actor is the sole incumbent. As De Swaan observes: "The assumption, implicit in the policy scale, is, of course, that the two opposite wings of the coalition will not join forces (think of vote trading: the author) against the pivotal actor" [De Swaan (1973, p. 330)]. It also leads to situations in which ideologically widely diverging parties are preferred in a coalition just because of this balancing.

32. Interesting in this context is the following conclusion drawn by Wagner: "To focus exclusively upon aggregate variables, however, is to set aside a substantial part of the phenomena to be examined. There is far more to the political business cycle than the use by government of changes in aggregate spending at different points in the electoral cycle to buy votes. Political manipulation revolves around individual rather than aggregate variables. Cycles result as a by-product of the efforts of politicians to by votes through micro-economic actions that generate readjustments in the structure of relative prices. Even when unemployment is adressed politically, it is rarely in the form of general increases in aggregate demand. It is far more frequently in the form of specific programs to increase the real incomes of particular persons. Macro-economic consequences may result *ex post*, but the *ex ante* impetus for the policy is micro-economic or micro-political in

orientation" [Wagner (1977, p. 407)]. See also Bernholz (1966).

33. In his discussion of the Status Quo in Germany, Friedrich Engels remarked that those estates or classes that due to their professions represented a branch of production, shared the political power in proportion to their number, wealth and share in total production of the country; see Hennig *et al.* (1974, p. 329).

34. The measures may also prove to be useful for authoritative bodies other than government or state.

35. In the following chapter, where we report on some numerical experiments, an example will be given of an economy (with elections and compulsory voting) approaching an equilibrium, where due to $\sigma(t)^2 \to 0$ for all h,k, the (two) political parties grow to the same size and are alternately incumbent because of slight economic disturbances.

36. Compare Mazmanian (1974, p. 139): "Disaffected groups, when withdrawing their support from the traditional parties, hesitate to coalesce with their longstanding adversaries and are thus open to appeals from other sources. Third parties appear in response to the needs of the disaffected transitional groups". Interesting are also some of the findings of Pinard (1975) regarding 'third parties'. To avoid a long digression we give some quotations from Pinard's case study of the rise of the Social Credit Party in Canada. "The results (.) reveal the existence of strong relationships between changes in economic conditions and the support of a new political movement" (*op. cit.*, p. 118). Pinard mentions three types of economic changes that are in his view important in this respect (*op. cit.*, pp. 108-119). "The most important seems to be short-term deteriorating conditions after relatively long-term periods of prosperity". "A second type of change is the long-term regular lowering of one's financial position"; "when long- and short-term deterioration are combined (.) the potential for revolt (.) reaches its highest point". "A third type of situation might also lead to protest movements. This occurs when the gradual improvement of a group's lot, though expected to continue, finally levels off". "Long-endured poverty, to the extent that it does not involve changes in one's economic conditions, is not a factor of political movements". Pinard also found that one need not be affected personally or in one's family to feel discontented. The threat that what people saw around them might soon affect them seemed to be sufficient to spur people to join the protest party (*op. cit.*, pp. 108-109). Recall in this context the discussion on 'pocket-book' and class-oriented voters; see Subsection 5.2.2. Pinard stresses the importance of class factors (see *op. cit.*, p. 219), such as the particularly strong working class base of the party, which is interesting in itself because of the conservative character of the Social Credit Party. All this seems to accord with our approach in so far as the importance of changes in economic conditions and social classes is concerned. The way Pinard fits these factors into an explanation of the rise of the third party is different, and, in our view, unsatisfactory, however. Space does not permit us to elaborate this statement here.

37. Note, however, that as the valuation of the political groups is also based on the parameters a and b, which represent other than economic factors, there may be other reasons for revolutions (and new political groups). Think of ethnic and religious causes in case of large scale migration, for example; newcomers may find the political system totally unrepresentative in these respects.

38. Think of Marx' theory of increasing pauperization.

39. The only formal approach to revolutions that we know of is Tullock (1974b). In Tullock's view the crucial factor in revolutions is the revolutionary's calculus of the discounted value of (private) reward and punishment; the collective goods - and, although Tullock does not seem to draw this conclusion, the collective bads - on the effectuation of which the ordinary revolutionary's influence is taken to be extremely small, drop out of his calculus to participate or not. The formula used by Tullock for the revolutionary's calculus is equivalent to the voter's calculus formula shown in note 5 of this chapter. With Tullock's theory the occurrence of revolutions seems to be hard to explain, however. It may be useful for the explanation of the behaviour of leading revolutionaries that have an appreciable effect on the course of the revolution, or for the analysis of *coups d'état*.

40. See Appendix 2a.

41. Define:

$$\dot{w}_{ki}(f) \equiv ln\left[\frac{\bar{\bar{w}}_k(t_2-f+1)}{\bar{\bar{w}}_k(t_2-f)}\right], \quad \dot{\hat{w}}_{kh}(f) \equiv ln\left[\frac{\hat{\bar{\bar{w}}}_{ko_h}(t_2-f+1)}{\hat{\bar{\bar{w}}}_{ko_h}(t_2-f)}\right],$$

$$\dot{w}_{kh}(f) \equiv ln\left[\frac{\bar{\bar{w}}_k(t_3-f+1)}{\bar{\bar{w}}_k(t_3-f)}\right], \quad \dot{\hat{w}}_{ki}(f) \equiv ln\left[\frac{\hat{\bar{\bar{w}}}_{ko_i}(t_3-f+1)}{\hat{\bar{\bar{w}}}_{ko_i}(t_3-f)}\right],$$

where the party index attached to 'hatted' variables denotes by which party the promises are made. In exactly the same way we define $\dot{e}_{ki}(f)\ldots\dot{\hat{e}}_{ki}(f)$, $\dot{x}_{ski}(f)\ldots\dot{\hat{x}}_{ski}(f)$, by substituting e and x_s respectively for $\bar{\bar{w}}$.

Let, furthermore,

$$c_k(f) \equiv c_k(t_m-f+1) \quad , \bar{c}_k(2) \equiv \bar{c}_{ko_i}(t_2) \quad , \hat{\bar{c}}_k(2) \equiv \hat{\bar{c}}_{ko_h}(t_2),$$

$$\underline{c}_k \equiv (c_k(1),..,c_k(n)) \quad , \bar{c}_k(3) \equiv \bar{c}_{ko_h}(t_3) \quad , \hat{\bar{c}}_k(3) \equiv \hat{\bar{c}}_{ko_i}(t_3),$$

then,

$$\underline{u}(T) \equiv [1, \dot{w}_{ki}(1), \dot{e}_{ki}(1), \dot{x}_{ski}(1),\ldots, \dot{w}_{ki}(n), \dot{e}_{ki}(n), \dot{x}_{ski}(n),$$
$$\dot{\hat{w}}_{ki}(1), \dot{\hat{e}}_{ki}(1), \dot{\hat{x}}_{ski}(1),\ldots, \dot{\hat{w}}_{ki}(n), \dot{\hat{e}}_{ki}(n), \dot{\hat{x}}_{ski}(n), \dot{\hat{w}}_{kh}(1),$$
$$\dot{\hat{e}}_{kh}(1), \dot{\hat{x}}_{skh}(1),\ldots, \dot{\hat{w}}_{kh}(n), \dot{\hat{e}}_{kh}(n), \dot{\hat{x}}_{skh}(n), \dot{w}_{kh}(1), \dot{e}_{kh}(1),$$
$$\dot{x}_{skh}(1),\ldots, \dot{w}_{kh}(n), \dot{e}_{kh}(n), \dot{x}_{skh}(n)] \quad \text{and}$$

$$\underline{v} \equiv [-(a_k/b_k), (1/b_k)\underline{c}_k\otimes\underline{\varepsilon}_{kg}, (1/b_k)\hat{\bar{c}}_k(3)\underline{c}_k\otimes\underline{\varepsilon}_{kg}, -(1/b_k)\hat{\bar{c}}_k(2)\underline{c}_k\otimes\underline{\varepsilon}_{kg},$$
$$-(1/b_k)\bar{c}_k(3)\underline{c}_k\otimes\underline{\varepsilon}_{kg}]',$$

where ⊗ stands for Kronecker product.

42. In this context, it should be mentioned that quite a number of studies have appeared, recently, on the distribution of collective goods; see e.g., Aaron and McGuire (1970), Maital (1979).

43. See, e.g., Bell, Edwards, and Wagner (1969), Cartwright and Zander (1968), Dahl (1972), Rothschild (1971), Van Doorn (1957).

44. The application of the interview method to government decision-making is strongly critisized in Ancot and Hughes Hallett (1978, pp. 16-17).

45. In collectivities in which votes are the major determinant of policies one might also consider the use of the Shapley-Shubik and Banzhaf indices of voting power, which measure the importance of agents to the outcome of the voting process; see, e.g., Brams (1975, Ch. 5).

NOTES TO CHAPTER 6

1. Notice that the denominator cannot vanish, for if $\Delta E_{3-k}(T-1) = 0$ then $E_4(T-1) > 0$ should hold, since $\Delta E_k(T-1) > 0$ and the number of capitalists is constant.

2. Suppose that the type of state for which the equilibrium exists is a pure capitalist type of state, i.e. $\lambda_{3s} = 1$, and that $\varepsilon_{33} = 1 - \varepsilon_{31} > 0$, $E_1 = \bar{\bar{E}}_1 > \underline{E}_1$. In that case, a change in the type of state that is sustained by the dominant party (through the manipulation of ε_{kg}) may not be feasible, as a change in ε_{31} may demand a change in σ, which would disturb the equilibrium, [see (4A7)], while a decrease in ε_{33} - leaving ε_{31} unchanged - would lead to a decrease in $E_1^d(t)$ (see Subsection 4.5.1, point 6).

3. As regards the first part, see the previous remark. For the latter part, suppose that $E_1 = \bar{\bar{E}}_1 = \bar{E}_1$, $d\bar{\bar{E}}_1/dE_2 \geq 0$ [see (4B4)], and recall the content of remark 4.

4. It should be remarked that $[P_k(t_m-f+1) - P_k(t_m-f)]/P_k(t_m-f)$ was used instead of $ln\ [P_k(t_m-f+1)/P_k(t_m-f)]$ in eq. (5.5) for the experiments.

NOTES TO CHAPTER 7

1. Instructive in this respect is Lang's study of the relationship between the pharmaceutical industry and the state in Canada and Great Britain; see Lang (1974), in particular p. 165.

2. See, e.g., Key (1955, p. 24), Van Doorn (1966, pp. 44-61). Note that we do not demand - as Key seems to do - that the group is *formed* to influence the collectivity in question. Thus, according to our definition, a firm can function as a pressure group *vis-à-vis* the state, although it is not established for the purpose of influencing the behaviour of the state.
Van Doorn discusses some other, disputed, restrictions on the use of the concept.
An individual agent can be considered as a limiting case of a collectivity.

3. Instructive case studies are Lang (1974), Lynch (1971), Sampson (1974, 1976). See further, for example, Domhoff (1979), Edwards (1955), Johansen (1979), Key (1955), Mason (1969), Miliband (1973a), Posner (1974), Walker (1943).

4. In this context we should also mention the (empirical) studies on political campaign contributions which bear out the same suggestion; see Pittman (1977), Welch (1980).

5. Zusman, for example, simply assumes that the government aims at minimal subsidy costs.
The characteristic is less valid for Pincus' study as it at least refers to a relationship between elected politicians and interests of voters.

6. Think of studies on profit rates and concentration ratios; see Bain (1959, p. 295) for a discussion of this approach.

7. Of such an index it stands to reason to demand that it ascribes maximum cohesiveness (valued one) to an individual (a one-member group). In a similar context, Pincus speaks of a fraction of an 'individual decision-making equivalent' on analogy with 'full-time male equivalent' in labour force studies [Pincus (1975, p. 759)].

8. There is a close relationship between the advertising of a product by a firm and a pressure group's 'advertising' of its objective threat intensity. The activities involved are often multidimensional in character (for example, there is a choice between media, and 'messages') and the information given may be correct as well as incorrect. Advertising studies and models [see Kotler (1971), Schmalensee (1972)] may, therefore, also find an application in this research area.

9. One may think in this context of costs that have to be incurred to overcome 'free-rider' or 'prisoner's dilemma' types of problems. It is, furthermore, noted that property 6 has some affinity with the Nash Bargaining Solution to two-person co-operative games with zero threat payoffs; in both cases the product of the interest functions (P) of c_h and c_i is maximized. However, in our case no complete information is assumed, so that the outcome may still differ from the Nash Bargaining Solution. Also note that the Nash Bargaining Solution would again demand the maximization of the product of the interest functions of c_h and c_i when the effective threat intensities of the pressure groups would be equal but less than one. This latter aspect does not seem to be realistic for the interaction that is studied in this chapter; see our argumentation with respect to property 3 in the main text.

10. There are other specifications satisfying these properties; substitute, for example, $\left[{}_{c_h}\Pi_{c_i}^{c_h}(t)\right]^2$ for ${}_{c_h}\Pi_{c_i}^{c_h}(t)$ in the nominator.

11. For a similar statement in the context of advertising, see Schmalensee (1972, p. 213).

12. Having found some evidence of a negative correlation of trade association resources (staff, budget) and concentration ratios in a study of trade associations in the U.S., Stigler puts the question whether very large companies undertake many of the activities allocated to associations in less concentrated fields [Stigler (1974), pp. 364-365)]. Our

tentative answer would be that they do, for reasons given in the main text.

13. This situation can be said to hold, for example, for a pharmaceutical company in Great Britain; see Lang (1974).

14. The former may be required, e.g., to get one's product registered to begin with; the latter may be the consequence of the requirement that one should be a member of the trade association in order to become, officially, a bargaining partner of the state.

15. Visibility as a problem for a large firm in this context is mentioned by a number of authors; see, e.g., Edwards (1955, p. 346), Pittman (1977, p. 39), Salamon and Siegfried (1977, pp. 1032 and 1033).

REFERENCES

Aaron, H., and M. McGuire (1970), "Public Goods and Income Distribution", *Econometrica*, 6, pp. 907-920.
Aarrestad, J., (1978), "On the Optimal Development of Knowledge-Based Industries and the Educational Sector in a Small Open Economy", *International Economic Review*, 19, pp. 379-394.
Alavi, H., (1972), "The State in Post-Colonial Societies: Pakistan and Bangladesh", *New Left Review*, 74, pp. 59-81.
Albrow, M., (1970), *Bureaucracy*, Pall Mall Press, London.
Altvater, E., (1972), "Zu einigen Problemen des Staatsinterventionismus", *Probleme des Klassenkampfs*, S. 1-53.
Altvater, E., (1976), "Vorm, middelen en grenzen van het ingrijpen van de burgerlijke staat", *Te Elfder Ure*, 22, pp. 457-487.
Ancot, J.P., and A.J. Hughes Hallett (1978), "A General Method for Estimating Revealed Preferences", discussion paper 7817/G, Institute for Economic Research, Erasmus University, Rotterdam.
Anderson, P.S., (1961), "The Apparent Decline in Capital-Output Ratios", *Quarterly Journal of Economics*, pp. 615-634.
Arcelus, F., and A.H. Meltzer (1975a), "The Effect of Aggregate Economic Variables on Congressional Elections", *American Political Science Review*, 69, pp. 1232-1239.
Arcelus, F., and A.H. Meltzer (1975b), "Aggregate Economic Variables and Votes for Congress: A Rejoinder", *American Political Science Review*, 69, pp. 1266-1269.
Arrow, K.J., (1962), "The Economic Implications of Learning by Doing", *Review of Economic Studies*, 29, pp. 155-173. Reprinted in J.E. Stiglitz and H. Uzawa (eds.), *Readings in the Modern Theory of Economic Growth*, M.I.T. Press, Cambridge (Mass.), 1969, pp. 210-228.
Arrow, K.J., (1963), *Social Choice and Individual Values*, Yale University Press, New Haven (first edition, 1951).
Arrow, K.J., and F.H. Hahn (1971), *General Competitive Analysis*, North-Holland, Amsterdam.
Arrow, K.J., and T. Scitovsky (eds.) (1969), *Readings in Welfare Economics*, Irwin, Homewood, Illinois.
Aumann, R.J., and M. Kurz (1978), "Power and Taxes in a Multi-Commodity Economy (Updated)", *Journal of Public Economics*, 9, pp. 139-161.
Axelrod, R., (1970), *Conflict of Interest*, Markham, Chicago.

Bacon, R., and W. Eltis (1978), *Britain's Economic Problem: Too Few Producers*, 2nd edition, MacMillan, London.
Bacon, R., and W. Eltis (1979), "The Measurement of the Growth of the Non-Market Sector and its Influence: A Reply to Hadjimatheou and Skouras", *Economic Journal*, 89, pp. 402-415.
Bain, J.S., (1959), *Industrial Organization*, Wiley, New York.
Bannock, G., Baxter, R.E., and R. Rees (1979), *Economics* (The Penguin Dictionary of), second edition, Penguin Books, Harmondsworth.
Baran, P.A., (1973), *The Political Economy of Growth*, Penguin Books, Harmondsworth.
Baran, P.A., and P.M. Sweezy (1968), *Monopoly Capital*, Penguin Books, Harmondsworth.
Barro, R.J., and H.I. Grossman (1976), *Money, Employment and Inflation*, Cambridge University Press, Cambridge.
Barry, B.M., (1970), *Sociologists, Economists and Democracy*, Collier-MacMillan, London.
Bartlett, R., (1973), *Economic Foundations of Political Power*, The Free Press, London.
Baumol, W.J., (1965), *Welfare Economics and the Theory of the State*, second edition, Bell and Sons, London.
Bell, R., Edwards, D., and R. Wagner (eds.) (1969), *Political Power*, Free Press, New York.
Bernholz, P., (1966), "Economic Policies in a Democracy", *Kyklos*, 19, pp. 48-79.
Bernholz, P., (1972, 1975, 1979), *Grundlagen der politischen Oekonomie*,

1. Band (1972), 2. Band (1975), 3. Band (1979), Mohr, Tübingen.
Black, D., (1958), *The Theory of Committees and Elections*, Cambridge University Press, Cambridge.
Blankart, B., (1975), "Zur ökonomischen Theorie der Bürokratie", *Public Finance*, 30, pp. 166-183.
Blinder, A.S., and R.M. Solow (1974), "Analytical Foundations of Fiscal Policy", in A.S. Blinder, *et al.*, *The Economics of Public Finance*, The Brookings Institution, Washington D.C., pp. 3-115.
Bloom, P.N., and P. Kotler (1975), "Strategies for High Market-Share Companies", *Harvard Business Review*, November-December, pp. 63-72.
Bloom, H.S., and H.D. Price (1975), "Voter Response to Short-Run Economic Conditions: The Asymmetric Effect of Prosperity and Recession", *American Political Science Review*, 69, pp. 1240-1255.
Boddy, R., and J. Crotty (1975), "Class Conflict and Macro-Policy: The Political Business Cycle", *Review of Radical Political Economics*, 7, pp. 1-19.
Borcherding, T.E., (1977), "One Hundred Years of Public Spending, 1870-1970", in T.E. Borcherding (ed.), *Budgets and Bureaucrats: The Sources of Government Growth*, Duke University Press, Durham, North Carolina, pp. 19-44.
Bottomore, T.B., (1970), *Elites and Society*, Penguin Books, Harmondsworth.
Braam. G.P.A., (1973), *Invloed van bedrijven op de overheid*, Boom, Meppel.
Brams, S.J., (1975), *Game Theory and Politics*, Thee Free Press, New York.
Brennan, G., and J.M. Buchanan (1978), "Tax Instruments as Constraints on the Disposition of Public Revenues", *Journal of Public Economics*, 9, pp. 301-318.
Breton, A., (1974), *The Economic Theory of Representative Government*, Aldine, Chicago.
Buchanan, J.M. (1967), *Public Finance in Democratic Process*, University of North Carolina Press, Chapel Hill.
Buchanan, J.M., and G. Tullock (1962), *The Calculus of Consent*, University of Michigan Press, Ann Arbor.
Bush, W.C. and A.T. Denzau (1977), "The Voting Behavior of Bureaucrats and Public Sector Growth", in T.E. Borcherding (ed.), *Budgets and Bureaucrats: The Sources of Government Growth*, Duke University Press, Durham, North Carolina, pp. 90-99.

Cameron, D.R., (1978), "The Expansion of the Public Economy: A Comparative Analysis", *American Political Science Review*, 72, pp. 1243-1261.
Campbell, A., *et al.* (1965), *The American Voter*, Wiley, New York.
Carchedi, G., (1977), *On the Economic Identification of Social Classes*, Routledge & Kegan Paul, London.
Cartwright, D., (1968), "The Nature of Group Cohesiveness", in D. Cartwright and A. Zander (eds.), *Group Dynamics*, Harper and Row, New York, 1968, pp. 91-109.
Cartwright, D., and A. Zander (1968), "Power and Influence in Groups: Introduction", in D. Cartwright and A. Zander (eds.), *Group Dynamics*, Harper and Row, New York, pp. 215-235.
Castles, F.G., (1974), "Political Stability and the Dominant Image of Society", *Political Studies*, 22, pp. 289-298.
Chamberlin, E.H., (1962 [1933]), *The Theory of Monopolistic Competition*, Harvard University Press, Cambridge, Mass.
Coleman, J.S., (1971), "Internal Processes Governing Party Positions in Elections", *Public Choice*, 2, pp. 35-69.
Comanor, W.S., (1976), "The Median Voter Rule and the Theory of Political Choice", *Journal of Public Economics*, 5, pp. 169-177.
Commissie van de Europese Gemeenschappen (1976), *Vergelijkende tabellen van de stelsels van sociale zekerheid, Algemeen stelsel*, 9e uitgave.
Courant, P.N., Gramlich, E.M., and D.L. Rubinfeld (1979), "Public Employee Market Power and the Level of Government Spending", *American Economic Review*, 69, pp. 806-817.
Cross, J.G. (1969), *The Economics of Bargaining*, Basic Books, New York.
Crotty, J.R., (1973), "Specification Error in Macro-Econometric Models: The Influence of Policy Goals", *American Economic Review*, 63, pp. 1025-1030.

Dahl, R.A., (1971), *Polyarchy*, Yale University Press, New Haven.
Dahl, R.A., (1972), "Power", in D.L. Shills (ed.), *International Encyclopedia of the Social Sciences*, vol. 11, New York, pp. 405-415.
Dahrendorf, R., (1976), *Class and Class Conflict in Industrial Society*, Routledge & Kegan Paul, London.
Dallemagne, J-L, *et al.* (1974), *Critiques de l'économie politique, L'inflation*, Maspero, Paris.
Davis, O.A., Dempster, M.A.H., and A. Wildavsky (1966), "A Theory of the Budgetary Process", *American Political Science Review*, 60, pp. 529-547.
Davis, O., Hinich, M., and P. Ordeshook (1970), "An Expository Development of a Mathematical Model of the Electoral Process", *American Political Science Review*, 64, pp. 426-448.
Den Hartog, H., *et al.* (1975), "De structurele ontwikkeling van de werkgelegenheid in macro economisch perspectief", *Preadvies voor de Vereniging voor de Staathuishoudkunde*, Martinus Nijhoff, 's-Gravenhage.
Denison, E.F., (1967), *Why Growth Rates Differ*, The Brookings Institution, Washington.
De Swaan, A., (1973), *Coalition Theories and Cabinet Formations*, Ph.D. thesis, Amsterdam, (published by Elsevier, Amsterdam, 1973).
De Swaan, A., and R.J. Mokken (1980), "Testing Coalition Theories: The Combined Evidence", in L. Lewin and E. Vedung (eds.), *Politics as Rational Action*, Reidel, Dordrecht.
Devletoglou, N.E., (1968), "Thresholds and Rationality", *Kyklos*, 21, pp. 623-636.
De Vries, B., (1978), "Het draagvlak van de economie", *Economisch Statistische Berichten*, 63, no. 3141, pp. 138-142.
Djilas, M., (1971), *The New Class*, Thames & Hudson, London.
Dobb, M., (1972), *Studies in the Development of Capitalism*, Routledge and Kegan Paul, London.
Dobb, M., (1973), *Theories of Value and Distribution*, Cambridge University Press, Cambridge.
Domencich, T.A., and D. McFadden (1975), *Urban Travel Demand*, North-Holland, Amsterdam.
Domhoff, G.W., (1967), *Who Rules America*, Prentice-Hall, Englewood Cliffs.
Domhoff, G.W., (1979), *The Powers That Be*, Vintage Books, New York.
Dougherty, C.R.S., (1974), "On the Secular Macro-Economic Consequences of Technical Progress", *Economic Journal*, 84, pp. 543-566.
Downs, A., (1957), *An Economic Theory of Democracy*, Harper and Row, New York.
Downs, A., (1967), *Inside Bureaucracy*, Little, Boston.
Dunning, J.H., and F.J.B. Stilwell (1978), "Theories of Business Behaviour and the Distribution of Surplus Profit", *Kyklos*, 31, pp. 601-623.

Edwards, C.D., (1955), "Conglomerate Bigness as a Source of Power", in C.D. Edwards (ed.), *Business Concentration and Price Policy*, Princeton University Press, Princeton, N.J.
Egozi, M., (1973), "An Elementary Model of the Determination of the Level of Public Expenditure and the Distribution of the Tax Burden", *Public Finance*, 28, pp. 259-277.
Emmanuel, A., (1979), "The State in the Transitional Period", *New Left Review*, 113-114, pp. 111-131.
Engels, F., (1846) *Deutsche Zustände*, MEW, Bd.2, S. 564-584, Dietz Verlag, Berlin, 1976.
Engels, F., (1847), *Der Status Quo in Deutschland*, MEW, Bd.4, S. 40-57, Dietz Verlag, Berlin, 1977.
Engels, F., (1892), *Der Ursprung der Familie, des Privateigentums und des Staats*, MEW, Bd.21, S. 30-173, Dietz Verlag, Berlin, 1975.
Esser, J., (1976), "De staatstheoriediskussie in West-Duitsland", *Te Elfder Ure*, 22, pp. 436-456.
Evans, M.K., (1969), *Macroeconomic Activity*, Harper and Row, New York.

Fair, R.C., (1978), "The Effect of Economic Events on Votes for President", *Review of Economics and Statistics*, 60, pp. 159-173.
Farquharson, R., (1969), *Theory of Voting*, Yale University Press, New Haven.

Ferejohn, J.A., and M.P. Fiorina (1974), "The Paradox of Not Voting: A Decision Theoretic Analysis", *American Political Science Review*, 68, pp. 525-536.

Festinger, L., (1968), "Informal Social Communication", in D. Cartwright and A. Zander (eds.), *Group Dynamics*, Harper and Row, New York, 1968, pp. 182-191.

Fiorina, M.P., (1977), "An Outline for a Model of Party Choice", *American Journal of Political Science*, 21, pp. 601-625.

Fisher, F.M., (1970), "Quasi-Competitive Price Adjustment by Individual Firms: A Preliminary Paper". *Journal of Economic Theory*, 2, pp. 195-206.

Fisher, F.M., (1972), "On Price Adjustment without an Auctioneer", *Review of Economic Studies*, 39, pp. 1-15.

Foley, D.K., (1978), "State Expenditure from a Marxist Perspective", *Journal of Public Economics*, 9. pp. 221-238.

Fox, K.A., Sengupta, J.K., and E. Thorbecke (1973), *The Theory of Quantitative Economic Policy*, North-Holland, Amsterdam.

Freeman, M., (1972), "Review Article: Theories of Revolution", *British Journal of Political Science*, 2, pp. 339-359.

Frey, B.S., (1968), "Eine politische Theorie des Wirtschaflichen Wachstums", *Kyklos*, 21, pp. 70-99.

Frey, B.S., (1971), "Why Do High Income People Participate More in Politics", *Public Choice*, 11, pp. 101-105.

Frey, B.S., (1974a), "A Dynamic Theory of Public Goods", *Finanzarchiv*, 32, pp. 185-193.

Frey, B.S., (1974b), "The Politico-Economic System: A Simulation Model", *Kyklos*, 27, pp. 227-253.

Frey, B.S., (1977a), *Moderne Politische Oekonomie*, Piper, München (in English: *Modern Political Economy*, Wiley, New York, 1978).

Frey, B.S., (1977b), "On the Political Economy of Public Service", in M.S. Feldstein and R.P. Inman (eds.) *The Economics of Public Services*, MacMillan, London, pp. 415-434.

Frey, B.S., (1978), Politico-Economic Models and Cycles", *Journal of Public Economics*, 9, pp. 203-220.

Frey, B.S., (1979), "Politometrics of Government Behavior in a Democracy", *Scandinavian Journal of Economics*, 81, pp. 308-322.

Frey, B.S., and H. Garbers (1971), "'Politico-Econometrics' - On Estimation in Political Economy", *Political Studies*, 19, pp. 316-320.

Frey, B.S., and L.J. Lau (1968), "Towards a Mathematical Model of Government Behaviour", *Zeitschrift für Nationalökonomie*, 28, pp. 355-380.

Frey, B.S., and F. Schneider (1978a), "A Politico-Economic Model of the United Kingdom", *Economic Journal*, 88, pp. 243-253.

Frey, B.S., and F. Schneider (1978b), "An Empirical Study of Politico-Economic Interaction in the United States", *Review of Economics and Statistics*, 60, pp. 174-183.

Frey, B.S., and F. Schneider (1978c), "Economic and Personality Determinants of Presidential Popularity", *Empirical Economics*, 3, pp. 79-89.

Friedlaender, A.F., (1973), "Macro Policy Goals in the Postwar Period: A Study in Revealed Preference", *Quarterly Journal of Economics*, 87, pp. 25-43.

Friedman, B.M., (1979), "Optimal Expectations and the Extreme Information Assumptions of 'Rational Expectations' Macromodels", *Journal of Monetary Economics*, 5, pp. 23-41.

Friedman, J.W., (1977), *Oligopoly and the Theory of Games*, North-Holland, Amsterdam.

Friedman, M., (1976), "The Line We Dare Not Cross: The Fragility of Freedom at 60%", *Encounter* (November).

Galbraith, J.K., (1967), *The New Industrial State*, Hamish Hamilton, London.

Gamson, W.A., (1961), "A Theory of Coalition Formation", *American Sociological Review*, 26, pp. 373-382.

Gerstenberger, H., (1976), "De wording van de burgerlijke staat", *Te Elfder Ure*, 22, pp. 488-503.

Gevers, L., and S. Proost (1978), "Some Effects of Taxation and Collec-

tive Goods in Postwar America", *Journal of Public Economics*, 9, pp. 115-137.
Gold, D., Lo, C., and E. Wright (1975), "Recent Developments in Marxist Theories of the Capitalist State", *Monthly Review*, October, pp. 29-43 (part I), November, pp. 36-51 (part II).
Goode, R., (1979), "Limits to Taxation", Paper for International Institute of Public Finance, 35th Congress, Taormina.
Goodhart, C.A.E., and R.J. Bhansali (1970), "Political Economy", *Political Studies*, 18, pp. 43-106.
Goodman, S., and G. Kramer (1975), "Comment on Arcelus and Meltzer, The Effect of Aggregate Economic Conditions on Congressional Elections", *American Political Science Review*, 69, pp. 1255-1266.
Gough, I., (1975), "State Expenditure in Advanced Capitalism", *New Left Review*, 92, pp. 53-92.
Gramsci, A., (1971), *Prison Notebooks*, Lawrence and Wishart, London.
Griliches, Z., (1964), "Research Expenditures, Education, and the Aggregate Agricultural Production Function", *American Economic Review*, 54, pp. 961-974.
Guggenberger, B., (1974), "Oekonomie und Politik - Die neomarxistische Staatsfunktionenlehre", *Neue Politische Literatur*, pp. 425-471.
Gurley, J.G., (1971), "The State of Political Economics", *American Economic Review* (Papers and Proceedings), 61, pp. 53-65.

Hadjimatheou, G., and A. Skouras (1979), "Britain's Economic Problem: The Growth of the Non-Market Sector?", *Economic Journal*, 89, pp. 392-401.
Haley, M.R., and J.M. Kiss (1974), "Larger Stakes in Statehouse Lobbying", *Harvard Business Review*, January-February, pp. 125-135.
Halm, G.N., (1970), *Economic Systems*, third edition, Holt, Rinehart and Winston, London.
Hanushek, E.A., and J.E. Jackson (1977), *Statistical Methods for Social Scientists*, Academic Press, London.
Harcourt, G.C., (1974), *Some Cambridge Controversies in the Theory of Capital*, Cambridge University Press, London.
Harsanyi, J.C., (1963), "A Simplified Bargaining Model for the n-Person Cooperative Game", *International Economic Review*, 4, pp. 194-220.
Heimann, E., (1968), *History of Economic Doctrines*, Oxford University Press, London.
Helleiner, G.K., (1977), "Transnational Enterprises and the New Political Economy of U.S. Trade Policy", *Oxford Economic Papers*, 29, pp. 102-116.
Helmers, H.M., *et al.* (1975), *Graven naar Macht*, Van Gennep, Amsterdam.
Hennig, E., *et al.* (1974), *Karl Marx/Friedrich Engels - Staatstheorie*, Ullstein, Frankfurt/M.
Hensher, D.A., and L.W. Johnson (1981), *Applied Discrete-Choice Modelling*, Croom Helm, London.
Hey, J.D., (1974), "Price Adjustment in an Atomistic Market", *Journal of Economic Theory*, 8, pp. 483-499.
Hibbs, Jr., D.A., (1977), "Political Parties and Macroeconomic Policy", *American Political Science Review*, 71, pp. 1467-1487.
Hirschman, A.D., (1970) *Exit, Voice and Loyalty*, Cambridge, Mass.
Holt, C.C., (1962), "Linear Decision Rules for Economic Stabilization and Growth", *Quarterly Journal of Economics*, 76, pp. 20-45.
Hoogerwerf, A., (1979), *Politicologie: Begrippen en Problemen*, Samsom, Alphen aan den Rijn.
Hordijk, L., Mastenbroek, A.P., and J. Paelinck (1976), "Contributions récentes a l'étude empirique de fonctions de préférence collectives", *Revue d'économie politique*, pp. 505-534.
Hotelling, H., (1929), "Stability in Competition", *The Economic Journal*, 39, pp. 41-57.

Intriligator, M.D., (1971), *Mathematical Optimization and Economic Theory*, Prentice-Hall, Englewood Cliffs, N.J.

Jacquemin, A.P., and H.W. de Jong (eds.) (1976), *Markets, Corporate Behaviour and the State*, Nijhoff, The Hague.
Jessop, B., (1977), "Recent Theories of the Capitalist State", *Cambridge Journal of Economics*, 1, pp. 353-373.
Johansen, L., (1968), *Public Economics*, North-Holland, Amsterdam.
Johansen, L., (1974), "Establishing Preference Functions for Macroeconomic Decision Models", *European Economic Review*, 5, pp. 41-66.
Johansen, L., (1979), "The Bargaining Society and the Inefficiency of Bargaining", *Kyklos*, 32, pp. 497-522.
Johnston, J., (1975), "A Macro-Model of Inflation", *Economic Journal*, 85, pp. 288-309.
Jorgenson, D.W., and Z. Griliches (1967), "The Explanation of Productivity Change", *Review of Economic Studies*, 34, pp. 249-283.

Kalecki, M., (1971), "Political Aspects of Full Employment", in: *Selected Essays on the Dynamics of the Capitalist Economy 1933-1970*, Cambridge University Press, Cambridge, pp. 138-146.
Kapteyn, A., and V. Halberstadt (1979), "The Notion of Minimum Income", Center for Research in Public Economics, Report 78.26, Leyden.
Keller, W.J., (1976), "A Nested CES-Type Utility Function and its Demand and Price-Index Functions", *European Economic Review*, 7, pp. 175-186.
Key, Jr., V.O., (1955), *Politics, Parties, and Pressure Groups*, Crowell, New York, 3rd. edition.
Kiewiet, D.R., (1980), "Accounting for the Electoral Effects of Short-Term Economic Fluctuations: The Role of Incumbency-Oriented and Policy-Oriented Voting", paper presented at the Annual Meeting of the Public Choice Society, San Francisco.
Kinder, D.R., and D.R. Kiewiet (1979), "Economic Discontent and Political Behaviour: The Role of Personal Grievances and Collective Economic Judgements in Congressional Voting", *American Journal of Political Science*, 23, pp. 495-527.
Kirchgässner, G., (1979), "Popularity of the Government and the Opposition in a 2-Party and a 3-Party System", paper presented at the Arne Ryde Symposium on Theories of Economic Institutions, Lund.
Koch, K., (1979), "De nieuwe marxistische staatstheorie: (Her)ontdekking van de grenzen van een structureel-functionalistisch paradigma", *Acta Politica*, 14, pp. 3-70.
Kornai, J., (1971), *Anti-Equilibrium*, North-Holland, Amsterdam.
Kornai, J., (1979), "Resource-Constrained Versus Demand-Constrained Systems", *Econometrica*, 47, pp. 801-819.
Kotler, P., (1971), *Marketing Decision Making*, Holt, Rinehart, and Winston, New York.
Koutsoyiannis, A., (1979), *Modern Microeconomics*, 2nd edition, MacMillan, London.
Kramer, G.H., (1971), "Short-Term Fluctuations in U.S. Voting Behavior 1896-1964", *American Political Science Review*, 65, pp. 131-143.
Kydland, F., (1975), "Noncooperative and Dominant Player Solutions in Discrete Dynamic Games", *International Economic Review*, 16, pp. 321-335.

Laclau, E., (1975), "The Specificity of the Political: The Poulantzas-Miliband Debate", *Economy and Society*, no. 1.
Lancaster, K., (1973), *Modern Economics*, Rand McNally, Chigago.
Lang, R.W., (1974), *The Politics of Drugs*, Lexington Books, Lexington, Mass.
Leiserson, M.A., (1966), *Coalitions in Politics*, Doctoral dissertation (mimeographed), Yale University, New Haven [(cited in De Swaan 1973)].
Leiserson, M.A., (1968), "Factions and Coalitions in One-Party Japan: An Interpretation Based on the Theory of Games", *American Political Science Review*, 57, pp. 770-787.
Lenin, V.I., (1918), "The State and Revolution", in *V.I. Lenin, Selected Works*, Volume 2, Foreign Languages Publishing House, Moscow, pp. 301-399.
Lenin, V.I., (1919), "The State", in *V.I. Lenin, Selected Works*, Volume 3,

Foreign Languages Publishing House, Moscow, pp. 277-293.
Lepper, S.J., (1974), "Voting Behavior and Aggregate Policy Targets", *Public Choice*, 18, pp. 67-81.
Lindbeck, A., (1975), "The Changing Role of the National State", *Kyklos*, 28, pp. 23-46.
Lindbeck, A., (1976), "Stabilization Policy in Open Economies with Endogenous Politicians", *American Economic Review* (Papers and Proceedings), 66, pp. 1-19.
Lipsey, R.G., and P.O. Steiner (1975), *Economics*, Harper and Row, New York, 4th edition.
Lucas, Jr., R.E., (1976), "Econometric Policy Evaluation, A Critique", *Journal of Monetary Economics*, Supplement Series, 1, pp. 19-46.
Luce, R.D., and H. Raiffa (1957), *Games and Decisions*, Wiley, New York.
Lynch, D., (1971), "Economic Power and Political Pressure", in: Rothschild (1971), pp. 158-166; excerpted from D. Lynch, *The Concentration of Economic Power*, Columbia University Press, 1946, Chapter 10.

MacIver, R.M., (1966), *The Modern State*, Oxford University Press, Londen.
MacRae, C.D., (1977), "A Political Model of the Business Cycle", *Journal of Political Economy*, 85, pp. 239-263.
Magdoff, H., (1969), *The Age of Imperialism*, Monthly Review Press, New York.
Maital, S., (1979), "Measurement of Net Benefits from Public Goods: A New Approach Using Survey Data", *Public Finance*, pp. 85-95.
Mandel, E., (1973), *Der Spätkapitalismus*, Suhrkamp Verlag, Frankfurt am Main.
Marschak, J., and R. Radner (1971), *The Economic Theory of Teams*, Yale University Press, New Haven.
Marx, K., (1843), *Kritik des Hegelschen Staatsrecht*, MEW, Bd.1., S. 203-333, Dietz Verlag, Berlin, 1976.
Marx, K., (1852), *Der achtzehnte Brumaire des Louis Bonaparte*, MEW, Bd.8, S. 110-207, Dietz Verlag, Berlin, 1975.
Marx, K., (1859), *Zur Kritik der politischen Oekonomie*, Dietz Verlag, Berlin, 1972.
Marx, K., (1871), *Der Bürgerkrieg im Frankreich*, MEW, Bd.17, S. 313-365, 493-610, Dietz Verlag, Berlin, 1976.
Marx, K., and F. Engels (1848), *Manifest der kommunistischen Partei*, Dietz Verlag, Berlin, 1968.
Mason, E.S. (ed.) (1969), *The Corporation in Modern Society*, Harvard University Press, Cambridge, Mass.
Mazmanian, D.A., (1974), *Third Parties in Presidential Elections*, Brookings Institution, Washington D.C.
McMillan, J., (1978), "A Dynamic Analysis of Public Intermediate Goods Supply in Open Economy", *International Economic Review*, 19, pp. 665-678.
Meade, J.E., (1952), "External Economies and Diseconomies in a Competitive Situation", *Economic Journal*, 62, pp. 54-67.
Meltzer, A., and M. Vellrath (1975), "The Effects of Economic Policies on Votes for the Presidency: Some Evidence from Recent Elections". *Journal of Law and Economics*, 18, pp. 781-799.
Merkies, A., and T. Nijman (1980), "Preference Functions of Dutch Political Parties", paper presented at the Econometric Society World Congress, Aix-en-Provence.
Merton, R.K., (1968), *Social Theory and Social Structure*, The Free Press, New York.
Michels, R., (1962), *Political Parties*, The Free Press, New York.
Milbrath, L.W., and M.L. Goel (1977), *Political Participation*, second edition, Rand McNally, Chicago.
Miliband, R., (1970), "The Capitalist State - Reply to Nicos Poulantzas", *New Left Review*, no. 59, pp. 53-60.
Miliband, R., (1973a), *The State in Capitalist Society*, Quartet Books, London.
Miliband, R., (1973b), "Poulantzas and the Capitalist State", *New Left Review*, no. 82, pp. 83-92.
Miliband, R., (1977), *Marxism and Politics*, Oxford University Press,

Oxford.
Miller, G.J., (1977), "Bureaucratic Compliance as a Game on the Unit Square", *Public Choice*, 29, pp. 37-51.
Mills, C. Wright (1956), *The Power Elite*, Oxford University Press, London.
Mokken, R.J., and F.N. Stokman (1976), "Power and Influence as Political Phenomena", in B. Barry (ed.), *Power and Political Theory*, Wiley, London, pp. 33-65.
Monroe, K.R., (1979), "Econometric Analysis of Electoral Behavior: A Critical Review", *Political Behavior*, 1, pp. 137-173.
Morgenstern, O., (1972), "Thirteen Critical Points in Contemporary Economic Theory: An Interpretation", *Journal of Economic Literature*, 10, pp. 1163-1189.
Mosley, P., (1976), "Towards a 'Satisficing' Theory of Economic Policy", *Economic Journal*, 86, pp. 59-72.
Mueller, D.C., (1976), "Public Choice: A Survey", *Journal of Economic Literature*, 14, pp. 395-433.
Mueller, D.C., (1979), *Public Choice*, Cambridge University Press, Cambridge.
Musgrave, R.A., (1969), *Fiscal Systems*, Yale University Press, London.
Musgrave, R.A. and P.B. Musgrave (1973), *Public Finance in Theory and Practice*, McGraw-Hill, Kogakusha, Tokyo.
Musgrave, R.A., and A.T. Peacock (eds.) (1967), *Classics in the Theory of Public Finance*, MacMillan, London.
Muth, J.F., (1961), "Rational Expectations and the Theory of Price Movements", *Econometrica*, 29, pp. 315-335.
Myrdal, G., (1953), *The Political Element in the Development of Economic Theory*, Routledge and Kegan Paul, London.

Nash, J., (1950), "The Bargaining Problem", Econometrica, 18, pp. 155-162.
Nash, J., (1953), "Two-Person Cooperative Games", *Econometrica*, 21, pp. 128-140.
Nerlove, M., and K.J. Arrow (1962), "Optimal Advertising Policy Under Dynamic Conditions", *Economica*, 29, pp. 129-142.
Nieburg, H.L., (1966), "The Contract State", reprinted from: *In the Name of Science*, in D. Mermelstein (ed.), *Economics: Mainstream Readings and Radical Critiques*, Random House, New York, 1970, pp. 203-211.
Nijkamp, P., and W.H. Somermeyer (1971), "Explicating Implicit Social Preference Functions", *Economics of Planning*, 11, pp. 101-119.
Niskanen, W.A., (1974), *Bureaucracy and Representative Government*, Aldine, Chicago.
Nordhaus, W.D., (1975), "The Political Business Cycle", *Review of Economic Studies*, 42, pp. 169-190.

O'Connor, J., (1972),"Scientific and Ideological Elements in the Economic Theory of Government Policy", in E.K. Hunt and J.G. Schwartz (eds.), *A Critique of Economic Theory*, Penguin Books, Harmondsworth, pp. 367-396.
O'Connor, J., (1973), *The Fiscal Crisis of the State*, St. Martin's Press, New York.
OECD (1978), *Public Expenditure Trends*, Paris.
Offe, C., (1972), *Strukturprobleme des kapitalistischen Staates*, Suhrkamp Verlag, Frankfurt am Main.
Okun, A.M. (1973), "Comments on Stigler's Paper" [see Stigler (1973)], *American Economic Review* (Papers and Proceedings), 63, pp. 172-177.
Olson, M., (1965), *The Logic of Collective Action*, Harvard University Press, Cambridge (Mass.).
Orzechowski, W., (1977), "Economic Models of Bureaucracy: Survey, Extensions, and Evidence", in T.E. Borcherding (ed.) *Budgets and Bureaucrats: The Sources of Government Growth*, Duke University Press, Durham, North-Carolina, pp. 229-259.

Peabody, R.L., and F.E. Rourke (1965), "Public Bureaucracies", in J.G. March (ed.) *Handbook of Organizations*, Rand McNally, Chicago, pp.802-837.
Peacock, A.T., and J. Wiseman (1961), *The Growth of Public Expenditures in*

the United Kingdom, Princeton University Press, Princeton, N.J.
Pejovich, S., (1978), *The Codetermination Movement in the West*, Lexington Books, Toronto.
Phlips, L., (1974), *Applied Consumption Analysis*, North-Holland, Amsterdam.
Pinard, M., (1975), *The Rise of a Third Party*, McGill-Queen's University Press, Montreal (enlarged edition).
Pincus, J.J., (1975), "Pressure Groups and the Pattern of Tariffs", *Journal of Political Economy*, 83, pp. 757-778.
Pittman, R., (1977), "Market Structure and Campaign Contributions", *Public Choice*, 31, pp. 37-52.
Pommerehne, W.W., (1978), "Institutional Approaches to Public Expenditure", *Journal of Public Economics*, 9, pp. 255-280.
Posner, R.A., (1974), "Theories of Economic Regulation", *Bell Journal of Economics and Management Science*, 5, pp. 335-358.
Poulantzas, N., (1969), "The Problem of the Capitalist State", *New Left Review*, no. 58, pp. 67-78.
Poulantzas, N., (1973), "On Social Classes", *New Left Review*, no. 78, pp. 27-54.
Poulantzas, N., (1974), *Fascism and Dictatorship*, NLB, London.
Poulantzas, N., (1976), "The Capitalist State: A Reply to Miliband and Laclau", *New Left Review*, no. 95, pp. 63-83.
Poulantzas, N., (1978a), *Political Power and Social Classes*, Verso, London.
Poulantzas, N., (1978b), *Classes in Contemporary Capitalism*, Verso, London.
Prais, S.J., and C. Reid (1976), "Large and Small Manufacturing Enterprises in Europe and America", in Jacquemin and De Jong (1976), pp. 78-94.
Pryor, F.L., (1968), *Public Expenditures (in Communist and Capitalist Nations)*, Irwin, Homewood, Illinois.

Quinn, J.F., (1979), "Wage Differentials among Older Workers in the Public and Private Sector", *Journal of Human Resources*, 14, pp. 41-62.

Radner, R., (1972a), "Normative Theories of Organization: An Introduction", in C.B. McGuire and R. Radner (eds.). *Decision and Organization*, North-Holland, Amsterdam, pp. 177-188.
Radner, R., (1972b), "Teams", in C.B. McGuire and R. Radner (eds.), *Decision and Organization*, North-Holland, Amsterdam, pp. 189-215.
Rees, A., (1980), "Improving Productivity Measurement", *American Economic Review* (Papers and Proceedings), 70, pp. 340-342.
Reuber, G.L., (1964), "The Objectives of Canadian Monetary Policy, 1949-1965. Empirical Trade-offs and the Reaction of the Authorities", *Journal of Political Economy*, 72, pp. 109-132.
Riker, W.H., (1962), *The Theory of Political Coalitions*, Yale University Press, New Haven.
Riker, W.H., and P.C. Ordeshook (1968), "A Theory of the Calculus of Voting", *American Political Science Review*, 62, pp. 25-42.
Riker, W.H., and P.C. Ordeshook (1973), *An Introduction to Positive Political Theory*, Prentice-Hall, Englewood Cliffs, New Jersey.
Ritzen, J.M.M., (1977), *Education, Economic Growth and Income Distribution*, North-Holland, Amsterdam.
Robinson, J., (1970), "Capital Theory Up to Date", in E.K. Hunt and J.G. Schwartz (eds.), *A Critique of Economic Theory*, Penguin, Harmondsworth.
Roll, E., (1973), *A History of Economic Thought*, Faber and Faber, London, 4th. edition.
Romer, T., and H. Rosenthal (1979), "The Elusive Median Voter", *Journal of Public Economics*, 12, pp. 143-170.
Rose-Ackerman, S., (1975), "The Economics of Corruption", *Journal of Public Economics*, 4, pp. 187-203.
Rothschild, K.W. (ed.) (1971), *Power in Economics*, Penguin Books, Harmondsworth.
Ruys, P., (1974), *Public Goods and Decentralization*, Tilburg University Press, Tilburg.

Salamon, L.M., and J.J. Siegfried (1977), "Economic Power and Political Influence: The Impact of Industry Structure on Public Policy", *American Political Science Review*, 71, pp. 1026-1043.

Sampson, A., (1974), *The Sovereign State*, Coronet Books, Hodder Fawcett, London.

Sampson, A., (1976), *The Seven Sisters*, Bantam Books, New York.

Samuelson, P.A., (1954), "The Pure Theory of Public Expenditure", *Review of Economics and Statistics*, 36, pp. 387-389.

Samuelson, P.A., (1955), "Diagrammatic Exposition of a Theory of Public Expenditure", *Review of Economics and Statistics*, pp. 350-356.

Samuelson, P.A., (1976), *Economics*, MrGraw-Hill, New York, 10th. edition.

Sato, K., (1967), "A Two-Level Constant-Elasticity-of-Substitution Production Function", *Review of Economic Studies*, 34, pp. 201-218.

Scherer, F.M., (1970), *Industrial Market Structure and Economic Performance*, Rand McNally, Chicago.

Schmalensee, R.L., (1972), *The Economics of Advertising*, North-Holland, Amsterdam.

Schneider, F., (1978), *Politisch-ökonomische Modelle*, Hain, Königstein.

Schumpeter, J.A., (1947),*Capitalism, Socialism, and Democracy*, Allen and Unwin, London, revised second edition.

Schumpeter, J.A., (1972), *History of Economic Analysis*, Allen und Unwin, London.

Scitovsky, T., (1971), *Welfare and Competition*, Allen and Unwin, London, revised edition.

Selten, R., (1971), "Anwendungen der Spieltheorie auf die Politische Wissenschaft", in H. Maier, K. Ritter, U. Matz, *Politiek und Wissenschaft*, Verlag C.H. Beck, München, pp. 287-320.

Sen, A.K., (1970), *Collective Choice and Social Welfare*, Holden-Day, San Francisco.

Shonfield, A., (1970), *Modern Capitalism*, Oxford University Press, New York.

Shubik, M., (1970a), "On Different Methods for Allocating Resources", *Kyklos*, 23, 1970, pp. 332-337.

Shubik, M., (1970b), "A Curmudgeon's Guide to Microeconomics", *Journal of Economic Literature*, 8, pp. 405-434.

Simaan, M., and J.B. Cruz, Jr. (1973), "On the Stackelberg Strategy in Nonzero-Sum Games". *Journal of Optimization Theory and Applications*, 11, pp. 533-555.

Smith, A., (1970[1776]), *The Wealth of Nations*, Dent, London.

Sraffa, P., (1960), *Production of Commodities by Means of Commodities*, Cambridge University Press, Cambridge.

Stigler, G.J., (1966), *The Theory of Price*, MacMillan, New York, 3rd. edition.

Stigler, G.J., (1972), "Economic Competition and Political Competition", *Public Choice*, 12, pp. 91-106.

Stigler, G.J., (1973), "General Economic Conditions and National Elections", *American Economic Review* (Papers and Proceedings), 63, pp. 160-167.

Stigler, G.J., (1974), "Free Riders and Collective Action: An Appendix to Theories of Economic Regulation", *Bell Journal of Economics and Management Science*, 5, 1974, pp. 359-365.

Strotz, R.H., (1957), "The Empirical Implications of a Utility Tree", *Econometrica*, 25, pp. 269-280.

Stuurman, S., (1978), *Kapitalisme en burgerlijke staat*, SUA, Amsterdam.

Sweezy, P.M., (1968), *The Theory of Capitalist Development*, Monthly Review Press, New York, (first printing, 1942).

Sweezy, P.M., and H. Magdoff (1972), *The Dynamics of U.S. Capitalism*, Monthly Review Press, New York.

Takayama, A., (1974), *Mathematical Economics*, Dryden, Hinsdale, Illinois.

Taylor, M., (1971), "Mathematical Political Theory", *British Journal of Political Science*, 1, pp. 339-382.

Taylor, M., (1972), "On the Theory of Government Coalition Formation", *British Journal of Political Science*, 2, pp. 361-388.

Taylor, M., (1976), *Anarchy and Cooperation*, Wiley, London.

Taylor, M., and M. Laver (1973), "Government Coalitions in Western Europe", *European Journal of Political Research*, 1, pp. 205-248.
Theil, H., (1964), *Optimal Decision Rules for Government and Industry*, North-Holland, Amsterdam.
Theil, H., (1971), *Principles of Econometrics*, Wiley, New York.
Theil, H., (1972), *Statistical Decomposition Analysis*, North-Holland, Amsterdam.
Therborn, G., (1977), "The Rule of Capital and the Rise of Democracy", *New Left Review*, 103, pp. 3-41.
Tinbergen, J., (1956), *Economic Policy: Principles and Design*, North-Holland, Amsterdam.
Tufte, E.R., (1978), *Political Control of the Economy*, Princeton University Press, Princeton.
Tullock, G., (1974a), "Dynamic Hypothesis on Bureaucracy", *Public Choice*, 19, pp. 127-131.
Tullock, G., (1974b), *The Social Dilemma: Economics of War and Revolution*, Center for Study of Public Choice, Blacksburg.
Tweede Kamer (1979), *Innovatie: Het overheidsbeleid inzake technologische vernieuwing in de Nederlandse samenleving*, zitting 1979-1980, nrs. 1-2.

Van Benthem van de Berg, G., (1976), "The Interconnection between Processes of State and Class Formation", *Acta Politica*, 11, pp. 289-311.
Van den Doel, J., (1978), *Democratie en Welvaartstheorie*, 2e druk, Samsom, Alphen aan den Rijn. (In English: *Democracy and Welfare Economics*, Cambridge University Press, Cambridge, 1979).
Van der Geest, L., (1977), "Het vastleggen van economisch-politieke oordelen in een doelstellingsfunctie", *Economisch Statistische Berichten*, 65, pp. 994-999.
Van Doorn, J.A.A., (1957), "Sociologische begrippen en problemen rond het verschijnsel macht", *Sociologisch Jaarboek*, 11, pp. 73-135.
Van Doorn, J.A.A., (1966), *Organisatie en Maatschappij*, Stenfert Kroese, Leiden.
Van Eijk, C.J., and J. Sandee (1959), "Quantitative Determination of an Optimum Economic Policy", *Econometrica*, 27, pp. 1-13.
Van Winden, F.A.A.M., (1976), "De interactie tussen staat en bedrijfsleven", *Bedrijfskunde*, 48, pp. 368-375.
Van Winden, F.A.A.M., (1979a), "State, Private Sector, and Political Parties", Report 79.12, Centre for Research in Public Economics, Leyden University; presented at the Arne Ryde Symposium on Theories of Economic Institutions, Lund (1979), and at the Econometric Society World Congress, Aix-en-Provence (1980).
Van Winden, F.A.A.M., (1979b), "A Two-Sector, Two-Department Model of the Interaction between State and Private Sector", Centre for Research in Public Economics, Report 79.19, Leyden University; presented at the Public Choice Society Meetings in San Francisco and Florence, 1980.
Van Winden, F.A.A.M., (1980), "The Interaction between State and Firms", *Oxford Economic Papers*, 32, pp. 428-452.
Van Winden, F.A.A.M., and B.M.S. van Praag (1981), "A Dynamic Model of the Interaction between the State and the Private Sector", *Journal of Public Economics*, 16, pp. 53-86; abstracted in *Economics Letters*, 1, 1978, pp. 225-229.
Verdoorn, P.J., (1952), "Welke zijn de achtergronden en vooruitzichten van de economische integratie in Europa, en welke gevolgen zal deze integratie hebben, met name voor de welvaart in Nederland?", *Preadvies voor de Vereniging voor de Staathuishoudkunde*, Martinus Nijhoff, 's-Gravenhage.
Vermaat, A.J., (1979), "De draagvlak-theorie nader beschouwd", *Maandschrift Economie*, 43, pp. 201-217.
Von Neumann, J., and O. Morgenstern (1944), *Theory of Games and Economic Behavior*, Princeton University Press, Princeton.

Wagner, R.E., (1977), "Economic Manipulation for Political Profit: Macroeconomic Consequences and Constitutional Implications", *Kyklos*, 30, pp. 395-410.

Walker, E.R., (1943), *From Economic Theory to Policy*, University of Chicago Press, Chicago.
Watson, W.G., (1978), "Bacon and Eltis on Growth, Government, and Welfare" (review article), *Journal of Comparative Economics*, 2, pp. 43-56.
Weatherford, M.S., (1978), "Economic Conditions and Electoral Outcomes: Class Differences in the Political Response to Recession", *American Journal of Political Science*, 22, pp. 917-938.
Weber, M., (1972 [1922]), *Wirtschaft und Gesellschaft*, fünfte, revidierte Auflage, Mohr, Tübingen.
Welch, W.P., (1980), "The Allocation of Political Monies: Economic Interest Groups", *Public Choice*, 35, pp. 97-120.
Wood, J.H., (1965), "Linear Decision Rules for Economic Stabilization and Growth: A Comment", *Quarterly Journal of Economics*, 79, pp. 310-316.
Wright, E.O., (1976), "Class Boundaries in Advanced Capitalist Societies", *New Left Review*, 98, pp. 3-41.
Wright, G., (1974), "The Political Economy of New Deal Spending", *Review of Economics and Statistics*, pp. 30-38.
WRR (1979), "De publieke sector: ontwikkeling en waardevorming", Wetenschappelijke Raad voor het Regeringsbeleid, Staatsuitgeverij, 's-Gravenhage.

Yaffe, D., (1976), "De staat en de kapitalistische krisis", *Te Elfder Ure*, 22, pp. 398-419.

Zechman, M.J., (1979), "Dynamic Models of the Voter's Decision Calculus: Incorporating Retrospective Considerations into Rational-Choice Models of Individual Voting Behavior", *Public Choice*, 34, pp. 297-315.
Zusman, P., (1976), "The Incorporation and Measurement of Social Power in Economic Models", *International Economic Review*, 17, pp. 447-462.

AUTHOR INDEX

SUBJECT INDEX